Thinking Through Tourism

ASA Monographs

ISSN 0066-9679

1. *The Relevance of Models for Social Anthropology*, ed M. Banton
2. *Political Systems and the Distribution of Power*, ed M. Banton
3. *Anthropological Approaches to the Study of Religion*, ed M. Banton
4. *The Social Anthropology of Complex Societies*, ed M. Banton
5. *The Structural Study of Myth and Totemism*, ed E.R. Leach
6. *Themes in Economic Anthropology*, ed R. Firth
7. *History and Social Anthropology*, ed I.M. Lewis
8. *Socialization: The Approach from Social Anthropology*, ed P. Mayer
9. *Witchcraft Confessions and Accusations*, ed M. Douglas
10. *Social Anthropology and Language*, ed E. Ardener
11. *Rethinking Kinship and Marriage*, ed R. Needham
12. *Urban Ethnicity*, ed A. Cohen
13. *Social Anthropology and Medicine*, ed J.B. Loudon
14. *Social Anthropology and Law*, ed I. Hamnett
15. *The Anthropology of the Body*, ed J. Blacking
16. *Regional Cults*, ed R.P. Werbner
17. *Sex and Age as Principles of Social Differentiation*, ed J. La Fontaine
18. *Social and Ecological Systems*, ed P. C. Burnham and R.F. Ellen
19. *Social Anthropology of Work*, ed S. Wallman
20. *The Structure of Folk Models*, ed L. Holy and L. Stuchlik
21. *Religious Organization and Religious Experience*, ed J. Davis
22. *Semantic Anthropology*, ed D. Parkin
23. *Social Anthropology and Development Policy*, ed R. Grillo and A. Rew
24. *Reason and Morality*, ed J. Overing
25. *Anthropology at Home*, ed A. Jackson
26. *Migrants, Workers, and the Social Order*, ed J.S. Eades
27. *History and Ethnicity*, ed E. Tonkin, M. McDonald and M. Chapman
28. *Anthropology and the Riddle of the Sphinx: Paradox and Change in the Life Course*, ed P. Spencer
29. *Anthropology and Autobiography*, ed J. Okely and H. Callaway
30. *Contemporary Futures: Perspectives from Social Anthropology*, ed S. Wallman
31. *Socialism: Ideals, Ideologies and Local Practice*, ed C.M. Hann
32. *Environmentalism: The View from Anthropology*, ed K. Milton
33. *Questions of Consciousness*, ed A.P. Cohen and N. Rapport
34. *After Writing Culture: Epistemology and Praxis in Contemporary Anthropology*, ed A. James, A. Dawson and J. Hockey
35. *Ritual, Performance, Media*, ed F. Hughes-Freeland
36. *The Anthropology of Power*, ed A. Cheater
37. *An Anthropology of Indirect Communication*, ed J. Hendry and C.W. Watson
38. *Elite Cultures*, ed C. Shore and S. Nugent
39. *Participating in Development*, ed P. Sillitoe, A. Bicker and J. Pottier
40. *Human Rights in Global Perspective*, ed R.A. Wilson and J.P. Mitchell
41. *The Qualities of Time*, ed W. James and D. Mills
42. *Locating the Field: Space, Place and Context in Anthropology,* ed S. Coleman and P. Collins
43. *Anthropology and Science: Epistemologies in Practice*, ed J. Edwards, P. Harvey and P. Wade
44. *Creativity and Cultural Improvisation*, ed E. Hallam and T. Ingold
45. *Anthropology and the New Cosmopolitanism: Rooted, Feminist and Vernacular Perspectives,* ed P. Werbner

Thinking Through Tourism

Edited by
Julie Scott and Tom Selwyn

Oxford • New York

English edition
First published in 2010 by
Berg
Editorial offices:
First Floor, Angel Court, 81 St Clements Street, Oxford OX4 1AW, UK
175 Fifth Avenue, New York, NY 10010, USA

Library of Congress Cataloging-in-Publication Data

A catalogue record for this book is available from the Library of Congress.

British Library Cataloguing-in-Publication Data

A catalogue record for this book is available from the British Library.

ISBN 978 1 84788 531 9 (Cloth)
978 1 84788 530 2 (Paper)

e-ISBN 978 1 84788 759 7 (Institutional)
978 1 84788 787 0 (Individual)

Typeset by JS Typesetting Ltd, Porthcawl, Mid Glamorgan
Printed in the UK by the MPG Books Group

www.bergpublishers.com

Contents

List of Figures   vii

Acknowledgements   viii

Notes on Contributors   ix

Foreword
Margaret E. Kenna   xiii

1   Introduction: Thinking Through Tourism – Framing the Volume
        Julie Scott and Tom Selwyn   1

2   Contours of a Nation: Being British in Mallorca
        Hazel Andrews   27

3   The Sex of Tourism? Bodies under Suspicion in Paradise
        Susan Frohlick   51

4   Belonging at the Cottage
        Julia Harrison   71

5   Tourists, Developers and Civil Society: On the Commodification
        of Malta's Landscapes
        Jeremy Boissevain   93

6   Enchanted Sites, Prosaic Interests: Traders of the Bazaar in Aleppo
        Annika Rabo   117

7   Tropical Island Gardens and Formations of Modernity
        David Picard   139

8   Of Jews, Christians and Travellers in Crete: Recovered 'Roots',
        Unwanted 'Heritage'
        Vassiliki Yiakoumaki   161

Contents

9 Tourist Attractions, Cultural Icons, Sites of Sacred Encounter:
Engagements with Malta's Neolithic Temples
Kathryn Rountree   183

10 'Hotel Royal' and other Spaces of Hospitality: Tourists and
Migrants in the Mediterranean
Ramona Lenz   209

11 Anthropology, Tourism and Intervention?
Simone Abram   231

Postlude
Nelson Graburn   255

Index   259

List of Figures

2.1   Cafe-bar eateries with 'British' names   38

2.2   A sign for cooking like mum   39

2.3   A cafe sign proclaiming British identity   39

4.1   Haliburton County location map   74

5.1   Like bleached skeletons, the speculative apartment developments on Point Tigné stare across Marsamxett Harbour at Valletta   107

9.1   The key Neolithic temple sites in Malta   186

9.2   Façade of Ḣaġar Qim   190

9.3   Summer Solstice 2006, Mnajdra. Archaeologist addressing tour group   193

9.4   Maltese Pagan priestess at Ḣaġar Qim temple   197

9.5   Maltese Pagan at southern Mnajdra temple   198

9.6   Conservation 'tent' covering Ḣaġar Qim   202

Acknowledgements

The Editors would like to thank past and present colleagues at London Metropolitan University, particularly Jonathan Karkut and Raoul Bianchi, for collaboration and discussion over the years; Richard Fardon for suggesting a tourism theme for the ASA's conference; and Paola Parravicini and Juliet King-Malik, for their hard work on the index. On behalf of Susan Frohlick we are grateful to the Social Sciences and Humanities Research Council of Canada, for providing funding for the research behind her chapter, as well as to the support of many people in Costa Rica. Finally, she has asked us to acknowledge the late Emily Howell and Emily Eagan and we express our deepest condolences to their families.

Notes on Contributors

Simone Abram has been Reader at the Centre for Tourism and Cultural Change at Leeds Metropolitan University since 2008. Her research moves between questions of mobility and the bureaucracy of settlement. Published books include *Tourists and Tourism*, *Rationalities of Planning* and *Anthropological Perspectives on Local Development*. Two new books, *Culture and Planning* and *The Elusive Promise* (edited with Gisa Weszkalnys) will be published in 2010.

Hazel Andrews is a Senior Lecturer in Tourism, Culture and Society in the Centre for Tourism, Consumer and Food Studies at Liverpool John Moores University. With a particular focus on practices of embodiment, consumption, habitus and place, Hazel's research and publications have examined social and symbolic constructions of national, regional and gendered identities in the context of British tourists to Mallorca. Her current research involves the application of theories of existential anthropology to understandings of tourists' experiences and an examination of discourses of nationalism in tourism imagery. Hazel is a co-founder and an editor of the *Journal of Tourism Consumption and Practice*. Recent publications include: "'Tits Out for the Boys and No Back Chat': Gendered Space on Holiday', in the *Journal of Space and Culture* and 'Tourism as a Moment of Being', in *Suomen Antropologi*.

Jeremy Boissevain (b.1928) is Emeritus Professor of Social Anthropology, University of Amsterdam. His field research in Malta, Sicily, Montreal and Amsterdam has included local politics, ethnic relations, small entrepreneurs, ritual change and, currently, the impact of tourism and civic reaction to environmental degradation. His books include *Saints and Fireworks: Religion and Politics in Rural Malta* (London: 1965, Malta: 1993), *The Italians of Montreal: Social Adjustment in a Plural Society* (Ottawa: 1970), *Friends of Friends: Networks, Manipulators and Coalitions* (Oxford: 1974), *A Village in Malta* (New York: 1980) and *Hal Kirkop* (Malta: 2006); and the edited collections (with John Friedl) *Beyond the Community: Social Process in Europe* (The Hague: 1975); (with Hans Vermeulen) *Ethnic Challenge: The Politics of Ethnicity in Europe* (Göttingen: 1985); (with Jojada Verrips) *Dutch Dilemmas: Anthropologists Look at the Netherlands* (Assen: 1989); *Revitalizing European Rituals* (London: 1992); *Coping with Tourists: European Reactions to Mass Tourism* (Oxford: 1996); (with

Tom Selwyn) *Contesting the Foreshore: Tourism, Society and Politics on the Coast* (Amsterdam: 2004). Translations of his work have appeared in Dutch, French, Italian, Spanish, Hungarian, Japanese and Polish.

Susan Frohlick is Associate Professor in the Anthropology Department and adjunct faculty in the Women's and Gender Studies Program at the University of Manitoba in Winnipeg, Canada. Her main field of research is heterosexuality, tourism, intimate relations, subjectivity and global processes. Her recent publications include articles in *Mobilities, Tourist Studies, City & Society, Gender, Place & Culture*, as well as several book chapters. She is currently writing a book about heterosexual subjectivity in the context of women's travel sex in Costa Rica, based on fieldwork carried out in 2005 to 2008.

Nelson Graburn is Professor Emeritus of Anthropology and Curator of North American Ethnology, Hearst Museum, Berkeley, USA. He teaches graduate and undergraduate courses on art, culture change and tourism. He is widely published in these areas, including *Ethnic and Tourist Arts* (1976), *To Pray, Pay and Play: The cultural structure of Japanese tourism* (1983) and *Relocating the Tourist* (2001). He is a founding member of the International Academy for the Study of Tourism, active in the International Sociological Association's research panel on tourism and on the editorial board of Annals of Tourism Research.

Julia Harrison (DPhil, Oxon) is Professor of Anthropology and currently Director of the Frost Centre for Canadian Studies and Indigenous Studies at Trent University, Ontario, Canada. She teaches and conducts research on issues of representation in museums and other public displays of culture, on the nature of the tourist interaction and experience, and most recently, on the Ontario cottage culture experience. Prior to coming to Trent she had a sixteen-year career in the museum field in Canada and Australia. Her book *Being a Tourist* (UBC Press) was published in 2003; she recently co-edited (with Regna Darnell) a volume called *Historicizing Canadian Anthropology* (UBC Press, 2006). She has published in a range of museum and anthropology journals, including a guest edited (with Sue Frohlick) (2008) special issue of *Tourist Studies*, called *Engaging Ethnography in Tourist Research*.

Margaret Kenna is retired Professor of Social Anthropology, Swansea University. Having carried out research in Greece over the past forty years, her main fields of interest include: kinship, ritual, migration and tourism. Her major publications are: *Greek Island Life: Fieldwork on Anafi* (2001) and *The Social Organisation of Exile: Greek Political Detainees in the 1930s* (2001). Publications on tourism include 'Return migrants and tourism development', *Journal of Modern Greek Studies* 11 (1993): 60–74.

Ramona Lenz holds a Masters degree in Cultural Anthropology/European Ethnology, Political Science and Religious Studies. Since April 2004 she has been research and teaching associate at the Institute of Cultural Anthropology and European Ethnology of the University of Frankfurt/Main. In 2009 she completed her doctoral thesis on *Mobilities in Europe: Migration and Tourism in Crete and Cyprus in the context of the European border regime.* Her main fields of research are transnationalism, Europeanization, mobilities, migration, tourism, the Mediterranean and gender studies. Recent publications include (with Mone Spindler) 'National Report: The Case of Germany' in *Integration of Female Domestic Workers, Strategies of Employment and Civic Participation* (University of Nicosia Press: 2008); 'Challenging and Confirming Touristic Representations of the Mediterranean: Migrant Workers in Crete' St Antony's College, University of Oxford, Ramses Working Paper Series, Working Paper 4/06 (2006); and 'Fake marriages as a Threat for the Nation – Migrant Sex Workers in Cyprus' in Alice Szczepaniková, Marek Canek and Jan Grill (eds), *Migration Processes in Central and Eastern Europe: Unpacking the Diversity.* (Prague: Multicultural Center, 2006).

David Picard is a Senior Research Fellow at CRIA (Centro em Rede de In- vestigacão em Anthropologìa), at the University Nova of Lisbon, Portugal, and also remains attached to the Centre for Tourism and Cultural Change (CTCC) at Leeds Metropolitan University where he has been working since 2002. With a PhD in anthropology from the University of La Réunion, Indian Ocean, he has been a Visiting Scholar at the Institute for Development Research, Madagascar, and the Anthropology Department of the University of California, Berkeley, United States. Major research interests are in phenomenological and political anthropology, tourism, environmental conservation and ethnographic filmmaking. Publications include *Festivals, Tourism and Social Change* (for which he served as a co-editor; Channel View, 2006); *Tourism, Culture and Sustainable Development* (which he co-authored; UNESCO, 2006); *The Framed World: Tourism, Tourists and Photo- graphy* (for which he served as a co-editor; Ashgate, 2009); and *Tourism, Magic and Modernity: Cultivating the Human Garden* (Berghahn, forthcoming 2010).

Annika Rabo is Professor in the Department of Social Anthropology, Stockholm University. She has conducted research on various topics in the Middle East, mainly Syria, and since the late 1970s her main focus has been on state–citizen relations. She has published widely on civil society, education and gender, and her edited books include (with Marie Carlson and Fatma Gök) *Education in Multicultural Societies*; (with Dawn Chatty) *Organizing Women*; and (with Bo Utas) *The Role of the State in West Asia.* Her book *A Shop Of One's Own – Independence And Reputation Among Traders In Aleppo* was published by I. B. Tauris in 2005.

Kathryn Rountree is Associate Professor of Social Anthropology at Massey University. Her research focuses primarily on ritual and religion, especially Neo-Paganism; pilgrimage and tourism; and contemporary discourses in relation to archaeological sites. She is author of many articles on these themes and two books: *Embracing the Witch and the Goddess* (Routledge, 2004) and *Crafting Contemporary Pagan Identities in a Catholic Society* (Ashgate, 2010).

Julie Scott is Senior Research Fellow in Tourism, Culture and Development at London Metropolitan University. Her work, with its particular focus on Cyprus and the Mediterranean, explores the role of memory and 'intangible heritage' in conflict and post-conflict societies. She has also published on casino tourism, female entrepreneurship and employment in the tourism industry, and the material practice of project implementation. She convened a major EU project creating a database of oral history and cultural practice in a network of twelve Mediterranean cities, and has worked in an applied capacity on numerous tourism and heritage related projects. Her published work has appeared in anthropology and tourism books and journals, including the *Journal of Mediterranean Studies*, *History and Anthropology*, *Annals of Tourism Research*, and the *International Journal of Heritage Studies*.

Tom Selwyn is Professorial Research Associate and Teaching Fellow at the School of Oriental and African Studies, University of London, where he teaches graduate and undergraduate courses on the anthropology of tourism. He founded the first Masters degree course in the Anthropology of Tourism in the UK at the University of Surrey (Roehampton) in 1992 and was a founder member of the NGO Tourism Concern. He has directed two research and development projects on pilgrimage, tourism, and the cultural industries – in Bosnia-Herzegovina and Palestine – for the EC's TEMPUS Programme. He is widely published in the field, including *The Tourist Image* (1996), (with J. Boissevain) *Contesting the Foreshore* (2004) and (with M. Kousis and D. Clark) *Contested Mediterranean Spaces* (2010). He was awarded the Lucy Mair Medal by the Royal Anthropological Institute in 2009.

Vassiliki Yiakoumaki (PhD, New School for Social Research) is Lecturer in Social Anthropology at the University of Thessaly (Volos), Greece. Her area of research is ethnic groups, minorities and multiculturalist politics in Europe, and she has written on topics such as Mediterranean cultures, Jewish identities and cultural politics of food. She has conducted research for the European Programme Mediterranean Voices/Euromed Heritage II, and has published in journals (*South European Society & Politics*, *Journal of Modern Greek Studies*) and edited volumes (*Visual Interventions* edited by S. Pink 2007; *Contested Mediterranean Spaces* edited by M. Kousis, T. Selwyn and D. Clark 2010).

Foreword

Margaret E. Kenna

Introduction

In this brief Foreword, at the suggestion of the editors I reflect on the dialogue I have had with the anthropology of tourism, a dialogue grounded in long-term empirical experience of the same fieldwork site for over forty years (the small Cycladic island of Anafi, just to the east of Santorini).

The Anthropologist as Tourist, Traveller and Theoretician

When I first went to carry out research in Greece in the spring of 1966, I was careful to differentiate myself from tourists and travellers in a way I now recognize to be a reaction to the threat of 'contamination' to my mission, which I saw as in some way morally superior to the search for pleasure and recreation which I assumed characterized these others. From what I have read (Errington and Gewertz 1989), this attempt to mark difference of essence and intent has been common among other researchers, as well as among academics in other disciplines ('you've come to whale-watch, but I'm a cetologist').

I was not in Greece, I told myself, to sunbathe, to read Fowles's *The Magus* or translations of Kazantzakis's *Zorba* on the beach or on the decks of inter-island ferries; I was there to become a real anthropologist, to carry out participant observation, to live with local people all year round, winter as well as summer. I might look like a typical backpacker but I felt that I was different. I became aware that some of these other visitors to Greece, like myself, also saw themselves as different, but my interpretation then was that this was a rationalization of their economic position (usually coupled with age). Backpackers[1] claimed that they were there to experience the 'real Greece', and that those who travelled in air-conditioned coaches, or had cabins with bunks rather than sleeping on deck, were missing some kind of authenticity in their encounter with places and people. The question of what constituted 'the "real" Greece', and how best to find it, gained salience for me much later; at that time I assumed that I would have access to it through long-term participant observation fieldwork.

I was not confident enough then, however, to anthropologize the situation I found myself in and to problematize the different kinds of tourists and travellers I met and in contrast to whom I tried to assert a different identity. Even if I had done this, I think I would have felt that the focus of my studies should be the local people not the visitors.[2]

Although Nunez's article on 'weekendismo'[3] had been published three years earlier (Nunez 1963), I was then completely unaware of any anthropological studies of, or thinking about, tourism. Erik Cohen's typologies of tourists and tourism experiences were yet to be published (1974, 1979), as were his writings on the connections between tourism and pilgrimage (1992), in which he differentiated between pilgrims 'seeking the Centre' (1992: 58), and tourists who are either looking for a contrast with their everyday lives, or, at the other extreme, trying to find an alternative to it – 'seeking the Other', whether for recreational or existential reasons. As beings inhabiting the zone of liminal antistructure (Turner 1973), pilgrims and tourists are alike: 'If a pilgrim is half tourist, a tourist is half pilgrim' (Morinis 1992: viii). And maybe the anthropologist is a partly a pilgrim too – seeking the Centre, which might be thought of as the key themes of the community being studied. Indeed, it has been claimed more recently that in '… their search for (authentic truths) in the "world out there", it is easy to see that tourists resemble … the social scientist' (Graburn and Barthel-Boucher 2001: 154; their brackets, my omissions).

Empirical Experience and the Need to Theorize

During this first fieldwork (1966–7), fewer than ten people came to Anafi who could be classified as tourists or travellers. Not surprisingly, they were nearly all backpackers, carrying sleeping bags and basic supplies, in case they could not find a place to sleep or anything to eat. And the islanders were certainly not set up to receive, nor did they seem even to welcome, the arrival of these visitors.[4] The topic of tourism hardly featured in the material written up from this period.

However, the anthropology of tourism forced itself on my consciousness in 1974 when electrification, coupled with some repairs and improvements to the harbour which allowed steamers to dock directly at the jetty, brought tourism to the island. Anafiot migrants returned from Athens to open restaurants and cafés, while locals began to convert storehouses to offer to the increasing numbers of foreign and domestic tourists as rooms to rent, and then began to purpose-build such rooms. From 1989, lorries and refrigerated trucks could reach the outskirts of the village on a newly constructed road, which replaced the donkey-track, up which scooters, but not cars, had bumped their way since 1974. Village houses now had piped water and were connected to a sewerage system. Tourism-related enterprises took another quantum leap forward: now rooms to rent had en-suite bathrooms, and there were apartments with kitchenettes. Tavernas and restaurants now began to differentiate their menus and to offer 'specialities'. The road provided further opportunities for locals too, as its route opened up areas of land on the way to, and around, the village which had been previously impossible to reach. Some of these newly accessible building-sites, particularly those on steep hillsides, were developed into multi-storey apartment blocks, with panoramic views, and new village neighbourhoods were thus established. In each cluster, one apartment would provide a daughter's dowry, and the rest would bring her in an income when rented during the summer season. Outside the season, the large number of schoolteachers appointed to teach at the newly created secondary school and sixth-form college[5] provided a smaller but steady income. Within another decade, a network of unpaved 'agricultural' roads, constructed with money from European Union grants for the development of peripheral areas, contributed not only to the resurgence of agriculture, but also to the repair and renovation of country cottages, and to the building of new holiday retreats for migrants who found the village too noisy during the tourist season. As a result, new neighbourhoods were emerging outside the village as well as in it, and new kinds of social relationships were being established. Reading material on 'locals' and 'outsiders' in tourism-related enterprises elsewhere, it seemed to me that those who had written on this topic could not have had long-term in-depth knowledge of local communities and the relationships between people. Otherwise they might have asked the question how these outsiders had found out about the opportunities to set up tourist enterprises, and thus the researchers would have discovered that there were many kinds of already established ties between these 'outsiders' and people in the local community (see Kenna 1993). In the material I had collected, these ties were predominantly based on having a common place of origin. Migrants whose parents or grandparents had gone to the city to find work now brought their urban-acquired capital with them to take advantage of each decade's improvements on the island. But they had urban contacts (friends, neighbours, employers, fellow employees) who also recognized the economic opportunities of a newly developing tourism-oriented summer seasonal economy. So even those who could indeed be classified as 'outsiders', turned out to have some kind of link with islanders or migrants which explained their presence running a bar in the village or a mini-market at the harbour, in a building rented from a local contact. Knowledge of long-running enmities between village families, of local schisms and factions, also helped to explain why some of these outsiders' enterprises were actively promoted by some islanders – as a way of taking custom away from those with whom they were on bad terms as much as of supporting someone whom they felt they had 'sponsored' to come to the island.

Before the road was finished in 1989, most villagers were able to provide roughly the same 'product' to tourists (a room to rent, meals composed of similar ingredients). The creation of a personal relationship between a room renter or taverna owner and customers attempted to ensure that the tourist returned to them next time, and not to any other provider of the same service. I had witnessed this in Athens in the streets where shop after shop offered exactly the same stock, whether electrical cable, plastic pipe, or zips, buttons and ribbons. Men went to particular electrical supply shops, and women to specific haberdashers, as a result of familiarity and of long-term relationships, often established in previous generations. Prices were adjusted, or additional services provided, to ensure that these relationships continued. Just so, on Anafi, new relationships (in island terms) were being built up between service providers, based on an urban pattern (which itself was based on patterns brought from the places of origin of migrants to the city).

Seeing Oneself (and One's Environment) as Seen by Others

Starting off in a similar fashion (trying to create a repeat-customer relationship), another kind of relationship was also being established, and that was between villagers with rooms to rent and domestic and international holidaymakers who were becoming 'regulars', booking for the same week or fortnight every year (almost a kind of timeshare). Some of these had a much more detailed knowledge than I did of the changes which had taken place over the years between my visits to the island, and some of them knew much more than me about the family from whom they regularly rented accommodation. I became aware that I could no longer make claims to possessing encyclopaedic authoritative information about the island – this was worse than the unease that I had experienced twenty years earlier with the backpackers!

But this time I was able to diffuse the sense of threat by speculating about these relationships. Were these 'friendships'? Or were they defined and regarded in different terms by the two sets of participant? For example, a Dutch couple who had been coming every Easter for a decade said that they had a warm personal friendship with the owners of the rooms they rented; one year they had brought with them and left behind a coffee-maker, which was now ceremoniously unpacked and put in 'their room' each year before their annual visit. They were always invited to the family's Easter celebrations and given fresh vegetables and fruit from their garden, gifts which were reciprocated with specialities from Holland, and, of course, colour photographs of the couple and their children and of picturesque views of the island. But was this perceived as a friendship by the room-renters?

These ponderings overlapped with thoughts arising out of changes I had noticed in the celebrations of the island patron saint's festival day. The improvements in facilities that had led to the return of migrants and the development of tourism had also resulted in larger numbers of people attending this festival (usually regarded as important in demonstrating the power of the saint in attracting devotees (see also Kenna 1992). After the morning service on the day of the festival, the patron saint's icon (miracle-working holy picture) was carried in procession three times anticlockwise around the church where it was housed. Over the years I noticed that there was an increase in the number of people wanting to take photographs, and later, video-recordings of this event. Some were islanders, and some were migrants, both feeling that they had superior claims over others to do this because of their special relationship with their patron saint. These concerns began to clash with the desire of foreign tourists (and with domestic tourists from other parts of Greece, who seemed to regard themselves as observers rather than as participants) to capture images of what they seemed to regard as a particularly authentic example of traditional island custom.[6] They jostled with each other, and with Anafiots, for positions from which to film. Comments were made that the festival was turning into a tourist attraction and the procession into a 'photo-opportunity' rather than retaining its character (exactly what this character was provided an issue for debate, with islanders and migrants split into a number of factions).

Outside-in and Inside-out

These thoughts about what constituted authenticity also overlapped with a part-icular understanding I was reaching about Greek Orthodoxy, which seemed to me (and, I later discovered, to other scholars who worked in Greece) not to be particularly concerned with the internalized conscience and with guilt, but rather with avoiding public shame and with comporting oneself in accordance with public expectations (which on the island usually lagged behind urban mores).[7] What was important to the islanders was a socially acceptable performance, whatever one's personal feelings were. There were, of course, occasions when what I considered to be 'real emotions' were openly displayed (the happy glow of a young woman finally engaged to the young man of her choice; the uncontrollable grief of the female relatives of a teenage girl, who had been killed in a fall from a donkey and then down a rocky ravine), but proper behaviour by the protagonists seemed to be the key aspect of positively evaluating others' actions and words, and therefore became a guiding principle of the main actors' behaviour. So if the islanders themselves were not particularly concerned with sincerity and authenticity but rather in a reasonable representation of socially appropriate behaviour, how could these notions of evaluation from the anthropology of tourism be applicable? If most behaviour was 'performed authenticity' what counted as 'genuine' and 'sincere'?

I found myself returning to texts which I had studied as an undergraduate, including articles by Meyer Fortes based on his research among the Tallensi of West Africa (Fortes 1959, 1961). In one he muses on two religious and ethical conceptions, mutually opposed, 'different cosmological doctrines about the universe, and different conceptions of the nature of man and his relations with spiritual powers' (1959: 11). The story of Oedipus deals with the notion of fixed and inescapable fate, in the face of which questions of responsibility and guilt are irrelevant. The story of Job ends with Job accepting God's authority without resentment, seeing it as benevolent in intention even when used punitively – just as the Tallensi accept without question that ancestors are just and that men have no choice but to submit to them (1959: 59). 'This is the essence of filial piety' (1959: 59).

In the other article, clearly linked to these thoughts on Job, Fortes considers the notion of *pietas* (filial piety – 'faithfulness to duties naturally owed to parents and relatives', what he elsewhere calls 'the axiom of amity' in kinship relationships) and the role of conformity to custom in overriding personal feelings and even ethically grounded behaviour: 'Morality in the sense of righteous conduct does not count. All that matters is service and obedience ... [not good deeds, but] conformity with the basic moral axioms in fulfilling the requirements of all social relationships' (1959: 51; my interpolation].

These ideas relating to unquestioned axioms of customary behaviour illuminated for me the islanders' carrying out of an expensive cycle of rituals for the souls of their parents and other deceased relatives, regardless of the quality and content of the relationship when the person was alive. Here, I felt it could be argued, the focus was on performance ('fulfilling requirements' in Fortes's terms) in front of an audience – or, more strictly, viewers – of members of their own community. These ideas were equally suggestive in coming to some kind of understanding of the new kinds of relations which were being created on Anafi with short-term and long-term tourists, the attempt to forge a link to ensure a return visit to a cafe or taverna during the tourists' stay, or to rented rooms the next time they came to the island.

Further insights came from writers who interpreted local hosts' behaviour in terms of seeing themselves through tourists' eyes. The Anafiot villagers were now looking at the island landscape, and areas of the village, as if they were themselves tourists, evaluating their own surroundings in ways that they had not done before, as an 'object of consumption rather than merely production' (Bianchi 2003: 19). Cafés and bars that had views facing the west were now being promoted as places to sit and have an early evening drink while watching the sunset (this had been the case for decades on the neighbouring island of Santorini); rooms with views over the south coast were recognized to be more desirable for summer visitors than those facing inward (much less cold and windy than in the island winter). Beaches, and even the action of the sea itself, were evaluated in terms of potential for tourist activities – from the more usual swimming and sunbathing to wind-surfing and kayaking. Springtime bookings from birdwatchers and wild-flower enthusiasts (an area of the island had been given a special status under a European 'Natura 2000' programme) were encouraging active responses to develop ecotourism.

Just as the Anafiot environment now meant something different to Anafiots because it had a different meaning to visitors, so, in a similar fashion, islanders presented themselves differently. They behaved towards visitors as 'traditional island people' still practising the traditional Greek defining characteristic of hospitality (*filoksenia*) – a word which in Greek literally means 'love of strangers/foreigners/guests'.[8] Whether tourists were or are now regarded on Anafi as constituting a different category from either strangers or guests, the newly emerging type of 'customer oriented' behaviour, as described above, attempts to create good-humoured relationships, which might even be defined as 'friendships', and which would engender feelings of personal obligation. Each party in this relationship, or in the interaction of an encounter, might well have culturally different notions of what was constituted, and yet enough common ground to make it work.[9]

Authenticity and Performance

I am inclined to agree with Damer (2004), writing of the Dodecanese island of Symi, that 'tourist performances are constructed in a creative synthesis of human agency between locals and tourists', something which he labels 'social dialectics' (2004: 224). He describes and discusses a scene in a Symiaki taverna, run by a local, where other locals, mostly elderly relatives of the proprietor, come, as if to a theatre, for some 'free entertainment' (2004: 219). This entertainment is provided by the tourists, but also by their interaction with the proprietor, who 'performs' for them and with them. These old men sometimes participate themselves in this entertainment by singing with the taverna owner, and therefore giving the other customers the sense that they are almost eavesdropping on 'the inside of local culture' (2004: 219). The locals have fun, so do the tourists, they both have a 'commitment to participation' in order to enhance the 'tourist experience on Symi' (2004: 221). In other words, both locals and tourists 'amplify' their performances in these dialectically negotiated encounters with each other to create something that everyone enjoys (2004: 223; see also Taylor 2001: 9[10]). Tourists 'have seen *something* of the cultural intimacy of locals, usually only their tourism-oriented lives, which *is* constructed, and *is* partial, but it is real enough for most tourists' (Damer 2004: 224; emphasis in original).

With respect to the Anafi material, I would argue that because most non-locals, whether Greek domestic tourists or foreigners, do not (usually) know who among the other people in cafes and tavernas are island migrants (some running the enterprise, others there as customers), they interpret the conviviality, singing and dancing there as 'traditional island behaviour' which they have been able to witness, and have been lucky enough to take part in – an 'authentic experience' of 'the real Anafi' (what they imagine was 'traditional' behaviour – note the conflation of authenticity and tradition). As is probably the case on Symi, such jollification is not characteristic of islanders' behaviour out of season, except on festival days or at weddings. It is, however, typical summer holiday behaviour during the tourist season, and, in the past, occurred occasionally during the summer visits of Anafiot migrants. So, like Damer, and Wang (1999), I would argue that what is happening is as 'authentic' as it needs to be to satisfy both the tourists and other visitors, who are 'performing' as much as the locals are. Indeed, if one accepts that 'authenticity' is an essentially Western notion, grounded in a historical context relating to ideas of the individual; and that the label 'sincerity' depends on ideas of acting outwardly in conformity with inner feelings and self-knowledge (Trilling 1972), then these are inappropriate concepts to make sense of behaviour in a context like that on Anafi (or indeed among the Tallensi) where public performance is evaluated without reference to its relationship in expressing private feelings.

On this basis, it could be argued that societies and cultures which place a high value on appropriate behaviour rather than inner truth, on what might be called the performance of outward forms ('going through the motions'), have no initial problem with 'performing' for tourists. Authenticity, and sincerity, only become problematic as they become more Westernized. And thus, notions of 'being true' to the 'essential nature' of something, be it a dance form or an architectural style, begin to creep in. People cannot help but equate 'authenticity' in their cultural forms with the past, and with notions of 'tradition'. They also take on board Western notions of being true to themselves, of the hypocritical nature of acting in one way while believing or thinking something else. In other words, authenticity, however it may be defined as an analytical category, at an 'emic' level is socially constructed.[11]

Conclusion

This brings the discussion back to the situation with which it began: the assertion of a specific identity in the face of ambiguity and category confusion. The material presented here suggests that questions of authenticity and clear category membership arise in conditions of change and uncertainty. Just as in 1966 I could not feel confident about my identity as an anthropologist when it had not yet been established, nor sure of how to define 'the real Greece' when I had so little experience of the country and its people, so the Anafiots are beginning to question who 'counts' as a 'real islander', and what is 'authentically Anafiot'. While the legal appellation 'permanent resident', to establish voting rights, can include various degrees of residence on the island, the question of who counts locally as an islander, so as to have a recognized, legitimate, voice in discussions and local decision-making, whatever their legal status, is problematic. Does it include those migrants who come only in the summer to run tourism-related enterprises? Or is it restricted to those people who live on the island outside the tourism season (even if they go to Athens for the winter months), or should it be confined to those who live on the island all year round? Who defines what is, or was, an island custom? Not surprisingly, the majority of those who want a more encompassing definition are those who would be excluded if a narrower one was introduced. And, ironically, my own status as an anthropologist is legitimized by having field-notes and photographs dating back over the past forty years which could be used to validate certain definitions of local customs and behaviour.

Notes

1. This word was not in common usage in the UK back in the 1960s, although the distinction between tourist and traveller was gaining currency. At that time, although a Greek word for 'rucksack' (*sakidhio*) existed, there was no word equivalent to 'backpacker', and even today if *sakidhioforos* – rucksack carrier – were to be used, it has been suggested to me by Greek friends that it would probably describe a specific person's luggage rather than apply to a general category of traveller.
2. This typical anthropological focus on the 'hosts' was also a way of avoiding being defined by others, or crossing over into a sociological interest in the 'guests', at a time when the anthropology of the Mediterranean area was highly contentious, and by some considered not to be reputable anthropology at all. It was only when I took up my first academic post, in 1968, in a joint department of Sociology and Anthropology, that I began to feel comfortable with ignoring these disciplinary boundaries.
3. This is usually cited as a seminal publication in the history of tourism studies. It is sobering to reflect on the time it took to acquire this status when 'impact

factor' evaluation occurs nowadays almost the moment something appears in print.

4. This is probably because of the island's history as a place of political exile (Kenna 2001a). While the Greek word for 'tourist' (*touristas*, plural *touristes*) was used in Athens, they were referred to in country places, and on most islands, as 'strangers' (*kseni*), a word with a meaning relative to context, which could apply to foreigners (non-Greeks), or to non-locals, that is, Greeks from the next island or even the next village. Ticket-stubs for those leaving the island in 1966, usually with islanders' names written on them, recorded that a *ksenos*, or on one occasion *enas lordos* (a 'Lord', i.e. an Englishman) had bought them. The word 'tourist' was never used (see Kenna 2001b: 24).

5. This was part of a government initiative to try to halt rural depopulation. The teachers who opted to come to the island, and to volunteer for other such 'punishment postings', were rewarded (like the doctor and nurse) with appointments later to the places of their choice.

6. There is not space to consider here what might happen if tourists became interested in, and wanted to watch and film, memorial services or even exhumations as examples of 'authentic' local customs.

7. Nor is there space to develop a discussion about notions of the person and of individualism within Christian Orthodoxy, and in Greece (but see, for example, Hirschon 1989: 240; see also Clough 2006).

8. To elucidate which of these was meant when the word *ksenos* was used, Anafiots would either say *mousafiris* (invited guest, as to a private party), or designate the person's nationality or regional identity within Greece. There is now plenty of evidence that in some parts of Greece, there has developed a very clear-cut distinction between tourists/strangers and guests (see, for example, Zarkia 1996, writing about the island of Skyros).

9. I wonder if this is enough to warrant further examination of Damer's contention that 'Some locals *are* friends with some tourists' (2004: 217).

10. '... the moment of interaction may become the site in which value is generated' (Taylor 2001: 9).

11. This word, like 'tourist', has only recently entered the vocabulary and discourse of local people on Anafi (possibly because of the tourism and business management courses that some young people are taking). As Damer says, in many years of researching tourism in the UK and elsewhere, 'authenticity' is not a word he had ever heard.

References

Bianchi, R.V. (2003), 'Place and Power in Tourism Development: Tracing the Complex Articulation of Community and Locality', *PASOS – Revista de Turismo y Patrimonio Cultural* 1(1):13–32.

Clough, P. (2006), '"Knowledge in Passing": Reflexive Anthropology and Religious Awareness', *Anthropological Quarterly* 79(2): 261–83.

Cohen, E. (1974), 'Who is a tourist? A conceptual clarification', *Sociological Review* 22: 527–55.

Cohen, E. (1979), 'A phenomenology of tourist experiences', *Sociology* 13: 179–201.

Cohen, E. (1992), 'Pilgrimage and Tourism: Convergence and Divergence', in Alan Morinis (ed.), *Sacred Journeys: the Anthropology of Pilgrimage*, Westport, CT: Greenwood Press, pp. 47–61.

Damer, S (2004), 'Signifying Symi: Setting and Performance on a Greek Island', *Ethnography* 5(2): 203–28.

Errington, F and Gewertz, D. (1989), 'Tourism and Anthropology in a Post-Modern World', *Oceania* 60: 37–54.

Fortes, M. (1959), *Oedipus and Job in West African Religion*, Cambridge: Cambridge University Press.

Fortes, M. (1961), 'Pietas in Ancestor Worship' (the Henry Myers Lecture, 1960) *JRAI* 91(2): 166–91.

Graburn N.H.H. and Barthel-Boucher, D. (2001), 'Relocating the Tourist', *International Sociology* 16(2): 147–58.

Hirschon, R. (1989), *Heirs of the Greek Catastrophe: the Social Life of Asia Minor Refugees in Piraeus*, Oxford: Clarendon Press.

Kenna, M.E. (1992), 'Mattresses and Migrants: a Patron Saint's Festival on a Small Greek Island over Two Decades', in J. Boissevain (ed.), *Revitalizing European Rituals*, London: Routledge, pp. 155–72.

Kenna, M.E. (1993) 'Return Migrants and Tourism Development', *Journal of Modern Greek Studies*, 11: 75–95.

Kenna, M.E. (2001a), *The Social Organisation of Exile: Greek Political Detainees in the 1930s*, Amsterdam: Harwood Academic Publishers.

Kenna, M.E. (2001b), *Greek Island Life: Fieldwork on Anafi*, Amsterdam: Harwood Academic Publishers.

Morinis, A. (ed.) (1992), *Sacred Journeys: the Anthropology of Pilgrimage*, Westport, CT: Greenwood Press.

Nunez, T. (1963), '"Weekendismo" in a Mexican village', *South Western Journal of Anthropology* 34: 328–36.

Taylor, J.P. (2001), 'Authenticity and Sincerity in Tourism', *Annals of Tourism Research* 28(1): 7–26.

Trilling, L. (1972), *Sincerity and Authenticity*, London: Oxford University Press

Turner, V. (1973), 'The Center Out There: Pilgrim's Goal', *History of Religions*, 12(1):191–230.

Wang, N. (1999), 'Rethinking Authenticity in Tourism Experience', *Annals of Tourism Research* 26(2): 349–70.

Zarkia, C. (1996), 'Receiving Tourists – but not Guests – on a Greek Island', in J. Boissevain (ed.), *Coping with Tourists: European Reactions to Mass Tourism*, Oxford: Berghahn, pp. 143–173.

Introduction

Thinking Through Tourism – Framing the Volume
Julie Scott and Tom Selwyn

The three broad aims of this Introduction are to frame the essays presented here in terms of their institutional, epistemological and theoretical contexts and contours; to introduce each essay within a conceptual framework that brings out some of the continuities between them; and to reflect on the contributions anthropology, tourism, and tourism studies make to each other.

Contexts and Contours

Institutional Contexts

The ASA's sixty-first annual conference, *Thinking Through Tourism*, marked four noteworthy departures. Firstly, while, in the course of its history, the ASA has deliberated on a wide range of topics at its annual conferences, this was the first on (or near) the subject of tourism. In her foreword to this volume, Margaret Kenna suggests that part of the reason for this absence derives from the fact that, over a period of three or more decades, the subject of tourism has trodden a rocky path to recognition as a legitimate area of anthropological enquiry in the UK. A second departure was that the conference was the first ASA annual conference to be held in one of the post-1992 'new' universities in the UK – one that, moreover, had no anthropology department of its own. The third was the fact that the conference drew a wider than usual spectrum of participants from beyond traditional anthropology departments: from business schools, schools of tourism and hospitality, departments of geography, architecture and cultural (including 'cultural heritage') studies, and museums; and from sixth-form school students studying anthropology as part of their International Baccalaureate curriculum.[1]

The fourth departure derives from one of the features of the working lives and practices of a good number of anthropologists engaged in research in tourism. In addition to writing academic contributions to journals and books, they routinely become engaged in policy work with private and/or public institutions, including government ministries, and multinational organizations. This is why we include one essay (by Abram) in the present collection that addresses head on the question of 'intervention' by anthropologists in the tourism field and draws out the ethical, epistemological and political dilemmas faced by those who have moved into, or move in and out of, 'applied' fields of tourism consultancy of one kind or another. Applied work in tourism policy fields is not unrelated to one of the threads linking new universities lacking anthropology departments, tourism studies and contemporary anthropology itself: namely the changing landscape of funding for social-scientific research. At both national and European levels there are recurrent policy steers towards 'relevance' and 'impact' (the latter term presently finding prominence in the discourse of the forthcoming research assessment exercise in the UK). Part of the relevance of this work is seen by the EC in terms of arguable linkages between tourism and economic, social, and political development, including post-conflict development, in the regions involved. Such programmes of work come with substantial funds, which makes them attractive to the universities that host them.[2]

These separate yet, we suggest, related features, are key to understanding what anthropology contributes to the study of tourism and, conversely, what anthropology may learn about itself from 'thinking through tourism' – the twofold aims of the conference. Before introducing our chapters, then, we start by reflecting on the intellectual and institutional contexts in which the anthropology of tourism finds a place. This involves, inter alia, tracing some of the congruencies and tensions that emerge from the close relationship between them, and considering the nature of the environments in which they are practised, researched and taught. We suggest that this exercise reveals ambivalences at the heart of contemporary anthropology towards its object as well as its aspirations for a wider public role.

Epistemological Contexts

Avoidance Relationship or Unholy Alliance?   Anthropologists and tourists do similar things: they travel, spend temporary periods away from home, gather experiences and souvenirs, and tell stories about them when they get home. Numerous commentators have drawn attention to the kinship between them (Burns 1999) but it is a kinship that many others have preferred to ignore. Crick (1995) suggests that comparison with tourists is potentially so threatening that for many anthropologists

> ... the idea cannot be held in consciousness. Thus, in a discussion of anthropology in the context of other adventurer/travel roles, Peacock can list 'spies' and 'missionaries' but fails to mention tourists ... What is so forgettable or appalling about tourists that provokes these overreactions and avoidances? After all, in our recent reflexive phase,

we have been likened to other identities such as con-men, voyeurs and clowns ... which might, on first glance, appear to be even less palatable than the tourist comparison. (Crick 1995: 206–7)

Evidently, it is the very similarities that trouble anthropologists. The differences, suggests Crick, are primarily of degree (length of stay; level of language competence; nature of local interaction; the medium and language of storytelling) rather than of kind. Anthropologists may simply be unable to accept that they are just another particularly sophisticated type of traveller; that locals will most likely classify them as such; and that the ethnographic monographs and scientific reports they produce on their return home could be considered just another form of travel writing (Crick 1995). But underlying the classic avoidance relationship described by Crick is a deeper-seated tension. If anthropologists are no longer uniquely placed in terms of access to distant places and people, what then, to echo the question posed by Eriksen (2005), is the difference between anthropology and a piece of intelligent journalism (or travel writing)? Tourism, in other words, calls into question anthropology's ethnology-based authority – only, it seems, to reincorporate it and reinvest it with a spurious authority within tourism discourse (cf. Bruner 2005).

Critical voices from within anthropology have alleged too close a dependence on ethnography as its prime justification and distinguishing feature. Hart (2004), for example, deplores the failure to find an alternative to '[anthropologists'] original *raison d'être* ... the study of "primitives"', and the subsequent trend towards the fragmentation of issue-driven ethnography. His provocative characterization of anthropology's current *raison d'être*, as 'long-term, empty-headed exposure to strangers wherever they live' (2004: 4) could equally be a caricature of the more earnest types of tourist. In an early and now classic essay 'Tourism as a Form of Imperialism', Dennison Nash (1989) draws attention to the continuities and structural similarities between tourism and imperialism, and the parallels with anthropology's roots in colonialism need not be laboured here. But while the intellectual and political certainties of colonial-era anthropology have given way to more equivocal critical reflexivity, 'tourism' is accused of being unencumbered by self-doubt, continuing to embrace the narratives, confidence and certainties of earlier anthropological generations, and drawing on ethnographic authority to authenticate its nostalgic versions of colonialism.[3] This is a world in which the troubling ethnicity of minority populations inhabiting the cities of the developed world is transformed into the exotic, colourful traditions of the Third World, performed for tourists by 'ex-primitives' (MacCannell 1992), and validated by a 'co-opted' ethnographic voice (Bruner 2005). Earlier anthropologists' accounts may serve as templates for the invention of cultural performances for tourists, as Tilley (1997) discovers, along with an audience of fellow anthropologists, in a village in Vanuatu; or anthropologists may be sought as tour guides, to structure and interpret the tourists' experience for them (cf. Bruner 1995, 2005; Wallace 2005). Bruner writes revealingly of his own experiences as a guide leading small groups of middle-aged North American cultural tourists around Indonesia, where he had spent three years conducting ethnographic fieldwork. For Bruner, his stint as a tour guide was a way of doing fieldwork among tourists; for the tour company, his credentials as a professor of anthropology were part of the brand – a symbol and guarantee of the seriousness and quality of the tour. But, as he discovers, when he is sacked for introducing sessions where he leads the group in deconstructing their touristic experience, what the tour company wants is an old-fashioned '1930s realist ethnographer, not one who was beginning a journey to postmodernism' (Bruner 2005: 4). Tourism, he concludes, is happy '... chasing anthropology's discarded discourse, presenting cultures as functionally integrated homogeneous entities outside of time, space, and history', but structurally unable to accommodate its contemporary paradigms (2005: 4).

The 'Black Box'   As Kenna observes in her foreword, most anthropologists in the 1960s and 1970s were content to ignore the presence of tourism and tourists on 'their' turf. To the extent that anthropologists noticed tourism at all, it was largely in terms of its local 'impacts'. A 'black box' approach was adopted to the subject of tourism itself, which was treated as another variety of industrial input, albeit particularly rapid and radical in its effects on rural communities (cf. Greenwood 1972; Redclift 1973).

From the late 1970s anthropologists began to unpack this black box and to look directly at tourism itself. In the process, different categories of tourist, styles of travel and development trajectories were identified (e.g. Cohen 1974; Smith 1989). Indeed the production of typologies of tourism and tourists not only resulted in more sophisticated analyses than had been possible when tourism was treated as an undifferentiated input, but effectively put paid to the notion (prevalent in some of the best known early examples of the anthropology of tourism) that tourists, and hence a figure termed 'the tourist', derived from the same mono-lithic category. This stereotype was further undermined by ethnographic research, which drew attention to the phenomenon of domestic tourism, and the fact that the very people traditionally studied by anthropologists could themselves be tourists, both at home and abroad (e.g. Graburn 1983; see also Leite and Graburn 2009). Anthropologists also began explicitly to acknowledge the need to avoid imposing value judgements on the effects of tourism, and to evaluate them against local ideas of development that are the outcome of negotiation and conflict over time (cf. Boissevain 1977; Nash 1981; de Kadt 1990; Wood 1993). However, until the early 1990s or so, anthropological approaches remained largely rooted in ideas of 'bounded' communities and 'cultural islands' which also characterized tourism discourse (Eriksen 1993; Scott 1995); and even the development of critical concepts, such as cultural commodification (Cohen 1988; Greenwood 1989) initially reinforced rather than challenged underlying functionalist assumptions about culture and authenticity. Tourism did not yield the theoretical breakthroughs sought by anthropologists engaged in its research (cf. Nash 1981) despite a fizzy period when some postmodernist analyses grasped and shook up existing paradigms and found in tourism an ideal metaphor for the proliferation and accelerated circulation of meanings and images, mobilities, scapes and flows, under conditions of globalization. As Crick already noted in 1995: 'in our present post-modernist, mass communications world we have very much seen a universalization of a mode of perception and being which might be termed "touristic"' (1995: 206). Tourism and its interstices – including such 'heteretopias' as hotels and airports (cf. Augé 1995; Chambers 2000; Gordon 2008), as well as the imaginary spaces of touristic interaction that Bruner terms 'border zones' (Bruner 2005) – have become quintessential arenas for 'capturing' contemporary processes and relationships.

The study of tourism likewise pushes anthropologists into increasingly inter-stitial areas of practice, engaging with a wide range of actors, knowledge claims and competing expert discourses, and expanding the range of 'local' informants to include tourists, tourism practitioners, developers, entrepreneurs and managers, officials, professionals and specialists of varying hues. Anthropologists of tourism are not alone in finding that actors from 'the field' can also become powerful interlocutors 'at home'; nor that an apparently shared technical vocabulary masks a semantic slippage in the deployment of key terms, pitting anthropologists in an unequal struggle with other, institutionally more entrenched specialist discourses, for control of meaning in the public sphere (a point taken up by Lenz and Abram in this volume). The public life of the 'culture' concept offers a particularly pertinent illustration of how outmoded anthropological models – for example, the Tylerian view of culture as a 'whole way of life of a group or society' (Wright 1998: 8) – can be appropriated and misapplied by non-anthropologists pursuing a range of agendas, from the justification of organizational reform for the purposes of achieving top-down management control (Wright 1998: 8), to the embedding of corporate ethno-national identities and associated rights in Ireland (Finlay 2006), or the creation of a symbolic vocabulary to promote European unity (Shore 2000).

Tourism thus presents anthropology with both threats and opportunities. Of the more than 50 per cent of British PhDs in anthropology who, according to recent research by Spencer, Jepson and Mills (n.d.), now find employment outside conventional anthropology departments, a good proportion of these are working on tourism-related themes, in the kind of multidisciplinary settings we referred to above. Public familiarity with tourism – in contrast to the general level of public ignorance surrounding anthropology, and what anthropologists do (cf. Caplan

2005) – may offer a route to raising the visibility of anthropology, attracting new students to its study, and all the good things that flow therefrom. At the same time, opportunities to broaden and popularize are often regarded with suspicion by anthropologists, not only because of the perceived risks of oversimplification, misrepresentation and misappropriation, referred to above; but also due to the anxiety surrounding what Mars (2004) identifies as a kind of structural tendency towards disciplinary centrifugalism, bringing with it the fear that the core will be emptied of its distinctively anthropological content. This anxiety cuts both ways: a meeting of social anthropologists working in multidisciplinary departments, convened with C-SAP[4] support at London Metropolitan University two years before the ASA conference, highlighted the growing number of academics, producing 'anthropological' theses and supervised by conventionally trained anthropologists, who now define themselves as 'anthropologists' without ever having studied in a traditional anthropology department – but worry about whether they have the 'right' to do so. For many of those teaching and researching in multidisciplinary and largely vocationally oriented settings, questions of what constitutes, and how to maintain, anthropological integrity and 'authenticity' – among colleagues from other disciplines who frequently share the misconceptions of the public at large about what anthropology is and does – have become a matter for daily negotiation (Scott and Lugosi 2005).

Theoretical and Thematic Architecture

Leisure, Culture, Hospitality

Having privileged some of the epistemological distinctions and overlaps between ways that tourists, anthropologists and others think, we may now direct our attention to the pool of descriptive terms and theoretical issues that, given the nature of the subject, routinely engage anthropologists of tourism. Looking backwards at the development of anthropological studies of tourism and sideways at our essays and other contemporary writing in the subject (Selwyn 2007) we suggest that the subject's foundations are located within the anthropological study of three broad fields: leisure, culture and hospitality.

Leisure   Marcel Mauss took a step towards signalling the sociological importance of leisure when, in 1898 and following his realization that leisure is as socially and economically significant as work, he joined a Parisian co-operative society known as *L'Avenir de Plaisance*, The Future of Leisure. Perhaps this small fact allows us to incorporate Mauss into the ancestral pantheon of the founding influences of the anthropology of tourism. More plausibly, however, the first substantial sociological essay on the subject was Veblen's (2007 [1899]) *Theory of the Leisure Class*, a work that unquestionably is one of the founding building blocks of our subject. The importance of Veblen's work lies in the way he places the leisure practices of the leisure class – including 'knowledge of dead languages', ceremonies and ritualistic and mannered displays, extravagant house decorations, 'correct spelling', fashion and brand names, 'games and sports, and fancy-bred animals, such as dogs and race-horses' – within their social and politico-economic contexts. Veblen's argument was that forms of conspicuous leisure consumption such as these both marked and legitimized social status.

We suggest that our own essays pay tribute to Veblen partly by taking his insights a good deal further than he did. The world has changed in the 100 or so years since he published his book. We are all (to put it too simply) conspicuous consumers now. The leisure practices described in this book are involved in symbolizing more complex sets of sociocultural statuses, dispositions, collectivities and solidarities than those described by Veblen. He was mainly concerned with the division between the working class and the bourgeoisie. We are concerned with all sorts of social divisions (class certainly, but also ethnic, national, gender and age related, and so on) as well as ideological and cultural formations. Harrison, for example, describes how her Canadian informants use their holiday lakeside homes symbolically to define the essence of what it means to be a 'true Canadian'. In rather similar vein, Andrews points towards the implications for the formation of British nationalism in the leisure practices of the mass tourism resorts in Mallorca.

Culture   Culture is one of the most unmanageable and slippery terms ever to make it into the lexicon of anthropological discourse in general and the anthropology of tourism in particular. However, since the term is routinely attached to expressions such as cultural heritage and cultural identity, we cannot, and would not wish to, sweep it under the carpet. Apart from anything else, we tend to teach our students that, along with 'nature', culture is one of the staples of tourism. Furthermore, culture occupies centre stage in much of the scholarly writing on the subject of tourism. For example, there have been lengthy discussions about cultural authenticity (MacCannell 1989; Selwyn 1996), cultural commoditization (Graburn 1976; Greenwood 1989; Meethan 2001), the uses of cultural performance in the tourism industry (Boissevain 1996; Bruner 2005), the uses of cultural creativity in contemporary economic development (Richards 2007) and so on. All these point both to the longevity and potency of the term, and also to the difficulties it poses. Questions and problems tumble forth. Is there a distinction to be made between 'real' and 'fake' culture? What are the implications of the arrival in the global market place of cultural artefacts from the third and fourth worlds? Should we pay particular attention to the fact that different persons interpret the same cultural monument or site in different ways – and, if so, why should we do this? How might we use the ubiquitous expression 'cultural heritage' in a way that opens up (rather than closes down) discussion of the complex economic, political and social questions that attend its use?

Chapters by Yiakoumaki, Rountree and Rabo in this volume address these questions as they tease out the commercial, political, social and personal relationships surrounding cultural heritage sites in Crete, Malta and Aleppo. In each of these cases, we see how the different sites, and the tourist itineraries in which they are embedded, articulate personal and collective memories, the goals of local and regional elites, and the agenda of nation-states and transnational entities such as the EU – to link a Cretan town with the Israeli state building project; incite Maltese hunters to acts of vandalism against the island's Neolithic sites; and transform the economic calculations of market traders in Aleppo's *souk*. These ethnographic interrogations of the politics of heritage construction and inscription open up cultural heritage as a category and invite further exploration of the processes connecting quotidian life, emergent identities and their representation with the landscapes and practices of heritage listing and mapping; leading us, in turn, into questions of agency, and its distribution and deployment in strategies of visibility and concealment, memory and forgetting.

Hospitality   Early on in its development, Smith (1977) and colleagues framed the anthropology of tourism in terms of relationships between 'hosts' and 'guests', by so doing establishing hospitality, that most anthropological of topics, as one of the starting points of the subject. Fifty years earlier, Hocart's (1927) essay on classical hospitality had propelled the subject into the anthropological limelight, effectively opening up space for later anthropological elaborations – by Pitt-Rivers (1977) and others (Kanafani 1983, for example) – on the sociocultural principles of classic and modern forms of Mediterranean and Middle Eastern hospitality. More recently we have had O'Gorman's (2008) Hocartian socio-historical considerations of the subject, reminding us that hospitality has always played a pivotal role in the making of social relations in both ancient and modern societies. Although the host/guest paradigm is no longer used in the way it was originally conceived by Smith et al., the term 'hospitality' itself continues to occupy a central role in the study of tourism, the so-called 'hospitality industry' lying at the heart of contemporary tourism in various ways.

The chapter by Lenz in the present volume, however, explores a context in which hospitality, as a process involving, in O'Gorman's (2008) words, 'friend-ships and alliances between persons, between communities, and between nations', is inverted and becomes its own antithesis. The hotel used to house 'illegal' and unwanted migrants in a Mediterranean island places its inhabitants in a virtually contaminated space. Here they are effectively barred from the kind of relationships with neighbours on the island that they might have expected from assuming that traditional principles of Mediterranean hospitality were at work there. Instead they are condemned to perpetual strangerhood and social isolation. Apart from raising uncomfortable questions about the fragility of principles – hospitality being one – that we might like to think are an integral part of our civilizational repertoire (to borrow a phrase from O'Gorman) Lenz's chapter effectively underlines the fact that the boundaries of the anthropology of tourism need to encompass consideration of mobile populations that occupy the same or proximate spaces to those inhabited by tourists.

Spaces, Images, Objects, Bodies

We have argued that leisure, culture and hospitality (arguably *the* mode of sociocultural exchange most often rhetorically associated with tourism) and the practices associated with each constitute the broadest fields underpinning the general scope of the anthropology of tourism. Our chapter writers approach these areas by using slightly more precise organizing and thematic tools that belong to a slightly lower level of abstraction. Identifying them helps us to move towards the heart of the subject – not least because the terms involved derive from long histories of work in the mainstream of social anthropology. Thus, as we look over the collection as a whole, we propose that all our chapters are focused, in various different ways, upon the relationships between spaces, images, objects and bodies (cf. Selwyn 2007).

All the essays in the volume are concerned with various kinds of spaces. There are the geographical spaces such as coasts, lakes, market places, hinterlands of tourist nightlife and leisure consumption, and so on. Then there are the political spaces that Abram discusses in which power is exercised and expressed over tourist related issues, most of which feed back directly into geographical spaces. Thus we have the vulnerable coastlines of Malta upon which prey the property developers described by Boissevain; the relatively intimate spaces of the Aleppo *souk*, which is the focus of life and social relationships for the market traders visited by Rabo; the tropical trees, hotels pools and spas of Picard's islands; and so on. All are subject to economic, political and cultural processes, which are at once local, regional and global. Thus Malta's coasts are fought over by private property developers (many with investment funds from outside the island), the national government, non-governmental local and regional environmental bodies and movements, regional and global regulatory systems of trade emanating from such bodies as the European Union and World Trade Organization, as well as other transnational institutions. The urban fabric of Aleppo rests on an uneasy accommodation between the interests of local and international conservation networks, the long-distance commercial links and economic calculations of the market traders, and the response of a range of entrepreneurs and investors to the diverse expectations of a heterogeneous mix of visitors, which includes a growing number of regional tourists in addition to the local traders. Picard's tropical island spaces are part of a much broader global canvas in the formation of the modernist and postmodernist imaginations.

Images have long been of interest to anthropologists of tourism (Crick 1989; Selwyn 1996), literally cascading as they do over the surfaces of the tourist project: in brochures, postcards, photographs, TV documentary and commercial productions, and so on. Under the surface lurk such historical and modern examples of tourist related imagery as Orientalist stereotypes (Edwards 1996) and the images evoked by the texts of travel diarists and travel writers. In our own case we have some very powerful evocations of images: of the murdered tourist girls in Costa Rica in 2000 described by Frohlick; of the old town of Chania described by Yiakoumaki, with its harbour and 'timeless' narrow backstreets; of the neat bungalows of Harrison's Canadian lake. Each of these (along with many others that we could pick out from our collection) has the potency to mobilize strong feelings relating to and shaping assumptions about young independent women, a generalized 'Mediterranean', and imagined communities of symbolic kin.

Tourist worlds are also full of objects. These include credit cards, passports, suitcases, souvenirs, museum exhibits, the paraphernalia of the beach – balls, flags, fishing rods, deck chairs, sun hats – and so forth. In our own case, we also have such exemplars of the material culture of tourism as products displayed in a market, sacred and symbolic instruments in a synagogue in a tourist town, prehistoric stone monuments, buildings (from built religious sites to hotels) and even food, for there are many examples of 'objects of desire' to be found in our collection – including the products that make up a full English breakfast in Magaluf – sausages, eggs, baked beans, bacon, toast and so on.

Finally, as several of our chapters clearly show, the human body plays a seminal role in tourist practices in ways that are explored in more detail in several parts of what follows.

Contents

Bearing in mind the architectural contours described above, we may now introduce the chapters that make up the contents of this volume.

Hazel Andrews describes some of the more prominent ideas and practices to be found in the Mallorcan resort of Magaluf. This is a destination incorporated into the charter tourism circuit catering predominantly for British tourists. She describes how a spirit of British nationalism (flavoured by northern English idioms) emerges from the daily rhythms of the resort, showing how this derives from the symbolic articulation between the spaces, bodies and images to be found there. She thus describes how the streets, shops, restaurants, beaches and other spaces in Magaluf are filled with evocative, familiar and 'homely' imagery – in the names of cafes, TV films on show, menus and so on. She goes on to describe how displays of routinely sexualized tourist bodies find a way into this landscape and how, at certain strategic (and alcohol fuelled) moments of high symbolic potency (in theatrical and participatory performances at nightclubs, for example) the whole imaginative construction is pitched in opposition to images and evocations of *other* nationalisms (including, among others, Spanish and French). Moreover, such imaginative cocktails as these, concocted as they are in the resort, are served in a general atmosphere of energetic consumerism – products of interest to the tourist population are piled high and deep in the resort's shop windows. A quizzical observer might conclude that Rupert Murdoch himself would be proud of his robustly and competitively sexualized (specifically breast directed) anti-European Brits rehearsing their nationalist scripts over a 'full English' breakfast.

Susan Frohlick turns her attention towards the role of the body, in particular the sexualized female body, as it appears in the anthropology of tourism, in the discourses of the tourism industry and in media reports about tourism. Noting, *en passant*, the astonishing fact that 'pleasure, generally, is an aspect of tourist experience that has been squelched in tourism studies', she observes that although there have been some anthropological studies on tourism and gay/lesbian sex, about what is termed 'sex tourism', and about sex, tourism and health, there has been remarkably little about the place of 'everyday sexuality' in 'everyday tourism'. This is so despite the fact that, as in life, sexualities, sexual relations – sex generally – is, in many respects, one of the foundations of tourism. She tells the story of two female American students who were murdered by a group of three young Costa Rican men while the women were on a shopping trip to a town near their holiday accommodation. The group car-jacked their vehicle, intending to use the car for a robbery. Frohlick surveys the subsequent international and local media reports of the incident and shows how the dead bodies of the two women were used to peddle a (false) story about young white tourist women looking for sex in the nightclubs and beaches of the Caribbean. The media implied that the women were, in effect, victims of their own erotic intentions. Frohlick builds on this particular and sad story to explore the multivalent quality of the body itself. It is 'social, political, subjective, objective, discursive, narrative, and material all at once'. In the case of the two women, their bodies became the centrepieces of a moral panic (dispersed in the USA and Costa Rica alike) about young white women's sexuality and irresponsibility that, among other things, masked the 'real' story about contemporary Costa Rica and the 'deep flaws in its corrupt governance and justice systems, its racism, and growing economic disparities in the context of late twentieth century neo-liberalism'. Looking at the relations between the story's actual and imagined spaces (trans-border territories, nightclubs, jungles), images (of sexualized young American women in relation to young black local men) and the dead bodies on the roadside themselves, we should perhaps be surprised to learn from Frohlick that, by its routine avoidance of everyday sex and pleasure, and its concomitant tendency to medicalize and/or exoticize sex in the context of tourism, the anthropology of tourism itself shares certain characteristics with the popular media. Our quizzical observer might, once again, spy a distant media magnate figure lurking just over the horizon with a hint of a smile on his face as he surveyed the scene.

Julia Harrison's essay on Canadian lakeside second homes and the ideas and practices of their owners reminds us that the study of second homes and their social, cultural and economic implications is an increasingly important part of the anthropology of tourism. She describes the thematic setting of the chapter in terms of the formation of national identity in an environment sculpted by relationships between landscapes, their iconographies and the human bodies that inhabit them. The Haliburton region of Ontario is rocky and full of trees and lakes. It is a place that many of its contemporary inhabitants think of as a quintessential 'Canadian' landscape. By disporting themselves in canoes, by swimming and playing by the lakes, cottage owners nostalgically call up memories of early nineteenth-century pioneers who 'made' and fashioned Canada and Canadian identity by clearing land, farming, working hard and building small lakeside log houses. These pioneers were 'northern' people, and they were 'tough, strong and hardy'. They were thought to be 'real Canadians'. But our quizzical observer may have just caught sight of the way that a collection of very strange and alien bodies – belonging to a Muslim youth group – were regarded after the group purchased a small lakeside resort. One response among existing cottage owners nearby was to imagine that the group might be an al-Qaeda cell. Another was to assert to passers-by that the Muslim group members would be innately incapable of using the lake in any recognizable way (none possessed canoes or swimming costumes it seemed), whilst the equanimity of a third response was based on the assumption that group members would keep themselves to themselves, thus leaving most of the lake and its banks to those who really did know how to disport themselves there.

Jeremy Boissevain is concerned with the ways in which the coastal spaces of Malta are being consumed and effectively destroyed by property developers. He describes how the Maltese tourist authorities are seeking to emphasize to new (and richer) visitors the attractions of Maltese natural attractions, including coasts and walking paths beside and above them, as a way of moving Maltese tourism away from the charter market. He argues that such an effort clearly needs a sound environmental policy capable of protecting and conserving the natural landscape on which these expectations are based. However, in case after case, he demonstrates how the accelerating pace of property development is able to overcome both statutory regulatory building policies and popular resistance. The authorities thus not only appear two-faced (on the one hand proclaiming the value of protected natural spaces, on the other allowing building development on them) but actually powerless in the face of property developers, many with financial muscle from way beyond the shores of the island. Boissevain suggests a multi-stranded and closely intertwined context in the form of a catalogue of characteristics of Maltese political culture that will be familiar to Mediterraneanists and others working in areas shaped by political patronage, nepotism, amoral familism and weak civil society. Turning her gaze to Malta, our quizzical observer would be forgiven for concluding that one segment of Maltese society is presently in the process of consuming another: that the political classes, backed by global capital, are effectively eating up those precious natural and cultural assets (belonging to the majority of the population) that constitute the essential basis for an economy highly dependent on tourism.

Annika Rabo's chapter on 'Old Aleppo' takes us to the World Heritage listed *medina* and introduces us to the diverse groups of people – traders, tour guides and entrepreneurs, intelligentsia, politicians and bureaucrats, as well as a heterogeneous mix of tourists – who draw on the *souk* for their living, their sense of identity, for entertainment, enchantment, or for their prosaic daily needs. Rabo's account reveals a strong line of continuity in the tradition of trading, and the regional and international networks in which these trade links situate the bazaar. Tourism, in the eyes of the traders, is but the latest manifestation of this evolving commercial activity – with the difference that it also entails trade in the symbolic representations associated with the enchantment of the medina, represented both by the objects being traded (many of which are bought in specifically for the tourist market) and the environment and way of life. The calculations of the traders are complicated not only by the complexity of the symbolic economy in which they are increasingly forced to operate, but also by their ambivalent relationship with the state, a major actor in the 'modernization' and remodelling of Aleppo's urban space for the purposes of channelling leisure and tourism investment in the city. While the state relies on the traders for the reproduction of public space in 'Old Aleppo', the evident indifference of the traders to the bazaar as a place of 'enchantment' contrasts with their strong attachment to it in other ways, and parallels the mismatch between the 'Arabian Nights' version of the medina, sought by the *ajaanib* (European) foreign tourists – and the more nuanced associations of the Arab (Syrian, Iraqi, Jordanian, Lebanese), Turkish and Iranian tourists, who far outnumber them.

Following Rabo's analysis of the Aleppo bazaar, David Picard examines another symbolic economy into which producers and tourist consumers are drawn mainly for the benefit of the latter's enchantment. Here the setting is the tropical gardens of Indian Ocean islands, particularly that of La Réunion. Picard suggests that gardens constitute not only the basis for the islands' tourism offer but also a much broader symbolic backdrop to (global) modernist thought itself. For him, gardens 'produce images to think the world'. Gardens tell stories about meaning and order in a fragmented world, about calming the uncertain spatialities and temporalities of modern life and providing instead 'meaningful frameworks' and symbolic worlds for predominantly Western tourists to dip into during the course of their leisure time. He looks in some detail at the gardens and architectural layouts of hotels in La Réunion, arguing both that they are subject to a discernible standardization of design – in which sense they appear as 'Fordist' in their manufacture – but that they also call up memories of ancient biblical *pardesim* (Hebrew: 'orchards') including the most central of all symbols of aesthetic and moral value in Western thought, the garden of Eden. Thus, alongside such utopian projects as the conservation efforts in the centres of ancient cities or the grounding of a museum in La Réunion on the basis of the island's 'miracle' of 'cultural diversity', gardens form the objects of 'utopian projection' that are essential features of the legitimation of Western modernism itself. Eden awaits at the end of the road of the Washington consensus. Meanwhile, of course, tourists and others will need to keep their minds off such uncomfortable features of the socio-economic landscape of La Réunion as an unemployment rate of 40 per cent.

The Cretan city of Chania, like Aleppo, offers an insight into the translocal processes behind the production of localities in tourism destinations, but in this case, the emergence of a particularly controversial 'local' heritage site poses a more direct, fundamental challenge to local residents' sense of their collective past and identity. The synagogue of Etz Hayyim (Hebrew: 'tree of life') is virtually the last reminder of an historic Jewish presence in Chania, which ended with the sinking of a transportation ship en route to Auschwitz in 1944. Vassiliki Yiakoumaki's sensitive analysis peels back the narrative layers surrounding the fate of the Jews and the markers of their physical presence; the rehabilitation of the synagogue; and its re-emergence as 'heritage', reinforcing the sense of a palpable absence in Chania's contemporary urban landscape. The growing international visibility of the synagogue, due to its incorporation into European itineraries of Jewish memory sites, is at odds with the pervasive silence and invisibility in which it is shrouded at the local level, and which reflects, in part, the persisting problem of 'Otherness' in the construction and representation of Greek national identity. Yiakoumaki demonstrates how the dissonant heritage represented by Etz Hayyim helps to achieve consonance, at the public level, with the discourses of rights, minorities and multiculturalism authorized by distant centres of power, such as the European Union, which, she argues, have not yet found acceptance at the level of the local and the private. As an expression of the 'local' heritage of Chania, Etz Hayyim, she concludes, is 'unwanted, but cannot be disowned'.

The transformation of landscapes as a result of their incorporation into the lists, itineraries and transnational political entities of world heritage inscription, tourism, and the European Union, is further explored in Kathryn Rountree's chapter on Malta's Neolithic monuments. The temples, as indeed the countryside generally, have traditionally been little appreciated by the Maltese, either aesthetically, or as a source of identity or prestige, the latter being largely derived from the colonial heritage of the Knights of St John and the Catholic Church (see also the chapter by Boissevain in this volume). On the other hand, the countryside is the setting for one practice that is *very* important in terms of Maltese self-image, namely, hunting; but with the restrictions and protective measures put into place as a result of UNESCO listing, and Malta's entry into the European Union in 2004, this is now a prohibited activity. Rountree shows us how the remapping of the Maltese countryside closes down certain spaces, while opening up others – a process which is locally contested through competing practices, which have the Neolithic temples as their focus. Tourism brings a new dimension in the form of goddess tours, which reinterpret the monuments as numinous places of worship, incorporating them into the sacred geography of Europe, and thus opening up a small space for Malta's own nascent pagan movement, alongside a movement of Maltese artists and writers, to connect with a pre-colonial collective past.

Ramona Lenz directs our attention to the infrastructure underpinning international tourism, in order to offer a critique of the analytical categories used by anthropologists and tourism practitioners. She argues that the host/guest paradigm is inadequate for analysing the commercial relations of production and exchange characterizing the global 'hospitality industry' today; nevertheless, these terms remain entrenched in tourism management language and approaches to labour market issues. Drawing on her fieldwork in Cyprus and Crete, Lenz highlights the contradictions between, on the one hand, the economic realities to which tourism is subject – such as its reliance on a globalized pool of cheap labour, or its vulnerability to extreme seasonal fluctuations – and, on the other, the nostalgic rhetoric of 'hosts' and 'guests' on which the tourism industry draws in its marketing material; which makes 'hospitality' a quality of a 'native' population (rather than a skill that can be acquired), while privileging a particular type of (paying) traveller as a bona fide 'guest'. This contradiction emerges particularly strongly in Lenz's analysis of the 'Hotel Royale' in Crete. Out of season, the hotel becomes a detention centre for 'illegals' picked up trying to enter the European Union. These migrants use the same infrastructure as the hotel's summer guests and enable the hotelier to earn some out of season income. Lenz's material demonstrates clearly how tourism both constitutes, and is constituted by, myriad categories of mobile populations, and challenges tourism practitioners to reflect that more complex reality in their literature and practice.

Lenz's argument is picked up, and its implications for anthropological theory and practice developed, in Simone Abram's chapter on the nature of anthropological intervention in tourism. Abram raises a number of questions that go to the heart of anthropology as a calling, and the tension between anthropology's role in representing, and acting on, the 'real world'. While anthropology's ethnographic tradition ensures a continuing commitment to linking theory and practice in general, the terms on which anthropologists can intervene in real world processes – and, indeed, the dominant understanding of what constitutes the real world itself – are, she argues, defined largely by others, and mediated through the language of commerce and consultancy. Thus the scope for anthropological intervention in tourism is generally restricted to that of subsidiary cultural specialists, a role that downgrades the value of academic knowledge, and dismisses the usefulness (or practicality) of a theoretically informed critical anthropological practice. Drawing on examples taken from the anthropology of development and land use policy advocacy, Abram makes a strong case against the dichotomizing of academic/pure and applied/useful knowledge, arguing that the best prospects for anthropological intervention in tourism lie in broadening the scope of anthropological research and taking it beyond the impact-related studies favoured by consultancy to the sites and technologies where power is located and tourism policy determined.

Before concluding, and in preparation for the slightly fuller development that follows, we may briefly rehearse how our volume's chapters have used and addressed some of the elements and issues we identified at the start of this section. There is a consistent interest, for example, in how spaces in general, leisure spaces in particular – including landscapes, seascapes, cityscapes – are commercially and otherwise transformed in response to tourism. Then there is the issue of the ways that tourist-related images find their way into structures of feelings and imagination about the nature of society and culture. Bodies themselves (both live and dead) appeared as vehicles that embody ideas, values and narratives about a wide variety of subjects from sexual to national identity. Objects (from products in the bazaar to megalithic stone monuments to burnt-out jeeps to the ingredients of the bars and cafes of tourist resorts) have been described that carry sentiments ranging over nostalgic desire for former worlds and aspirations for future ones, the boundaries of moral universes, symbolic (and sometimes edible) imagined building blocks of social and cultural communities. Hospitality wove its way through several, if not all, chapters coming up against (in the cases of the chapters by Lenz and Frohlick) its nemesis.

Thinking Through Tourism

We began this Introduction by noting the institutional contexts that have shaped the relatively recent upsurge of research into and teaching of the anthropology of tourism, and by describing the architecture of our volume. This, we argued, rested upon several framing terms, all of which have anthropological lineages well beyond tourism studies themselves. As we come towards the end of this Introduction, we need to return to the issues we discussed at the beginning.

We may forge one question out of the several issues we raised. This has two closely linked parts. The first part concerns the areas of general social anthropological concern to which the anthropology of tourism has contributed. What claims, exemplified by the present collection of chapters, might the field make with regard to its contribution to anthropological theory and practice? The second concerns the basis for the authority of anthropology vis-à-vis the thought and work of others including (among many others) tourists themselves, journalists and (recalling the debate in 1996 between professional anthropologists for and against the motions that 'cultural studies will be the death of anthropology'[5]) experts in cultural studies. Looked at this way, both its parts appear to merge into a single question that has to do with the political economy of anthropological knowledge.

One account of the state of anthropology at the conclusion of the twentieth century (Moore 1999) picked out several features of the discipline that strike familiar chords in the present context: the concern with the ethnographic and theoretical spaces between the global and the local, questions of cultural and personal hybridity, cultural transformation, politics of identity and what Moore terms the 'governmentalization' of anthropology. She goes on to note the burgeoning career in anthropology of the body, and reflects on anthropological preoccupations with representation, objectivity and subjectivity, wondering whether these concerns are linked to what she describes as 'post-modern retreats from theory'.

In a more recent reflection on the discipline, Harrison (2008) describes a theoretical and ethnographic domain within which the work presented in this volume fits well:

> Anthropologists are less likely to think of 'culture' in terms of bounded, fully integrated, and static systems, and they are more inclined to ponder cultural processes, dynamics, and conflicts grounded in uneven fields of power that cross the contested boundaries of nation-states and peoples. In an age of heightened globalism and transnationalism, many of the peoples with whom anthropologists work are repositioning and re-identifying themselves as agents of continuity and discontinuity within diasporas, borderlands, and other contexts of interculturality. (2008: 7)

We might notice that this succinct overview already points towards a gap between anthropology and cultural studies, for if Rapport (1997: 26) is correct in describing the latter in terms of a project interested in 'large-scale collective discourses' that link communities, classes, nations (and so on) 'into single cultural groupings', anthropologists (including our own authors) clearly also routinely engage with such contextual questions as how such discourses are used, by whom, for what purposes, and in what contexts.

The anthropological landscape described by Moore and Harrison is clearly familiar to all of us in this volume, as is the relevance of Rapport's view of cultural studies. From the particular point of view of the anthropology of tourism, however, we see little evidence of 'retreat from theory', and on the contrary we would like to claim not only that the authors represented here, as well as others in the field, are making substantial theoretical contributions, but also that the anthropology of tourism is well placed to continue so to do.

Nash (2007) recalls that, following the ethnographically based beginnings of the anthropology of tourism, there followed a longish period, from 1976 onwards (which stretches into the present) during which time several now very well known stars of tourism studies have come up with a variety of heady insights into global tourism and its works. It has sometimes seemed as if the study of tourism has provided us with some sort of Aladdin's cave of insights into contemporary global capitalism (and its consequences for identity and culture) and, moreover, that these insights may be expressed in an appealing, relatively programmatic and readily digestible form. Thus we have treatises on tourism and 'authenticity' (MacCannell 1976), 'escape' (Cohen and Taylor 1976), 'the gaze' (Urry 1990), 'consumption' (Urry 1994) and so on. But, as Meethan (2001) has surely correctly observed in relation to consumption (but equally applicably to the others) these bubbly terms actually mean little unless carefully grounded ethnographically.

We suggest that the above works (and others like them) by leading international scholars working in various university departments have successfully (and brilliantly) laid the foundation for an energetic and altogether exhilarating tradition of cultural studies in tourism, exemplified by a journal such as *Tourism Studies*, the first issue of which contained a plea by Franklin and Crang (2001) for a theoretical reinvigoration of the subject. Yes indeed. But, for us, the specifically *anthropological* tradition of tourism studies, particularly following the most significant post 1970s boost it experienced in 1994 with the publication of Crick's *Resplendent Sites, Discordant Voices*, has been, gradually but with increasing confidence, building a substantial body of ethnographically rooted theoretical work and possibilities for the future. Crick's ethnography of the Sri Lankan town of Kandy was the first full-length monograph with tourism as the determining theme and, for us, it marked (quite precisely) a point of bifurcation between anthropological studies of tourism and those by practitioners of cultural studies. Crick's authoritative intervention has given rise to a substantial collection of ethnographic studies of tourism (Waldren 1996; Edensor 1998; Tucker 2002; Nadel-Klein 2003; Cole 2007; Duke 2007; Pitchford 2008; Kolas 2008; Costa 2009). By placing the present volume unequivocally in this tradition, we propose, without demur, that whatever else it is, the anthropology of tourism is distinguished by its commitment to ethnography and ethnographic detail.

But, to emphasize the point, this is not to suggest that in its commitment to ethnography, the anthropology of tourism is 'retreating from theory'. Quite the reverse is the case. The challenge for us at this point in this Introduction, therefore, is summarily to outline *both* the ethnographic *and* theoretical engagement that our volume has with tourism.

While we will take the majority of our cues from our own authors, we would like first to agree with Nash (2007: 8) that the anthropology of tourism sits within an intellectual tradition associated most closely with two classic socio-logical projects. One follows Durkheim by looking at the nature of collective representations. The other follows Marx's insistence that the principal subject of the social sciences is the structural and processual relationship between 'material base', social structure and ideology.

Looking, then, at our own chapters and taking them together, we may find a considerable theoretical coherence (along the lines indicated by Nash) that exemplifies the capacity of the anthropology of tourism dynamically to connect up material and representational worlds by describing some of the structural and processual relations between them. Thus, for example, Picard's suggestion that the postcolonial economic transformation of La Réunion has moved the island from the old colonial world into the political and symbolic economy of what Wallerstein (2004) has termed the 'modern world system' encourages us to ask whether we can say anything along these lines about some of the other tourist destinations described here and the techniques and technologies involved in fitting them out as economic and symbolic servants to the neo-liberal global economy. How is it done? How resisted? What cracks and contradictions may be observed? Similarly, the chapters by Andrews, Harrison, Lenz and Frohlick, offer food for further reflection on the mechanisms, meaning and experiential content of boundary construction and transgression, by showing how holiday spaces link a heightened sense of class, regional and national identity with feelings and values attached to different types of consumption; create an industrial infrastructure which draws on and reinforces ambiguous and contradictory ideas about identity and alterity, the 'welcome' and the 'unwelcome' other; and convey potent messages about the sexualized and dangerous nature of the border which separates the rich North and the poor South.

Moving to the chapters by Boissevain, Abram, Rountree, Yiakoumaki and Rabo, the picture becomes more complex, as the writers probe the complicated relationships between local and global capital, tourism and heritage investment, and what might broadly be termed 'civil society' (cf. Hann and Dunn 1996). Boissevain's discussion of the relation between finance capital and (as far as regulation of property development is concerned) a weak state also speaks of a critical moment in the development of a civil society seeking to hold the political classes to account. As an institution of civil society, this is a field in which universities and academics are necessarily players, and not just observers, as Abram's chapter reminds us. For Rountree, Yiakoumaki and Rabo, the Neolithic temples, the Chania synagogue and Aleppo market place are sites where nationalist, Orientalist and religious stereotypes are being challenged in various ways by various different kinds of actors: religious innovators in a conservative state, traders establishing new business links well beyond state boundaries, tourists themselves.

The above represents an extremely partial reading of the complex and numerous issues raised in our chapters, and the fields into which they enter, which include nationalism, relations between capital and the state, social movements, landscape symbolism, Orientalism, the place of tourism in the global neo-liberal world, the political economy of sex and sexuality, questions of intervention, religious innovation, borderlands and many more.

They reveal a picture of a tourism industry composed of systems of relations and sets of ideas and practices that straddle material (land, sea, buildings and other material objects, physical bodies, etc.) and representational (images, icons, media products, embodied ideas, etc.) worlds. As we have shown, each of the chapters in its own way keeps a foot in each world and (crucially) articulates the relation between the two. In most cases this is done by focusing on those global and local spaces and actors in which private and public interests, from those of property investors and tour operators to political movements and parties and agents of the state, do battle to determine the nature of the natural, physical, social and symbolic worlds in which they live, work and offer to tourists. It is a bracing place for the anthropologist to be as she exercises her particular ways of seeing, understanding, and intellectually, ethically and politically positioning herself.

Notes

1. The Royal Anthropological Institute (RAI) has recently succeeded in assisting and enabling the school authorities in the UK to establish an A level in Social Anthropology (further details from RAI website: http://www.therai.org.uk).
2. For example, the two editors of this volume, together with colleagues from universities and research institutions in Europe and the Mediterranean, have taken part in several large research and development projects part-funded by the European Commission in the Mediterranean and Balkan regions.
3. This is not to overlook the fact that tourism exists in many diverse forms, as the chapters in this volume demonstrate; but while narratives of colonial

nostalgia underpin some varieties of tourism experience more explicitly than others, they are, arguably, never entirely absent. Cf., in this volume, Andrews's discussion of international sun, sea and sand tourism; and Harrison's discussion of domestic tourism in Canada, where the presence of the 'exotic' other in the Canadian heartland is perceived as troublingly out of place.

4. C-SAP (subject network for Sociology, Anthropology and Politics) is based at the University of Birmingham and is one of twenty-four subject networks funded by the UK Funding Councils for Higher Education as part of the Learning and Teaching Support Network. See http://www.c-sap.bham.ac.uk (accessed 28 October 2009).

5. Cf. Wade 1997.

References.

Augé, M. (1995), *Non-Places: Introduction to an Anthropology of Supermodernity*, London: Verso.

Boissevain, J. (1997), 'Tourism and Development in Malta', *Development and Change* 8: 523–38.

Boissevain, J. (1996), 'Ritual, Tourism, and Cultural Commodification in Malta: Culture by the pound?' in T. Selwyn (ed.), *The Tourist Image: Myths and myth making in tourism*, Chichester: Wiley, pp. 105–20.

Bruner, E. (1995), 'The Ethnographer/Tourist in Indonesia' in M.-F. Lanfant, J.B. Allcock and E.M. Bruner (eds), *International Tourism: Identity and Change*, London: Sage, pp. 224–41.

Bruner, E. (2005), *Culture on Tour: Ethnographies of Travel*, Chicago: University of Chicago Press.

Burns, P. (1999), *An Introduction to Tourism and Anthropology*, London: Routledge.

Caplan, P. (2005), 'In Search of the Exotic – A Discussion of the BBC2 Series Tribe', *Anthropology Today* 21(2): 3–7.

Chambers, E. (2000), *Native Tours: The Anthropology of Travel and Tourism*, Prospect Heights, IL: Waveland Press.

Cohen, E. (1974), 'Who is a Tourist? A Conceptual Clarification', *Sociological Review* 22(4): 527–55.

Cohen, E. (1988), 'Authenticity and Commoditization in Tourism', *Annals of Tourism Research* 15(3): 371–86.

Cohen, S. and Taylor, L. (1976), *Escape Attempts: The Theory and Practice of Resistance to Everyday Life*, London: Allen Lane.

Cole, S. (2007), *Tourism, Culture and Development: Hopes, Dreams and Realities in East Indonesia*, Clevedon: Channel View.

Costa, K.A. (2009), *Coach Fellas, Heritage, and Tourism in Ireland*, Walnut Creek, CA: Left Coast Press.

Crick, M. (1989), 'Representations of International Tourism in the Social Sciences: Sun, sex, sights, savings, and servility', *Annual Review of Anthropology*, 18: 307–44.

Crick, M. (1994), *Resplendent Sites, Discordant Voices: Sri Lankans and international tourism*, Chur: Harwood.

Crick, M. (1995), 'The Anthropologist as Tourist: an Identity in Question' in M.-F. Lanfant, J.B. Allcock and E.M. Bruner (eds), *International Tourism: Identity and Change*, London: Sage, pp. 205–23.

De Kadt, E.J. (1990) 'Making the Alternative Sustainable: Lessons from development for tourism', Institute of Development Studies Discussion Paper 272, University of Sussex.

Duke, P.G. (2007), *The Tourists' Gaze, the Cretans' Glance: Archaeology and Tourism on a Greek Island*, Walnut Creek, CA: Left Coast Press.

Edensor, T. (1998), *Tourists at the Taj: Performance and Meaning at a Symbolic Site*, London: Routledge.

Edwards, E. (1996), 'Postcards: Greetings from another world', in T. Selwyn (ed.), *The Tourist Image: Myths and Myth Making in Tourism*, Chichester: Wiley, pp. 197–222.

Eriksen, T.H. (1993), 'In Which Sense Do Cultural Islands Exist?', *Social Anthropology* 1(1B): 133–48.

Eriksen, T.H. (2005), 'Nothing to Lose but our Aitches', *Anthropology Today* 21(2): 1–2.

Finlay, A. (2006), 'Anthropology Misapplied? The Culture Concept and the Peace Process in Ireland', *Anthropology in Action* 13(1–2): 1–10.

Franklin, A. and Crang, M. (2001), 'The Trouble with Tourism and Travel Theory', *Tourist Studies* 1: 5–22.

Gordon, A. (2008), *Naked Airport: A Cultural History of the World's Most Revolutionary Structure*, Chicago: University of Chicago Press.

Graburn, N. (ed.) (1976), *Ethnic and Tourist Arts: Cultural Expressions from the Fourth World*, Berkeley, CA: University of California Press.

Graburn, N. (1983), *To Pray, Pay and Play: The Cultural Structure of Japanese Domestic Tourism*, Aix-en-Provence: Centre des Hautes Etudes Touristiques.

Greenwood, D. (1972), 'Tourism as an Agent of Change: A Spanish Basque Case', *Ethnology* 11: 80–91.

Greenwood, D. (1989), 'Culture by the Pound: An Anthropological Perspective on Tourism As Cultural Commoditisation', in V.L. Smith (ed.), *Hosts and Guests: The Anthropology of Tourism*, 2nd edition, Philadelphia: University of Pennsylvania Press, pp. 171–85.

Hann, C. and Dunn, E. (eds) (1996), *Civil Society: Challenging Western Models*, London: Routledge.

Harrison, F.V. (2008), *Outsider Within: Reworking Anthropology in the Global Age*, Urbana, IL: University of Illinois.

Hart, K. (2004), 'What Anthropologists Really Do', *Anthropology Today* 20(1): 3–5.

Hocart, A.M. (1927), 'The Divinity of the Guest', *The Life-Giving Myth and Other Essays*, London: Methuen, pp. 78–87.

Kanafani, G. (1983), *Aesthetics and Ritual in the United Arab Emirates*, Beirut: American University Press.

Kolas, A. (2008), *Tourism and Tibetan Culture in Transition: A place called Shangrila*, London: Routledge.

Leite, N. and Graburn, N. (2009), 'Anthropological Interventions in Tourism Studies', in J. Tazim and M. Robinson (eds), *The Sage Handbook of Tourism Studies*, London: Sage, pp. 35–64.

MacCannell, D. (1976) *The Tourist: A New Theory of the Leisure Class*, New York: Schocken.

MacCannell, D. (1989), Introduction to Special Edition on Semiotics of Tourism, *Annals of Tourism Research* 16: 1.

MacCannell, D. (1992), *Empty Meeting Grounds: The Tourist Papers*, London: Routledge.

Mars, G. (2004), 'Refocusing with Applied Anthropology', *Anthropology Today* 20(1): 1–2.

Meethan, K. (2001), *Tourism in Global Society: Place, culture, consumption*, New York: Palgrave.

Moor, H.L. (ed.), (1999), *Anthropological Theory Today*, Cambridge: Polity.

Nadel-Klein, J. (2003), *Fishing For Heritage: Modernity and Loss along the Scottish Coast*, Oxford: Berg.

Nash, D. (1981), 'Tourism as an Anthropological Subject', *Current Anthropology* 22: 461–79.

Nash, D. (1989), 'Tourism as a Form of Imperialism', in V.L. Smith (ed.), *Hosts and Guests: The Anthropology of Tourism*, 2nd edition, Philadelphia: University of Pennsylvania Press, pp. 37–52.

Nash, D. (ed.) (2007). *The Study of Tourism: Anthropological and sociological beginnings*, Amsterdam, Elsevier.

O'Gorman, K.D. (2008), 'The Essence of Hospitality from the Texts of Classical Antiquity', University of Strathclyde. PhD thesis.

Pitchford, S. (2008), *Identity Tourism: Imagining and Imaging the Nation*, Bingley, UK: Emerald.

Pitt-Rivers, J. (1977), *The Fate of Shechem or the Politics of Sex*, Cambridge: Cambridge University Press.

Rapport, N. (1997), 'Opposing the motion that "Cultural Studies will be the Death of Anthropology"', in P. Wade (ed.), *Cultural Studies will be the Death of Anthropology*, Group for Debates in Anthropological Theory, Manchester: GDAT, pp. 22–32.

Redclift, M.R. (1973), 'The Future of Agriculture in a Spanish Pyrenean Village and the Decline of Communal Institutions', *Ethnology* 12: 193–202.

Richards, G. (ed.) (2007), *Cultural Tourism: Global and local perspectives*, Binghampton, NY: Haworth.

Scott, J.E. (1995), 'Sexual and National Boundaries in Tourism', *Annals of Tourism Research* 22(2): 385–403.

Scott, J.E. and Lugosi, P. (2005), 'Spreading the Net – Anthropology in Non-Anthropology Departments', *Anthropology Today* 21(5): 22–3.

Selwyn, T. (ed.) (1996), *The Tourist Image*, Chichester: Wiley.

Selwyn, T. (2007), 'The Political Economy of Enchantment: Formations in the Anthropology of Tourism', *Suomen Antropologi*, 2: 48–71.

Shore, C. (2000), *Building Europe: The Cultural Politics of European Integration*, London: Routledge.

Smith, V.L. (ed.) (1977), *Hosts and Guests: The Anthropology of Tourism*, Philadelphia: University of Pennsylvania.

Smith, V.L. (1989), 'Introduction', in V.L. Smith (ed.), *Hosts and Guests: The Anthropology of Tourism*, 2nd edition, Philadelphia: University of Pennsylvania Press, pp. 1–17.

Spencer, J., Jepson, A. and Mills, D. (n.d.), 'Where do all the Anthropologists go? Research training and "Careers" in Social Anthropology', available online at http://www.theasa.org/news/careers_research.doc (accessed 28 October 2009).

Tilley, C. (1997), 'Performing Culture in the Global Village', *Critique of Anthropology* 17(1): 67–90.

Tucker, H. (2002), *Living With Tourism: Negotiating Identities in a Turkish Village*, London: Routledge.

Veblen, T. (2007 [1899]), *The Theory of the Leisure Class: An Economic Study in the Evolution of Institutions*, New York: MacMillan.

Wade, P (ed.) (1997), *Cultural Studies will be the Death of Anthropology*, Group for Debates in Anthropological Theory, Manchester: GDAT.

Waldren, J. (1996), *Insiders and Outsiders: Paradise and Reality in Mallorca*, Oxford: Berghahn.

Wallace, T. (ed.) (2005), *Tourism and Applied Anthropologists: Linking Theory and Practice*, NAPA Bulletin: University of California Press.

Wallerstein, E. (2004), 'The Rise and Future Demise of the World Capitalist System', in F.J. Lechner and J. Boli (eds), *The Globalisation Reader*, Oxford: Blackwell, pp. 63–69.

Wood, R.E. (1993), 'Tourism, Culture and the Sociology of Development', in M. Hitchcock, V.T. King and M.J.G. Parnwell (eds), *Tourism in South East Asia*, London: Routledge, pp. 48–70.

Wright, S. (1998), 'The Politicization of "Culture"', *Anthropology Today* 14(1): 7–15.

Urry, J. (1990), *The Tourist Gaze: Leisure and Travel in Contemporary Societies*, London: Sage.

Urry, J. (1994), *Consuming Places*, London: Routledge.

–2–

Contours of a Nation

Being British in Mallorca

Hazel Andrews

Introduction

This chapter is concerned with the ways in which understandings of a national identity, in this case British,[1] are articulated in a particular setting, that of two charter tourism resorts – Palmanova and Magaluf – on the Mediterranean island of Mallorca. I argue that the context of the holiday allows people to engage with representations and experiences that respond to a particular understanding of British identity derived from food and drink consumption, social space and the body. The complex and interesting questions relating to identity are an ongoing concern for social anthropologists not least because of the concept's ambiguities and multilayered nature – gender, class, sexual, national – both in terms of self and/or group. Within all of these are questions of social allegiance, and issues of how one distinguishes oneself or one's group from that of the other and where and how boundaries between these are seen to lie. Such points are particularly pertinent in an increasingly mobile world, in which forces relating to globalization are argued, by some, to undermine old certainties and points of collective identity. Indeed, according to Bauman, the responsibility for identity formation has fallen increasingly on the shoulders of the individual, which in turn has led to a focus on a seeking out of a collective. He states 'the precariousness of the solitary identity building prompts the identity-builders to seek pegs on which they could hang together their individually experienced fears and anxieties and perform the exorcism rites in the company of the other, similarly afraid and anxious individuals' (2002: 19–20). What makes the current study especially stimulating to consider is that some of the forces of globalization – in particular integration with the European Union, migrant workers, processes of devolution and so on – have been argued to undermine a sense of collective British identity in the home world.[2] However, upon removal to a different physical space (e.g. Mallorca) that sense of national identity becomes more pronounced and effervescent.

This removal to a different place falls in line with Tapper's argument that 'ident-ities, ethnic and other, are flexible, negotiable, multiple and always situational'

(2008: 101). In addition, as Brück notes, 'people always have the resources to produce alternative interpretations of a context.... Hence, the relationships, events, and places that constitute the self can be strategically evoked in a highly contextual and contingent realization of selfhood' (2001: 655).

The idea of a situational identity has strong resonance, in my view, with the work of Bourdieu and the notion of habitus, and particularly that of a disrupted habitus (Jackson 1989, 2005; Andrews 2009a). A disruption to habitus occurs when what might be classed as everyday rhythms are punctuated by, for example, a particular event – an initiation ritual or, in the present case, the taking of a holiday.[3] In the illustration under discussion here, my argument is that due to a disruption to the habitus and the heightened sense of self, in terms of group and individual identity, brought into focus by the machinations of the tourism industry the latent possibilities of national identity find outlets and potentialities for greater expression. Using this theoretical base provides a subtler and deeper insight into the nature of identities created through tourism than much of the discussion in the tourism studies literature has thus far allowed.

Understandings of who tourists are have tended to centre on categorization of tourists by typologies (cf. Cohen 1974, 1979; MacCannell 1976; Wickens 2002) and psychological dispositions (cf. Pearce 1982). More specifically, the inter-connections between tourism and constructions of identity have received rather less attention. Notable exceptions include Selwyn's (1996a) examination of the relationship between landscape and the creation of an embodied and embedded Jewish identity through *tiyoulim* (walking tours) in the Israeli countryside. Work by Desforges has considered the way in which long-haul tourism experiences can be seen as a form of cultural capital that is consumed for the purposes of 'articulating about identity and life-style' (2000: 942). Magelssen (2002) examined the manner in which ideas of America and Americanness were expressed by the 1950s' American tourism industry. The way in which sites of tourists' consumption practices are gendered and therefore reinforce ideas of masculinity and femininity has been explored in relation to narratives presented as part of Stirling's heritage (Edensor and Kothari 1994; Aitchison, 1999).

With specific reference to ideas of Englishness, there is Palmer's (1998, 1999, 2003) focus on three key heritage sites in the south-east of England, which explores the way that Englishness is experienced through tourism. In her examples, the practice of tourism raises awareness and reinforces ideas of national identity. Arranz (2006) has also interrogated notions of Englishness, and Britishness, through a semiological examination of some of the official promotional material produced by the English Tourism Council and Visit Britain.

This paper rests on my own investigations into the ways in which identity is socially constructed, symbolized and embodied by British charter tourists to Mallorca (Andrews 1999, 2000, 2002, 2005, 2006). I also examine how these ideas of Britishness are in part provided, and manipulated by, the tourism industry and other facilitators of tourists' experiences in the resorts. The idea that providers of tourists' experiences might have a hand in constructing ideas of Britishness finds resonance with Selwyn's work on the political economy of enchantment, in which he argues that the processes involved in, and the elements designed to attract tourists to, destinations, are premised on a symbolic exchange, and that part of this enchantment derives from 'an industry fuelled, inter alia, by ideas, values, and symbolic structures the purposes of which are to enchant, that is to shape imaginations, interpretations, and memories, and to otherwise enhance cognitive and emotional transformations' (2007: 49). I shall argue that the symbolic world of Magaluf and Palmanova sets out to enchant its visitors with ideas of Britishness.

The ethnographic detail upon which my argument rests results from several periods of participant observation, between 1998 and 1999, among the predominately British tourists who holiday in Magaluf and the conjoining resort of Palmanova. I begin by providing a brief outline of the context of study, providing the field (Bourdieu 1993) of action so to speak. I shall then proceed to consider three key aspects of social life: space, the social body, and food and drink. It is the relationship between, and interpenetration of, these that articulate identity. The discussion that follows on from these will weave some of the threads from each together in order to reflect on the nature of 'Britishness' being signalled and exhibited in Mallorca, and to draw a conclusion.

Field of Action

The island of Mallorca is situated off the east coast of the Spanish peninsula, in the north-west Mediterranean, and is the largest of the Balearic Islands. Tourism provides the main source of income for the Balearics. The development of tourism as an economic activity began at the start of the twentieth century with expansion rapidly underway by the 1950s and 1960s. By the middle of the 1970s, the islands were well established as mass[4] tourism destinations, receiving 8 million annual visitors by 1995, 6 million of whom visited Mallorca (Bardolet 1996). Statistics show a continued increase so that in 2005 the Balearics received in excess of 11 million tourists of which over 8 million went to Mallorca.[5] Magaluf and Palmanova are two of six coastal resorts in the municipality of Calvià, which is in the south-west of the island. The other resorts are Illetes, Peguara, Portal Nous, and Santa Ponça. There are also two inland historical towns: Calvià and Capdella.

Although Palmanova and Magaluf can be understood as two separate *places* in terms of name, there is not a neat spatial division between them, and they run into one another. They were among the first resorts to witness tourism development, with two hotels in place by 1930 (Selwyn 1996b). Such has been Calvià's success with tourism that in 1996 the municipality was the richest in Spain and one of the richest in Europe (Selwyn 1996b). The Spanish National Institute of Statistics reported that in July 2008 Calvià was the lead municipality for bed occupancy out of the whole of Spain.[6] Over the years, the local authority has made many improvements to the physical nature of the two resorts: for example, building a promenade that runs virtually alongside the full length of the beaches making it possible to walk from one end of Palmanova to the far end of Magaluf, almost without interruption. Other initiatives have included (1) the removal of high rise block hotels, (2) the establishment of the post of Tourism Ombudsman within Calvià Council to deal with issues and complaints specific to tourism, and (3) traffic calming with the establishment of a way-one system. The extent to which the municipality has endeavoured to address environmental concerns and ensure the sustainability of the resorts has won it awards. Further, as far as possible, the council has pursued a policy that separates residential facilities from tourist facilities. Thus the two resorts are in place to serve tourists' needs in terms of accommodation, places to eat, shops, entertainment facilities and so on. However, the functioning of the resorts is very much underpinned by the relationship between the hotels and the tour operators, as there is a situation of dependency upon the tour operators to supply the tourists. The head of the local hotel association advised me that 'the relationship between the hotels and the tour operators is the most important, and the most important tour operator is Thomsons'.

Magaluf and Palmanova are predominately 'British'. There are several reasons why I make this assertion. Firstly, the majority of tourists staying in the resorts derive from one of the four entities of the UK. This includes a very wide geographical spread from Cornwall to Aberdeen and everywhere in between. However, from my observations and encounters a large proportion of the tourists hailed from the north-east of England, and Manchester and its environs. Secondly, the majority of these tourists arrive as part of an organized holiday led by one of the UK's leading tour operators,[7] for example, First Choice and Thomsons, who also employ British workers as their representatives in the resorts. Such is the dominance of British operators that whole hotels are given over entirely to their custom. Thirdly, the dominant language of communication is English, in part attributable to the sheer number of native English speakers present, which includes an expatriate community, many of whom are involved in the tourism industry, as well as seasonal British workers and, of course, the tourists. The use of the English language relates to cafe-bars' menus; TV programmes; newspapers – including those from the UK, for instance *The Sun* – and the local *Majorca Daily Bulletin*. Fourthly, the food and drink available caters to British tastes, with the provision and sale of exported British milk, bread, meat, breakfast cereals and beers. In some cases, it is possible to buy an imperial pint and to spend pounds sterling. Fifthly, Britishness is displayed in an overt way, in the flying, for instance, of the Union Jack flag; but also, in more subtle ways, through the choices and dispositions evinced by the tourists. In addition the mediators of their experiences exploit a sense of a national identity and the dangers of the other by highlighting points of difference and drawing attention to the possibilities of risk attendant on being in the presence of the other. As well as being British, I would also categorize the tourists visiting the two resorts as mainly white, heterosexual and working class. Very few tourists holiday alone, thus the population is composed of friendship and kinship groups, the former often being single sex. There is a slight change during the winter low season, when more single males are present.

As already noted, Magaluf and Palmanova, although separate resorts, merge into one another. The whole area is bounded: firstly, inland by a motorway running between the resort of Andraitx further to the west and the capital of Palma to the east; and secondly, the edge of the land and sea form a natural perimeter. The distinctive character of Magaluf is one of a 'party' destination with its numerous cafe-bars and nightclubs that attract a youthful tourist in the style of Club 18–30. It is also underwritten by ideas of self-gratification in all sorts of ways, including alimentary and sexual. Such is the extent of the latter that it has earned the resort the nickname of 'Shagaluf'. The main road in Magaluf, Punta Balena, is dominated by numerous shops that sell a wide range of goods ranging from souvenirs and postcards to clothes and jewellery. Many of the shops are packed tightly together, and the numerous stands exhibiting wares outside of many of the shops give an impression of variety and choice. Mixed in with these shops are cafe-bars, nightclubs, amusement arcades and food outlets, including several that can be described as 'fast food', for example, KFC and Burger King.

Palmanova exhibits some of the characteristics of Magaluf, but as Andrews points out 'it is considered by many of the tourists who stay there to be slightly more "upmarket", with some people referring to the "badly behaved" tourists in Magaluf as "animals"' (2006: 222). Certainly Palmanova has fewer nightclubs and therefore attracts fewer tourists looking for a Club 18–30 style holiday. And, even if they were accommodated in Palmanova, they would be more than likely to concentrate their actions in Magaluf, which provides more of the facilities that they are looking for. As such, Palmanova tends to attract older people and a family-based clientele. However, in reality, neither resort can be demarcated in any exclusive way based on tourist typology, and both exhibit similar characteristics that make them landscapes driven by the promotion and action of various forms of consumption (Andrews 2006).

In both resorts there are plentiful activities that tourists can take part in, including sunbathing, hiring a moped, paragliding, riding an inflated banana, or, if staying in a hotel, games and activities led by hotel entertainers. There are numerous tours and excursions organized by tour operator representatives (reps), which are also available through local travel agencies. These include, for example, tours to the east of the island to visit the underground caves, excursions to markets based in Inca and Andraitx, and general island tours to admire the scenery. In addition there are organized trips to night-time entertainment venues both inside and outside of the resorts, and tour operator rep marshalled bar crawls around Magaluf.

Another important feature of both resorts relates back to their identification as British. I have already given several reasons why I make this claim in the observation that there are many signals of ideas relating to Britishness. Some of these signals relate to the ways in which the resorts are encoded in a quite literal sense in the naming of places, in a fashion that is reminiscent of places geographically, or mythically, located in the UK.

Name that Place

In his discussion of sheep farming in hill farms of the Scottish Borders, John Gray calls for greater consideration of the ideas of place making and the role of a 'sense of place' in that process. He describes the acts of shepherds in naming features of the hills and cuts in which their sheep graze. 'As a referential practice, going around the hill also includes acts of naming places' (2003: 236). Gray quotes the geographer Porteous as saying, 'One familiar method of directing or controlling the external environment is the act of naming.... Naming is a powerful act. By naming landscape features ... we in part possess them' (1990: 72 in Gray 2003: 236). Gray goes on to attest that the naming of places by shepherds 'tames' the natural environment of the hills, and in so doing acts in 'transforming them into places where they feel at home' (2003: 237).

This is a key concept to understanding the nature of Magaluf and Palmanova as places that are imbued with a sense of Britishness, for, as Gray also notes, the sense of home affected by the hill farmers 'becomes the basis for their identity' (2003: 237). In Magaluf and Palmanova, it is not simply the naming of places that reinforces a sense of place, ownership and belonging, but also laying claim to the space by the internal décor. For example, one pub called the Geordie Pride, which is in Magaluf, is, in terms of its actual physical space, a small bar (as many of the bars are). Inside there are football shirts and scarves from the Newcastle team pinned to the walls and ceilings. There are also pictures of the team on the wall. The feeling is that it is like a shrine, and it is recognizable immediately to tourists who derive from Newcastle and support the local football team.

My argument here is that, on one level, the naming of specific places within Magaluf and Palmanova after a British fashion becomes an acquisition of those spaces, by the, often expatriate, proprietors, as British. In so doing they are creating an environment that, in crude marketing terms, doubtless speaks to a British audience, but at a deeper, more symbolic level, is also creating that space as British, and laying bare an aspect of self-identity by externalizing, in the Durkheimian sense, a facet of their inner world. By choosing such establishments over others, the tourists are also complicit in this homemaking project. For although tourism has been discussed as a search for difference and alterity (for examples, see MacCannell 1976 and Urry 1990), in this environment the tourists have chosen it as their holiday destination because it is not too distant from a feeling of home, or matches their fantasies of what home is, or should be. As one elderly, retired female tourist proclaims, 'I feel more at home here than I do in England.' In this respect the tourism industry has successfully enchanted (Selwyn 2007) its clientele.

It is not possible to name every single establishment in the two resorts here, but an extract from a table categorizing some of the names is given to demonstrate (Table 2.1). That some names in the table appear in more than one category speaks of the poly-vocal nature of symbols, evoking or relating to varying aspects of, in this case, ideas of Britishness. In this respect, we might refer back to Tapper (2008) and be reminded that identity is contingent upon context. By way of example, an interpretation of one of the categories, that of 'Cosy England', might include the following: the purpose of grouping these names together is to conjure up images of rural England in a past time. Daniels notes that 'landscape has played a key role in articulating English identity' (1991: 98) and that the associated image, constructed mainly in the last century, is one of a 'vernacular, agrarian, home-counties countryside' (1991: 98). Again, it is not possible to examine every name in detail. However, there are some general observations that can be made. Many of the names are linked to a time before mechanization – Coach and Horses Inn, The Plough and Mail Coach, for example. The use of the word 'Inn', as in the first name, and also used elsewhere (e.g. the Welcome Inn) is evocative of past times. The idea of welcome that is intimately linked to ideas of hospitality (Andrews 2000) speaks of a *gemeinschaft* community that forms part of the names' enchantments. A sense of loss in relation to a gemeinschaften sense of social cohesion echoes Bauman's observations that identity building has become an individual project.

To try to invoke further a sense of place and atmosphere in the two resorts, and draw attention to the sense of social solidarity encountered in the resorts, I continue by outlining the atmosphere and experience found in one of the many cafe-bars in Magaluf: The Britannia Pub.[8] I visited the Britannia Pub with a Glaswegian, Nancy, an eighteen-year-old worker in the resort.

On entering the pub it is very crowded with middle-aged men and women on a golfing holiday.[9] As we walk around the bar and through the crowd, Nancy directly bumps into

Table 2.1 Extract from a categorization of place names in Magaluf and Palmanova.

Comic	Military/Heroes	Familiar British	Cosy England	National / Regional/Ethnic Identity	Royalty	Birds	Mythology/ Fantasy
Nutters	Bar Trafalgar	Arfur's	Coach and Horse Inn	Windsor	Windsor	Mucky Duck	Robin Hood
Popeyes Fun Pub	Lord Nelson	Windsor	The Local British Pub	Britannia Pub	Kings Arms	The Green Parrot	Fantasy Island Bar
Jokers Pub	The Three Musketeers	Fred's Fish and Chips	The Cottage Pub	Bar Piccadilly	Prince William	Roosters Fish and Chips	Robinson Crusoe
Benny Hills Party Pub	Duke of Wellington	Hard Times	The Plough	O'Malleys Irish Tavern	Queens Bar		Casanovas
Peter Sellers Disco Fun Pub	Robin Hood	Ministry Club	Mail Coach	Sospan Fach	The Rose & Crown		Camelot Pub
Del Boys Pub	The Falklands	The Office	The Oak	The Tartan Arms	Lady Diana		Oasis Pub

one of the younger males in the crowd. Everyone is drinking and dancing. One couple is engaged in a continual kiss even as they dance, although at one point he lifts her into the air. One man falls over and he hits his back as he goes down. Later another man falls on his back, he bends his knees up over his chest and other members of the crowd spin him around. One man keeps coming up to me and tries to get me to dance. Later he points towards his penis. Eventually he takes his belt off and starts pulling it in-between his legs and rubbing his crotch. The dancing continues and everyone is swaying and rocking together. At one point it feels as though we are on a boat in choppy seas. The movement seems to be quite fast and there is an intensity and excitement about the atmosphere. Nancy dances with the young man she bumped into and he buys her two red roses.

The name of the cafe-bar – Britannia – is also worth considering, as it alludes to a sense of militarism. There is a category of names that stands out in its connection with a British military history. It is striking not simply because of the high number of establishments with such an association – for example, The Duke of Wellington, or the Lord Nelson – but also because of their concentration in one location, that of Magaluf. The military association of these names is based on the idea that they are all in some way connected with ideas of conflict – and usually of conflict between the UK and her European neighbours – heroism and military might.[10] Within this, a name like Three Musketeers does not make an obvious fit, based as it is on the French novel by Alexandre Dumas. Nevertheless the fictional characters share some common traits with those drawn from factual events. For example, the bravery and heroism exhibited by all the protagonists, the ability to overcome adversity and be triumphant in the face of greater numbers – only three musketeers against many. Both Wellington and Nelson faced bigger naval fleets and armies. The message contained in these names is that the British can look defeat in the face and win, by use of superior tactics, greater strength and bravery. Further, central to all of this is the defence of the establishment, the upholding of 'normative' law and order, as represented in the central figures of a king or queen. There are, of course, other categories with their own appeal. Ideas pertaining to a British sense of humour are well represented, and the use of figures from the popular imagination undoubtedly features in the promotion of such places. A place that is instantly recognizable, albeit only in its name, offers the comfort of familiarity and sense of safety. However, what further marks out the military names is the fact that the conflicts they refer to are in effect acted out in the resorts, and thus become embodied as part of the tourists' experiences and sense of who they are in the context of their holiday. As Bender notes, '[l]andscapes are created by people – through their experience and engagement with the world around them' (1993: 1).

One way in which tourists engage with the representations of the world around them in Magaluf is through the expression of the conflicts, alluded to in these names, which become manifest in a hugely popular night-time entertainment event, aimed predominately at British tourists. Pirates Adventure (and its associated Family Pirates for a younger audience) is a retelling of British conflicts with Spain and France, drawing on genuine historical figures including, for example, Sir Francis Drake, Sir Henry Morgan and Jacques Lafitte. The basic premise of the show's story line is that the French (mainly represented in the form of Jacques Lafitte) have taken possession of some Moroccan gold that rightfully belongs to the British[11] as represented in the figures of Drake, Morgan and their associates in the play. Battles and celebratory parties are enacted largely through the medium of skilful acrobatic performances by the French side, until they are finally vanquished and Jacques Lafitte disposed off into the mouth of a waiting and obliging shark. In relation to constructions of national identity, the features in the show are significant because as Carter, Donald and Squires (1993) point out, the creation of ideas of identity in the present often rely on narratives of nationalism which are rooted in the past. A similar observation is also made by Holtzman (2006) in relation to memory in a discussion concerning the relationship between food and memory in which he notes 'the subjective ways that the past is recalled, memorialized, and used to construct the present' (2006: 363).

The audience is not only reminded of the historical relations of hostility between the French and British, but also, through the use of characters including Sir Francis Drake, of other conflicts with the Spanish. In addition, negative references are made about German people, drawing on the stereotypical tale regarding sun beds. For example, in one audience participation game, the prize is that of a beach towel with the Pirates Adventure logo depicted on it. On handing out the prize, the compère advises 'put that on the sun bed and no Germans will bother you, but you'll have to get up early.' Further, the tourists become implicated in this process of othering through audience participation games. As Crouch, Aronsson and Wahltstrom contend, 'space ... at least in part is constructed and signified by the tourist. Moreover ... space is a medium through which the tourist negotiates her or his world, tourism signs and contexts, and may construct her or his own distinctive meanings' (2001: 254). Thus the actions and dispositions of the tourists become as relevant to the constructions of identity as the performance. Throughout the show the audience is encouraged to abuse Jacques Lafitte and to call him a 'French bastard'. Indeed, his appearance on stage, even at the point of the final applause, is accompanied by chants of 'you French Bastard' from the audience. On other occasions, he is variously described as 'evil', 'a pillock' or 'a poof'. At the beginning of the show, the audience is divided into four sections with each section being allotted a British pirate to cheer for throughout the show, and particularly during the enacting of conflict. The various sections of the audience shout, cheer and clap for their designated captain, and there is an atmosphere of excitement. The first half of the performance, which is based largely on the antics of the British pirates, ends with an interval. During this time, the meal that is part of the package for the show is brought out and consumed. Thus the interval marks a reuniting of the audience from their various teams, as they all come together to share in the eating of food. During this time, some members of the audience enact mock battles of their own with the plastic swords they have purchased on the way in. The overall point is that the tourists undertake to engage with the articulation of identity displayed in the show. Far from being voyeuristic bystanders, they inform the storytelling. To borrow from Geertz (1973), Pirates Adventure becomes a story they tell themselves about themselves.

I have made reference to the use of a meal to bring about a sense of unity, the sharing of a common purpose and eating the same food. The importance of food and meals as both a communicator and re-enforcer of identity is deep rooted as a vehicle of analysis in social anthropology, as Holtzman attests there is a 'voluminous body relating food to ethnic or other forms of identity' (2006: 361).

Eating Home

We are reminded by Kuper that '[c]ooking and eating can be a way of travelling to foreign countries' (1997: x). In other words, we are able to know the other through the ingestion of their food and drink and the adoption of particular cooking techniques. Insights into social relations and understandings of identity have for a long time been examined by anthropologists through the symbolic meanings of cooking food, the food itself and its circulation.[12] Holtzman claims that, more recently, 'much of the burgeoning literature on food in anthropology and related fields implicitly engages with issues of memory' (2006: 361). He argues that one of the advantages of examining the link is that it considers how food is experienced not only on an intellectual level but also physically and emotionally, which he rightly points out aligns itself with Bourdieu's concept of habitus. In relation to national identity, Holtzman observes, 'food is often used explicitly in the invention of national identities' (2006: 368) and that in general 'integration into the European Union (EU) has been a particularly important arena tying food to notions of memory and historical consciousness, particularly the threat of homogenization of national and regional difference' (2006: 369). While I am not concerned directly with memory, Holtzman's observations nevertheless prove useful for my analysis because the experience of food and drink is important in Magaluf and Palmanova. For example, the search for a 'proper cup of tea' because 'they [the Spanish] can't make it' acts as an expression of difference between ideas of 'us' and 'them'. In addition there is the seeking out of British food produce, because as Douglas (a black male tourist from Birmingham in his thirties) says about his hotel breakfast 'the toast is lacking in texture and the bacon

Figure 2.1 Cafe-bar eateries with 'British' names.

and sausages are not like the English versions. The sausages are like the ones in hot dogs.'

One of the defining characteristics of the landscapes of the two resorts is the availability of 'British' foods, and the advertisement of that availability. So, for example, the names of eateries and cafes not only appeal to a sense of home; but also proclaim the nationality of their ownership (see Figure 2.1). By way of further enticement, the establishments often state their ability to provide meals that are cooked in the style of home, and specifically of one's mother, as illustrated in Figures 2.2 and 2.3.

Both Figures 2.2 and 2.3 utilize the Union Jack flag to symbolize their Britishness. Of particular interest in Figure 2.3 is the use of a homely, portly looking female figure serving up the home cooked food. The significance of the use of a mother figure will be explored in my final discussion.

To focus specifically on what food is eaten, it is possible to identify not just meals – for example, the fry-up and roast dinner – but also British ingredients – sausages, bacon, milk, breakfast cereals and fish from the North Sea.[13] As Rory, the son of a fish and chip bar owner, explained, the reason why fish has to be imported is because the sort used in his father's concern is caught in the North Sea, frozen straight away, and then flown to Mallorca within twenty-four hours. He advises that although there are cod in the Mediterranean, they are too salty

Figure 2.2 A sign for cooking like mum.

Figure 2.3 A cafe sign proclaiming British identity.

to be used,[14] and therefore, in order to meet customer demand for a certain taste, the fish has to be imported. Flying in the cod, thus allowing the familiar to be provided, restricts the hunger for something different and promotes the desire for something the same. In a different example, some tourists will enquire if the water used for making ice cubes is local or bottled. If it is the former, the ice is rejected. To illustrate: a woman among one group of tourists sitting at a bar discussing their next drink was unsure that she wanted another drink. When her husband suggested that she might like an ice lolly instead, she screwed up her nose and commented 'but it would be made from their water.' To return to Kuper, cooking and eating may be a way of knowing the other, but it is also a way of knowing the self. A sense of place is also informed by food choices – for example, the connection between fast food and modern urban environments versus the quaint quiet tea-room of the rural locale (Bell and Valentine 1997). In Magaluf and Palmanova, the sense of place is informed by food choices, the rejection of local food in favour of imported 'British' foodstuffs. The wish not to consume difference is based on a recognition of ideas of otherness, which are both symbolized and performed in attitudes and dispositions towards food and drink in the two resorts.

The old maxim 'we are what we eat' applies not only to the metaphorical associations of representing personhood and identity through what is consumed,[15] but also to the physical nature of our bodies. The connection between food and body shape is also directly related to space. Consumption habits demarcate cultural boundaries and give form to spatial scales. In addition, the size of our bodies determines how much space we physically occupy. It is to bodies that I now turn.

British Bodies

Our relationships with the wider social world can be explored through our bodies. What is evident is that we can use an analysis of the social body both as a medium of symbolic expression through what the body and how it is adorned represents (Hertz 1973), and gain insights into the embodied nature of systems and understandings of external social relations (e.g. Gell 1996) which derive from our habitus and form a way of 'being' in the world.

Sunbathing is both a way of being in the world and, via the transformation of the skin, produces a symbolic representation of identity. As Carter claims, it is a symbol of tourist consumption, and it is 'an important symbol of the visual consumption of others' (1997: 144). The majority of sunbathing takes place in Palmanova and Magaluf around hotel and apartment swimming pools and balconies, and on the beaches. For one tourist in Palmanova the acquisition of a suntan was seen as a symbol of wealth and status. She explains that she sunbathes for a couple of hours a day with her daughter but that, 'I can't just lie there like some of them, and anyway when I get back to the UK I'll end up covering it up when I go to court [she is a magistrate] in case anyone thinks I have lots of money.' For Douglas (referred to above in relation to cooked breakfasts), the symbolic significance of skin colour is as a marker of distinction in terms of his ethnicity. I met Douglas sitting at a drinks kiosk on one of the promenades that runs alongside one of the beaches in Palmanova. Douglas is black. He is on holiday with his white, female partner and their little girl. Upon meeting Douglas his family are sunbathing on the beach. However, although he has done some sunbathing, on the days that I encounter him he is always drinking by the kiosk while his family are on the beach. He says 'I bet you can't tell if I've got a tan or not'. When I ask him why he is not spending time on the beach, he replies 'if I get much darker I'll end up looking like an African. If she [his partner] wants to get a tan that's her business.' Thus the way in which the colour of skin becomes a marker of identity for Douglas is to distinguish him from a particular group.

The act of sunbathing tells us something else about the nature of touristic experiences and identities. As Douglas declares, 'here [Mallorca] I can lie out in the sun and totally relax.' The idea of total relaxation is often expressed in terms of 'vegin out' as one young, white male tourist explains about his and his girlfriend's activities 'we've mainly been *sunbathing*, just lying on the beach vegin' out ... boring but I just wanted to completely veg out.' In her analysis of gardening practices in the English North, Degnen observes the 'reciprocal parallels between human bodies and intentionality and those of plants' (2009: 151). In extending her argument further, she observes that plants are often used, in the words of Rosaldo, 'to speak of humans' (1972: 91 cited in Degnen 2009: 154). What I am suggesting here is that likening oneself to a vegetable speaks of a way of being in the world. The idea of 'vegin' out' (being like a vegetable: inert, close to the ground, unthinking and unfeeling) suggests a link with nature – a vegetable is devoid of the attachments of culture. Physically lying down and being close to the ground is concomitant with relaxing and not having to think about the demands of the quotidian world the tourists have left behind.

As part of the tourism industry's attempts to enchant, the body and its functions – but particularly those that are related to sex – are primary sites. So, for example, during the tour rep organized bar crawls,[14] participants are invited to take part in games called 'sexual positions' in which they are required to simulate various sexual intercourse poses. In a similar game played as part of hotel entertainment, balloons are used both as pretend penises and breasts. With regard to the former, contestants must demonstrate their agility and speed to burst the balloons in the designated sexual position. The foregrounding of the body in this manner and the emphasis on speed and skill serve to feed into ideas of sexual availability and excess which, in part, characterizes both resorts, but Magaluf in particular. Part of this enchantment is also derived from the availability of the female breast(s).

Bare female breasts are everywhere in the two resorts, on postcard images, aprons, souvenirs, beaches, and as part of the night-time entertainment. One example is in Pirates Adventure where during the playing of an audience participation game female members of the audience are invited, cajoled and berated with the mantra 'get your tits out for the boys' (Andrews 2009b). The breast is a poly-vocal symbol standing for nourishment, consumption, mother, comfort, nation, freedom and so on. In addition, in the context under discussion here, it is an object for male titillation and consumption and helps to define the spaces of the two resorts in a 'normative' gendered framework premised as it is on heterosexual relationships. Thus women are objects, there for the satisfaction and gratification of men, and this stands out in contrast to the strength and heroism of men signalled in the military references found in place names in Magaluf and the story of Pirates Adventure. Perhaps more than any other symbol in the two resorts the breast is the most potent in standing for what it means to be British, as such it is used in my final discussion to draw the threads of the ethnography together.

Suckling the Nation

The significance of the breast in this context is that it unites all three elements of the social world under discussion. Firstly, it is a part of both female and male bodies, although it is a more convincing symbol of femininity than masculinity. Indeed, Yalom (1997) argues that the breast is the defining part of the female body. Secondly, in its various representations and actual physical presence, the breast informs a sense of place. Thirdly, it is directly linked to ideas of consumption and nourishment. As Yalom (1997) notes, in both the Jewish and Christian traditions the breast is honoured as the provider of milk and its ability to nourish infants; as such it has been used allegorically for the care of whole religious or political communities. The provision of milk speaks of kinship and social relations. Its role as an agent of social unification is found in Islamic Law under which people are related by blood, marriage and milk (Khatib-Chahidi 1992).

The ubiquitous presence of the breast and thus, by association, milk suggests that the holiday is about relationships, the creation of new encounters and opportunities to build upon existing familial and friendship connections, as well as being indicative of a common bond shared by the tourists in relation to national identity. Milk as the first food infantilizes the tourists; as such they are the children of the nation. In other respects and linked to the idea of the nation, the breast is a reminder of the values of home: love, intimacy and nurturing, all factors that the disoriented tourist needs for a sense of security. The breasts depicted in the postcards are always available and ready for sucking. They do not appear to be the 'bad' breast described by Klein that frustrates and angers as it is withheld and unavailable for lactation (Yalom 1997).[17] Thus the breast and its milk become signifiers of the satisfaction of needs, desires and wants that exist at a most basic level.

The symbolic link between women and ideas of nation serve to sexualize and eroticize the latter (Cusack 2003). The over-valorizing of the breast in the resorts firmly entrenches ideas of women as sexual beings. In connections to nation, women's bodies become a part of a collective body and their abuse (e.g. rape) a way of violating the nation. Valerius contends '[t]here is a close correspondence between the nation and women's bodies, whether they are material bodies biologically reproducing the nation ... or targets of ethnic rage and humiliation' (2003: 43). The role of women as reproducing the nation is argued by Das to be distinct from that of men. Men, she argues, are assigned a role in which they 'should be ready to bear arms for the nation and be ready to die for it' (2008: 285), whereas 'women's reproduction is seen to be rightly belonging to the state ... so as citizens they are obligated to bear "legitimate" children who will be, in turn, ready to die for the nation' (2008: 285).

Conclusion

I have argued that the tourists' home-world is characterized by feelings of loss, impotence and insecurities in the face of outside foreign influences, to which we might also add the emergence of the free market and the erosion of the welfare state. Thus the collective idea of the nation that the tourists are being able to buy into in the contexts of Magaluf and Palmanova through the symbolic and embodied manifestations of Britishness is, itself, uncertain. There is no guarantee that it will always be present for people, especially if they do not conform to specific roles in terms of their bodily abilities, gender orientations or as active consumers. By contrast, the mother is supposed to love and care for her child regardless of their circumstances or aptitudes. She is a steadfast figure who should always be present for her children to satisfy their needs and desires. This places her in a powerful position; she also has the capacity to disown, withdraw and punish. Thus she is both the 'good breast' and the 'bad breast'. The ambiguity in her role, and by corollary, her relationship with her children makes her a figure to challenge, even to punish for not being eternally 'good' or for simply being a form of authority. Thus the mother as nation in Palmanova and Magaluf is not only set up to be admired (which is one interpretation of the ubiquitous presence of the breast), but also to be torn down, humiliated and ultimately subjugated to the will of her children as in the demands to 'get your tits out for the boys'.

All of these symbols and performances inform the lexicon of 'sex and death, reproduction and war, [which] become part of the same configuration of ideas and institutions through which the nation-state sets up defences to stave off the uncertainty emanating from dangerous aliens and from the ravages of time' (Das 2008: 285).

In tracing the contours of Britishness presented and experienced in the setting of Magaluf and Palmanova, I have identified its presence and performance through food and drink practices; and the representations and experiences of space, in particular the drawing upon a sense of militarism from past conflicts to inform a sense of identity in the present. In relation to the body, I have argued that it is a vehicle of symbolic expression about self identity, but also through bodily practices it speaks of what it means to be on holiday. The focus on a sexualized body, and particularly the role of the breast, shifts my argument towards an understanding of a sexualized Britishness that relies on traditional, normative gender roles in which women take on the function of domestic reproducer of the nation. By contrast, men must be ready to die willingly for its survival. The resulting view of Britishness in this context is one underscored by violence – the recourse to the various acts of war associated with the building of empire are used to enchant and inform a sense of identity in the present helping to fuel existing bloody conflicts and those doubtless yet to come.

Notes

1. I want to note the difficulty inherent in discussions of ideas of Britishness or British identity, particularly given that it is often the case that the terms English and British, United Kingdom and Britain are conflated to cover all of the countries and separate identities that make up these concepts. Also I heed Tapper's warning of 'essentialization and imprecision' (2008: 100). However, from a methodological point of view, in Magaluf and Palmanova it is not easy to disaggregate the individual 'nations' that make up the United Kingdom, or indeed regions, unless these were clearly identified by the tourists concerned, and where possible these identities are reflected in the chapter. However, there is also a need to think about the tourists collectively and thus the terms British, Britain and UK are used for discussion purposes. In this respect, I follow O'Reilly's example drawn from her study of the British ex-pat community on the Costa del Sol: 'I use British to apply to those English, Scottish, Welsh and Irish people who are identified, either through their actions or words, as British nationals' (2000: 167).

2. Lunn, for example, observes '[g]reat concern is frequently expressed about the loss of British sovereignty which seems implicit in a greater acceptance of European integration' (1996: 84).

3. For a more detailed discussion of the ritualistic nature of holiday taking, see Graburn's (1989) seminal paper.

4. Another word that is perhaps in need of contextualization is that of mass. Reference to mass tourism has its roots, as Holden (2005) indicates, in the idea of bringing leisure travel to the masses as a result of the process of industrialization. Rates of tourism have grown considerably since this era and with increased technological advances its reaches are in many diverse environments some of which might be labelled, for instance, as 'fragile' (e.g. Weaver 1995) in which case a mass need not refer to 'masses'. Given this, the term 'charter tourism' seems more appropriate.

5. http://www.mallorcaweb.co./news/2006/01tourism-balearic-islands-2005 (accessed 15 October 2008).

6. http://www.euroweeklynews.com/news/10888.html (accessed 15 October 2008).

7. Given the horizontal and vertical integration of aspects of the tourism industry within national and across national boundaries, ideas of a distinctly UK operator are likely erroneous. For example, Thomsons is owned by German-based company TUI.

8. Britannia is the Latin name for Britain. The personification of the land mass was first used by the Romans on coinage in which Britannia was depicted as a female figure sitting on a globe and holding a shield and spear. The motif was picked up again by Charles II (Brewer 1988; Odhams Encyclopaedia 1961). The image continues to be used on some Bank of England notes and coinage in the present day. The symbol of Britannia with sword and shield militarizes her. At the same time her seated position also makes her a more passive figure, and while she undoubtedly connotes patriotism and conquest (as in 'Britannia rule the waves') her role as a mother figure also casts her as a defender and protector.

9. One point about 'golfing holidays' is that they are often used, by men, as a cover for extramarital relationships, according to one informant. It is therefore not clear if the women would describe themselves as being on a golfing holiday or if they were the partners of the men.

10. Regardless of the historical accuracy of the terms of UK and British in relation to when some conflicts took place.

11. The show is an example of the way in which the terms British and English become conflated. It is the case that the patrons of the performance are drawn from British tourists following the definition outlined above. However, the historical figures in reality existed before the act of union and therefore speak

of a distinctly English rather than British history. Nevertheless they are used by the performers to present a united British front in opposition to the French.

12. For examples, see Lévi-Strauss (1964, 1997), Douglas (1975, 1984, 1987), Selwyn (1980), Caplan (1997) and Archetti (1997). In relation to drink and drinking practices, there is Douglas's (1987) edited collection, and more recently Wilson's (2005) volume, which links varied forms of drinking practices to aspects of identity in a range of different cultural contexts.

13. Although fish caught in the North Sea cannot necessarily be labelled British as such, the point in highlighting the creatures' point of origin is that they are associated with what is eaten in the UK and also are differentiated from fish found in the Mediterranean.

14. The reality is that there are no cod in the Mediterranean (Bramwell 1977).

15. Which, as Barthes points out, is 'a system of communication, a body of images, a protocol of usages, situations and behaviour' (1975: 50).

16. For a more detailed description of bar crawls, see Andrews (2005).

17. There is an exception to this rule in a postcard that depicts a breast dangling tantalizing above the open mouth of a man buried, apart from his head, in sand, the breast his source of nourishment just out of reach.

References

Aitchison, C. (1999), 'Heritage and Nationalism: Gender and the Performance of Power', in D. Crouch (ed.), *Leisure/Tourism Geographies: Practices and Geographical Knowledge,* London: Routledge pp. 59–73.

Andrews, H. (1999) 'We Are What We Eat', *In Focus*, Summer 1999 no.3, Tourism Concern, London, pp. 24–5.

Andrews, H. (2000), 'Consuming Hospitality on Holiday', in C. Lashley and A. Morrison (eds), *In Search of Hospitality: Theoretical Perspectives and Debates,* Oxford: Butterworth Heinemann, pp. 235–54.

Andrews, H. (2002), 'A Theme Park for the Brits Behaving Badly', *Times Higher Education Supplement,* 19 July 2000, p. 22.

Andrews, H. (2005), 'Feeling at Home: Embodying Britishness in a Spanish Charter Tourist Resort', *Tourist Studies* 5(3): 247–66.

Andrews, H. (2006), 'Consuming Pleasures: Package Tourists in Mallorca', in K. Meethan, A. Anderson and S. Miles (eds), *Tourism, Consumption and Representation,* Wallingford: Cabi, pp. 217–35.

Andrews, H. (2009a), 'Tourism as a "Moment of Being"', *Suomen Antropologi* 34(2): 5–21.

Andrews, H. (2009b), '"Tits Out for the Boys and No Back Chat": Gendered Space on Holiday', *Space and Culture* 12(2): 166–82.

Archetti, E.P. (1997), *Guinea-Pigs: Food Symbol and Conflict of Knowledge*, Oxford: Berg.

Arranz, J.I. Prieto (2006), 'Rural, White and Straight. The ETC's Vision of England', *Journal of Tourism and Cultural Change* 4(1): 19–52.

Bardolet, E. (1996), Balearic Islands General Information, IBATUR Conselleria de Turisme Govern Balear.

Barthes, R. (1975), 'Toward a Psychosociolgoy of Contemporary Food Consumption', in E. Forster and R. Forster (eds), *European Diet from Pre-Industrial to Modern Times*, London: Harper and Row, pp. 47–59.

Bauman, Z. (2002), 'Space in the Globalizing World', in E. Krausz and G. Tulea (eds), *Starting the Twenty-first Century: Sociological Reflections and Challenges*, London: Transaction Publishers, pp. 3–24.

Bell, D. and Valentine, G. (1997), *Consuming Geographies: We Are Where We Eat*, London: Routledge.

Bender, B. (1993), 'Stonehenge – Contested Landscapes (Medieval to Present Day)', in B. Bender (ed.), *Landscape: Politics and Perspectives*, Oxford: Berg, pp. 1–17.

Bourdieu, P. (1993), *The Field of Cultural Production: Essays on Art and Literature*, Cambridge: Polity Press.

Bramwell, M. (ed.) (1977), *Atlas of the Oceans*, Guildford: Colour Library Books Ltd.

Brewer, E.C. (1988) *The Dictionary of Phrase and Fable,* Leicester: Galley Press.

Brück, J. (2001), 'Monuments, Personhood and Power in the British Neolithic', *JRAI* 7(4): 649–67.

Caplan, P. (1997), 'Approaches to the Study of Food, Health and Identity', in P. Caplan (ed.), *Food, Health and Identity*, London, Routledge, pp. 1–31.

Carter, E., Donald, J. and Squires, J. (1993), 'Introduction', in E. Carter, J. Donald and J. Squires (eds), *Space and Place: Theories of Identity and Location*, London: Lawrence and Wishart, pp. vii–xv.

Carter, S. (1997), 'Who Wants to be "Peelie Wally"? Glaswegian Tourists' Attitudes to Sun Tans and Sun Exposure', in S. Clift and P. Grabowski (eds), *Tourism and Health: Risks Research and Responses*, London: Pinter, pp. 139–50.

Cohen, E. (1974) 'Who is a Tourist?: A Conceptual Clarification', *Sociological Review*, 2: 527–55.

Cohen, E. (1979), 'A Phenomenology of Tourist Experiences', *Sociology* 13: 179–201.

Crouch, D., Aronsson, L. and Wahltstrom, L. (2001), 'Tourist Encounters', *Tourist Studies* 1(3): 253–70.

Cusack, T. (2003), 'Introduction', in T. Cusack and S. Bhreathnach-Lynch (eds), *Art, Nation and Gender: Ethnic Landscapes, Myths and Mother-Figures*, Oxford: Blackwell, pp. 1–11.

Daniels, S. (1991), 'Envisioning England (Review Article)', *Journal of Historical Geography* 17(1): 95–9.

Das, V. (2008), 'Violence, Gender, and Subjectivity', *Annual Review of Anthropology* 37: 283–99.

Degnen, C. (2009), 'On Vegetable Love: Gardening, Plants and People in the North of England', *JRAI* 15(1): 151–67.

Desforges, L. (2000), 'Travelling the World: Identity and Travel Biography', *Annals of Tourism Research* 27(4): 926–45.

Douglas, M. (1975), 'Deciphering a Meal', in M. Douglas (ed.), *Implicit Meanings: Essays in Anthropology*, London: Routledge and Keegan Paul, pp. 249–75.

Douglas, M. (1984), *Food in the Social Order*, New York: Basic Books.

Douglas, M. (1987), *Constructive Drinking: Perspectives on Drink from Anthropology*, Cambridge: Cambridge University Press.

Edensor, T. and Kothari, U. (1994), 'The Masculinisation of Stirling's Heritage', in V. Kinnard and D. Hall (eds), *Tourism: A Gender Analysis*, Chichester: John Wiley, pp. 164–85.

Geertz, C. (1973), *The Interpretation of Cultures*, New York: Basic Books Inc.

Gell, A. (1996), 'Reflections on a Cut Finger: Taboo in the Umeda Conception of the Self', in M. Jackson (ed.), *Things as They Are: New Directions in Phenomenological Anthropology*, Bloomington, IN: Indiana University Press, pp. 115–27.

Graburn, N.H.H. (1989), 'Tourism: The Sacred Journey', in V. Smith (ed.), *Hosts and Guests: The Anthropology of Tourism*, 2nd edition, Oxford: Blackwell, pp. 21–36.

Gray, J (2003), 'Open Spaces and Dwelling Places: Being at Home on Hill Farms in the Scottish Borders' in S. Low and D. Lawrence-Zuñiga (eds), *The Anthropology of Space and Place: Locating Culture*, Oxford: Blackwell, pp. 224–44.

Hertz, R. (1973), 'The Hands', in M. Douglas (ed.), *Rules and Meanings: The Anthropology of Everyday Knowledge*, Harmondsworth: Penguin.

Holden, A. (2005), *Tourism Studies and the Social Sciences*, London: Routledge.

Holtzman, Jon D. (2006), 'Food and Memory', *Annual Review of Anthropology* 35: 361–78.

Jackson, M. (1989), *Paths Toward a Clearing: Radical Empiricism and Ethnographic Inquiry*, Bloomington, IN: Indiana University Press.

Jackson, M. (2005), *Existential Anthropology: Events, Exigencies and Effects*, Oxford: Berghahn.

Khatib-Chahidi, J. (1992), 'Milk Kinship in Shi'ite Islamic Iran', in V. Maher (ed.), *The Anthropology of Breast-Feeding: Natural Law or Social Construct*, Oxford: Berg, pp. 109–32.

Kuper, J. (1997), 'Preface', in J. Kuper (ed.) *The Anthropologists' Cookbook*, London: Kegan Paul, pp. x–xiii.

Lévi-Strauss, C. (1964), *The Raw and the Cooked*, Harmondsworth: Penguin.

Lévi-Strauss, C. (1997), 'The Roast and the Boiled', in J. Kuper (ed.), *The Anthropologists' Cookbook*, London: Kegan Paul, pp. 239–48.

Lunn, K. (1996), 'Reconsidering Britishness: The Construction and Significance of National Identity in Twentieth-Century Britain', in B. Jenkins and S.A. Sofos (eds), *Nation and Identity in Contemporary Europe*, London: Routledge, pp. 83–100.

MacCannell, D. (1976), *The Tourist: A New Theory of the Leisure Class*, London: The Macmillan Press.

Magelssen, S. (2002), 'Remapping American-ness: Heritage Production and the Staging of the Native American and the African American as Other in "Historyland"', *National Identities* 4(2): 161–78.

Odhams (1961), *The Modern Encyclopaedia*, London: Odhams Press.

O'Reilly, K. (2000), *The British on the Costa Del Sol: Transnational Identities and Local Communities*, London: Routledge.

Palmer, C. (1998), 'From Theory to Practice: Experiencing the Nation in Every-day Life', *Journal of Material Culture* 3(2):175–99.

Palmer, C. (1999), 'Heritage Tourism and English National Identity', Unpublished PhD Thesis, University of North London, London.

Palmer, C. (2003), 'Touring Churchill's England: Rituals of Kinship and Belonging', *Annals of Tourism Research* 30(2): 426– 45.

Pearce, P.L. (1982), *The Social Psychology of Tourist Behaviour*, Oxford: Pergamon.

Selwyn, T. (1980), 'The Order of Men and the Order of Things: An Examination of Food Transactions in an Indian Village', *International Journal of the Sociology of Law* 8: 297–317.

Selwyn, T. (1996a), 'Atmospheric Notes from the Fields: Reflections on Myth-collecting Tours', in T. Selwyn (ed.), *The Tourist Image: Myths and Myth Making in Tourism*, Chichester: John Wiley and Sons, pp. 147–61.

Selwyn, T. (1996b), 'Tourism Culture and Cultural Conflict: a case study from Mallorca', in C. Fsadni and T. Selwyn (eds), *Sustainable Tourism in Mediterranean Islands and Small Cities* Malta: Medcampus in European Tourism Project.

Selwyn, T. (2007), 'The Political Economy of Enchantment. Formations in the Anthropology of Tourism', *Suomen Antropologi* 32(2): 48–70.

Tapper, R. (2008), 'Who are the Kuchi? Nomad self-identities in Afghanistan', *JRAI* 14(1): 97–116.

Urry, J. (1990), *The Tourist Gaze: Leisure and Travel in Contemporary Societies*, London: Sage.

Valerius, J. (2003), '(Dis-)Embodying the Nation: Female Figures, Desire and Nation Building in Early Twentieth-century Finland', in T. Cusack and S. Bhreathnach-Lynch (eds), *Art, Nation and Gender: Ethnic Landscapes, Myths and Mother-Figures*, Oxford: Blackwell, pp. 83–52.

Weaver, D.B. (1995), 'Alternative Tourism in Montserrat', *Tourism Management* 16(8): 593–604.

Wickens, E. (2002), 'The Sacred and the Profane: A Tourist Typology', *Annals of Tourism Research* 29(3): 834–851.

Wilson, T.M. (ed.) (2005), *Drinking Cultures*, Oxford: Berg.

Yalom, M. (1997), *A History of the Breast*, London: Harper Collins.

Internet Sources

http://www.euroweeklynews.com/news/10888.html (accessed 15 October 2008).

http://www.mallorcaweb.co./news/2006/01tourism-balearic-islands-2005 (accessed 15 October 2008).

–3–

The Sex of Tourism?

Bodies under Suspicion in Paradise
Susan Frohlick

Introduction: the sex of tourism?

[Female sex tourists] are just whoremongers, horny ... they want one thing, like the rest of us.

From 'Orient Expat', an online discussion forum

Is sex + tourism always equal to sex tourism? Has the 'sex' of tourism come only to mean 'one thing'? In an era of economic globalization, sexual commodification and international travel, sex tourism is an increasingly widespread phenomenon. Yet, analyses of the *sexuality* of tourism have not moved far beyond important but circumscribed critiques of the global political economy that structures and enables sexual desire and the touristic quest for material-erotic exchanges with the exotic Other. Anthropologists have contributed nuanced ethnographies that elucidate the exploitative scenarios associated with sex tourism, notably the inequities of the global sex trade and the power imbalances enacted in these transactions embodied through race, gender, class and sexuality (e.g. Brennan 2004; Padilla 2007).

My analysis offers an examination of the linkages of sex and tourism from a different perspective, looking at ways in which sex tourism can cast a menacing shadow on the bodies of particular travellers – and as a kind of spectre hides as much as it explains. By raising the possibility that visitors to particular destinations are likely there for 'only one thing', inflammatory representations such as the one above, from a thread about 'women who travel for sex' on a website called 'OrientExpat', participate in the eroticization (and moralization) of sociability between tourists and locals. In this sense, as my example will demonstrate, the possibility that tourist–local relations within paradisiacal 'hot spots' must certainly be of a sexual nature is a powerful schema that places some tourists under suspicion. I am expressly interested in the figure of 'the female sex tourist', constructed as an icon of post-feminist consumer culture with its tropes of freedom and choice and 'energetic personal empowerment' (Tasker and Negra

–51–

2007: 3), and as such an allegory of the inherent dangers of women's sexual pleasure and erotic desire.

In this chapter I argue that there is much going on regarding sex and sexuality within tourism domains that warrants anthropological enquiry. However, the focus has been on sex tourism and on the experiences of men, women and children in the global South who are sexual labourers for Northern tourists. Although anthropological accounts of sex tourism are valuable because of the particularities they present and the critiques they offer of the search for pleasure that takes place within inequitable economies and structures of power, anthropology has not done as well yet at examining the 'dense webs of socially meaningful moralities' (Pigg and Adams 2005) in which sexuality plays out within tourism. Moreover, because anthropology of tourism has been largely concerned with the impacts of tourism on local people, combined with the problem that 'anthropology has always trafficked in the sexuality of the people we study ... their sex, the sex of "the Other"' (Kulick 1995: 3), tourists have not made the best research subjects (Frohlick and Harrison 2008). A broader issue that I only begin to address here is how, on the one hand, tourism is a highly eroticized practice, fantasy and imagery, where commercial sex and sexual leisure are becoming increasingly widespread and quotidian, and on the other hand, anthropological studies of tourism have not yet examined these fantasies and representations and their crosscut meanings through analyses of sexuality.

There are many likely reasons why anthropology has yet to tackle the enormity and complexity of social realities in which sexuality impacts upon nearly every facet of tourism and, in many places in the world, tourism impacts many facets of sexuality. I sketch out three here. First, embodiment more generally has not been a strong focus in anthropological approaches to tourism. The messy, subjective and intimate corporeal bodily processes of travel and human experience have been largely ignored. 'Tourist experience' as a set of embodied practices is reduced largely to gazing, and more recently to performing, which includes ways of dressing, carrying the body and so forth – all potential expressions of sexuality but as yet unexplored in ethnographic engagements. Moreover, male bodies remain the normative performing active mobile tourist subject. Related to this, bodies that are recognized as sexual within anthropology are regarded as medicalized and largely pathologized bodies; we see this in terms of the predominance of AIDS/HIV-focused studies of sexuality that have been largely the purview of medical anthropology (Vance 1991). Second, the bulk of studies are derived predominantly from gay and lesbian studies and theoretical approaches that prioritize erotic desire and pleasure and view sexuality as utopian and transgressive and thus as apart from everyday life and the 'domain of mundane sociality' (Rival, Slater and Miller 1998: 296). Given that pleasure more generally is an aspect of tourist experience that has been squelched in tourist studies (although see Harrison 2003), the outcome has tended to be accounts of sex-as-exploitative or deviant (such as paedophilia and child sex tourism) rather than examinations of the linkages between everyday sexuality and 'touristic sexuality' (Frank 2007) or 'erotic hospitality' (Andrews, Roberts and Selwyn 2007). Third, in spite of its visibility as a dimension of everyday life, in media especially, sexuality and sex remain for the most part a set of acts and experiences that are relegated to the domain of the personal, and often a taboo subject. In many parts of the world, including North America, sex is regarded a private matter, a dirty thing, not to be talked about in public unless sanitized by medical or education 'experts'. Foucault argued that 'for Western subjects, sex is "the secret"' (in Kulick and Wilson 1995: 12), which means that for anthropologists dependent upon strategies of participant observation and confidentiality, sex is tricky research ground to tread, and as Kulick and Wilson (1995) claim sex is a messy, unsettling, 'a between thing'.

By way of bringing the body to ethnographic investigations of tourism, I raise one example here, a tragic event that has bothered me a great deal, which took place a few years before I arrived in Costa Rica in 2005 to carry out research on the sexual and intimate relationships of European and North American women with local men. Two American women were murdered while travelling in a region of Costa Rica renowned for female sex tourism. While their assailants were found guilty and charged (and thus justice was served?) a hazy but palpable doubt lingered, expressed in media representations and local stories, about the women's culpability for their own violent deaths, as I will explain. Women's sexuality and sexual agency coupled with border crossing and the production of desire implicit to tourism has everything to do with the vestigial tracings of victim-blaming in this case. Like a parable warning women travellers to stay home and not be sexual, their story offers a moral lesson rather than a treatise on the deep and systemic flaws in Costa Rica's education, health care, justice, immigration and labour institutions, and its entrenched racism, corruption and increasing economic disparities in the context of late twentieth and twenty-first century neo-liberalism (Palmer and Molina 2004). The main purpose of this chapter is to offer a reframing of this event in order to challenge taken-for-granted relationships between sex and tourism in anthropology and a wider public imaginary, to show how representations as moral discourses are complicit in the formation of sexual identities and subjects, and how pernicious these can be: Lived realities and social worlds are, of course, much more complex. In other words, I hope to show that 'sex tourism' is not just one thing.

Women Travellers and Cross-Border Sexual Desire: Despicable Subjects?

Sex tourism is associated with masculine subjectivity and privilege – with imperialism, militarism, adventure, mobility and 'innate sex drive' (Enloe 1989). Yet, as Craik puts it, the 'connection between tourism and sexual desire has not been the sole province of males seeking females' (1997: 132). The advent of female sex tourism has piqued much curiosity in the public imagination. Plays, movies, books and other popular culture depict a phenomenon traced to about the late 1970s at the convergences of mass global tourism, sexual liberation and second wave feminism. As Western women began touring to non-Western destinations and developing countries in the global South and engaging in dalliances with local men desired for their alterity and exotic masculinities, a new subject emerged: the female sex tourist. An iconic image invested with assumptions and contradictory meanings about white feminine heterosexual sexuality (e.g. empowered, liberated, exploitative, masculinized, aggressive, hyper-feminine, vulnerable), 'the female sex tourist' presents a challenge for thinking through women's (hetero)sexual pleasure (Aston 2008: 181) and, I argue, anthropology's relationship to sexuality and travel more generally.

A growing body of literature maps out the historically and socially contingent patterns and practices of women's cross-border cross-cultural desires and encounters, including Scandinavian women in the Gambia (Wagner 1977; Ware 1997), European women in Egypt (Jacobs 2006), Japanese women in Bali (Dahles and Bras 1999) and Nepal (Yamaga 2006), Dutch women in Indonesia (Dragojlovic 2008), Australian and European women in Thailand (Malam 2008), and American and Canadian women in Latin America and the Caribbean (Meisch 1995; Pruitt and LaFont 1995; Frohlick 2007). The translocal contexts in which women travellers express heterosexual desire for Other men and masculinities structure and shape these encounters in diverse ways such that, among other things, the materiality of the exchanges and culturally embedded forms of intimate sociality and ties vary across destinations as well as across 'sending nations'. Dutch women attracted to Balinese men in Indonesia are influenced by a colonialist nostalgia that does not affect Japanese women attracted to Kuta surfers. Canadian women's sexual relations with Afro-Caribbean men in Costa Rica are mediated by discourses of multiculturalism and cultural diversity back home in Canada, as well as by local hybrid Latino and English-Caribbean discourses of *machismo*, and so forth. The emergent ethnographic record thus demonstrates that the phenomenon commonly and sometimes even blithely referred to as 'female sex tourism' is in reality too complex and diverse to be accurately described under such an overarching and troublesome label.

For other reasons as well this rubric is more misleading than helpful. A main issue has to do with its analytical purchase. While the particularities of these ethno-cartographies of gendered cross-border sexual desire are evident, at the same time a key commonality is the veiled nature of the monetary aspects of the relationships (Ryan and Hall 2001) or, as I have argued, how the exchanges beyond sex acts and cash that pass hands between foreign women and local men are fluid (Frohlick 2007). By this I refer to the overall difference in the social organization and political economy of women's sexual pleasure and leisure compared to men's. Quibbling over typologies of female sex tourists, such as the 'situational' versus 'one nighter', as identified by Phillips (1999), or the 'vanilla' sex versus 'hardcore' female sex tourist (O'Connell Davidson and Sanchez Taylor 2005), does little to resolve the conceptual dilemma wherein sex tourism entails monetary exchange and femininity disavows paying for sex. It may be more accurate then to think of the transactionality of sexuality that occurs through cross-border sexual encounters, which may include the negotiation of payment for sex as well as the negotiation of sexual knowledge and other aspects of sexuality, rather than presuming women's acceptance of the role of paying client or sexual consumer that adheres to the term 'female sex tourist'. The analytical challenges to the anthropology of tourism are to find ways to engage in the underlying issues presented by the new formations of tourist subjects and sexual actors that emerge in the context of globalization and transformations in intimate relations, sexual leisure practices, 'new sexualities', and women's economic and consumer-based power. In this chapter I hope to demonstrate that one of these underlying issues is the way that women become targets for accusations of sex tourism in part because of the pernicious stereotypes both 'home' and 'away' that link white heterosexual femininity with salaciousness (see also Meisch 1995; Ebron 1997; Ware 1997; Alexeyeff 2008).

Numerous cultural productions of female sex tourism reflect a kind of anxiety in the public's imagination over the potential reach of women's sexual desire as the normativity of women's tourism and number of female tourists increases. Again, the connection between tourism and sexual desire is complex. Representations depicting 'travelling women who love foreign men' exemplified in the book, *Romance on the Road* (Belliveau 2006), construct a rather predacious sexuality applauded by global feminist travel discourses that uncritically view women's travel sex as liberating. Feminist scholarship focused on the political economic and racial inequities of women's material-erotic exchanges with non-Western non-white marginalized men construct what I call 'despicable sexualities', that is, a view of white feminine heterosexuality as disdainful (notably, O'Connell Davidson and Sanchez Taylor 2005). In popular media including websites and films such as *Rent-a-Rasta*, the female sex tourist is depicted as a pathetic figure, where her longings for sexual conquest in tropical poverty-stricken countries like

Haiti and Jamaica hinge on failure to win a man back home in Canada or Britain or failure to embody the aesthetics of normative feminine beauty.

All in all these representations indicate the degree to which women travellers (especially those travelling without men or solo) to foreign countries are closely scrutinized, regardless of individual proclivities for sexual relations with local men or, more generally, individual sexual desires, identities and practices. While men's erotic desires while on holiday may not be tolerated, notions of normative masculinity naturalize associations of sexual appetite and consumption with men. Travel and sexuality (especially sexual agency) are both masculine domains (Enloe 1989); women who travel are regarded as out of place and their sexuality is automatically under suspicion.

It is within this complex and contradictory terrain of the real-and-imagined, celebrated-and-despised figure of 'the female sex tourist' in the early twenty-first century where women travellers are situated globally and locally. This is certainly the case in Costa Rica, a country that welcomes women tourists and is lauded as one of the top destinations in the world for women tourists, yet whose policies regarding the regulation of women's sexuality including the lack of public sexual health education, access to contraception and abortion, and Catholic stance against pre-marital sex present a number of disjunctures (and health risks) for its visitors from the global North socialized within a culture of safer sex and reproductive rights discourses (see also Romero-Daza and Freidus 2008). Women who do engage in sex while on holiday may be especially unaware of these social and cultural realities because of the Costa Rican government and tourism industry's channelling of tourism education and resources on anti-child sex tourism campaigns – campaigns that are directed at men and the most heinous of touristic sexuality. Women who do not engage in sexual activity with locals are not beyond reproach or surveillance in that the associations of white feminine sexuality with promiscuity, sexual aggression and prostitution are rampant. At the same time, the expectation that one's sex life is nobody else's business derives from deeply held (white, middle-class?) cultural notions about the privacy and secrecy of sex (Friedl 1994). The premise that 'all sexuality falls under a normative regime of some sort' (Rival, Slater and Miller 1998: 316) is where I want to begin to interrogate the sex of tourism, by showing how the identity of two American women shot to death while on a trip to Costa Rica was situated within such regimes.

The Shootings of Two American Women Travellers in Costa Rica

In 2000, two nineteen-year-old women, Emily Howell and Emily Eagan, had travelled to Costa Rica as part of a study abroad program with an American university, a popular means of travel to Costa Rica for many young adult foreign tourists. While visiting a beach community on the Atlantic coast known as Puerto Viejo, the women were killed one evening after they had left their lodging in their rental car to do some shopping in town. The women's deaths were particularly tragic in that they were not killed by an accident such as drowning, relatively common in the area, or in a car accident, circumstances which would not have made their passing any less mournful but, perhaps, their deaths more bearable or at least comprehensible. Rather, the women were shot dead by one or more of three local men associated with their murders in what appears to be a set of horribly unfortunate occurrences that unfolded on that particular evening.

My focus here is not on investigating the facts of all that transpired that led to their deaths, although the complex truth is of great importance to me. Rather, I focus on the social imagination and interpretations of the event wherein before and after their deaths the women were represented in the media as particular subjects situated in a particular time and place. In other words, my interest in the women and the events surrounding their tragic deaths is in the trafficking of images of them as tourists, as women and as subjects situated within a touristic milieu through normative linked ideas about gender, travel and sexuality, and the implications of these linked notions.

Media attention was widespread for some months after their murders, but I didn't hear about them until 2005, when a local resident vaguely alluded to 'the murders of two foreign women' in her explanation of escalating violence in the area as the reason for tourism slowing down. In subsequent visits, I became friends with a woman, Shaun, who had been a close friend with both Emilys, and she generously agreed to share her knowledge the event, both in terms of how her friends came to be killed and the local and international responses to their grisly deaths. My account is based on dozens of English-language print and online media stories, my fieldwork in Costa Rica between 2005 and 2008, and most centrally, my conversations with Shaun in late 2008. Although Shaun's own careful analysis is echoed in many ways here, any mistakes and misinterpretations of the events are entirely my own.

A somewhat detailed but still insufficient version of what is likely to have happened is that the women were carjacked outside a night club in Puerto Viejo, a few miles from the *cabina* they had rented. Three male youths between the ages of fifteen and nineteen, who were looking to steal a car to drive out of town and possibly back to San José, the capital city of Costa Rica, where they lived, about a four-hour drive away, must have thought the rental jeep was a good choice. Because they didn't know how to drive a stick shift, the teens needed the women to drive the standard-transmission sport utility vehicle for them. Between the time they stole the car and took the women hostage outside the club on the Sunday evening and the time the corpses were found the following day, the youths had possibly raped one of the women and shot both of them dead a few miles north of Puerto Viejo. Apparently the assailants had continued to drive the SUV themselves, and made it undetected through a police checkpoint along the highway in spite of the fact that something was seriously awry (a carjacking, at the very least). They evidently required the services of a tow truck some time later because they had by then either burned out the vehicle's transmission or run out of gas. When a tow truck driver spotted the blood in the SUV, one of the youths forced him at gun point to burn the car and then all three of the youths disappeared from the scene of the multiple crimes. Two of the three assailants were located and subsequently tried in the local courts and found guilty of the murders. The sixteen-year-old, a minor, was given a sentence of fourteen years, just six months short of the maximum sentence for a minor; the eighteen-year-old was given the maximum prison sentence of thirty-five years for aggravated murder.

News of the shooting deaths of two American women by Costa Rican men in a Caribbean tourist town in Costa Rica was immediate and widespread. University newsletters and international press (including *Newsweek*, *People*, the *Los Angeles Times*, *The Miami Herald* and *CNN*) carried the gruesome and horrifically tragic story, a news item that was trafficked well beyond English-language print media. It is understandable that the injustice of the violent deaths of innocent persons, especially ones so young, would incite such an outpouring of emotion and moral outrage. Yet, as my interlocutor pointed out, consideration of what might be a rather different set of motivations that fed the media frenzy is called for. Just weeks prior to the murders of Emily Howell and Emily Eagan, other foreigners had been killed in Costa Rica. Those killings had not received nearly the amount of media attention nor the duration of interest shown to the case of 'the two Emilys' (Zarembo 2000: 45). Why, indeed, was there so much coverage?

Bodies under Suspicion

There are too many details of this particularly sordid case to consider adequately in this chapter. Here I focus on the attention paid by the media to the specific descriptions of the women's bodies, or rather corpses, when found the morning after the carjacking and fatal shootings. A *CNN* online posting is striking in this regard, but not exceptional. It reads in part:

> The women's bodies were found along a highway near the town of Cahuita, about 145 kilometres (90 miles) east of San Jose, the capital. Their rented SUV was found burning near their bodies.... The girls apparently met the suspect at 10pm Sunday in the beach town of Limon, said Rogelio Ramos, Costa Rica's minister of security. The town is popular with tourists. Their bodies were found at 1:30pm Monday. One was nude; the other had had some of her clothing removed. Neither had been robbed, but both appeared to have been assaulted sexually, police said.

Several misrepresentations in this news report are worth pointing out: the vehicle was in fact found in another region of Costa Rica and not 'near the bodies' nor 'burning near the bodies'; the women did not 'meet' but rather were abducted by the suspects; the name of the town where the women were abducted and their car stolen was Puerto Viejo and not 'Limon' (a larger city north of Puerto Viejo and also the name of the Atlantic province); and, of course, the women undoubtedly *had* been robbed – their vehicle had been taken from them against their will. I leave aside the issue of the alleged sexual assaults for now. The sloppy news reporting is troublesome. The numerous mistakes are one thing, but the language used and the emphasis placed on 'the women's bodies' is especially troubling. Notably, the reports comment on the state of the bodies, whether they are dressed or undressed, and on their location – 'along a highway' and (inaccurately) *'near* the *burning* [rather than burnt] SUV'. What kind of picture is painted through these words and emphases?

Another article, appearing on *The College Media Network*, also places emphasis on the state of the bodies and their location:

> *The bodies* of the two young women, schoolmates from Antioch College in Ohio, were found March 13 in *a roadside clump of jungle* about a mile north of the Caribbean town of Cahuita. They were shot a total of five times at close range. They were last seen leaving a disco in the town of Puerto Viejo, a few miles south of Cahuita, about 12:30 that morning. (Garvin 2000a; emphasis added)

This report presents 'the bodies' as though 'they' are alive, choosing 'a roadside clump of jungle' to be found in, 'leaving' and presumably going to 'a disco' prior to being found 'a mile' outside of the 'Caribbean town'. The details of the shootings – the number of times the women were shot, and the proximate closeness of the women to their killers – are likely intended to portray the innocence of victims incomprehensibly murdered. An alternative interpretation suggests that these same descriptions serve to construct the victims of multiple acts and forms of violence within a moral order where gendered, raced and sexed bodies belong in certain places and not others. Thus at the same time that these descriptions render a picture of innocent individuals, they also call into question the propriety of female travellers in a Central American country by virtue of their positioning outside of this moral order.

By highlighting the locations of the women's bodies prior to their deaths ('leaving a disco', 'north of Cahuita') and the corpses afterwards ('in a roadside clump of jungle', 'north of Cahuita'), and mixing up the temporality of events such that the corpses and living persons appear simply as 'bodies' here and there in different parts of a tourist area, the accounts serve to associate the women with highly salient signifiers of touristic sensual desire and pleasure-seeking – the jungle, a nightclub, the Caribbean. Time, too, plays into the questioning of the women and their mobility within these spaces. In particular, the quibbling in different articles over the time the women left the nightclub (was it 12.30 a.m.? was it 1.30 p.m.? etc.) calls into question a particular moral order where particular subjects belong particular places. In other words, through this language and intimation the 'half-naked' bodies of two American women found on a roadside clump of jungle near a Caribbean town in Costa Rica are rendered suspect in so far as explanations for their violent deaths are sought in the women's actions, their travels, and speculation over the possible sexual nature of their interactions with local men and, possibly, male youth. The women are, in a sense, 'undressed' by the media, a point I further elaborate on.

Undressing Women's Bodies: Murder, Sex and Tourism

> Women's bodies have historically provided a fertile terrain for imagining, reasserting, or contesting the porous boundaries of moral worlds. (Masquelier 2005: 2)

I return now to the troubling issue of the alleged sexual assaults and how particular images deployed by the media, using innuendo and provocation, effectively sexualizes the women posthumously. Many of the news accounts question whether or not during the course of events leading to their deaths the women were sexually assaulted. Vague and contradictory statements illustrate the apparent urgency in which it seemed necessary to raise the possibility of rape or sexual violence prior to and irrespective of more conclusive information being made available. I provide a sampling here of how this quandary played out.

In some accounts, the claim that the women had been sexually violated was based on the speculation presumably offered by local police that, because the women had not been robbed, they must have been used for sex. An article in a major Canadian newspaper and another in a major American newspaper both state, 'Police believe *there was a sexual attack* ... noting that valuables had not been taken. Credit cards, clothing, and other belongings were found near the bodies ...' (*The Globe and Mail*, 16 March 2000; and *The New York Times*, 15 March; emphasis added). A *CNN* report echoes the police's belief, linking the apparent facts with what seems to be a commonsensical conclusion, 'One [of the bodies] was nude; the other had had some of her clothing removed. Neither had been robbed, but *both appeared to have been assaulted sexually*, police said ...' (*CCN.com*, 16 March 2000; emphasis added).

In contrast, some articles use the same facts (of the women's state of dress or undress) to present a different conclusion – asserting that sexual assaults did not likely occur. For instance, an article in *People* says, 'Though Howell's body was nude, there was *no sign that either women had been sexually assaulted ...*' (Hewitt 2000, p. 173; emphasis added). A regional paper, the *Michigan Daily*, presents a statement from a family member who appears duly concerned about any negative judgement of her sister's character as well as the likelihood that a framing of the deaths as sex-related will obscure the wider context of crime in Costa Rica. The reporter quotes Sara Eagen as saying, 'We have been told *it is not a sex crime*. My sister was found fully clothed ... We would like to clarify that' (Kaufman 2000: 1).

However, the majority of accounts, such as this one in the *Los Angeles Times*, present the facts more dubiously, not claiming with any certainty that sexual assault occurred but nevertheless summoning the likely possibility: 'Eagen was partially clothed ... [Howell] was naked. Police found no semen in their bodies but have not completely discounted *the possibility of rape ...*' (Darling 2000: A1). The American weekly news magazine, *Newsweek*, did not state explicitly but rather inferred the probability of rape, speculating that 'while published reports said *neither girl had been raped*, one was left naked and the other was nearly naked' (Zarembo 2000: 45; emphasis added).

These quandaries over what counts as evidence of sexual assault serve to implicate the Costa Rican male youth in more than crimes against personal property (the stolen and burnt SUV) but rather in the more reprehensible sex crimes against their female abductees. Did the men rape the women or not? This would be an incredibly difficult answer to anticipate for the local community in which the crimes took place and, especially, for the families of the victims struggling to make sense of the fragments of stories circulating as rumour and gossip and to parse together the truth from delayed statements doled out by the investigation team in Costa Rica. It is an important question to be asking for the personal regard of the suffering of the individuals involved and their kin, and also for the wider social issue of misogyny and violence against women. Many people had a stake in the story that would eventually come out as the authoritative account and public explanation for the incomprehensible violence against innocent tourists. The North American reporters would have been situated within these complex machinations for control of the story, a national and transnational political economy dependent upon tourism revenues, and a government needing to project a good image.

It is within this context that a kind of violence against the women (and Northern women in general) is perpetuated by the media accounts in spite of the best intentions of reporters seeking to claim the innocence of the university students on a study tour in a foreign country. I want to show how the American women's bodies can be seen to have been 'undressed' by the language and representations used in the media accounts and thus to have been posthumously subjected to discursive acts of sexualization that hinge on understandings of women's bodies as 'fertile terrain' for the negotiation of moral boundaries (Masquelier 2005). It is in this sense that I suggest that the particular media descriptions focusing on the apparent 'given-ness' of the women's bodies are complicit in a wider harm that subjugates and subordinates women for their sexual agency and in particular women as tourists and travellers.

The accounts provide a clue as to the kinds of moral panic that ensued over the shootings on many different scales – at the level of family, community, government, international institutions and so on. As I explain above, murders of other tourists had taken place in the months prior to these and had not received nearly the same attention nor become part of the social memory to the depth that the deaths of the American women had, at least in my conversations with local residents. A partial explanation of the disparate weightiness of the victims can be found in the compelling language of the media reports, which highlights the vulnerability of the young, unchaperoned, female travellers which is compounded by the disconcerting evidence (however contradictory the facts appear) that one or both of their bodies were found stripped or partially stripped: Were they dressed, half dressed, fully clothed, half naked, nearly naked, entirely nude, or what? Yet a different but equally crucial question to consider here is: Why is this aspect of their well-mediated story so prominent? Are their gendered, vulnerable, assaulted and exposed bodies – and the troubling descriptions of them – part of the reason as to why the story was so popular and frantic?

I ask these questions not to diminish the brutality the women suffered but rather to interrogate the focus on the bodies, indeed what amounts to a fixation, and the possible implications of this fixation in the objectification of feminine sexuality that is a form of symbolic violence. To put this another way: How did the bodies act as a 'social skin' or 'morally charged medium' on which 'identities and relations are made visible, or, conversely, erased' (Masquelier 2005: 5)?

Feminist and anthropological theories of the body take meanings of bodies to be far from straightforward or god-given, suggesting instead that bodies 'come into being' and 'are social, political, subjective, objective, discursive, narrative, and material all at once' (Farquhar and Lock 2007: 5). In spite of their polyvalence and historicity, however, as 'signifying forms of cultural life' bodies are fundamental to what Douglas referred to as 'the building blocks for enforcing social order' (in Farquhar and Lock 2007: 5) and what Turner conceptualized as 'the social skin' wherein the bodily surface serves as an 'effective instrument and means of reasserting moral boundaries' (in Masquelier 2005: 5). Masquelier applies this idea to a feminist analysis of gender, nakedness and difference, arguing that 'gender is a central axis of difference through which ideas of dirt, pollution and immodesty can be instantiated. Women's bodies have historically provided a fertile ground for imagining, reasserting, or contesting the porous boundaries of moral worlds' (2005: 4). She looks at how clothing or its lack thereof is a 'morally charged medium' because clothing gives people their ethnic, social and moral identity to 'be denuded, stripped, or divested [of clothing] is to be dispossessed of something one ought to have ... being unclothed means finding oneself in a degrading position' (2005: 15). This scholarship draws a distinction between stripping as 'wilful disrobing' and being denuded, where those denuded do not control the process, and between nudity as an aesthetic, an 'ideal body' rooted in Western thought, and nakedness as evidence of sexual depravity and indulgence.

If women's bodies are complex moral grounds on which identities, selfhood and human dignities are upheld, resisted, contested or robbed through the myriad social processes of dressing and undressing, being denuded or disrobing, then the idea that the women's bodies were denuded or made naked by the press (as well as by their assailants) shows how this kind of eroticization serves as a chimerical distraction to normative regimes of sexual regulation. Underpinning the quandary over the women's clothed/unclothed bodies as evidence of male sexual abuse was the related and in some ways much more sensitive issue of whether young single women should be allowed to travel so far from home unaccompanied, and the sexual impropriety and transgressions that international border crossing seemingly entails.

Affecting Sexuality: the Hitch-Hiker Story

> Moral panics rarely alleviate any real problem because they are aimed at chimeras and signifiers. (Rubin 1984: 297)

The media images and representations provoked emotional and contradictory reactions in the local community. In a sense, the bodies became a battle ground over the good and bad of global tourism. On the one hand, the half-dressed, half-stripped, undressed bodies of young foreign women who travelled to Costa Rica as part of a university program with dreams of relocating shortly after their arrival came to represent tourism as a form of innocence and romantic quest for paradise (where its inherent benefits include self-knowledge and the betterment of the world). On the other hand, innuendoes that the women were 'asking for it', which I detail below, accused all female tourists of sexual aggression towards local residents unable to defend themselves against the onslaught of tourism and its attendant moral degradation. Therefore, in sorting out the positive from the negative aspects of the presence of international tourists in this area and Costa Rica more broadly, the aftermath centred on the *effect* of the murders on the tourism economy. Foreign journalists, Costa Rican nationals and local residents alike discussed the implications of 'the bad press' on the local tourism economy, that is, the fear that the widespread news of the murders would curtail international tourist visits to the area and perhaps even the rest of the country. Additionally, at issue in the international press were the consequences of the murders of two American women in a foreign country for study abroad programs at universities and other educational institutions in the United States, specifically, the question of personal safety for members and consumers of such programs.

In this analysis, I want to shift the focus away from the effects to the *affect* of the accounts, a shift that complicates questions of the influence of bad news on tourism and the safety of independent youth travel to how the accounts are productive in the formation of things made sexual. It is in representations, images, language – discourses – that meanings of sex are organized, and how 'certain acts, relationships, or situations' are constituted as 'sexual' (Cameron and Kulick 2006: 5). These accounts were not neutral, for language is 'an important element in political struggles around sexuality' (Cameron and Kulick 2006: 5).

Reporters looking for a story about gender, sexuality and tourism found one. Apparently when post-mortem tests could not support speculation that the women had probably been taking drugs that evening, the machinations of media and need by the local and national authorities to produce a plausible explanation turned to the fabrication that the young tourists *must have been* looking for a party, given that it was 'late' and 'dark' and that the women were in a 'strange' place that they 'didn't understand'. Various guesses as to how and why the women first came into contact with the young men still circulated when people talked about the murders five years later. I heard rumours that the women met the men in the bar that night, and, to the contrary, that they had been friends with the men for days before they took them in their jeep that evening. The commonest story, however, was that on their way to the store the women *must have* picked up the men, who *must have* been hitch-hiking, because the women *must have* wanted to party with the trio of Costa Rican male teenagers.

'The hitch-hiking story' depicting clueless, flirtatious, party girls in spring break mode is a very different story from the less titillating scenario where random tourists were carjacked. 'Don't pick up hitch-hikers' is an allegorical warning for all women who ought to know better. In a foreign country, the common-sense advice goes: women have all the more reason to be fearful of strangers and to restrict their movements. Going out late at night, well past dark, picking up aimless young men from a bar or by the side of a desolate countryside road in a Latin American country ... What *were* the women doing? As my interlocutors explained, many local residents (both Costa Ricans and expatriates) who had anxiously followed the news came to the following foregone conclusion: It was very unfortunate that the women had gotten involved with strange men from San José not knowing anything about them, and had risked their lives by acting inappropriately, especially in Latin America where, echoing gender stereotypes which did not reflect actual local social worlds, 'everyone knows that only men go into bars'. That the women were categorically regarded as 'female sex tourists' is manifested explicitly in one especially offensive account entitled 'Recklessness of tourists alarming Costa Ricans: Many women put selves in danger, residents lament' (Garvin 2000b), which I quote at length here.

The reporter from *The Miami Herald* begins his story like this:

> The sight of the young blond gringa, standing on the roadside in the gathering dusk with her thumb in the air, made Ricardo Gonzalez bang the steering wheel of his truck in fury. 'Two girls murdered, and still the rest of them are out here like nothing happened!' he exclaimed. 'I'm telling you, señor, we don't have a crime problem! We have a problem with American girls who go looking for trouble' (Garvin 2000b).

Garvin describes a fear voiced by some local people 'that the publicity over the killings will strangle a blooming tourist industry in one of the country's most underdeveloped areas'. The fear is compounded, he posits, because of

> the one strain of that breed [of tourist], the young women seeking romance, often leavened with generous helpings of marijuana and cocaine that are readily available ... a potent mixture that many business people in the area say makes young people take risks they would never dare at home in the United States or Europe. Some of the most outspoken critics are hotel owners who say they frequently shoo away the men from the beach brought home by their young female guests ... (Garvin 2000b)

He quotes numerous hotel owners who chastise 'girls who come here looking for sex', 'looking for danger' and 'for walking on the beach with someone they just met'. Although the reporter defends the reputation of the dead American women, using testimony from the owners of the hotel where the women stayed before they were murdered who 'never saw them intoxicated' or buying drugs, and who assure the readers that 'the Emilys were not among [the tourists who come looking for sex]', they 'didn't bring guys back to the hotel', the suspicion is nevertheless evoked, through the particular language used, about how, most likely, they had been 'asking for it'.

The panic over the potential loss of tourism is refracted onto the 'girls who come here looking for sex' and thus transformed into a moral panic over foreign women's sexual agency, pleasure and danger, and their culpability rather than any number of systemic factors that contributed to the lethal violence and criminality of the Costa Rican youth. By virtue of the women's feminine subjectivity as travellers far from home on their own who ought to have acted according to norms of proper femininity, by American or Costa Rican gender codes, and their identities as American tourists, *gringas*, and thus sluts and whores, through sleight of hand they become the object, the chimera, of a moral panic. (Recall that the other tourists' deaths had not generated the same level of media attention.) A resounding message in the media, through the discursive act of undressing the women, as I have suggested above, was that women's sexuality is a dangerous thing (e.g. 'should we really be sending our young women out into the world un-chaperoned?').

The fixation on the women's bodies and the state of the corpses, which get read as statements of the women's mores (body surfaces of women read off as testaments to their sexuality and therefore to their purity, their virginity and so on), takes the focus away from the complicated political economic realities in which the women became much more than passive victims in a random crime. In their investigations of European women vacationers in the Gambia, Ware and Ebron both argue that representations in popular culture (newspapers, women's magazines) and local narratives about white femininity and 'allegorical figures of female travel' (Ebron 1997: 233) can have 'profound effects for concrete women' because they become part of social relations (Ware 1997: 150). For Ebron, images of Northern women as 'uncontrolled sex zealots' serve as 'parables that express national anxieties over power differences between Africa and Europe, between men and women' and, effectively, transform all tourist women into 'potential sexual partners' (1997: 224).

Conclusion: Politics of Sexuality in Costa Rica

Female tourists presumably ... 'are just whoremongers, horny, want one thing'. Sex tourism supersaturates a place like Puerto Viejo, Costa Rica – a sleepy but hip sort of cosmopolitan town inhabited by people from something like forty different nationalities and a popular backpacking, surfing and ecotourism destination for adventure-seeking 'alternative' travellers from the global North – in such a way that particular subjects and bodies are narrated, inscribed, invested with sexual agency, intent, meaning, culpability by virtue of association, innuendo, implication. In contrast to the Pacific coast renowned as a sex tourist destination for American men (and female prostitutes from San José), the remote Atlantic area has gained a reputation and cachet with European and North American female tourists for its attractive and sexually available 'Caribbean' men. Many but certainly not all foreign women do hook up with local men for casual encounters as well as longer term relationships when they arrive as tourists, volunteer workers, yoga instructors, massage therapists, university students and so on. My larger research project investigates the transformations of sexualities and emotions that are played out in these cross-border cross-cultural attractions and encounters. These are complex relationships to sort out. Racial stereotypes on both sides (white femininity and black masculinity) structure the mutual desire. Women's economic status and physical mobility is compromised when they choose to stay illegally past the expiry of their tourist visas and take up poorly paying jobs.

Male violence is prevalent in many women's experiences. Numerous women I interviewed told me about their own or other women's rapes or near-rapes and physical assaults, and numerous assaults that were made public occurred during the period of my fieldwork.

These realities, which of course are not unique to Costa Rica or even Central America, are not contradictory to, but rather intersect with, the moralizing accusations levelled at women tourists, and point to the ways local and translocal systems of sexuality regulate women's bodies – which is a far cry from post-feminist claims for travel sex as sexual liberation or for the achievement of male privilege through travel. I have tried to show that women's sexual pleasure and heterosexual femininity remains under suspicion in the context of global tourism in spite of any headway made as far as gender equality in economic and education spheres at home, a suspicion that requires further investigation if we want to understand sexuality and tourism as linked processes more fully, and, more specifically, the ways in which travel discourses espousing travel as liberation, discourses about female sex tourists as exploiters, and discourses that place all female travellers as sexual zealots converge. 'Female sex tourist', I argue, can be a chimera that might say as much about fears about women's sexuality as about exploitation of men, at least in some parts of the world. Sex + tourism is not what it seems at face value, and the job of anthropology, as always, is to delve deeply past the smoke and mirrors.

I conclude by explaining how, rather than a loss of tourist income, the local community actually gained as a result of the media exposure over the murders of the two American women on study abroad programs. Indirectly at least, the tragedy brought about an infusion of resources including a much-needed police station to an area of Costa Rica historically neglected by the San José politicians, a police station, which, prior to 2000, residents had requested many times but had not been granted. In a sense, then, the bodies were implicated in the politics of sexuality in Costa Rica. There were multiple ways in which the young foreign women and their bodies were used: to sell the idea of travel as sexual liberation, by post-feminist popular culture and the tourism industry, of which the university international study abroad programs are a part; to steal a car and to exert masculine aggression and violence; to sell newspapers and gain readers; and, to divert attention away from social issues in Costa Rica, including a long history of government corruption and inequitable allocation of resources to the Caribbean region where the majority of the black Costa Rican minority population live. Attention placed on the alleged antics of white women tourists, especially those as naïve and sexually 'loose' as university-age 'girls', diverts attention from questions of social ills and moral wrong-doings closer to home: What were the men doing far from home without enough money to get back to San José? How did they manage to get through a police checkpoint (with blood in the car that the tow truck driver couldn't help but see)? Why did it take these deaths and the fabricated media stories (about young women taking risks travelling alone at night and picking up strange male hitch-hikers) to get a response to community needs? Finally, I, too, used the women's bodies as an extreme and sensationalistic example, perhaps, but one that illustrates poignantly the fluid boundaries between the everyday and the extraordinary, between domains of mundane sociality and the sexually charged, and between the private acts and public regimes by which sex and sexuality is regulated, in and through global tourism.

References

Alexeyeff, K. (2008), 'Are You Being Served? Sex, Humour and Globalisation in the Cook Islands', *Anthropological Forum* 18(3): 287–93.

Andrews, H., Roberts, L. and Selwyn, T. (2007), 'Hospitality and Eroticism', *International Journal of Culture, Hospitality, and Tourism Research* 1(3): 247–62.

Aston, E. (2008), 'A Fair Trade? Staging Female Sex Tourism in Sugar Mummies and Trade', *Contemporary Theatre Review* 18(2): 180–92.

Belliveau, J. (2006), *Romance on the Road: Traveling Women Who Love Foreign Men*, Baltimore: BeauMonde Press.

Brennan. D. (2004), *What's Love Got To Do With It? Transnational Desires and Sex Tourism in the Dominican Republic*, Durham, NC: Duke University Press.

Cameron, D. and Kulick, D. (2006) 'General Introduction', in D. Cameron and D. Kulick (eds), *The Language and Sexuality Reader*, New York: Routledge, pp. 1–12.

Craik, J. (1997), 'The Culture of Tourism', in C. Rojek and J. Urry (eds), *Touring Cultures: Transformations of Travel and Theory*, New York: Routledge, pp. 113–36.

Dahles, H. and Bras, K. (1999), 'Entrepreneurs in Romance: Tourism in Indonesia', *Annals of Tourism Research* 26(2): 267–93.

Darling, J. (2000), 'Tourist Deaths Cast Cloud in Costa Rica', *Los Angeles Times*, 20 March.

Drajojlovic, A. (2008), 'Dutch Women in Bali: Contested Notions of Citizenship and Gender in Dutch-Bali Intimacies', paper presented at the American Anthropological Association meetings, San Francisco, November.

Ebron, P. (1997), 'Traffic in Men', in M. Grosz-Ngaté and O. Kokole (eds), *Gendered Encounters: Challenging Cultural Boundaries and Social Hierarchies in Africa*, New York: Routledge, pp. 223–44.

Enloe, C. (1989), *Bananas, Beaches, and Bases: Making Feminist Sense of International Politics*, Berkeley, CA: University of California Press.

Farquhar, J. and Lock, M. (2007), 'Introduction' in M. Lock and J. Farquhar (eds), *Beyond the Body Proper: Reading the Anthropology of Material Life*, Durham, NC: Duke University Press, pp. 1–18.

Frank, K. (2007), 'Playcouples in Paradise: Touristic Sexuality and Lifestyle Travel', in M. Padilla et al. (eds), *Love and Globalization: Transformations of Intimacy in the Contemporary World*, Nashville: Vanderbilt University Press, pp. 163–85.

Friedl, E. (1994), 'Sex the Invisible', *American Anthropologist* 96(4): 833–44.

Frohlick, S. (2007), 'Fluid Exchanges: The Negotiation of Intimacy between Tourist Women and Local Men in a Transnational Tourist Town in Caribbean Costa Rica', *City & Society*, 19(1): 139–68.

Frohlick, S. and J. Harrison (2008), 'Engaging Ethnography in Tourist Research: An Introduction', *Tourist Studies*, 8(1): 5–18.

Garvin, G. (2000a), 'Costa Rican Police Identify Accomplices in Murders of Two American Teenagers', *The Knight-Ridder Tribune*, 5 April.

Garvin, G. (2000b), 'Recklessness of Tourists Alarming Costa Ricans', *The Miami Herald*, 19 March.

Harrison, J. (2003), *Being a Tourist: Finding Meaning in Pleasure Travel*, Vancouver: UBC Press.

Hewitt, B. (2000), 'Their Paradise Lost', *People*, 53(13): 173.

Jacobs, J. (2006), 'Tourist Places and Negotiating Modernity: European Women and Romance Tourism in the Sinai', in C. Minca and T. Oakes (eds), *Travels in Paradox: Remapping Tourism*, Lanham, MD: Rowman and Littlefield, pp. 125–54.

Kaufman, J. (2000), 'Ann Arbor Woman, Friend, Shot to Death in Costa Rica, *Michigan Daily*, 30 March.

Kulick, D. (1995), 'The Sexual Life of Anthropologists: Erotic Subjectivity and Ethnographic Work', in D. Kulick and M. Wilson (eds), *Taboo: Sex, Identity and Erotic Subjectivity in Anthropological Fieldwork*, New York: Routledge, pp. 1–28.

Malam, L. (2008), 'Bodies, Beaches, and Bars: Negotiating Heterosexual Masculinity in Southern Thailand's Tourism Industry', *Gender, Place and Culture* 15(6): 581–94.

Masquelier, A. (2005), 'Dirt, Undress, and Difference: An Introduction', in A. Masquelier (ed.), *Dirt, Undress, and Difference: Critical Perspectives on the Body's Surface*, Bloomington, IN: Indiana University Press, pp. 1–33.

Meisch, L. (1995), 'Gringas and Otavaleños: Changing Tourist Relations', *Annals of Tourism Research* 22(2): 441–62.

O'Connell Davidson, J. and Sanchez Taylor, J. (2005), 'Travel and Taboo: Heterosexual Sex Tourism in the Caribbean', in E. Bernstein and L. Schaffer (eds), *Regulating Sex: The Politics of Intimacy and Identity*, London: Routledge, pp. 83–99.

Padilla, M. (2007), *Caribbean Pleasure Industry: Tourism, Sexuality, and AIDS in the Dominican Republic*, Chicago: University of Chicago Press.

Palmer, S. and Molina, I. (2004), 'Introduction,' in S. Palmer and I. Molina (eds), *The Costa Rica Reader: History, Culture, Politics,* Durham, NC: Duke University Press, pp. 1–8.

Phillips, J. (1999), 'Tourist-Oriented Prostitution in Barbados: The Case of the Beach Boy and the White Female Tourist', in K. Kempadoo (ed.), *Sun, Sex, and Gold: Tourism and Sex Work in the Caribbean'*, Lanham, MD: Rowman & Littlefield, pp. 183–200.

Pigg, S. and Adams, V. (2005), 'Introduction: The Moral Object of Sex', in V. Adams and S. Pigg (eds), *Sex in Development: Science, Sexuality, and Morality in Global Perspective*, Durham, NC: Duke University Press, pp. 1–38.

Pruitt, D. and LaFont, S. (1995), 'For Love and Money: Romance Tourism in Jamaica', *Annals of Tourism Research* 22(2): 422–40.

Rival, L. Slater, D. and Miller, D. (1998), 'Sex and Sociality: Comparative Ethnographies of Sexual Objectification', *Theory, Culture & Society* 15(3–4): 295–321.

Romero-Daza, N. and Freidus, A. (2008), 'Female Tourists, Casual Sex, and HIV Risk in Costa Rica', *Qualitative Sociology* 31:169–87.

Rubin, G. (1984), 'Thinking Sex: Notes for a Radical Theory of the Politics of Sexuality,' in C. Vance (ed.), *Pleasure and Danger: Exploring Female Sexuality*, New York: Routledge.

Ryan, C. and Hall, M. (2001), *Sex Tourism: Marginal People and Liminalities*, New York: Routledge.

Tasker, Y. and Negra, D. (2007), 'Introduction: Feminist Politics and Postfeminist Culture', in Y. Tasker and D. Negra (eds), *Interrogating Postfeminism: Gender and the Politics of Popular Culture*, Durham, NC: Duke University Press, pp. 1–26.

Vance, C. (1991), 'Anthropology Rediscovers Sexuality: A Theoretical Comment', *Social Science and Medicine* 33(8): 875–84.

Wagner, U. (1977), 'Out of Time and Place – Mass Tourism and Charter Trips', *Ethnos* 42: 38–52.

Ware, V. (1997), 'Purity and Danger: Race, Gender, and Tales of Sex Tourism', in A. McRobbie (ed.), *Back to Reality? Social Experience and Cultural Studies*, Manchester: Manchester University Press, pp. 133–51.

Yamaga, C. (2006), 'Japanese Girl Meets Nepali Boy: Mutual Fantasy and Desire in "Asian" Vacationscapes of Nepal', MA thesis, Winnipeg: University of Manitoba.

Zarembo, A. (2000), 'Hell in a Heavenly Place', *Newsweek*, 135(13): 45.

–4–

Belonging at the Cottage
Julia Harrison

This chapter contributes to the anthropologies of tourism, nationalism and landscape. More specifically it engages three themes: how a group of domestic tourists express and experience national identity and mythology; the iconography of landscape, and the relationship between landscape and bodies; and the articulation of memory, belonging, meaning and emotion in a specific touristic context. This discussion sheds light on the symbolic, intellectual and emotional construction of 'home', something I conclude suggests a productive direction for the anthropology of tourism, a shift from looking at the relation between hosts and guests/'home' and 'away' to looking more precisely at the nature of 'home' in the touristic context.

Touristic travel is implicitly entangled with ideas of 'home' and 'away'. Much of the work of the anthropology of tourism has concentrated on the latter part of the experience, with particular emphasis on travel to distant places, destinations that could be labelled exotic from a Western point of view. Less consideration has been given to the experiences and meaning of these travels for tourists themselves. Those who travel 'at home' – domestic tourists – have been the most overlooked. In recent decades, however, the discipline of anthropology has extended its focus more consistently to include those 'at home'. Such a shift can provide a fruitful direction for the anthropological study of tourism/tourists. The touristic journeys on which I focus in this chapter are to places that appeal in large measure because they are *not* exotic; indeed they are characterized by the familiar and the known. In the local parlance the destination of these tourists is 'the cottage', a seasonal residence usually at most a two- to three-hour drive from the tourists' permanent homes.

These cottagers as they are generally known in the more southerly regions of the Canadian province of Ontario, or second-home tourists as Jaakson (1986) called them, are the focus of my discussion. They do not necessarily regard themselves as tourists, a categorization they see laden with an endless string of pejorative and trivialized notions. They do, however, acknowledge that they cannot be classed as locals, no matter how long or regularly they have been travelling to the region where their cottage is located. Local residents, in contrast, generally do see these seasonal visitors as a form of tourist (Dobrzenky 1985: 11; Jasen 1995; Stevens 2008a: 29; see also Hall and Müller 2004; Svenson 2004). In classifying cottagers as tourists it is important to highlight that their experiences are not inconsequential ones. As I have argued elsewhere, touristic experiences are embedded in dense and complex, even if at times contradictory, webs of meaning (Geertz 1973; Harrison 2003).[1]

Williams and Kaltenborn (1999) have suggested that the cottage is a place 'thick' with meaning (see also Jaakson 1986; Cross 1992; Sack 1997; Halseth 1998: 18ff; Chaplin 1999; Lofgren 1999: 139ff; Luka 2006: 171ff). My research further substantiates this point. I repeatedly heard sentiments such as 'my heart resides there'; 'it is my "real" home'; 'it is where I belong'. As one cottager said to me, 'Coming to the cottage is coming home to us.' The cottage was invested with much more emotional attachment than cottagers' city residences (see also Lofgren 1999: 139; Luka 2006: 171–4). I will elaborate here the idea that the cottage is seen to be a place with strong connections to personal and national history, and an iconographic Canadian landscape. I examine the attachment to this 'real' home, the cottage, as an extrapolation of the notion of the 'real' Canadian nation, and of being a 'real Canadian'. One key characteristic that I will argue these second-home tourists share with those who choose to travel to more distant locations is a desire to 'recover something that was lost' (Jasen 1995: 132). Both groups share a search for a past when somehow things seemed simpler, more authentic (Harrison 2003: 55–7). Each is merely looking for it in different places.

The entangled relationship between tourism, the tourist experience and nationalism is a powerful one and has been well documented in anthropology. Nationalist tropes and mythologies are standard fare at state sponsored historic sites, monuments, attractions, tourist zones and literature (see, for example, Handler and Gable 1997; Graburn 1998; Palmer 2003; Bruner 2005; Peers 2007). Analysis shows that these sites and experiences are powerfully and densely layered with complex narratives reinforcing class, gender, ethnic and cultural ideologies and structural inequalities within nation-states. The intermediaries in these narratives – tour guides and interpreters – play a central role in the dissemination, and at times the challenge to these narratives (Selwyn 1995, 1996). These sites and practices influence what tourists 'learn' about the histories, struggles and celebrated triumphs of nation-states, but also affirm the understandings – and often the acceptance of – state-driven nationalist ideals, mythologies and hegemonies by local citizens (Leong 1989). At a more informal level, nationalist discourses and struggles can play out more subversively at the level of interaction between tourist provider and tourist, sometimes unbeknownst to the latter (Bowman 1989). But the state is often only one player in the dissemination of such nationalist rhetorics in the touristic context, often working in concert with private corporations and citizens. The latter are often the tourists who visit, or in my discussion here, shape the 'destination' in concert with and in support of nationalist mythologies (see also Palmer 2003). In doing so, they construct through their own touristic practice what they understand to be an authentic national identity.

Cottagers who schooled me in what the cottage meant owned cottages in the Haliburton region in the Canadian province of Ontario, and had permanent homes in the Greater Toronto Area (GTA). Many understood themselves and their families to be 'real' cottagers. I will argue that for these individuals their cottage is a place redolent with a nostalgic nationalism, a sentiment made even more complex in a country such as Canada, which seems forever ridden with ambivalent – some would say conflicting – images of itself, and outpourings of anxiety when challenged to clearly articulate a strong sense of its national identity, beyond stating that it is not American (Campbell 2002: 83).[2] Overt expressions of a passionate nationalist fervour are not part of Canadian character. As a Canadian myself, and thus well aware of this national angst, I was struck by the large number of Canadian flags that seem to be flying in Haliburton when I first ventured there. Some of these standards were rather tattered and worn and hung on roughly hewn poles of varying heights and stability; others were startling in the brilliance of their red and white, mounted on erect and firmly fixed proper flagpoles. All were visible from the lakeshore, the veritable 'front entrance' of the cottage. These standards at Haliburton cottages suggested a literal expression of Billig's banal nationalism where repeatedly and without fanfare, 'the nation is indicated, or "flagged" in the lives of its citizenry' (1995: 6). I wondered what this uncharacteristic expression of Canadian nationalist sentiment was all about.

An Anthropologist in Cottage Country

In 1986, geographer Reiner Jaakson wrote a short, but seminal paper focused on the question, 'what [does] the second-home mean to the second-home tourist?' (Jaakson 1986: 367) Since the 1980s there has been a flurry of interest in this topic, the vast majority of this work being done in cultural geography, and most recently in social history (see, for example, Campbell 2005; Luka 2006: 38–40; Halseth 1998, 2004; Chaplin 1999; Williams and Kaltenborn 1999; Quinn 2004). As an anthropologist, I developed a research project to investigate this question with a localized group of cottagers, intending to build on this earlier work with a finely grained ethnographic approach. I turned my attention to a group of moderately affluent, predominantly Caucasian, middle-aged, multigenerational second-home-owners in the Haliburton region of Ontario (Figure 4.1) who own and regularly visit their cottage. These cottagers see Haliburton as the rocky/treed/lake-strewn quintessential 'Canadian' landscape. It was the loosely defined middle class who originally acquired cottages in Haliburton, a population that paralleled the earlier groups of tourists with whom I had done research (see Harrison 2003).

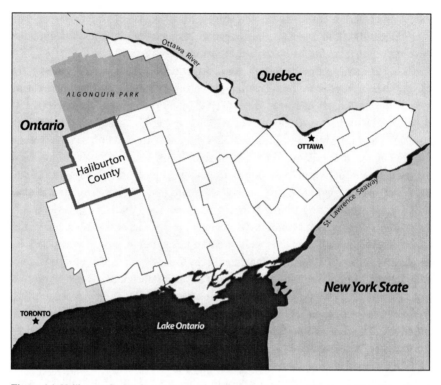

Figure 4.1 Haliburton County location map (courtesy of Department of Economic Development and Tourism, County of Haliburton).

For Canadians, summer offers a few short weeks of release from the harshness and rigours of the winter, a liminal period to be filled with hedonistic indulgences and fun-filled leisure pursuits. In the Greater Toronto Area (GTA) of Ontario, bumper-to-bumper traffic fills the freeways heading for 'cottage country' every Friday from mid-May to the Labor Day long weekend in September. An almost religious fervour drives southern Ontarians in this exodus as they frenetically try to ensure that not a moment of this 'sacred' time is wasted. To an outsider such a weekly 'pilgrimage' – now something many are extending beyond the summer months as they have 'winterized' their cottage – was a practice whose logic needed some explanation. In addition, newspapers and other media regularly engaged the topic of the increasing financial cost and responsibility of owning a cottage, yet continued to extol its overriding virtues. But as my feminist colleagues were quick to point out, a cottage was 'just another place of domestic labour' that they were loathe to take on. But these 'nay-sayers' were in a minority from what I had observed, and if I were to believe all that I heard in the local media. What was it that made this experience so appealing?

Statistically, cottaging does not seem to be a practice whose desirability is diminishing. The number of cottages in Ontario has increased at a rate of at least 10,000 per year since the late 1970s, when there were already an estimated 250,000 in the province (Priddle and Kreutzweiser 1977: 165). By the early years of the twenty-first century there were over 370,000 cottages in Ontario (Luka 2006: 134). This continual expansion still only includes about 7.5 per cent of the total Ontario population according to the 2006 census figures. Regardless, popular media and cocktail party chat affirms the notion that the cottage is the ideal venue in which to express one's commitment to the belief that summer and the cottage are indeed a special Canadian time and place. They also suggest that all Ontarians either own or have access to a cottage for at least some part of the summer. And if they do not, they wish they did.

The recreational enclaves around many of Ontario's 9,600 km of lake shoreline (Priddle and Kreutzweiser 1977: 165) are referred to as 'cottage country', but there really are several 'cottage countries' as these areas are widely dispersed across Canada's second largest province. I turned my attention to the cottage experience in the area known as Haliburton, a region characterized by the lakes, trees and magnificent outcroppings of the Precambrian rock characteristic of the Canadian Shield. My interpretation here is exclusive to this experience.[3]

The cottage experience in Ontario is going through a period of transition. In areas like Haliburton, where cottage development expanded significantly in the 1950s and 1960s, many cottages are now changing generational hands. This change can result in the sale of the cottage if siblings, many often with permanent residency thousands of miles from cottage country, cannot agree on matters concerning who gets to use the cottage when, or how it should be maintained, and who will pay for it, and whether or not it should be redeveloped, modernized or even brought into the postmodern world. These struggles can become intense and bitter, employing in the end the services of lawyers and the courts. A dramatic increase in the taxes that cottagers now pay to local municipalities has driven some families to sell their cottage, or at least rent it out for periods of the summer. Other cottagers have decided to live at the cottage full time and have renovated, or completely rebuilt it into a year-round home. Changes in federal tax laws have imposed a dramatically increased tax burden on many cottages to be paid at the time of any transfer of title.[4] Wild fluctuations in the price of fuel, and the global economic downturn at the end of the first decade of the twenty-first century have forced some cottagers to re-evaluate their ability to continue to travel to the cottage regularly (see Stevens 2008a: 56).

Consistently in my research I was directed to talk to those who had the longest history on any given lake, or at least those who had had a cottage there for many years. Most were quintessential examples of 'real' cottagers. It is important to note, however, that such 'real' cottagers, while shunning some contemporary developments which they saw as threatening the ethos of what the cottage was, were proud of two things: (1) what they considered as the 'essential' improvements that they had made over the years to their cottage, which included the addition of electricity, indoor plumbing, expanded and upgraded sleeping spaces to accommodate the growing generations of their family, screened in porches and improved water access; and (2) the fact that the character of the original cottage had been retained. Being a 'real cottager' was recognizing the personal/familial investment that went into the cottage, and appreciating the moral values which it was thus seen to embody. It was also knowing that the cottage was *the* quintessential Canadian experience (see also Luka 2006: 168–70).

'The province that thinks it's Canada'

A recent article in a Canadian national newspaper on the struggle that the province of Ontario currently faces in developing a strong regional identity was headed 'The province that thinks it's Canada' (Campbell 2008: A15). The article analysed the changing position of the province in the social, political and certainly economic topography of the nation in the first years of the twenty-first century. Unlike other parts of the country that have strong regional, and, in the case of Quebec, nationalist identities, Ontarians have historically seen themselves as Canadians first, and Ontarians second (Campbell 2008: A15). Such a mindset emerged particularly in the immediate post Second World War era when Canada's economy modernized and diversified, with Ontario at its centre (Courchene 2008). This reality enhanced Ontario's historically established legacy as the political and social force of the nation. Canada was Ontario to Ontarians. They had no sense of the province as simply a 'region' of Canada.

The British colony of Upper Canada as Ontario had been a dominant centre in the colonies long before confederation in 1867. The first wave of settlers had arrived in the late 1700s. Known as the United Empire Loyalists, they were loyal subjects of the British Crown, who fled the United States following the American Revolution. They sowed the seeds of the strong Anglo identity or 'Britishness' in Ontario, something fuelled by waves of immigrants from England, Scotland and Ireland throughout the nineteenth and twentieth centuries. Geographically Ontario is the second largest province but is the most populous and highly urbanized in the country. Toronto remains the nation's largest city with a population of nearly 4.5 million.[5]

Aesthetic representations aided in propagating the idea that the rocks, lakes and windswept trees of the Shield country of Ontario were *the* iconic Canadian landscape. Beginning in the 1920s, a group of artists – soon labelled the Group of Seven – spawned what some called a distinctly Canadian artistic style, depicting a distinctly Canadian landscape. Their widely disseminated images of this rugged landscape were interpreted to capture what lay at the nation's core. Little did they know that they were painting what would eventually become coincident with Ontario's cottage country (Osborne 1992; Campbell 2002: 73–5, 80).

Pioneers and 'Productive Leisure' in Ontario

A popular living history park just north of Toronto describes what a young pioneering couple confronted in 1816:

> 100 acres of land in the wilderness, clothed in majestic white pine, oak and elm trees, faced Daniel and Elizabeth [Stong] as they started their life's farming work together. They knew it took hard work to build a productive farm ... Clearing the land, they built their first home, a small log house ... and prospered.[6]

This narrative exemplifies the popular, if somewhat romanticized, understandings of the pioneer history of Ontario. This short description hints at little of the hard work the Stongs would have exerted to 'build a productive farm' from this densely forested land. Life in this era was more often characterized, as John Carroll, a Methodist preacher, recalled, 'frugal fare and *work, work, work*' (as quoted in Baskerville 2002: 75; emphasis added). Ralph Bunce has suggested, however, that such narratives about 'bygone lifestyles ... [are] fundamental ... [to Ontarian] values' (1994: 36). They produced a fundamentally 'utilitarian and functional' or, in MacGregor's terms, domesticated view of landscape (MacGregor 1985: 39; Bunce 1994: 36).

It was a return to the densely treed, rock-strewn and lake-filled landscape that had challenged – and in many cases defeated – pioneering efforts that drew an aesthetic response from post-war cottagers. But to fully experience the beauty, healing and inspirational properties of this unforgiving landscape, Haliburton cottagers of the 1950s and 1960s (and I would argue their descendants today) engaged the trope of the pioneers of earlier generations. Through their physical labours these mid twentieth-century middle-class 'pioneers' reclaimed this landscape as an affirmation of their social, cultural and economic position in the post-war world. Through their 'work, work, work', which in this context became what Chaplin (1999) calls 'productive leisure', they claimed their identity as 'real cottagers', and thus 'real Canadians'. Such referents imbue the cottage and the experience there with a nostalgic nationalism.

In the 1950s, geographer Roy Wolfe wrote:

> The great out-of-doors is, in Ontario, the out-of-doors against which the pioneers fought. Some of the activities that pioneers were, often with great hardship, forced

into, are now indulged in for pleasure ... thus in Ontario the cult of the wilderness is far from being exotic. It takes pleasure in experiences that were recently commonplace and difficult ... (1977: 22; see also Hall and Müller 2004: 8; Campbell 2005: 111; Luka 2006: 279, 291).

Wolfe (1977: 27) talks about the design and scale of the cottages of the immediate post Second World War era, details which describe the early cottages in Haliburton as having many parallels to the first log dwellings built by those such as the Stongs. But many of the links between the experiences of the Stongs and early Haliburton pioneers end here.

Settlement opened up in Haliburton in the 1860s, once all of the more access-ible – and in the end more arable – land north of Lake Ontario and Lake Erie had already been claimed by previous waves of settlers. Pioneers in Haliburton quickly came to understand that farming there was definitely 'work, work, work' and even then, often producing results too meagre to be sustainable. The sparsely soiled rocky landscape of Haliburton broke the backs, spirit and hearts of many of those who tried to cultivate it (Dobrzensky 1985). Lumber companies soon moved through the region, rapaciously felling the forests to fuel urban development across North America (Reynolds 1973). Once this finite resource was gone, the question remained as to how this land could be 'made productive', in light of the challenges it presented to agriculture and large scale lumbering.

After the Second World War the indomitable spirit of industrial capitalism, which historically drove the expansionist agenda in Canada, launched its next efforts to make the landscape of the Haliburton region 'productive' in earnest (see also Luka 2006: 282–3). The Crown and other landowners – including farmers who knew the limits of the productivity of their lands – began to sell cottage lots on Haliburton lakes. The area had been logged, and several cottagers told me of their ongoing efforts in the early days of their life at the cottage to clear the water, shore and even their lots of logs, stumps and other debris left behind by the logging industry. This work was in addition to the construction of the cottage or at least finishing the interior with proper walls and a basic kitchen, the creation of access routes to the water's edge, at times down a steep embankment to the lake (the only source of drinking water), and developing and constantly improving road and vehicle access points. Such labours did have links to early pioneer conditions. But any connection was heavily mediated by advancements in technology in place by the mid twentieth century. A chainsaw made clearing one's cottage lot much easier than the handsaws available to the pioneers, for example.

Such post-war experiences at the cottage were, following middle-class experiences in the 'wildness' of earlier eras, legitimated by the 'degree and quality of [relative] "primitivism" that was encountered there' (Jasen 1995: 105). Many of the cottagers I spoke with, particularly women, emphasized this quality when talking about their early days at the cottage in the 1950s and 1960s. Some, who spent their entire summers at the cottage while their husbands commuted from the city on the weekends, resented the enforced isolation and the labour of doing the family laundry in the lake, while their new 'modern' washing machine sat idle in the city. But life at the cottage was, they said, 'good for their children'. It was an investment in the children's future as it kept them safe from the evils of city life, while teaching them independence and self-reliance, things implicitly seen as good 'Canadian' values (see also Luka 2006: 166; Stevens 2008a: 52–3).

If land in Ontario was seen primarily in 'utilitarian and functional' terms, value was instilled in the cottage through the labour invested in it. Such sentiments resonated with trenchant Anglo Protestant ideologies about the value of hard work and acquisition of private property, central to the ethos of post-war Ontario (Warkentin 1966: 161; Luka 2006: 291; Stevens 2008a). The ongoing physical labour that life at the cottage entailed became re-imagined as a leisure activity (Chaplin 1999; Stevens 2008a: 48). Such labours captured the spirit of the much venerated, if at times highly romanticized, Ontario pioneer. As Merriman (quoted in Lowenthal 1989: 28) has pointed out, such nostalgic imaginings do not suggest that anyone wanted to actually return to the times of these pioneers. Their attraction is that they express a 'desire to get out of modernity without leaving it altogether'. Many of those I interviewed expressed a desire to experience a purer, simpler, more authentic life, something that the cottage was imagined to afford (Jaakson 1986; Williams and Kaltenborn 1999; Luka 2006; Stevens 2008a). Such sentiments capture imaginings of a previous time in history.

The ability to acquire a second home, a summer home, no matter how modest, replicated a privilege historically reserved only for the wealthier upper classes. The St Lawrence River Thousand Island area and the Muskoka region directly north of Toronto beginning in the late nineteenth century were two of the first areas where the tradition of summer homes developed in Ontario (Jasen 1995: 59–61, 116–26; De La Ruffinière and Farr 2004; Stevens 2008a: 30–3). But in Haliburton by the 1950s and 1960s, cottaging was well established as something in which the middle class could partake (see also Luka 2006: 152). It became, in some measure, a much more democratized experience, but even so, those of the lower classes, and certain racial and ethnic groups either could not, or chose not to, participate in the practice (see also Luka 2008; Stevens 2008a: 51). Acquiring a cottage spoke to a long-standing 'middle class fear of not succeeding' that had it roots in the late nineteenth century. It was then that 'leisure took its place as a central part of life, [and its] enjoyment became associated with personal success' (Jasen 1995: 113; see also Ehrenreich 1990). Acquiring a cottage was a mark of individual accomplishment.

Those who became cottagers in the immediate post Second World War era were carving out a new identity, something that brought them significant cultural and social capital, with only a relatively modest amount of economic investment. Owning a cottage, no matter how basic, quickly became a key marker in the status hierarchies of Ontario (Wolfe 1965, 1977). Its acquisition signalled that by the mid twentieth century some of those who were descendants of earlier pioneering generations had the economic and social stability to invest in such capitalized leisure pursuits. But equally important, being a cottager allowed such firmly entrenched urban dwellers a chance to own, in some cases reclaim a piece of, and a place in, what had become an iconic 'Canadian' landscape. These links defined these 'real cottagers' as 'real Canadians'.

Locating the Cottage: Views of the 'Canadian' Landscape

Hirsch (1995: 23) has argued that any landscape is 'not one absolute'; rather it must be understood as 'a series of related, if contradictory, moments ...', something that must be seen as a 'cultural process'. This is certainly true of what many considered the iconic Canadian landscape found in cottage country. Francis quipped of Canadians 'that nature in the raw scares the wits out of us', and as such we have an almost 'pathological response to the wilderness' (1997: 146). Nature in Canada, author and poet Margaret Atwood suggested, was a 'monster' to be domesticated, something that could be accomplished if one focused on those aspects that were 'amenable to human control' (Atwood 1972; McGregor 1985: 39, 26–46; see also Frye 1971; Bunce 1994: 1–14).

In tandem with the negative and fearful responses to the Canadian landscape is a counter-narrative. Altmeyer posits that Canadians in the period around the turn of the twentieth century also had a much more positive view of nature. She (as 'nature' was always feminized) was 'capable of soothing city-worn nerves and restoring health; ... [was] a treasurehouse [that] must be treated with greater respect; and [was] a Temple where one could again find and communicate with the Deity' (1976: 22). Excursions to this restorative, inspirational and nurturing place were well-established leisure practices by the early twentieth century in Ontario. In some regions of Ontario, the early roots of the cottage tradition had taken hold. It is worth noting, however, that the development in the late nineteenth century of a tradition of summer homes – they were far more than cottages – in these areas was initially by wealthy Americans, *not* Canadians (Bunce 1994: 86; see also Wolfe 1962). Was there some latent national ambivalence about establishing a more permanent, if seasonal, residency in such places?

What is pertinent to my discussion here is that Canadian/Ontarian excursions to 'nature', no matter what form they took in this period, were *not curtailed* by a competing vision of the Canadian landscape as a fearful and frightening place. Driven by the idea that a return to 'nature' would entail 'adventure, rejuvenation, or simple peace and quiet', and greatly aided by the technologies of modernity (Francis 1997: 146; Stevens 2008a), cottage ownership grew rapidly in Ontario, particularly in the post-war era. It can be argued that this interest in a retreat to nature was part of the anti-modernist movement that emerged in the twentieth century. The latter was both 'a critique of the modern ... but also a longing for the types of physical or spiritual experience embodied in utopian futures and imagined pasts' (Jessup 2001: 3; Stevens 2008b).

Appreciation and enjoyment of this landscape was enhanced by an active engagement with it. The phenomenological or the 'being-in-the-world' experience of such landscapes shapes nationalist mythologies (Csordas 1999). In Bender's words, '[b]y moving along familiar paths, winding memories and stories around places, people create a sense of self and belonging' (2001: 5), inscribing a collective memory of place (Connerton 1989). Selwyn (1995, 1996) demonstrates how structured tours through, and intimate physical work on the land, were important vehicles for cultivating intimate and deeply felt attachment and sense of belonging to a Zionist homeland/nation (see also Ingold 2000).

By the 1950s and 1960s, when the expansion of cottages took hold in Haliburton, intense physical labour and a range of manual skills – those of logging, construction, engineering, and eventually plumbing and electrical wiring – were useful in ameliorating any rather idealistic 'city-worn' understandings of this landscape and, at a practical level, to simply render functional one's newly acquired, and relatively primitive cottage. Labouring in the spirit of the pioneers of earlier eras offered both a pragmatic and conceptual model for the challenge this presented. It was also intended to define a certain moral character and incidentally a collective national spirit for 'real' cottagers/Canadians, paralleling what Selwyn (1995, 1996) has argued was a desire for both the physical labour on, and movement through, the Israeli 'wilderness' by Jewish immigrants, and later citizens.

Real Canadians at the Cottage, Nostalgic Nationalism

Places need to be seen as multilocal influenced by 'modernity ... history, and contemporary contexts' and shaped, understood and remembered in different ways by different groups who have a stake in any one locale (Rodman as quoted in Low and Lawrence-Zúñiga 2003: 15). Here my focus is on how a group of Ontario seasonal second-home tourists see a place – their cottage – and its position in a national narrative. I would argue that cottagers use their cottage 'to legitimize "their nation"', something Low and Lawrence-Zúñiga have observed is not limited to the processes and actions of the state (2003: 23). Angus (1997) argues that a strong popular sense of national identity emerged in Canada in the immediate post Second World War era. Others highlight that it reached its peak by the late 1960s and 1970s (Palmer 2009).

I would suggest it was and is a particular understanding of the Canadian nation that these cottagers affirmed. Tropes of history and the mythic pioneer engage the challenge of carving out one's place in what is seen as a beautiful but unforgiving landscape, and instil value – economic, emotional, social, aesthetic, nationalistic, moral – in a, or more aptly, their, 'idea of Canada' (Wolfe 1977; Luka 2006: 279). The Haliburton cottage and the experience of it express what Valenius calls a 'less conscious' nationalism when compared to 'official nationalism ... [that which is] expressed ... in the writings of politicians, historians, and other ideologues' (2004: 14). It is 'nationalism [that] suggests that nationhood is near the surface of contemporary life' (Billig 1995: 93). The physical, emotional, financial and generational resources invested in this experience foster a 'sentient or felt history' of this 'Canadian place' – the cottage (Palmer 2003: 427; see also Connor 1993: 384–5). Cottagers feel that they belong at the cottage, an experience far more powerful than any rational understanding of their citizenship within the Canadian nation-state (Palmer 2003: 427).

As I suggested above, these historical resonances were not necessarily those of the pioneer experience of Haliburton, as many of the latter group failed in their efforts to domesticate this landscape. This makes perfect sense since, as I discovered in my interviews, cottagers know little of the specific history of the Haliburton area. Rather, a more generic Ontarian/Canadian pioneer is invoked. The spirit and iconic status of early settlers, who prospered and thus achieved a particular social and economic positioning, are at play here. These pioneers, like the 'real cottagers', understood what 'real work' entailed. The latter, in the spirit of these pioneers, laboured long and hard to make this land 'productive', even if only for the practices of leisure, something which – as sociologists of leisure have long argued, and was obvious from what these 'real' cottagers told me – is a powerful means to inculcate social and cultural values. These Haliburton cottagers, in what could be called a 're-enactment of pioneering', and, by default, nation-building, understood the magnificence and opportunities embedded in the Canadian landscape, and, by association, the Canadian state. In Kedourie's (1960) and Smith's (1991) terms, they sought to connect with, and in some measure replicate the 'golden age' of nationalist development in Canada.

Skip ahead to the summers of midway through the first decade of the twenty-first century. What of those who have not been raised on such national tropes? The transitions I mentioned earlier about life in cottage country were in full swing. In her editorial in the October 2006 issue of the popular magazine *Cottage Life*, the editor observed, '... according to the letters we have received, this was the summer of disrespect' (Caldwell 2006: 11). It was the summer that the cottage renter rather than the owner appeared in larger numbers in cottage country, as many people were now forced to let their cottage to help pay increased property taxes. The renter, the short-term visitor, the owner 'new' to cottaging, 'real' cottagers argue, fails to understand what one called proper 'cottage etiquette' (MacLean 2006: 17). These transient/uninitiated populations are not aware of the unspoken rules about fast boats, loud music, and understandings of privacy that 'real' cottagers intuit, the latter somehow based on what is presumed to be primordial knowledge. They do not understand what it means to quietly contemplate the landscape, to gaze at the stars from a canoe at midnight, and they do not know, or appreciate, how much physical labour, but resultant sense of accomplishment, is generated in just keeping the cottage functional. They do not understand the layering of history, personal and otherwise, that is embedded in the cottage. In brief, they are ignorant of 'cottage culture'. They do not, it is thus assumed, embody the legacy of the successes of long-established Canadians.

Race and ethnicity can also set apart someone who does not know cottage culture.[7] When post 9/11 a Muslim youth group purchased a small resort on one lake in Haliburton, their arrival was greeted with a range of responses. A couple quipped that it could even be a cell of al-Qaeda. Others questioned why they were there at all as they did not know how to 'use' the lake, as they were never seen swimming, canoeing or even playing near the water. Others felt that they were the 'perfect' new residents as lacking any knowledge about how to be on the lake, they left it free for the 'real' cottagers.

Muro has suggested, 'nostalgia will come to the surface during epochs of intense social change' (2005: 575). Canada in 2008 is not the Canada of the 1950s and 1960s. Canada's immigration policies started to change dramatically in the 1960s. In 1962 the essentially racist 'all-white' immigration policy was abandoned, and a point system to encourage the flow of skilled immigrants was created. In the 1950s 84.6 per cent of immigrants were European by birth, but by the mid 1980s only 15.6 per cent of immigrants were born in Europe or the United Kingdom. By 2005 40 per cent of Canada's immigrants came from China, India, Philippines or Pakistan. Only 11 per cent of immigrants came that year from Europe and the United Kingdom.[8]

The Canadian, and specifically the GTA population, is now much more racially and culturally diverse than it has ever been before. The country's population is also much more urban as 80 per cent of Canadians now live in cities, with an even higher percentage for the province of Ontario. This 'new' population may challenge the classic, if not clichéd assumptions that the opportunity to watch the sun set over the rocky shores of tree-lined lakes with one's immediate family is somehow a primordial 'Canadian' desire. The assumed link between rusticity and pleasure is not to be taken for granted. These new Canadians do not have any connection to the mythic narratives of pioneer experience and all that was endured to lay the foundations of the Canadian nation. Rather, urban technologies, entertainments, and luxury might just be deemed central to any leisured experience.[9] Leaving one's home to live with more modest amenities may just not be that appealing. As a 'new' citizen told me, she had left her original homeland to get away from such basic conditions. Returning to them for the purposes of leisure was not something that interested her.

I was told that one of the things that cottagers valued about life at the lake was that they would find others like themselves there. This was something some felt they could not be certain of encountering in the multi-ethnic/racial/cultural spaces of their urban homes. I was told that, at the cottage, cottagers were surrounded by those who shared an appreciation of the outdoors, and a desire to escape the urban world. Cottagers came to see their neighbours at the lake as 'fictive kin'. Everyone would know the history of the cottages there, and they would see themselves as part of that history. They would know who the other 'real cottagers' were. They would know what it meant to be 'Canadian'. Such things would not have to be spoken; they would simply be known.

Some Haliburton cottagers were troubled by increased numbers of renters coming to cottage country. The latter are assumed to be of a different, that is lower, class, as they do not have the resources to purchase a cottage. But it was not only this group which was a disruptive presence. The other class cohort that was equally troubling was the 'nouveau riche' – those who have benefited from the unprecedented wealth accumulation experienced by some sectors of the former middle class in Canada in the 1990s and first decades of the twenty-first century – who were moving in, tearing down the more modest cottages of earlier eras, and building much larger and grander 'monster' or 'trophy' cottages (Svenson 2004: 74; Gordon 2006). Such 'improvements' frequently required extensive deforestation of the cottage lot (see also Luka 2006: 176–85). These cottages have the amenities of upscale urban dwellings. These new 'neighbours' seem to favour only the largest and noisiest watercraft. One's boat was no longer a means of transportation; it was a statement about the size of one's bank account. The lack of consideration of the impact such development has on one's neighbours was deeply offensive to those who consider themselves 'real' cottagers. And, while owning a cottage has always been a statement about one's social status, in the true Anglo-Saxon Protestant ethos of Ontario, it was one that was most respected if it was acknowledged, but at the same time quietly understated.

In contemporary theoretical terms, these 'real' cottagers, in the manner of the earlier settlers, are seeking to protect what Giddens has called 'ontological security … [those] feelings of security in the wide sense … the confidence that … human beings have in the continuity of their self-identity and the constancy of the surrounding social and material environments …' (1990: 92; see also 1991; Williams and Van Patten 2006: 35ff). Williams and Van Patten (2006: 36) argue, in reference to a similar group of Wisconsin cottagers, and again drawing on

Giddens (1991), that cottagers seek 'refuge from modernity's ... disorienting and fragmenting quality'. They do so by rooting themselves 'in the local'. For the 'real' cottagers I spoke with, I have argued that the 'local' embedded notions of a nostalgic nationalism for a Canada that that they never really knew, but one that exists in mythic understandings of those who laboured to build this nation. Such nostalgic longings, I would further suggest, have intensified in the context of the increased racial/cultural/ethnic diversity of the GTA in recent decades. This response is a good example of Shaw and Case's second condition of nostalgia, when a class or stratum of society perceives a loss of their 'previously privileged place' (1989: 3).[10]

Cottagers pondered, 'Can these newcomers become/are they real Canadians?' Does a brazen demonstration of one's wealth challenge a certain understatedness about being 'Canadian'? Is it possible to find any place where one can enjoy 'social and spatial exclusivity' anymore? Borrowing from Benedict Anderson (2006) I would have to suggest that responding to these questions requires an examination of the assumptions of race, culture and class naturalized in the imaginings of 'the' Canadian identity. Such a critique is missing from the mythic memory of Canada. Such absences, ironically, make more 'real' this imagined place, the cottage.

Conclusion: 'It's all about belonging'

Tourists, like refugees, migrant workers, immigrants, expatriates and other such groups, are taken to be the embodied evidence of claims that mobility is the dominant leitmotif of the early decades of the twenty-first century. But as Featherstone observed early in the process of critical reflection on the world through which such mobile populations move, 'one of the paradoxical consequences of the process of globalization ... is ... to familiarize us ... [with] the extensive range of local cultures' (Featherstone 1993: 169). I take the 'culture' of Haliburton second-home tourists to be one such 'local culture' that has had little anthropological examination. Appadurai charged that the 'new' task of ethnography is to understand 'the nature of *locality* as a lived experience in a globalized ... world ...' (1991: 52; emphasis added). In a volume engaged in a reflection on the state of the art of the anthropology of tourism, this chapter has examined one aspect of a destination that at least for many is 'thick' with meanings of home/nation. My research supports what Quinn (2004) has argued: second-home tourists raise as many questions about dwelling as they do about mobility. Second-home tourists, as with those who go much farther afield, support my earlier argument that 'home' is central to what makes touristic travelling 'away' meaningful (Harrison 2003: 139–63). This critical link also highlights the point that the mobility of the populations that I listed above, is always imagined to end, even if only temporarily, in a 'real' home. They are seen to belong somewhere. The truly 'homeless' person, or the popularly imagined 'nomad', are ultimately much more troubling, I would argue, as they are seen to demonstrate an absence of belonging.

My discussion in this chapter further complicates the relationship between home/away, or in Quinn's terms, dwelling/mobility in the context of touristic travel. It engages the complexities of who is seen to belong where in the mobile world of the twenty-first century, and by what measure belonging is calculated. The Haliburton 'real cottagers' I interviewed saw their cottage as symbolic of what it meant to be Ontarian, and by default, Canadian. Such imaginings are rooted at least in part in mythic notions of what the 'real Canada' is, a place made meaningful by the narratives of the labours and determination of pioneering generations and a place not obscured by class, racial, cultural and ethnic difference.[11] Quinn suggested that to date 'tourist mobility [has not] inspire[d] major theoretical questions regarding notions of belonging ...' (2004: 129). Research on domestic tourists, such as Haliburton cottagers, suggests that this might be changing.[12]

Studies of groups such as Canadian domestic tourists, who spend their time at cottages in the Haliburton region of Ontario, offer fodder for pushing the anthropologies of tourism, nationalism and identity, and landscape forward. In anthropology the latter, like the body, as Hirsch (1995: 1) observed, was for far too long a mere backdrop, a 'framing convention' to anthropological narrative and analysis, while those at home, such as these domestic tourists, were considered not 'exotic' enough for study. And while nationalism and identity are more long-standing interests in the field, more often than not these are subjects of greater interest 'away' rather than at 'home'. The intertwining of these themes in the meaningfulness of the experience of the domestic tourists I discuss here suggests that the privileging of the discourse and experience of mobility to 'arrive away' in the anthropology of tourism, needs to be counterbalanced with attention to the experience and discourses of home/dwelling – a landscape shifting with the complexities of cultural and nationalist imaginings at the end of the first decade of the twenty-first century.

Notes

1. I wish to acknowledge the support of the Social Science and Humanities Council of Canada; the Symons Trust; and the Frost Centre for Canadian Studies and Indigenous Studies, Trent University. On the meaningfulness of the cottage, Wolfe (1977); Jaakson (1986); Cross (1992); Williams and Kaltenborn (1999); Luka (2006); Plochkina (2006); Stevens (2008a, b).

2. I make my comments here with exclusive reference to a sense of national identity in Anglo-Canada.
3. See Harrison (2008) for a discussion of my methodologies.
4. See http://www.canretire.com for details (accessed 11 August 2008).
5. See http://www.thecanadianencyclopedia (accessed 11 August 2008).
6. See http://www.trca.on.ca/Website/TRCA/ParksAndCulture/Website.nsf/ WebPage/black_creek_About_history?OpenDocument&Language=EN (accessed 21 August 2008).
7. Luka (2006: 169) quotes an Ontario cottager, 'This is not a multicultural place ... it's predominantly WASP ... and I am sorry to say it, but I like it that way very much.' See also MacGregor (2008).
8. G. Bourchard, Institute for Public Policy Research. http://72.14.235.104/ custom?q=cache:AMrcVQNtdYgJ:www.irpp.org/miscpubs/archive/ bouchard_immig.pdf+bouchard&hl=en (accessed 22 August 2008).
9. Such sentiments are not restricted to all 'new Canadians', or to only this group.
10. The other two conditions include a view of time that is linear and secular and an availability of material items from the past (Shaw and Case 1989: 2–4).
11. The only 'ethnic/racial/cultural' difference that historically is recognized by Ontarians is that of the French in Quebec. But to many Ontarians they are just that, in Quebec, not in Ontario, the 'real' Canada.
12. Quinn (2004) offers her own work on Irish second-home owners to challenge this statement. See also McIntyre, Williams and McHugh (2006: 322).

References

Altmeyer, G. (1976), 'Three Ideas of Nature in Canada, 1893–1914', *Journal of Canadian Studies* 11: 21–36.

Anderson, B. (2006 [1983]), *Imagined Communities*, 2nd edition, London: Verso.

Appadurai, A. (1991), *Modernity at Large, Cultural Dimensions of Globalization*, Minneapolis: University of Minnesota Press.

Angus, I. (1997), *A Border Within, National Identity, Cultural Plurality, and Wilderness*, Montreal: McGill-Queen's Press.

Atwood, M. (1972), *Survival, A Thematic Guide to Canadian Literature*, Toronto: Anansi.

Baskerville, P. (2002), *Ontario, Image, Identity and Power*, Don Mills: Oxford Press.

Bender, B. (2001), 'Introduction' in B. Bender and M. Winer (eds), *Contested Landscapes, Movement, Exile and Place*, Oxford: Berg, pp. 1–20.

Billig, M. (1995), *Banal Nationalism*, London: Sage Publications.

Bowman, G. (1989), 'Fucking Tourists. Sexual Relations and Tourism in Jerusalem's Old City', *Critique of Anthropology* 9(2): 77–93.

Bunce, M. (1994), *The Countryside Ideal, Anglo-American Images of Landscape*, London: Routledge.

Bruner, E. (2005), *Culture on Tour, Ethnographies of Travel*, Chicago: University of Chicago Press.

Caldwell, P. (2006), 'Neighbour to neighbour', *Cottage Life* September/October, p. 11.

Campbell, C. (2002), '"Our Dear North Country", Regional Identity and National Meaning in Ontario's Georgian Bay', *Journal of Canadian Studies* Winter 37(4): 68–91.

Campbell, C. (2005), *Shaped by the West Wind, Nature and History in Georgian Bay*, Vancouver: University of British Columbia Press.

Campbell, M. (2008), 'Ontario struggles to decide whether or not it exists', *The Globe and Mail* Saturday 2 August: A15.

Chaplin, D. (1999), 'Consuming work/productive leisure, the consumption patterns of second-home environments', *Leisure Studies* 18: 41–55.

Connerton, P. (1989), *How Societies Remember*, Cambridge: Cambridge University Press.

Connor, W. (1993), 'Beyond Reason, the Nature of the Ethnonational Bond', *Ethnic and Racial Studies* 16(3): 373–89.

Courchene, T. (2008), 'Fiscalamity! Ontario, From Heartland to Have Not', *Policy Options* June: 46–54.

Cross, A.W. (1992), *The Summer House: A Tradition of Leisure*, Toronto: Harper Perennial.

Csordas, T. (1999), 'Embodiment and Cultural Phenomenology' in G. Weiss and H.F. Haber (eds), *Perspectives on Embodiment: The Intersections of Nature and Culture*, London: Routledge, pp. 143–64.

De La Ruffinière, P and Farr, D. (2004), *Ah, Wilderness! Resort Architecture in the Thousand Islands*, Kingston, ON: Agnes Etherington Art Centre.

Dobrzensky, L. (1985), *Fragments of a Dream: Pioneering in Dysart Township and Haliburton Village* Municipality of Dysart et al.

Ehrenreich, B. (1990), *Fear of Falling: The Inner Life of the Middle Class*, New York: Harper Perennial.

Featherstone, M. (1993), 'Global and Local Cultures', in J. Bird, B. Curtis, T. Putnam, G. Robertson, and L. Tickner (eds), *Mapping the Futures: Local Cultures, Global Change*, London: Routledge, pp. 169–87.

Francis, D. (1997), *National Dreams: Myth, Memory and Canadian History*, Vancouver: Arsenal Pulp Press.

Frye, N. (1971), *The Bush Garden: Essays on the Canadian Imagination*, Toronto: Anansi.

Geertz, C. (1973), *The Interpretation of Culture*, New York: Basic Books.

Giddens, A. (1990), *The Consequences of Modernity*, Stanford, CA: Stanford University Press.

Giddens, A. (1991), *Modernity and Self-Identity: Self and Society in the Late Modern Agel*, Stanford, CA: Stanford University Press.

Gordon, C. (2006), *Still at the Cottage*, Toronto: McClelland and Stewart.

Graburn, N. (1998), 'Work and Play in the Japanese Countryside', in S. Linhart and S. Freusteuck (eds), *The Culture of Japan as Seen Through Its Leisure*, New York: SUNY Press, pp. 195–212.

Hall, Michael and Müller, D. (2004), 'Introduction: Second Homes, Curse or Blessing Revisited', in M. Hall and D. Müller (eds), *Tourism, Mobility and Second Homes: Between Elite Landscape and Common Ground*, Clevedon: Channel View Publications, pp. 3–14.

Halseth, G. (1998), *Cottage Country in Transition: A Social Geography of Change and Contention in the Rural-Recreational Countryside*, Montreal: McGill-Queen's Press.

Halseth, G. (2004), 'The "Cottage Privilege": Increasingly Elite Landscapes of Second Homes in Canada', in M. Hall and D. Müller (eds), *Tourism, Mobility and Second Homes: Between Elite Landscapes and Common Ground*, Clevedon: Channel View Press, pp. 35–54.

Handler, R. and Gable, E. (1999), *The New History in an Old Museum: Creating the Past at Colonial Williamsburg*, Durham, NC: Duke University Press.

Harrison, J. (2003), *Being a Tourist: Finding Meaning in Pleasure Travel*, Vancouver: University of British Columbia Press.

Harrison, J. (2008), 'Shifting Positions', in S. Frohlick and J. Harrison (eds), *Engaging Ethnography in Tourist Research*. Special Issue *Tourist Studies* 8(1): 41–59.

Hirsch, E. (1995), 'Introduction', in E. Hirsch and M. O'Hanlon (eds), *The Anthropology of Landscape: Perspectives on Place and Space*, Oxford: Clarendon Press, pp. 1–30.

Ingold, Tim (2000), *The Perception of the Environment; Essays in Livelihood, Dwelling and Skill*, London: Routledge.

Jaakson, R. (1986), 'Second-Home Domestic Tourism', *Annals of Tourism Research* 13: 367–91.

Jasen, P. (1995), *Wild Things: Nature, Culture, and Tourism in Ontario 1790–1914*, Toronto: University of Toronto Press.

Jessup, L. (2001), 'Antimodernism and Artistic Experience: An Introduction', in L. Jessup (ed.), *Antimodernism and Artistic Experience: Policing the Boundaries of Modernity*, Toronto: University of Toronto Press, pp. 3–9.

Kedourie, E. (1960), *Nationalism*, London: Hutchinson University Press.

Leong, W.-T. (1989), 'Culture and the State: Manufacturing Traditions for Tourism', *Critical Studies in Mass Communication* 6: 355–75.

Lofgren, O. (1999), *On Holiday: A History of Vacationing*, Berkeley, CA: University of California Press.

Low, S. and Lawrence-Zúñiga, D. (2003), 'Locating Culture', in S. Low and D. Lawrence-Zúñiga (eds), *The Anthropology of Space and Place: Locating Culture*, Oxford/London: Blackwell, pp. 1–47.

Lowenthal, D. (1989), 'Nostalgia tells it like it wasn't', in C. Shaw and M. Case (eds), *The Imagined Past: History and Nostalgia*, Manchester: Manchester University Press, pp. 18–32.

Luka, N. (2006), 'Placing the "Natural" Edges of a Metropolitan Region through Multiple Residency, Landscape and Urban Form in Toronto's "Cottage Country"', unpublished PhD thesis in Geography, University of Toronto.

Luka, N. (2008), 'Waterfront Second Homes in the Central Canada Woodlands: Images, Social Practice, and attachment to Multiple Residency', *Ethnologica Europea* 37(1–2): 71–87.

MacLean, J. (2006), 'Letter to the Editor', *Cottage Life* November/December, p. 17.

MacGregor, R. (2008), 'Curious tales emerge about site of lakeside 2010 G8 Summit', *The Globe and Mail*, 25 August; available online at http://www. theglobeandmail.com/servlet/story/RTGAM.20080825.wmacgregor25/ BNStory/specialComment/home (accessed 26 August 2008).

McGregor, G. (1985), *The Wacousta Syndrome: Explorations in the Canadian Landscape*, Toronto: University of Toronto Press.

McIntyre, N., Williams, D. and McHugh, K. (2006) 'Multiple Dwelling: Prospect and Retrospect', in N. McIntyre, D. Williams and K. McHugh (eds), *Multiple Dwelling and Tourism: Negotiating Place, Home and Identity*, Cambridge, MA: CABI, pp. 313–22.

Muro, D. (2005), 'Nationalism and nostalgia: The Case of Radical Basque Nationalism', *Nations and Nationalism* 4: 571–89.

Osborne, B. (1992), 'Interpreting a Nation's Identity: Artists as Creators of National Consciousness', in A. Baker and G. Biger (eds), *Ideology and Landscape in Historical Perspective*, Cambridge: Cambridge University Press pp. 230–54.

Palmer, B. (2009), *Canada's 1960s: The Ironies of Identity in a Rebellious Era*, Toronto: University of Toronto Press.

Palmer, C. (2003), 'Touring Churchill's England: Rituals of Kingship and Belonging', *Annals of Tourism Research* 30(2): 426–45.

Peers, L. (2007), *Playing Ourselves: Interpreting Native Histories at Historic Reconstructions*, Lanham, MD: Altimira Press.

Plochkina, S. (2006), 'Construction and Disruption of Cottage Idylls: Kushog Lake Case Study', unpublished MA thesis, Trent University, Peterborough, ON.

Priddle, G and Kreutzwiser, R. (1977), 'Evaluating Cottage Environments in Ontario', in J. Coppock (ed.), *Second Homes: Curse or Blessing?* Oxford: Pergamon Press, pp. 165–79.

Quinn, B. (2004), 'Dwelling through Multiple Places: A Case Study of Second Home Ownership in Ireland', in M. Hall and D. Müller (eds), *Tourism, Mobility and Second Homes: Between Elite Landscape and Common Ground*, Clevedon: Channel View Publications pp. 113–30.

Reynolds, N. (1973), *In Quest of Yesterday: Haliburton County*, Minden, ON: The Provisional County of Haliburton.

Sack, R. (1997), *Homo geographicus: A Framework for Action, Awareness and Moral Concern*, Baltimore: The Johns Hopkins University Press.

Selwyn, T. (1995), 'Landscapes of Liberation and Imprisonment: Towards an Anthropology of the Israeli Landscape', in E. Hirsch and M. O'Hanlon (eds), *The Anthropology of Landscape: Perspectives on Place and Space*, Oxford: Clarendon Press, pp. 114–34.

Selwyn, T. (1996), 'Atmospheric Notes from the Fields: Reflections on Myth-collecting Tours', in T. Selwyn (ed.), *The Tourist Image: Myths and Myth Making in Tourism*, Chichester: John Wiley and Sons pp. 147–61.

Shaw, C and Case, M. (1989), 'The Dimensions of Nostalgia', in C. Shaw and M. Case (eds), *The Imagined Past: History and Nostalgia*, Manchester: Manchester University Press, pp. 1–17.

Smith, A.D. (1991), *National Identity*, Reno: University of Nevada Press.

Stevens, P. (2008a), 'Cars and Cottages: The Automotive Transformation of Ontario's Summer Home Tradition', *Ontario History* C(1): 26–56.

Stevens, P. (2008b), '"The Nature of Cottaging", Summer Homes and the Environment in Post-war Ontario', Paper presented at the 87th Meeting of the Canadian Historical Association, Vancouver BC, 3 June.

Svenson, S. (2004), 'The Cottage and the City: An Interpretation of the Canadian Second Home Experience', in M. Hall and D. Müller (eds), *Tourism, Mobility and Second Homes: Between Elite Landscape and Common Ground*, Clevedon: Channel View Publications, pp. 55–74.

Valenius, J. (2004), *Undressing the Maid: Gender, Sexuality and the Body in the Construction of the Finnish Nation*, Helsinki: Suomalaisen Kirjallisuuden Seura.

Warkentin, J. (1966), 'Southern Ontario: A View from the West', *Canadian Geographer* X(3): 157–71.

Williams, D. and Van Patten, S. (2006), 'Home *and* Away? Creating Identities and Sustaining Places in a Multi-centred World', in N. McIntyre, D. Williams, and

K. McHugh (eds), *Multiple Dwelling and Tourism: Negotiating Place, Home and Identity*, Cambridge, MA: CABI, pp. 32–50.

Williams, D. and Kaltenborn, B. (1999), 'Leisure Places and Modernity: The Use and Meaning of Recreational Cottages in Norway and the USA', in D. Crouch (ed.), *Leisure/Tourism Geographies, Practices and Geographical Knowledge*, London: Routledge, pp. 214–30.

Wolfe, R. (1962), 'The Summer Resorts of Ontario in the Nineteenth Century', *Ontario History* 54(3): 149–62.

Wolfe, R. (1965), 'About Cottages and Cottagers', *Landscape* 15(1): 6–8.

Wolfe, R. (1977), 'Summer Cottages in Ontario: Purpose-Built for an Inessential Purpose', in J. Coppock (ed.), *Second Homes: Curse or Blessing*, Oxford: Pergamon Press, pp. 17–33.

–5–

Tourists, Developers and Civil Society

On the Commodification of Malta's Landscapes

Jeremy Boissevain

As Marx warned years ago, *'Geography tends to become annihilated as a way of increasing the temporal flow of commodities'* (Hirsch 1995: 15)

This discussion describes how Malta's traditional architectural and natural heritage was first used to attract tourists and, later, to sell apartments and commercial space to speculators and locals and foreigners seeking holiday homes. Malta's political culture, in combination with blatantly commercial interests, is now threatening to destroy this heritage and with it the country's unique identity. Environmentalists and a growing segment of civil society are increasingly contesting this commercial assault on the country's landscapes.

Malta and its Landscapes

The Maltese Islands, with a population of just over 403,000 crowded onto 316 square kilometres, is the most densely populated nation-state in Europe. An annual influx of some 1.2 million tourists seeking accommodation and entertainment further increases the crowding. An appreciation of this high density and small scale is basic to understanding some of the environmental problems of Malta.

Malta gained its independence from Britain in 1964. Its government uses proportional representation to elect sixty-five MPs from thirteen five-member constituencies. Since independence two parties have dominated the political scene, which is characterized by fierce party loyalty and a winner-take-all policy. The Nationalist Party (PN) formed the government from 1962 to 1971, from 1987 to 1996 and again from 1998 to the present (2009). The Malta Labour Party (MLP) governed from 1971 to 1987 and briefly from 1996 to 1998. The small green party, *Alternattiva Demokrattika* (AD), is not yet represented at the national level though it has secured representation in a number of local councils.

Throughout recorded history Malta has been subjected to rulers who sought to control her strategic position and fine deep water harbours. In 1530, Emperor

Charles V handed over Malta and Gozo as a fief in perpetuity to the Sovereign Military Order of St John of Jerusalem, a powerful body of celibate nobles who lived according to vows to help the poor, care for the sick and wage war on those seen as the enemies of Christendom. They in turn were driven out by Napoleon in 1798, and Britain replaced the French officially in 1814.

Malta's built-up landscape still bears the stamp of its strategic location. The wealthy Knights of St John fortified the settlements around the Grand Harbour and built Valletta as their capital city on the barren peninsula dividing the Grand Harbour from Marsamxett. Their baroque palaces and public buildings, together with those of the island's nobility in Mdina, the Island's former hilltop capital, today are major tourist attractions. The British took over the property of the Knights and continued to fortify the islands.

Until the beginning of the nineteenth century all villages and towns, with the exception of the fortified settlements around the Grand Harbour, were located inland, well away from the coast (Boissevain 1986, 2001). Tightly clustered around enormous, cathedral-like churches, the houses had few windows to the street. Instead they looked inward to their private courtyards. This inland settlement pattern was common to much of the European Mediterranean and protected its habitants from both malaria and the incursions of corsairs seeking booty and slaves (Blok 1969). Seaborne dangers receded early in the nineteenth century, after the British navy had finally pacified the central Mediterranean. The dozen coastal parishes in Malta and Gozo, Malta's smaller sister island, were all established subsequent to this pacification. During this period the countryside, save for a few large farmsteads, scattered stone shelters, hunting hides and some megalithic remains, was devoid of man-made structures.

The attitude to landscape in the late 1950s was ambivalent. Few people lived in the countryside. Farmers, even those who possessed rural accommodation, usually returned to the villages at night. As in many other Mediterranean countries, the countryside was considered dangerous and uncivilized. Residence in the village centre conferred prestige, for built-up landscape was associated with 'civilization' (Silverman 1978). Bourgeois inhabitants of the towns looked down upon villagers, who in turn looked down on their farming neighbours. Farmers were regarded as uncivilized – *ta' wara l-muntanja* (literally, from behind the mountain). Most Maltese showed little interest in the countryside. Out in the country you were only likely to encounter farmers going to and from their fields, hunters and bird trappers and, occasionally, bands of boys playing near their village. Maltese families generally stayed away from the open country. It was not a recreational zone. The seaside was less threatening. In winter, Sunday drivers parked near each other along the coast, safely locked inside their cars and in the company of others. In summer they crowded together at popular swimming sites.

The countryside, because it was uninhabited, was also viewed as a foreboding, wild area and a convenient place to dump all manner of refuse. Old mattresses, tins, discarded clothing, dead animals and other rubbish littered the sides of country lanes and, often, main roads in Malta. Attitudes to the urban landscape were also ambivalent. The most imposing constructions of the Knights in Valletta and around the Grand Harbour housed the British Governor and the headquarters of various British military services. British service departments, branches of the Maltese government, various social clubs and commercial establishments, used other buildings, including parts of the fortifications. They were regarded as utilitarian buildings. Upkeep was the responsibility of the occupier. They were not sentimentally viewed as important constituents of the Islands' patrimony, as heritage. In fact, 'national patrimony' and 'heritage' were then totally foreign concepts.

This utilitarian attitude did not apply to the sacred landscape. The many churches were regarded as patrimony, not of the nation but of the parishes and the congregations they served. Parish churches were community symbols, treasure houses of collective memory. Their upkeep and embellishment were matters of often-fierce debate (Boissevain 1993: 13, 74–96). The numerous megalithic temples, ruins and catacombs, while shown to visitors, were generally poorly cared for. They were definitely not part of the sacred landscape. Locals viewed these monuments merely as curiosities, interesting parts of the landscape to be shown to visitors, but nothing special (Grima 1998: 36).

Tourists, Settlers and Builders

Britain began the rundown of its Maltese military establishment in the late 1950s. After independence in 1964, tourism began to be promoted in earnest as an alternative source of income. Between 1960 and 1970 annual tourist arrivals increased from 28,000 to almost 236,000. By 1980 they had reached 789,000 and by 1997 over one million. The advent of mass tourism had a severe, relentless impact on the landscape. Hotels and cheap apartment complexes mushroomed in disorderly fashion mainly but not exclusively in Marsalforn and Xlendi on Gozo and along Malta's eastern coast in Mellieha, St Paul's Bay, Bugibba, Qawra, Salina, St Julian's, Sliema, Marsascala and Birzebbugia.

Besides an extensive advertising campaign to attract tourists, the government also developed a successful programme to attract permanent settlers and new residents by means of low tax rates. Favourable tax rates, sun and domestic servants attracted these 'settlers', for the most part British retirees, including many former officials and expatriate residents from other former British colonies. The islands promised continuity of their comfortable colonial lifestyle. By the early 1970s some 4,000 had settled in and were beginning to have an important impact on local customs (Boissevain and Serracino Inglott 1979; Esmeijer 1984; Boissevain 1986). Some settlers sought out old farmhouses in the countryside. Most preferred the traditional courtyard-centred houses in the heart of the old villages or in the rougher, 'uncivilized' countryside. The 'settlers' also walked through the countryside for pleasure. In short, they showed an appreciation of the country's traditional urban and rural landscape that was new to Malta.

The demand for tourist and expatriate accommodation exacerbated the already acute housing shortage. The Malta Labour Party's promise to tackle this social problem contributed substantially to its election victory in 1971. The new government set about increasing the affordable housing stock. It constructed housing estates, apartment blocks, made available inexpensive building plots and facilitated mortgages. Rising affluence and the new measures enabled the masses, often together with relatives in cramped old-fashioned accommodation, to move into new apartments or increasingly, into their own newly built houses on the outskirts of their villages.

From the 1970s onward, Malta has been caught up in a frenetic building boom and become a permanent building site. Between 1957 and 1995 Malta's built-up area increased from 11 sq. km to 44 sq. km, or from 4.5 per cent to 18 per cent of the total land area. The average built-up area in Europe then was only 8 per cent. By 2007 it had increased to 29 per cent (MEPA 2007). The growing demand for tourist accommodation, archaic, punitive rent laws that left older housing stock empty and rampant speculation have generated overcapacity: 23 per cent of the urban housing stock was unoccupied in 1996 (Mallia 1994; Moviment ghall-Ambjent 1997).

The building boom not only encroached on scarce agricultural land. It quite literally consumed much of the countryside. New quarries, ready-mix concrete batching plants, many of them illegal, and uncontrolled illegal dumping of building debris have eaten away or covered vast areas of the country's limited terrain. Malta's clientelistic political culture facilitated the award of building permits to political clients, thus furthering rampant abusive building and subverting the enforcement of building regulations (also see Mallia 1994: 700–2).

Tourist arrivals increased rapidly. By 1970 tourist arrivals had risen from 64,750 in 1965 to 235,851, an increase of 27.5 per cent in five years. It was clear that Malta had adapted swiftly to mass tourism, an adaptation built on a number of factors. To begin with, not all of Malta's economic eggs were in the tourist basket. Malta had other sources of income, which included a giant commercial dockyard, a host of small manufacturing industries and, at least until 1979, when Britain closed its last military establishment on the island, a strategic location for which it had been paying £15 million a year. The standard of living in Malta was relatively high compared to other Mediterranean societies in the early 1960s. Consequently, the contrast between the lifestyle of tourists and Maltese was not particularly striking and thus did not provoke the friction based on envy reported elsewhere. Maltese were outward looking. For centuries they had been used to large numbers of foreign residents who maintained a different lifestyle. They learned to do their own thing – and in their own native language – while in face-to-face contact with foreign neighbours.

There was also a tradition of service. The transition from serving the British military to serving still mainly British tourists was one of degree. Maltese maintain their independence, even as waiters, chambermaids and shop assistants. As all who have been to Malta can testify, their indifference and often rudeness (especially of bus drivers) is often startling. Moreover, the high population density permitted the Maltese to absorb a large tourist influx without undue stress. They were used to crowded conditions and had acquired the social skills necessary to cope with these. Local friendliness and widespread knowledge of English, the lingua franca of the tourist industry, facilitated communication with tourists. Finally, the Labour government of the 1970s demonstrated a firm intention to dominate the tourist industry, rather than be dominated by it (Boissevain 1977).

Tourism continued to increase and by 1985 annual tourist arrivals reached 561,000. But lack of careful planning and enforcement persisted, resulting in a rampant sprawl of (often illegal) new buildings and destruction of natural habitat by illegal quarries and the dumping of building rubble in the countryside. Increasingly, sections of the public began to grumble and protest about environmental destruction and lack of adequate planning. In spite of being roughed up by politically motivated elements within the police force and Labour party activists resentful of any criticism of 'their' government, environmentalists began sporadic demonstrations. They protested, generally unsuccessfully, against uncontrolled building activity, rampant development of beach concessions, illegally built tarmac plants and the massive allocation of government building plots on agricultural land, notwithstanding the large amount of vacant property (Boissevain 1993: 153; Mallia 1994: 695; Boissevain and Theuma 1998: 101–2).[1]

Free Market, Commodification, Contention

Following the 1987 elections, the new Nationalist government uncritically introduced free market principles. This speeded up the privatization and thus the commodification of the environment. By abolishing the Labour government's strict import regime, which had prohibited the introduction of a long list of consumer goods ranging from chocolates to television sets, the new government stimulated unrestrained competitive consumerism. The government also began to address the dire environmental situation. By 1992 Malta finally had a Structure

Plan (1990), an Environment Protection Act (1991) and a Development Planning Act (1992) providing for a Planning Authority to administer and enforce the relevant legislation.

The government also moved to upgrade the tourist product by prioritizing the reputedly more affluent and environment friendly 'quality tourists' over the traditional sun, sand and sea tourists that hitherto had been the industry's mainstay (Horwath and Horwath 1989). Inadvertently the new Master Plan paved the way for a serious escalation of conflict. Responding to the plan's recommendations, the government actively stimulated the building of luxury hotels, housing for resident tourists and the construction of marinas. It urged excursions to the countryside in winter and spring and it promoted diving, golf and visits to monuments and traditional religious festivals. It staged invented pageants and re-enactments of historical military ceremonies. In short, the new policy actively commodified Malta's history and its natural, social and cultural landscapes. Unfortunately, government planners largely ignored the impact that the appropriation of environmental and cultural resources for luxury accommodation and leisure facilities like golf courses, multiple swimming pools, beach concessions and marinas could have on the environment and on public opinion (see also Ionnides and Holcomb 2001). The new policy stimulated increased destruction of the rural and coastal landscape and restricted access to the countryside and foreshore. Not surprisingly, these developments provoked conflict. The environmental NGOs, now tolerated by the Nationalist government, vigorously challenged all the new mega projects and related developments. They repeatedly clashed with the Planning Authority and developers over the new projects designed to attract quality-cultural tourists.

Without going into details, these are some of the major campaigns that were mounted after the mid 1990s: the Gozo Air Strip (1995–6); the Hilton Hotel-Portomaso extension and yacht marina (1995–2000); the Munxar Point St Thomas Bay Leisure Complex (1995); the Verdala Golf Course (1994–2004); the Siggiewi Cement Plant (1999); the Tuna Penning Project (1998–2001); the Xaghra l-Hamra Golf Course (2005 to 2007); the Ramla l-Hamra villa and hotel complex in Gozo (2006–8); the Qui-si-sana car park in Sliema (2002–9); the Mistra Bay Disco (2008–9); and the Bahrija Valley villa (summer 2009).

These campaigns involved petitions, demonstrations, technical reports, press briefings, lobbying local and European Union parliamentarians, establishing websites and umbrella groups to coordinate their activity. The umbrella group that led the campaign against the Verdala Golf course consisted of twenty different NGOs. All but two of the eleven campaigns – those opposing the Hilton-Portomaso extension-marina and tuna penning – were successful in that the projects were either withdrawn by the developers, frozen by the government or rejected by the planning authorities. This may well be a unique record of NGO success. Ongoing campaigns are currently targeting some mega development projects discussed further below.

Continuing Environmental Destruction[2]

At this stage one may well ask why, despite the new strict planning laws administered by the Malta Environment and Planning Authority (MEPA), did widespread, often illegal, building and general environmental destruction still persist? Alongside the government's structural bias in favour of the free market and private enterprise, and the building and tourist industries in particular, there are a number of Maltese customs and attitudes that are also responsible. Here I discuss ten, but there are undoubtedly more.

The first, and perhaps most obvious, is that until very recently the general public knew and cared very little about the countryside and were rather apprehensive about visiting it. They literally did not recognize its beauty and ecological importance. Hence they were indifferent to its pollution and the destruction brought about by its privatization.

Second, the Maltese family-centred world-view holds that any action undertaken to benefit one's family is justifiable, and expects others to behave in a similar way. This attitude has been called *amoral familism*,[3] and it has left lasting imprints and deep scars on the landscape. It leads to a disregard of the effects on others – neighbours, strangers and future generations – of actions undertaken to further the interests of self and family. It is part of the fabric of daily life in Malta. Among other things, it leads to indiscriminate dumping of rubbish beyond one's front door, for public spaces are regarded as no man's land. It also condones the illegal construction of buildings with total disregard for the laws and regulations established to protect the quality of life of others and the nation's environment. Amoral familism is opposed to the notion that individual rights and interests must sometimes be sacrificed for the common good. In short, it contradicts the principle that the state's building ordinances and zoning regulations should be obeyed because they are right and just.

Third, the notions of heritage and patrimony until recently were foreign to most Maltese and Gozitans. Many – if not most – still look upon much of the country's natural and monumental heritage as having to do with others – the Knights, the British, *il-Gvern* (Government), the tourists – with '*them*', not with '*us*'. It is a legacy of colonialism. The foreign powers that colonized the Maltese Islands were generally uninterested in promoting Maltese culture or pride in their country. The Maltese thus reached independence with a poor self-image and a cowed civil society that was barely acknowledged. However, slowly more people are beginning to explore the countryside, which for them has taken on a new meaning that approaches a sense of patrimony (see Grima 1997). Generally speaking, however, this interest is not shared by most villagers, or by residents in the working-class districts of the towns and cities. Landscape as an intrinsic component of national patrimony is not yet part of Maltese culture at the grass roots. It is there to be used for hunting, farming and building.

Fourth, the extreme importance that Maltese attach to owning a house is also relevant. In the words of a Maltese sociologist:

> An own house is a major and safe investment; a source of family pride; a fortress to protect its owners against an all-intrusive society where privacy comes at a premium; an heirloom for the children ... *[I]n the choice between construction for private gain and maintaining a historic asset for the common good, the choice for the former is, usually, a foregone conclusion.* (Baldacchino 2007: 99; emphasis added, JB)

Fifth, the pervasive system of patronage, clientelism, nepotism and a real or imagined network of friends-of-friends reinforces the firm belief that influential friends and relatives in government or political party can in return for loyalty, political support, favours or cash, obtain building permits, regularize abusive building activities, influence the judiciary and obscure other contraventions (Boissevain 1974; Mallia 1994: 698–701; Mitchell 2002). The very fact that illegal construction activities are so widespread, and that so few persons are successfully prosecuted and severely punished for this, validates this belief and encourages potential offenders to proceed without the necessary permission.

Sixth, the country's somewhat muddled and archaic legal system makes it extremely difficult for MEPA successfully to prosecute building offences and to remove illegal constructions, even if it had the resources to do so. The inability – and/or unwillingness – of the state to enforce its own building regulations encourages people to disregard them.

Seventh, fear of retaliation for reporting or testifying against someone. This leads to the Maltese version of Sicilian *omertà*: collusion through silence (see also Baldacchino 1997: 116–24; 2008: 42–3). This fear also reflects the lack of confidence in the ability of the state to protect the rights of its citizens, and thus it underlines the need to cultivate influential protectors. There may even occasionally be some empathy with the offender: *Halli lil kulhadd jimxi ghal rasu* (Let everyone go his/her own way). The fear of reprisal for public criticism of family, neighbours, colleagues, political party, government or the Church is ever present. It inhibits persons from standing up and disagreeing with, or even just questioning someone who is or may be more influential or powerful. This fear of others has muzzled the voice of civil society. But, very slowly, this fear is growing weaker. Fifty years ago few dared to sign their own name to letters to newspapers criticizing government agencies or officers. Now newspapers and blogs carry many signed critical letters. Most Maltese have personally experienced and/or know of persons who have been punished for criticizing their neighbours, superiors, government policy or influential persons, or for reporting some illegal activity. Common acts of retaliation include splashing paint on or setting fire to private vehicles or one's front door, refusal of a permit, denial of a deserved promotion, scholarship or contract, and for critical employees, an unpleasant transfer (or no work to do). Critical news media are cowed by withholding advertising and serving libel writs on editors, columnists and outspoken NGO activists. The harsh, often violent, reaction of the Labour government in the 1970s and 1980s to those criticizing its policies – such as the attack on environmentalists alluded to above – also severely subdued the voice of civil society (see also Boissevain 1993: 153; Mallia 1994: 695; Boissevain and Theuma 1998: 101–2). Such punishments are of course not unique to Malta. But in Malta the fear of retribution is pervasive. It is a characteristic of those who live in small interrelated communities in face-to-face contact with each other (see also Baldacchino 1997: 116–24; 2008: 42–3).

Eighth, the central government manipulates planning policy for party political ends. For example, in July 2006 the parliament, without public consultation and the strategic environmental assessment (SEA) study required by the European Commission, voted to extend the 1985 Development Zone boundaries by 2.3 per cent. Right after this contentious decision, prices across the entire property market shot up by a massive 32.17 per cent over the same month in the previous year (Vella 2008). This naturally delighted hundreds of small property owners, speculators, architects and developers who subsequently were able to obtain building permits in what were formerly 'green areas' and land outside the development zone (ODZ).[4] This decision undoubtedly helped the Nationalist Party to win the national elections held in March 2008. Local environmental organizations duly reported the transgression of the SEA directive to the European Commission, which then warned government that it would investigate the matter. As of May 2009, the Commission was still contemplating whether to start infringement procedures against Malta (Debono 2009).

Ninth, short-term planning combined with greed for quick profit is also a major cause of the destruction of the landscape. This short-term vision, in turn, is in part a consequence of the colonial legacy of relying upon more powerful others – until recently Britain, now the European Union – to take care of long-term problems. But it is also partly a consequence of the short planning span stimulated by the five-year electoral cycle. The greed is fuelled by the self-indulgence promoted by the fierce competitive consumerism stimulated by the free market policy promoted after the 1987 election.

Finally, the electoral system furthers the intertwining of interests between politicians, the planning authority, developers and builders. The small constituencies generate intense pressure on politicians competing for votes from the same small pool of constituents. One way for candidates to obtain votes is to (promise to) personally intervene with authorities on behalf of their constituents. Acquaintances working in the MEPA assured me that political pressure on them at times was severe.

Confronting the Building Industry

Three contentious environmental episodes made headlines in Malta between November 2007 and July 2009. They provide excellent examples of the intertwined and conflicting, vested interests of politicians, MEPA board members, architects and construction entrepreneurs discussed above, and the impact they can have on the environment. They also provide a glimpse of some of the activities the environmental NGOs undertake in confronting the constant pressure of the building industry and illustrate the essential role that NGOs now play in defending Malta's natural heritage.[5]

The Lidl Supermarkets

On 30 November 2007 Alternattiva Demokratika reported that once again, the Development and Control Commission (DCC – MEPA's review and appeals board, the members of which are appointed by the Prime Minister) had dismissed the negative recommendation of the Planning Directorate and approved an application for the construction of a huge supermarket between the tiny adjacent villages of Safi and Kirkop. The designated area consisted of hectares of arable land that had recently been cultivated and was scheduled as Outside the Development Zone (ODZ), thus not to be built on. *Alternative Demokratika* commented pointedly that, 'It is no use designating areas "outside the scheme" when the DCC (Development Control Commission) is able to overturn the technical and professional deliberations of MEPA's own staff.' MEPA had stated that 'the board felt that the supermarket provided an essential service to the communities of Safi and Kirkop'.[6]

On 12 December 2007, the Kirkop mayor emailed me about the supermarket and complained that MEPA had never consulted the Kirkop local council about the project. 'It is a shame. The "Contractor" [Malta's foremost builder, JB] bulldozed the fields in just three days. We cannot protect any Roman remains as he covered the whole ground with gravel. However, I doubt what we could do against the "Contractor", but at least we could have photographed the site before it was bulldozed and issued a press release that the area … is a sensitive archaeological site.' The following day the Maltese language newspaper *l-Orizzont* published a long letter from the mayor in which he strongly protested the building of the supermarket, arguing that 'we should protect the little land and heritage we have left' (*Nipprotegu l-ftit raba li fadal*).[7] Five days later, the mayor emailed that the 'Contractor' was 'working day and night to finish the LIDL German food mega supermarket'. There had also been excellent coverage on the Labour Party's television channel about his objection to the development. His sister had warned him that he was, 'risking being beheaded like St John the Baptist'. Was this tongue-in-cheek or an expression of her real fear that he could expect trouble for publicly criticizing the authorities and, especially, the 'Contractor', the country's most powerful building magnate? This person had, since 2003, applied for permits to build a total of seven Lidl supermarkets, of which five were ODZ. Among these, two were being built: the one in Safi and another in the neighbouring village of Luqa. The Luqa supermarket, like the one in Safi, had also been approved despite strong objections of MEPA's Planning Directorate. Both the Civil Aviation Department and the Malta International Airport had objected because its proposed location was in the Public Safety Zone of Runway 24. The Agriculture Department had also objected as the site consisted of good agricultural land.

The MEPA Deputy Chairman had originally submitted the Luqa supermarket application in her capacity as the architect of the 'Contractor' for whom she had been working since 2006. However, following a *Malta Today* report that highlighted a potential conflict of interest, she had asked another architect to supervise the project for the 'Contractor'.

At the end of February 2008 the entire DCC board resigned in the wake of the MEPA auditor's report on the Safi supermarket. The report had lambasted the board for unanimously approving the project despite a recommendation for refusal by the Planning Directorate on the grounds that 'Such a permit should have never been issued on land that was outside the development zone and that the scale of the project required an environment impact assessment, which had not been called for.' The chairman of Alternattiva Demokratika announced that AD would be applying pressure through the German Green party on the Lidl mother company not to go ahead with its plans in Malta.[8] The Malta Chamber of Planners promptly announced that the MEPA permit issued for the Safi supermarket could still be withdrawn under existing legislation. The Chamber observed that, inexplicably the DCC's justification for the permit was based on the premise that Kirkop and Safi and the surrounding villages *had to have* a supermarket and that the development did not conflict with agricultural policy and provided an essential service to the communities of the surrounding villages. The Chamber pointed out that these were not isolated villages and it therefore did not see the essential need to which the DCC referred. The Chamber concluded that the decision was in breach of Development Planning and that relevant articles (Act 1992 Article 13 (5) and Article 39A) in fact allowed the Authority to revoke the permit.[9]

In October 2008 the Safi supermarket opened and the radical NGO, Movement Graffitti, remarked that despite the pre-election controversy over the irregular manner in which the permission had been granted and which had forced the resignation of the DCC board, it was unbelievable that, 'no one lifted a finger to revoke the permit ... with the result that a huge tract of agricultural land has been forever destroyed'.[10] Disputes surrounding Lidl supermarkets continued. In May 2009 *Malta Today* reported that the safety of people parking their cars at the Lidl supermarket in Luqa might be at risk: a MEPA sign now warned the general public that *'This site is located within the direct path of low flying aircraft. The exposure to substantial health and safety risks, particularly in the event of an aircraft accident is hereby notified.'* The paper also reported that MEPA's auditor was investigating the approval of the Luqa supermarket. He started this investigation after the former owner of the site complained that MEPA had three times turned down his requests to develop the same land. The auditor then noted that 'Subsequently he sold his land the to the present developer (the "Contractor") who had no difficulty to obtain the development permit requested.'[11]

The Mellieha Bridge

On 6 January 2008, *Malta Today* reported that construction activity on a bungalow being renovated in a restricted green area of the Santa Marija Estate in Mellieha caused a landslide that damaged a bridge. The project had been approved despite the negative recommendation of the MEPA case officer. He had declared the construction unacceptable because the swimming pool, water reservoir, pool deck and driveway all encroached on a protected green area. Extensive bulldozing beyond the permitted footprint had caused the collapse of a bridge. The road was rendered unusable. The developer also obliterated other parts of the valley to make way for trucks and bulldozers, though this was not covered by the MEPA permit. The architect who planned and supervised the development was none other than the MEPA Deputy Chairman and the builder was her employer, the 'Contractor'.[12]

On 13 January 2008, the same newspaper announced that the Minister for the Environment had asked for the resignation of the MEPA Deputy Chairman because of her personal involvement with illegal development activities that led to the destruction in the Mellieha Santa Marija Estate. A former president of the Chamber of Architects and once chairman of the Development Control Commission, she had been promoted to her present MEPA post in December 2005. As already noted, by December 2006 she had been engaged as the 'Contractor's' architect for the construction of some of the Lidl supermarkets. This blatant combination of overlapping roles prompted the coordinator of *Flimkien Ghal*

Ambjent Ahjar (FAA – Together for a Better Environment) to exclaim, 'This is obscene! The Deputy Chairman is effectively on the payroll of Malta's biggest developer who has a track record of 82 environmental infringements. This is outrageous.'[13]

The Mistra Bay Disco

Four days before the Parliamentary elections on 8 March 2008, the leader of the Malta Labour Party announced that there had been an exchange of monies in the award of a MEPA permit for the development of a disco on ODZ land at Mistra Bay belonging to a prominent Nationalist MP noted for his keen interest in the environment. When questioned about this, the Prime Minster replied that he had asked the Commissioner of Police to investigate the allegation. He then sententiously proclaimed that land outside development zones must be steadfastly protected: 'ODZ is ODZ.' Asked whether he would revoke the permit issued for the 'Contractor's' Lidl supermarket in Safi, he said that he had no power to revoke the permit. 'That is why we want the law to be changed ... the law was designed to limit the influence of politicians and let the experts decide.'[14] As of August 2009, the results of the police investigation had not been made public.

Promoting Tourism: Themes, Images and Landscapes

From the early 1960s onwards, sun, sand and sea plus colourful fishing boats have been central to Malta's tourist promotion. In fact when the Labour Government assumed power in the 1970s it even changed the National Coat of Arms to reflect these themes. Previously, the National Coat of Arms had consisted of a shield showing an emblematic Maltese flag flanked by two dolphins. In 1975 the MLP changed this into a composition consisting of the sun, the sea, two crossed agricultural implements, a traditional boat (a *dghajsa*), a strip of sand and a prickly pear cactus. The National Tourism Board could have designed this, but in fact it was the winning entry of competition held among school children. After winning the elections in 1987, the Nationalist government changed the coat of arms back to a plainer version of the original, but without the dolphins.

The home page of the Malta Tourism Authority[15] displays the principal elements of Malta's maritime heritage now used to entice tourists to visit Malta. In March 2009 the following fifteen wide photographic scenes were shown on a continuous loop: Fort St Angelo seen from the surface of the Grand Harbour; Mdina viewed from fields below; a pristine beach with just two couples walking hand in hand; yachts anchored in a Comino bay; the St Julian's sea front; the Sliema sea front; an empty green hillside with the sea in the background; a colourful fishing boat (*luzzu*); a display of coloured fireworks; Marsamxett Harbour at the start of a yacht race; a villa in Gozo with sea view; a scuba diver approaching a wreck; the Verdala Palace; the Upper Barrakka in Valletta; a cruise liner alongside the Valletta waterfront. The principal promotional mantra of the Tourist Authority thus includes rest, empty spaces, tranquil beaches, aesthetic panoramas of sea and landscape, and historic and rural vistas. Of the fifteen scenes, eleven had an obvious maritime flavour; maritime themes are still key components of Malta's tourism marketing campaign.[16]

Tourists are not so naïve that they believe everything they read and see in the promotional material. Nonetheless the reality they discovered upon actually visiting Malta may come as something of a shock to many. In 2008, besides some magnificent vistas reminiscent of those they might have encountered on the Tourism Authority's website, they would have found that the beaches were scarce, horribly crowded and quite often filthy; that obtrusive odours and organic debris sometimes emanated from the many tuna cages located along in or near popular bays; that the roads were terribly congested and often in dangerously poor repair; that parts of the open countryside were often littered with all manner of refuse; that many picturesque rambling paths were closed to walkers by threatening hunters and bird trappers; that there was a giant still-smoking recently retired landfill – 'Mount Maghtab' – looming over the coast near Salina Bay; and that large billboards along the highways disturbed and often completely obscured coastal and inland vistas.

Most disappointing of all for first-time visitors will be the extent to which the shoreline and bays, already substantially urbanized by a cement collar of large hotels and higgledy-piggledy apartment blocks, were being further citified by a series of mega speculative property developments. In order to grasp the scale of the building taking place along the north east coast in 2009, a number of the major projects are briefly described below. All have been or are still being challenged by environmental NGOs.

Developments in Progress

In the near future, the 500,000 cruise passengers who annually visit Malta will pass *Smart City*, a new town being developed by Maltese, Dubai and United States entrepreneurs on the southern side of the entrance to the Grand Harbour, Malta's foremost maritime treasure. Smart City is to be built on 300,000 sq. m of land that includes part of Fort Ricasoli: 54 per cent will include office space for up to 11,000 ICT and business employees; 27 per cent will be a commercial area for hotels, shops, restaurants, cafes and other commercial outlets; and 24 per cent will become a residential zone, of which 19 per cent will accommodate 460 residential units in seven-storey blocks and 40 luxury villas with swimming pools and sea views.[17]

Looming over the north side of the entrance to Marsamxett harbour and facing Valletta is the nearly completed grim façade of the *Tigné Point Development* (Figure 5.1). This is to consist of 460 apartments to be crammed into several eleven-story blocks built around a commercial and recreational plaza. The apartments are advertised as 'Framed on three sides by the Mediterranean Sea, Tigné Point draws its inspiration from the interplay of light and water ... one is beset from all angles by a visual testimonial of man's interaction with the sea.'[18] Further into Marsamxett Harbour, the Midi Consortium's *Manoel Island* development is preparing to locate another 450 housing units, a modern yacht club, a luxury hotel, a casino, a sports centre a boat yard and a marina with 400 berths including some for super yachts. According to the Midi Consortium blurb: 'The €450 million, 44 hectare Manoel Island and Tigné Point development is Malta's most ambitious property regeneration project. These two prime sites are located in one of the island's most desirable residential areas. Within view of each other across Marsamxett harbour, Tigné Point and Manoel Island's fabulous locations are a guarantee of their enduring appeal.'[19]

Just behind the Tigné Point project other developers are erecting the twenty-storey apartment blocks of the *Fort Cambridge* complex for 341 apartments with 'spectacular views'. In March 2009 one small (90 sq. m) privately owned apartment was already being offered for sale at €395,000.[20] Situated further into Marsamxett harbour near the Gzira waterfront, the *Metropolis Plaza*, a €60 million development, was under construction. The three high-rise buildings of

Figure 5.1 Like bleached skeletons, the speculative apartment developments on Point Tigné stare across Marsamxett Harbour at Valletta. (Photo: Marc A. Morell, 2007.)

thirteen, twenty-seven and thirty-three floors incorporate residential, commercial, health and leisure facilities, and 500 underground parking spaces. Future residents have been promised 'spectacular views of Manoel Island, Sliema Creek and the sea beyond Valletta'. In November 2007, thirty-four residential units and some garage spaces in the South Tower sold for a total market value of €13.7 million within ten minutes of launch.[21]

A little further along the coast in St Julian's, the new *Pender Place* residential and commercial complex will consist of 16 villas and 330 apartments in three multi-storey blocks. Residents have also been promised spectacular views of Manoel Island, Sliema Creek and the sea beyond Valletta.[22] Further northwards along the coast, on Xemxija hill overlooking St Paul's Bay, the controversial Mistra Village Complex, a project by Kuwaiti developers Al Massaleh and Maltese contractors, will comprise three boomerang shaped eleven-storey towers into which 900 apartments will be packed. Many of the future residents will have spectacular views of the bay, but others, it seems, will just look at each other.[23]

On Mellieha Bay to the north, 120 luxury villa apartments in thirteen clusters of the *Tas-Sellum Development* are being built with three pools on the steep hill overlooking the bay. Residents of course are to be attracted by the 'superb sea and country views'.[24]

Still further to the north on Gozo, another controversial proposal, the *Qala Creek* mega project, is to be built in an abandoned quarry at Hondoq ir-Rummien, which had once been earmarked by the local council to be landscaped as a nature park. It is to comprise a hotel, a small 'traditional village' with 200 terraced residences, 60 self-catering flats, 25 villas and a yet-to-be-excavated marina for 150 yachts. Its residents will be able to make use of the minute adjacent beach that all Gozitans prize as their only swimming area sheltered from the Majjestral, the prevailing strong north-westerly wind. Altogether the project will be able to accommodate some 1,500 people. This is roughly the population of the small adjacent village of Qala.[25]

Another contentious project in Gozo is the *Ta'Cenc Golf Course, Villa and Nature Park*. This is to be located near an existing tourist complex on land designated as an Important Bird Area (IBA). It is to include a new hotel and thirty-eight new villas and bungalows overlooking Mgarr ix-Xini Bay in the existing Bird Sanctuary and, according to the proposal, would be located outside the permitted development. The proposal may also include a golf course and another hotel.[26]

These then are the projects that were underway or about to start in 2009. All have been or are being contested by NGOs. They involve the building of 4 hotels, 329 villas and terraced houses, 10 mega complexes housing 4,121 apartments and the construction of 2 marinas. All are being built either on the coast with sea views and alongside or overlooking bays and harbours. All have come into being in the new millennium and are clearly catering for foreigners, expats, resident tourists and affluent Maltese. With the exception of the Qala Creek project, they make no attempt to imitate or blend in with vernacular architecture as has been done in many tourist locations in the Middle East (Daher 2006: 18). On the contrary, they seem to be patterned on the modern cement mass tourist developments along the Spanish *costas*.

During the last decade there was a sharp increase in property purchased by foreigners looking for a Mediterranean second home. In fact, between 1998 and 2003 their purchases increased annually by 41 per cent. With Malta joining the European Union May 2004 there was constant growth in foreign purchases, of which 60 per cent were for apartments and 28 per cent for terraced houses.[27] Some Maltese are able to afford to purchase these new luxury seaside apartments to which they move in the summer or rent out. Property in Malta has always been regarded as a good, safe investment. Local property prices had been going up by between 6 and 10 per cent annually since the 1960s. Malta has a large, growing grey to black economy. Much of it was invested locally and abroad in property. While the Maltese economy stagnated after 2000, recording on average zero growth in GDP from 2001 to 2004, property prices boomed, reaching an average increase of 18.80 per cent in 2004. However, the price boom ended in 2008.[28] When it became possible to repatriate overseas savings without too many questions asked, many invested in building projects. This local investment increased as the entrance date to the European Union and its stricter fiscal and banking controls approached. As noted, the Maltese property market, and the Smart City and Mistra Village projects in particular, have also benefited from some of the Gulf's '$80 billion in liquidity awaiting investment' (Daher 2006: 51).

Conclusions

From the 1960s through the 1980s the sun, sand and sea panoramic vistas of the islands' coasts were used to attract settlers and tourists. Now these same aspects of Malta's maritime heritage, while still attracting tourists, have since the 1990s been extensively exploited by property speculators and building entrepreneurs to attract affluent local and foreign speculators and second homeowners. These new real estate ventures are changing the character of the inland and coastal landscape. This unique environmental heritage is irreversibly being urbanized and uglyfied. In the words of the vice-president of leading NGO Din l-Art Helwa, 'Fort Cambridge, Tigné Point and Pender Place represent institutionalised vandalism' (Scicluna 2007: 20). Such has been the progress of the commercialization of Malta's landscape.

The country's coastal zone is increasingly coming to resemble other over-developed Mediterranean coastal resorts. Malta as a picturesque tourist destination is losing out as these other resorts have far more and better beaches and extensive hinterlands. The new real estate developments are destroying the country's unique landscape and overwhelming its indigenous architecture, the very characteristics that give Malta a competitive edge to attract visitors interested in discovering something authentically traditional and different from the usual massive, built-up resorts of its aggressive, larger rivals in the region. This uniqueness is an essential element of its own identity and in the long run, the most precious resource with which to attract the tourists on which its economy heavily depends.

Besides the ongoing building activity of real estate speculators, the coast is also being desecrated by voracious tuna ranchers who have filled the entrance of many of the islands' bays and adjacent water with the greatest concentration of tuna pens in the Mediterranean (Boissevain 2004). Since 2000 this growing tuna industry has polluted the surrounding waters and has all but exterminated the Mediterranean's bluefin tuna stock.[29] Again this is an example of how commodification of a valued resource leads to its destruction.

In short, Malta is increasingly sacrificing important aspects of its heritage to local and foreign speculators. They profit from the poorly regulated property market, the failure of the majority of the country's citizens to recognize the import-ance of their own cultural and natural heritage and the weakness of a government entwined with the building industry. Can Malta continue to sell off this heritage, its family silver, to outsiders without destroying the essence of its own identity and the patrimony of future generations?

Is the discussion above merely the subjective discourse of a nostalgic foreigner who for the past fifty years has watched Malta progressively become more subservient to Mammon and slowly lose essential, irreplaceable elements of its identity? Many Maltese themselves are making the same observations. But their government is still ignoring their warnings – and so the desecration and great sell-out continues.

Still, could it be that the quite remarkable record that the environmental NGOs have achieved during the past decade in killing off nine out of eleven environ-mentally destructive projects is an indication that the political class has in fact begun to listen seriously to civil society? Be that as it may, at present Malta is suffering from paradigm paralysis.[30] It is high time for Malta's economic planners and politicians to follow the advice of Malta's chief lateral thinker (Debono 1967: 30) and to climb up out of the deep hole crowded with colleagues paralysed by the *prosperity-and-sustainable-development-through-building-more-and-more* paradigm and to look around for another paradigm before any more of Malta's natural landscapes are destroyed.

Acknowledgements

A version of this paper was presented to the conference on Ships, Saints and Sealore: Maritime Ethnography of the Mediterranean and Red Sea. National Maritime Museum of Malta, 16–19 April 2009.

I am most grateful to Dionesius Agius, Godfrey Baldacchino, Michael Briguglio, Timmy Gambin, Rachel Radmilli, Mario Salerno, Julie Scott, Tom Selwyn and Astrid Vella for their very helpful comments and suggestions. As always, my very special thanks to Inga for her constructive criticism and eye for the apt word.

Notes

1. The allocation of building permits despite a surplus of vacant properties is still ongoing. The Malta Environment and Planning Authority (MEPA) approved 65,737 new dwellings between January 1998 and May 2008 although more than 43,000 properties were completely vacant all year round (Debono 2008).
2. This section is largely based on Boissevain (2006).
3. The ethic of amoral familism is found throughout the Mediterranean region, the Middle East, Africa, Latin America and Asia. It is a reflection of the cultural and social importance attributed to kinship, especially where the state is unwilling or unable to protect its subjects against injustices. It exists in a particularly concentrated form in Malta because of the importance of the family and the close-knit, small-scale, face-to-face character of the crowded islands and the legacy of alien domination. E.C. Banfield (1958) first explored the concept of amoral familism. See Silverman (1968) and Miller and Miller (1974) for critical discussions of the idea.
4. In the five years between 2002 and 2006 MEPA approved permits for the building of almost 38,000 dwellings – a record 10,500 in 2006 (Scicluna 2007: 18).
5. http://www.maltatoday.com.mt/2007/12/23/n4.html.
6. http://www.maltatoday.com.mt/2007/12/23/n4.html.
7. http://www.l-orizzont.com.news2.asp?artid=40485.
8. http://dinlarthelwa.org./content/view/117/70.
9. http://www.dinlarthelwa.org.content/view/118/70/.
10. http://www.timesofmalta.com/articles/view/20081008/local/safi-supermarket-opens-despite-building-permit-controversy.
11. http://www.maltatoday.com.mt/2009/05/24/t7.html.

12. http://www.maltatoday.com.mt/2008/01/06/n12.html.
13. http://www.maltatoday.com.mt/2008/01/13/tl.html.
14. http://www.maltatoday.com.mt/04/06/n5.html. On 9 July 2009, the Prime Minister finally promulgated a long promised MEPA reform. Henceforth planning and environmental policies would be drawn up within the Office of the Prime Minster while enforcement would be at the centre of a better environmental policy that respected rights. Din L-Art Helwa protested that 'shifting responsibility for policy from MEPA back into the hands of ministers and politicians is a grave mistake ... It is a step back into the past.' http://www.midimalta.com; http://www.euvision.org/MIDI%20Consortium. pdf
15. http://www.visitmalta.com.
16. There are many other essential elements of Malta's maritime heritage that are not actively promoted to attract tourists. Memories of this heritage are housed in the Maritime Museum in Birgu. Among other elements they include the traditional fishing industry, boat repair and building, the famous Malta Dockyard, and scenes of fierce sea battles waged by the navies of the Knights and the British near Malta.
17. http://www.timesofmalta.com/articles/view/20080423/local/smartcity-to-have-larger-ict-component.
18. http://www.tignepoint.com/living.html.
19. http://www.midimalta.com; http://www.euvision.org/MIDI%20Consortium. pdf.
20. http://www.homesonsale.co.uk/fort_cambridge_direct_by_owner_sliema_tigne_malta-o68065-en.html.
21. http://www.timesofmalta.com/articles/view/20090315/business/green-light-for- metropolis-plaza.
22. http://www.pendergardens.com/penderville/content.aspx?id=29744.
23. http://www.foemalta.org/home/index.php/prs-archive/78-green-ngos-condemn-mistra-s-mega-project; http://www.maltatoday.com. mt/2008/06/11/n16.html.
24. http://tassellum.com/sellum/default.asp.
25. http://www.adgozo.com/?news=480&type=odz.
26. http://www.birdlifemalta.org/photos/otherfiles/268/pdf; http://www. projectgaia.org/media/26-08-08.html.
27. 'Foreigners may purchase property in Malta that is not for a prime residence (a second or holiday home), but one must pay a minimum price for an apartment, a house or a villa to be able to obtain an AIP (Acquisition of Immovable Property) permit which is granted by the Ministry of Finance and usually takes some 6–8 weeks. These prices are €174,703 for a house or villa or €98,066 for an apartment' (http://www.remax-malta.com/buying.aspx#pr2).

28. http://www.propertylinemalta.com/statistics.asp; http://www. globalpropertyguide.com/Europe/Malta.
29. For current developments, see http://www.maltatoday.co.mt/2008/7/06/ t1.html; http://www.maltatoday.com.mt;/2008/08/06/t6.html; http://www. maltatoday.com.mt /2008/08/24/t9.html; http://www.maltatoday.com. mt/2008/09/03/t7.html; http://www.maltatoday.com.mt/2008/09/14/t2.html; http://www.timesofmalta.com./articles/view/20080930/local/ag-finds-enough-evidence-to-arraign-owners-of-trawlers.
30. "[A] paradigm is a shared set of assumptions about how we perceive the world, allowing us to develop expectations about what will probably occur based on these assumptions. But when data falls outside our paradigm, we find it hard to see and accept. This is called the 'paradigm effect'. ... [When] the paradigm effect is so strong that we are prevented from actually seeing what is under our very noses we are said to be suffering from 'paradigm paralysis'" (Harrison 1994).

References

Baldacchino, G. (1997), *Global Tourism and Informal Labour Relations: The Small-scale Syndrome at Work*, London and Washington: Mansell.

Baldacchino, G. (2007), 'Jurisdictional Capacity and Landscape Heritage: A case Study of Malta & Gozo', *Journal of Mediterranean Studies* 17: 95–114.

Baldacchino, G. (2008), 'Studying Islands: On whose Terms? Some Epistemological and Methodological Challenges to the Pursuit of Island Studies', *Island Studies Journal* 3: 37–56.

Banfield, E.C. (1958), *The Moral Basis of a Backward Society*, New York: The Free Press.

Blok, A. (1969), 'South Italian Agro-Towns', *Comparative Studies in Society and History* 9: 21–135.

Boissevain, J. (1974), *Friends of Friends: Networks, Manipulators and Coalitions*, Oxford: Basil Blackwell.

Boissevain, J. (1977), 'Tourism and Development in Malta', *Development and Change* 8: 523–38.

Boissevain, J. (1986), 'Residential Inversion: The Changing Use of Social Space in Malta', *Hyphen* 5: 55–71.

Boissevain, J. (1993), *Saints and Fireworks: Religion and Politics in Rural Malta*, 3rd edition, with 1993 postscript, Malta: Progress Press.

Boissevain, J. (2001), 'Contesting Mediterranean Landscapes', *Journal of Mediterranean Studies* 11: 277–96.

Boissevain, J. (2004), 'Hotels, Tuna Pens and Civil Society: Contesting the Foreshore in Malta', in J. Boissevain and T. Selwyn (eds), *Contesting the Foreshore:*

Tourism, Society, and Politics on the Foreshore, Amsterdam: University of Amsterdam Press pp. 233–60.

Boissevain, J. (2006), 'Taking Stock after fifty years: Where to Now?' http://www.maltatoday.com,mt/2006/03/26.

Boissevain. J. and Serracino Inglott, P. (1979), 'Tourism in Malta', in Emanuel de Kadt (ed.), *Tourism: Passport to Development?* Oxford: Oxford University Press, pp. 165–284.

Boissevain, J. and Theuma, N. (1998), 'Contested Space. Planners, Tourists, Developers and Environmentalists in Malta', in S. Abram and J. Waldren (eds), *Anthropological Perspectives on Local Development*, London: Routledge, pp. 96–119.

Daher, R.F. (2006), 'Reconceptualizing Tourism in the Middle East: Place, Heritage, Mobility and Competitiveness', in R.F. Daher (ed.), *Tourism in the Middle East: Continuity, Change and Transformation*, Clevedon, Buffalo, Toronto: Channel View Publications, pp. 1–69.

Debono, E. (1967), *The Use of Lateral Thinking*, London: Jonathan Cape.

Debono, J. (2008), 'Building Boom: 65,373 new dwellings in 10 years', http://www.maltatoday.com.mt/2008/06/22.

Debono, J. (2009), 'Brussels still deliberating on ODZ', http://www.maltatoday.com.mt/2009/05/24/t10.

Esmeijer, L. (1984), *Marginal Mediterraneans. Foreign settlers in Malta: their participation in society and their contribution to development*, Amsterdam: Antropologisch-Sociologisch Centrum, University of Amsterdam.

Grima, R. (1997), 'Can we go to Ta'Kaccatura?' *Malta Archaeological Review* 2: 1–13.

Grima, R. (1998) 'Ritual Spaces, Contested Places: The case of the Maltese prehistoric temple site', *Journal of Mediterranean Studies* 8: 33–45.

Harrison, J. (1994), 'Paradigm Paralysis', http://www.mnsu.edu/comdis/kuster/Infostuttering/Paradigmparalysis.

Hirsch, E. (1995), 'Introduction. Landscape: Between Place and Space', in E. Hirsch and M. O'Hanlon (eds), *The Anthropology of Landscape: Perspectives on Place and Space*, Oxford: Clarendon Press, pp. 1–30.

Horwath and Horwath (1989), *The Maltese Islands Tourism Development Plan*, London: Horwath and Horwath.

Ionnides, D. and Holcomb, B. (2001), 'Raising the Stakes: Implications of Up Market Tourism Policies in Cyprus and Malta', in D. Ionnides, Y. Apostolopoulos and S. Sonmez (eds), *Mediterranean Islands and Sustainable Tourism Development: Practices Management and Policies*, London: Continuum, pp. 234–58.

Mallia, E.A. (1994), 'Land Use: An Account of Environmental Stewardship', in R. Sultana and G. Baldacchino (eds), *Maltese Society: A Sociological Enquiry*, Malta: Mireva Publications, pp. 685–705.

MEPA (2007), http://www.mepa.org.mt/Environment/index.htm?SOER/SOEI2.

Miller, R. and Miller, M. (1974) 'Are Familists Amoral? A test of Banfield's Amoral Familism hypothesis in a South Italian village', *American Ethnologist* 5: 515–36.

Mitchell, J.P. (2002), 'Corruption and Clientelism in a "Systemless System": The Europeanization of Maltese Political Culture', *South European Society & Politics* 7: 43–62.

Moviment ghall-Ambjent [Friends of the Earth] (1997), *Towards Sustainable Europe. Sustainable Malta: A Discussion Paper*, Valletta: Author.

Scicluna, M. (2007), 'The Environmental Deficit: A story of greed, political inertia and lawlessness' *Vigilo* 32 (October).

Silverman, S. (1968), 'Agricultural organization, social structure and values in Italy. Amoral familism reconsidered', *American Anthropologist* 70: 1–20.

Silverman, S. (1978), *Three Bells of Civilization: The Life of an Italian Hilltown*, New York: Columbia University Press.

Vella, M. (2008), 'Rationalisation of boundaries exploded property prices', http://www.maltatoday.com.mt/2008/07/02.

–6–

Enchanted Sites, Prosaic Interests

Traders of the Bazaar in Aleppo

Annika Rabo

> To walk around the Aleppo bazaar ... is like nothing else in the world. Experiencing
> it is to experience the East at its most romantic: it is the stuff that travellers' tales are
> made of. (Diab n.d.: 20)

The Aleppo bazaar – *souq* in Arabic – extends over 12 km and claims to be the
largest covered market in the Middle East. Despite urban growth, it is still central
to the economy of the city. Large-scale traders and small-scale shopkeepers,
industrial workshop-owners, ambulant food-sellers, customers and spectators mix
and mingle in this covered market. The old city of Aleppo – the *medina* – where
the covered market is situated, covers around 350 hectares. Since 1986 it has
been on the UNESCO World Heritage List,[1] and infrastructural development and
urban rehabilitation is taking place in the bazaar and the old city, partly to attract
European and regional tourists. Old Aleppo is packaged and sold for Western
tourists as an enchanted site by underlining its authentic, ancient and unspoiled
character. In the words of a booklet published by the Syrian Ministry of Tourism,
the covered Aleppo market alleys are like 'living museums which depict medieval
life' (1989: 147), where, according to a foreign guidebook, 'the traditions of the
Arab middle ages do not seem all that remote.... . It still works according to the
conventions of commercial life unbroken since Mameluke times' (Burns 1994:
28). But the people making a living in this market do not support such claims
(unless they can make money on them). Although they describe themselves as
'traditional', they certainly do not see their businesses as relics from the past eras.
Instead, they care about the bazaar because this is where they and others like them
meet and work, now, in the contemporary world.

In this article, these more prosaic interests of the bazaar traders will be in
focus.[2] I will argue that an analysis of how Aleppo traders talk about, and react to,
tourism and urban rehabilitation will throw light on their perceptions of space and
place. But, more crucially, such talk and such reactions can also be understood as
a way in which they work and rework their relations to political power-holders in
the city, in the capital, but also abroad. The voices of Aleppo tourists are largely

absent in this article. The gazes which will be scrutinized are not those of tourists but mainly those of traders drawn into hopes and fears of increased dependency on tourism.[3] But views of people working as tourist guides, travel agents and with urban rehabilitation will also be brought out in order to 'chart *local* configurations of economic and social transformations' (Selwyn and Boissevain 2004: 14).

To have sites on UNESCO's World Heritage List is prestigious, and Old Aleppo (and five other Syrian sites) are used by officials to tell national and international audiences that Syria has patrimony of importance for humankind. But the list simultaneously creates obligations to take care of and preserve this heritage in a suitable manner. This caretaking and preservation may easily develop into an inherently conservative force, which can be used in local, national and international power struggles over what history to promote for what purposes when 'heritage is already an interpretation of history, which is already an interpretation of the past' (Smith 2006: xiv). A focus on tourism and urban rehabilitation is thus an excellent window to analyse the political economy of contemporary Aleppo.

Before turning to the traders and their views on the bazaar, their city and the changes taking place, the long and rich history of Aleppo, and the profound changes that have taken place in the last half century, will be highlighted.

Urban History and Use of Space

Aleppo is the second largest city in Syria with a population of around 2 million, and it is the country's principal centre for trade and manufacturing. It is one of the oldest continuously lived-in places on earth – competing with the capital Damascus – and can boast of an extremely rich and complex history. Five hundred years ago, Aleppo was a significant node in a vast network of trade stretching across Asia and Europe. The city was well known to seekers of fame and fortune.[4] From the sixteenth to the eighteenth century, it was the most important Asian town in the Ottoman Empire; only Istanbul and Cairo had larger populations. At the end of the seventeenth century Aleppo probably had about 120,000 inhabitants. It was an important entrepôt in the long-distance silk trade, and many European merchants lived in the city.[5] After the opening of new European-controlled sea-routes to Asia and the gradual decline of long-distance caravans in the eighteenth century, Aleppo intermittently continued to thrive as an important trading centre for the surrounding region, including large parts of Anatolia. After the First World War, when new borders were drawn, it lost its earlier regional trading position.

Today Aleppo no longer straddles strategic trade routes, nor is it a centre of production of exquisite textiles. But although the city can now be considered as situated on the margins of the contemporary global economy, its traders and industrialists still have a great many links outside Syria, and the economic importance of Aleppo continues to be significant.

Aleppo has expanded around a natural mound. On this mound the citadel is found. It is the city's landmark and flagship attraction (cf. Maitland 2006: 29) and the most visited tourist site in all of Syria.[6] The mound has been used for at least 4,000 years, and the present citadel dates back to the tenth century. East of the citadel the enormous covered market begins. The bazaar – *souq* – is divided into various parts, each specializing in a particular trade. The bazaar has a great many very large khans, or caravanserais, used not least by people involved in long-distance trade. Some of these impressive khans date back to the fourteenth century. These buildings were historically storage houses, hotels and offices all in one. In the old city we also find scores of important and imposing old mosques. The Great Mosque dates back to the tenth century and it is centrally placed within the bazaar. It stands on grounds which have been the site for religious buildings for thousands of years.

The old city also contains a number of residential quarters, some containing large and magnificent houses built around one or two courtyards. But apart from the citadel, Aleppo's historical buildings are not of a scale and grandeur to be uniquely significant one by one. Rather, what makes Aleppo a singularly important urban centre is the enduring role of its historical city centre in the lives of its inhabitants. The great attraction of Aleppo is the old city as a totality (Rabo 2002: 173ff). This is not a living museum, but it is still – despite profound changes in the economy and urban fabric – a location infused with the continued economic and social importance of its users.

With the growth of the city far outside the old city and the central city quarters – a process which has accelerated in the last decades – commerce and trade can now be found in all parts of the city. The bazaar, however, is still very important as the centre for wholesale trade, with retail trade mainly geared to rural visitors and urbanites with 'traditional' lower class tastes. Aleppo is connected to a rich and fairly populous agricultural hinterland which affects its economy and way of life. If the harvest of wheat, barley, olives and lentils is good, then villagers have money to spend. They often use it to marry their children, and travel to Aleppo to buy the trousseaux for the bride. If the harvest is meagre, the bazaar suffers as well. The old city market is dominated by textiles of various kinds, but gold and fripperies, as well as household utensils, are also important merchandise.

From Demolition to Rehabilitation

In any city with a long continuous habitation, the urban structure will, naturally, change and develop over time. After 1822, when a devastating earthquake hit the city, modern quarters grew outside the old city. In the late nineteenth century, when Aleppo was still part of the Ottoman Empire, a German architect drew up a plan for the urban expansion of Aleppo. After the First World War, when Syria became a French mandate, a survey of the medina was made and ownership of plots and lots were established (Hreitani and David 1984: 13ff). But the structure of the medina did not change very much during the mandate. It was only after independence in 1946 that 'development' and 'modernity' affected the old city. In the 1950s an urban master plan was partly put into effect. New roads were created and old ones were widened to make access into the medina easier for lorries and cars. Parts of the medina were torn down to make way for higher and more modern buildings.

The Arab Socialist Ba'ath party, which came to power in Syria in a coup in 1963, continued this staunchly 'modernist' urban thinking for decades. Major mosques and more ancient sites were considered an important patrimony linking the present rulers to a glorious past, but the old urban morphology and bazaar fabric with its alleys and cul-de-sacs was viewed with suspicion. Such space was associated with inhabitants who represented urban traditionalism and resentment against the far-reaching social, political and economic changes instigated by the ruling party. Small traders and others working in the bazaar were considered both socially backward and politically reactionary, and viewed as allies of the Syrian bourgeoisie. Their assets were largely nationalized during the Syrian union with Egypt in 1958–61, or during the early years of Ba'ath rule. Many well-known notable families in Aleppo, who still had large houses in the old city, left them, and Aleppo, as a response to these new economic policies.

In the 1970s an old urban plan from the 1960s was revived, and plans for the demolition of buildings covering 9 ha in the old city, close to the new and more modern centre of Aleppo, were set up. In this so called *Bab al-Farraj project* there would be high-rise buildings for offices, shops and restaurants. This area had for centuries been inhabited by mainly poorer Aleppo Jews who had left Syria in the early 1950s. According to the authorities, the area had become dominated by criminals and prostitutes. The destruction of this area would thus not only eradicate traditional use of space in this part of the old city, but it would also eradicate a lifestyle viewed as a threat to modern Syria. Most city-dwellers greeted the news of this demolition with a shrug, but some well-known public figures started to campaign actively against the project, and for the preservation of the old city as a whole (David 1984). In 1977 they mobilized the Syrian Board of Antiquities to classify the whole of the old city as a historical monument. The following year this classification was extended to the old Christian quarters outside the historically walled city. But despite such activities, leading Ba'ath party members decided that 'modernization' should begin. In May and June 1979 demolition of the nine hectares took place.

A counter-tide was, however, gaining momentum. In the spring of 1980, a UNESCO mission – at the invitation of the Board of Antiquities – made a report on the problems and the future of the old city. Proposals and counter-proposals were made by various groups in the next few years. Finally, a new governor was installed in 1983, and with him a new less confrontational political climate was ushered in. The earlier plans were changed, and, instead, new smaller-scale and more preservationist plans were discussed. In 1986 the whole of the old city of Aleppo was placed on UNESCO's list of World Heritage. New winds were blowing. A more conservationist ideal, as well as the global importance of tourism, influenced architects, urban planners and politicians. Many Aleppians quickly came to express pride in the antiquity and continuous use and habitation of their old city.

In the early 1990s there were still over 100,000 inhabitants living in the old city of Aleppo, and it contained almost 24,000 shops and businesses. The old city extended along 300 km of alleys. To take care of and preserve this world heritage was, and still is, a staggering task. But some steps have been taken. In 1992 a *Project for the Rehabilitation of Old City of Aleppo* was launched. It is run by the city of Aleppo, but also sponsored by GTZ, the German Development Agency, and the (Kuwaiti) Arab Fund for Economic and Social Development.[7] This project aims to preserve the character of the old city, as well as to promote its economic and social development. The preservation aspect should not, according to the project, ignore the fact that the medina has constantly changed, and needs to change to enable it to continue as a viable, workable and habitable part of Aleppo. The promotion of economic and social development should not be at the expense of people working and living in the old city today.

In the late 1990s this project touched many of my bazaar informants by way of a new sewerage system which was laid down in the old city. Most of my informants in the medina had only a very vague idea of the presence and status of this project, or of its aims, goals and development. Generally speaking, the project was not part of their everyday concerns, nor a topic of conversation. The sewerage system – especially when trenches were dug and never filled in – was discussed, but although it was appreciated ('the sewage has not been improved since the time of the French Mandate') it was generally seen as yet another activity imposed from above, and not as a project activity to preserve and develop their working environment. Some specialists working for the project thought that users in the old city should contribute economically to infrastructure which benefited them. But others were of the opinion that a system of payment would only increase the corruption which was already rife in Aleppo (and in Syria in general). In the ensuing decade, however, knowledge about and interest in this urban rehabilitation project has spread in the medina, and also among traders who are not the immediate beneficiaries of its activities.

Since the late 1990s the rehabilitation project has also had an interest in the enhancement of Aleppo for tourism. This was especially noticeable in the old

Christian area (*Jdeide/Saliba*) slightly outside the old city walls. Some concerned Aleppians worried about the gentrification of parts of these quarters, whereby rich, mainly Christian traders – or Christian traders investing on behalf of Muslim traders – bought property and converted it for the purposes of leisure and tourism. But others saw this gentrification and cleaning up of the area as a positive sign. By now about a dozen of the old houses have been converted into smart hotels and locally popular but – from the perspective of the vast majority of Aleppians – expensive restaurants.[8] The restaurants, though different, are all resplendent with 'Oriental' designs and furniture. The waiters are dressed up in clothes that clearly signal 'folklore', and they serve elaborate Middle Eastern cuisine. In the hot season there is often live 'traditional' music and sometimes whirling dervishes entertain the guests. In the last decade more hotels and restaurants have opened in this quarter utilizing the same 'authentic' Oriental concept. Although my informants in the medina know about these hotels and restaurants, the vast majority do not visit them. This will be discussed in more detail below.

The People of the Contemporary Bazaar

Aleppo has historically been a polyglot, multi-ethnic and multi-sectarian city. But in the last half century the, in many ways, cosmopolitan character of the city has declined. Traders, shopkeepers and small industrialists in the bazaar areas have become more homogeneous; linguistically, religiously and ethnically. Christians and Jews used to be very important in the Aleppo market, but the Jewish minority has all but disappeared, as noted above. In the seventeenth century Christians constituted about a fifth of the population in Aleppo. Today the percentage is smaller, but it is probably still around 14 or 15 per cent.[9] Aleppo Christians are divided among more than a dozen denominations, all of which have their separate churches. The largest is the Greek Catholic, followed by members of the Armenian, Syrian and Greek Orthodox churches. Almost all Christian sects have churches in the part of the old city called *Jdeide* or *Saliba*.[10] In the nineteenth century well-off Christians and Jews were the first to move out of the old city and into the new 'modern' quarters.

When I started doing fieldwork in Aleppo at the end of the 1990s, most of the men who became my informants in the bazaar presented themselves as urban Arab Sunni Muslim and talked of themselves as 'traditional and conservative'. Most of my informants are seen, and see themselves, as epitomizing specific values and attitudes. They condone the separation of women and men on religious grounds and insist that their mothers, sisters, wives and daughters should not work outside the home. Their conservatism, they claim, is grounded in a 'fear of God'. They express the opinion that Syrian traders in general, and Aleppo traders in particular, are hard-working and clever. Trade is said to be 'the essence of everything'. The overriding aim of traders is to be independent from other traders, but mainly from the state (cf. Rabo 2005). Many, but not all, of my main informants trade in cloth and textiles. One informant, for example, worked in a large business selling spare parts for cars and agricultural machinery when I first got to know him. Another works in the wholesale and retail of picture frames. Many of my close informants sell household utensils.

Most of my informants work in the medina which has been the city's commercial centre for thousands of years. But they express no specific interest in the abstract idea of the medina or the bazaar. Nor are they interested in details about the long history of the city. They are, instead, staunchly here-and-now oriented. At the same time, however, they express very strong sentiments about the old city. The spatial organization of central Aleppo is very important for the traders in their everyday lives. The bazaar is inscribed into their activities and their very personae, just as the bazaar is being formed and shaped by their own use of it. Most of my informants talk about their attachment to their own particular section of the market. 'This is where we spend most of our time, and we see more of each other than we do of our wives and small children', as one trader explained. Shops and offices are not only used for work but are equally important as meeting places for friends and relatives. Access to the medina is not always easy, but my informants are keen to keep their shops and their office spaces. To have a shop or an office in the old city is an indivisible aspect of being someone, and particularly of being part of the people of the market. It indicates a trading continuity and trade survival and gives a trader a standing in this particular community.

Since the early 1950s the change in the use of space, and who uses that space, has, as described, been profound in Aleppo. Residential quarters have been converted into sites for commerce and industry, and the better-off, in particular, have deserted the medina. This process started already a century ago in the first wave of urban modernization, when apartment houses were built outside the maze-like medina. It reached a peak when urban notables, as mentioned, had much of their assets nationalized in the early 1960s. The move of the better-off away from the medina has been accompanied by a move into the area by mainly poorer rural migrants.[11] Since then, successive waves of migrants have settled in the increasingly degraded old city environment. The seamless fabric of the covered bazaar has been destroyed by the implementation of urban plans for opening up new wide roads. Furthermore, and more importantly, although the medina is the uncontested centre of Aleppo, for decades neither the bazaar, nor the residential quarters of the old city were particularly cared for by its users, or protected by the city bureaucrats.

As children, many of my middle-aged informants lived inside the old city in so-called Arabic houses: houses closed to the outside and the street, opening up to an inner courtyard surrounded by rooms. Only one of my informants, born in the early 1920s, still lives in such a house. The father of one of my close informants still lives in the old city, but in an ordinary apartment house. He moved into this when the Arabic house, which had accommodated a large extended family, was torn down in the late 1950s. His apartment was very close to the bazaar section where many of his sons and nephews and other close male relatives worked. He was thus able to visit them in their shops and offices on a daily basis. As the family had become more affluent, his sons and daughters and other younger relatives had moved to various more modern parts of Aleppo. When they move out of the city centre, many of my trader-informants re-create the social pattern of the old Arabic houses but in a new and different environment. It is quite common to find new apartment houses containing families that are closely related. Relatives will pool capital to build such houses, or fathers will finance a complete apartment house and give each son an apartment as they grow up and marry.

Since old Aleppo was put on the UNESCO World Heritage List, the open-courtyard houses have been protected, and special permission is required to tear one down. But destruction still continues, and most of my informants are not particularly upset by this. 'We can't save every building in the medina', one trader told me when we discussed the ways that investors manipulated the law. 'People have to make a living today, and not just look to history', he continued. Although some of my informants expressed nostalgia when talking about their childhood in these houses, most told me that they had no interest in acquiring one again. They liked the convenience of new and modern plumbing, and their wives found it easier to clean a modern apartment, they said. They did realize, however, that Western tourists were attracted to the medina environment partly due to its 'traditional' urban fabric.

Attracting Local, Regional and Foreign Visitors

Since the early 1990s, Open Door economic policies have increasingly perme-ated Syria under the patronage and control of the regime. The state, for example, is trying to attract foreign capital – mainly from other Arab countries and from Syrians living abroad – for investment in tourism and leisure activities. This policy has also made itself felt in Aleppo. Already in the early 1990s a special handicraft bazaar – sponsored by the Ministry of Tourism – had opened in one of the old khans close to the citadel. By the late 1990s, organized tourist groups had increased and a number of shops in the bazaar had converted their stock from merchandise geared to village and pastoral customers to items thought to attract foreign tourists. Tourist merchandise is produced less and less locally, or even nationally, but tends to be of a more generic character. Many shops in the bazaar now sell the kind of 'Oriental' things one can find from Istanbul to Hong Kong.

In the late 1990s people in the market and outside were largely optimistic about the future development of tourism. Many of my informants in the bazaar were of the opinion that tourism in Syria in general, and in Aleppo in particular, should and must increase, and that this would be good for the economy. With more tourism they would hopefully reap some benefits, they argued. The number of historical buildings, the rich history of Aleppo, its cuisine, ambience and low crime rate were put forward as important assets. One trader who had travelled extensively in other countries compared Syria and Aleppo favourably with what he had seen: 'What do these countries have that we don't have?' Another trader, however, who also travelled frequently abroad, claimed that Syria was not clean enough and did not have enough hotels suitable for ordinary tourists.

To most of my informants a tourist is an *ajaanib*: a foreigner, a non-Syrian, a non-Arab and mainly somebody from Europe. But most tourists in Syria are actually from the region, as the Syrian authorities realize. There have been, and continue to be, official initiatives and support to increase Arab and 'Islamic' tourism as well as tourism by Syrians living abroad. West European tourists, and tourists from South and North America and Australia visiting Syria, did not exceed 450,000 in 2006; while tourists from the Arab world and from Iran and Turkey reached more than 5.5 million.[12] Although relations between Syria and Lebanon are fraught with tensions and difficulties, Lebanese citizens constitute the largest category visiting Syria, and numbered almost 1.8 million in 2006 – a year in which many Lebanese fled to Syria as a result of the Israeli bombings in the summer.[13] In 2007, almost 1.5 million Lebanese visited Syria, indicating that traffic across this border is brisk and important. Although many Lebanese are not typical tourists, but rather come to visit family, the Lebanese are appreciated as 'good shoppers'. Syria is cheaper than Lebanon and many Lebanese who visit Aleppo also go shopping in the bazaar.

In 2006 over 800,000 Jordanians also visited Syria. Aleppo, however, does not benefit as much as Damascus from Lebanese and Jordanian visitors. In 2006 almost 1.3 million Iraqis visited Syria. The vast majority of these are, of course, refugees. Although many Syrians complain that these Iraqis drain the Syrian economy, and cause price hikes on housing and food, especially around Damascus, others stress that many Iraqis have infused the Syrian economy with money. Iranian tourism to Syria has also been significant since the early 1980s. This has mainly been tourism sponsored by the Iranian state and focused on pilgrimages to Shi'ite holy places in Damascus and its vicinity. But trade has obviously benefited greatly in the wake of this religious tourism. From a local Aleppo trade perspective, the Iraqi and Iranian tourism is, however, not very important. In Aleppo, it is, instead, Turkish visitors who are periodically significant and enhance the local economy.

In 2007 an agreement between Syria and Turkey made border crossing between the countries simpler, and in the spring of 2008 many Turkish tourists came to visit important religious and historical monuments in Aleppo and to shop, all in one day. The increased presence of Turks in the market made many traders and others in the bazaar suddenly remember quite a lot of Turkish. Old animosities towards the Turks and the Ottoman Empire were forgotten, and common links across the border were once again established (cf. Moubayed 2008).[14] In the medina, that spring, my informants did not classify the visiting Turks as 'foreigners' but rather as fellow Muslims, with whom they shared many commonalities.

How Important Are Tourists?

The Aleppo bazaar can be likened to a market for information where traders exchange views on their own and others' goods and merchandise. Traders are also keen classifiers of others, and all have views on the behaviour and shopping pattern of various kinds of customers, or possible customers. Traders who depend on tourists have very strong views on how people from different countries behave when shopping. Germans are liked because 'they quickly decide what they want and although they try to bargain, they never keep at it for long', according to Samir,[15] who is highly dependent on tourists. He liked Japanese the best. 'But there are few of them.... We get quite a lot of Italians here in Aleppo but they are the worst customers of all. They want to see every single item in your shop. They look and look and stay forever and in the end they hardly buy anything. They are rude as well and try to bargain endlessly.'

Khaled who sells silver jewellery in the gold bazaar has a more charitable view of tourists. He switched from gold to silver in the early 1990s and started to design 'Oriental' necklaces, earrings and bracelets. Khaled's customers are mainly tourists from Europe and Lebanon. But Syrians who are going abroad also buy jewellery from him to take along as presents. Khaled has been doing quite well and stresses that he has many steady customers who bring other customers to him. He also pays helpers who hunt the bazaar for tourists and bring them to him.

Tourists often enter the bazaar close to the citadel and follow the main street for a few hundred metres. This is the route most guides take their groups, and many traders have, as mentioned above, changed their merchandise to attract tourists rather than villagers. But the further one gets from this particular section, the fewer the shops selling things geared to tourists. There is, however, a tourist market growing up in the old Christian quarter. There is also the special tourist and handicraft market in an old khan opposite the entrance to the citadel, mentioned above. The location of this market should be quite strategic, but in the last decade many traders here have become more and more disgruntled. Some insist that tourist guides no longer bring groups through the khan. In 2007 many traders in this market claimed that the tourist market was so slow that it was hardly worth opening one's shop. 'There are no tourists' one informant in the handicraft market told me over and over. 'And the few who come do not shop. Before the tourists used to buy, but now they just look and pass. And we are getting no help and support from the state! We are told that tourism is good, but we have to bear the burden of lack of movement ourselves.'

But to most of my informants, tourists – however defined – are marginal to their businesses. Riyad, for example, is a fairly young trader specializing in the well-known Aleppo soap based on olives and laurel oil. His customers are mainly from the countryside, but since the Aleppo soap has won a certain reputation in Europe as 'natural', he tries to catch the occasional Westerners passing his shop. In 2007 he had a whole range of new soaps in nice packages displayed at the entrance of his small shop in the medina. These products were not of a very good quality but Riyad told me that he was trying them to see if they were more attractive to foreigners than the brown and not very elegant 'real' Aleppo soap. 'No harm in trying something new. But if I don't sell much I will not bother to get more.' Riyad would never switch to a line of products making him dependent on tourists only.

But although most traders are not directly involved in tourism, tourists – or the lack of them – and investment in projects for leisure, may affect them all the same. Hassan has a shop located where it could become an enormous economic asset if converted into a cafe or small restaurant. But he is not certain that the conversion from a conventional market street geared towards the local retail and wholesale market, to a street based on services and geared mainly towards visitors and tourists will come about, or be profitable. 'I am afraid! I think and I worry! Should I sell now or should I wait? Will the prices go up or down? But what if the tourists don't come? And perhaps prices will go down and not up with the tourists! So I am afraid and I keep thinking.' Hassan also told me that if this transformation comes about he would have to sell because he cannot see himself as the owner of a small cafe or restaurant serving others. 'I am too old to change my line of business, and having a cafe or restaurant is not what I want for my sons.' Hassan also claimed that serving alcohol is often necessary to make such businesses be really profitable, but for him this is out of the question for religious reasons.

Many of my worried informants underline that the external market cannot support all this emphasis on eating, drinking, sleeping and 'authentic shopping'. Nor are they convinced that local better off people will come to the city centre for amusement. The people in the old city itself are poor and of low social class, and thus rich people will not really be attracted to this area outside work, many traders argue. But other traders are of a different opinion. Some of my informants are very hopeful concerning the future of tourism and the development of leisure industry in Aleppo and they have borrowed enormous amounts of money to start new ventures in tourism-related activities. Rami, for example, has invested in a large four star hotel in the central part of the city, but outside the medina. The building started in 2002 and progressed quite slowly. I was told by others in the market that Rami had run out of money, but in 2008 the hotel had opened. 'But not officially', Rami told me when I passed by. 'We will have an official opening with great pomp and many important people. But since the hotel was finished and there was a great demand for rooms we have opened unofficially'. Rami was quite convinced that the hotel will be feasible, and cater for both foreign tourists interested in antiquities and history, and more local visitors who do not want to spend a fortune on five star hotels. The hotel is not 'Oriental' in its design, and he has no interest in linking his business to ideas of the enchantment of old Aleppo. He and his brothers are also going to invest in a tourist village outside Aleppo complete with bungalows, swimming pools, saunas and a fitness centre. In the early twenty-first century, when I doubted the economic viability of such a venture, he insisted that this village would attract not only local, but also regional and foreign interest.

But not all traders are as expansive. In 2006 Omar (with a partner living abroad) bought a piece of property strategically placed close to the citadel. Omar wanted to make this house into a restaurant and cafe with strongly 'Oriental' flavour. He was not gearing his business to mainly foreigners, but rather to a local public which he felt certain would come. He was not going to serve alcohol. 'It is true that alcohol will make a place more profitable, but I want this place to have a nice character where families will come and enjoy themselves.' In that year he told me that if he became too tired of running it himself, he would sell it. 'The way property-prices are going up around this area I should make a profit on that alone.' In 2008 he told me that he was really tired of this venture. He had never worked in the restaurant business before, and he was exhausted by having to oversee every little thing in the business. His wife complained as well. She never got to see Omar since he was working day and night. The market was slow, and he did not have as many customers as he hoped for. He would sell, but not at a loss, he told me. Omar was waiting for property prices to increase. 'This place will be very profitable in the future, but I might have to sell before that occurs.'

Even if my trader informants are not directly involved in tourist ventures, they generally welcome the idea that Europeans and others come as tourists and visitors and spend money in Aleppo. They also talk of themselves as friendly and hospitable towards strangers. But there are two interrelated issues where the presence of non-Muslim foreigners connects to local sensitivities. This concerns gendered public space and the presence of alcohol in that space.

Talking through Tourism: Gender and Alcohol

Aleppo is a spatially differentiated city where gender, age, class (or occupation), and ethnic and religious affiliation have an important bearing on who moves where and why, and who stops where and why. The most differentiated city is that between men and women, and there has been an indisputable increase in public gender segregation in the last decades. The increasingly 'Islamic' character of public space in Aleppo, epitomized by female veiling and a stress on gender differences, heightens the anxieties of many Christians in the city. The Syrian state gives equal rights to Christians and Muslims, and women and men are in many ways equal as citizens. But political opposition to the Ba'ath dominated state has increasingly taken on an Islamic character expressed particularly through gender separation and styles of dress. The global resurgence of Islamic movements, fed not least by the disastrous US and British policies in the Middle East, has also had a great impact on people in Aleppo.

In this atmosphere of self-styled and publicly expressed social conservatism, the question of alcohol has become an increasingly sensitive public issue in the city. Alcohol is produced in Syria, both in state and private factories. But it is mainly sold in shops in the Christian quarters and only Christians are licensed to sell it in shops or in restaurants. All hotels and restaurants found in the converted courtyard houses in the old Christian quarters of *Saliba/Jdeide* serve alcohol. Many of my self-styled conservative Muslim traders actually drink, but they do so privately among their close male friends. When tourist projects were discussed in the late 1990s and early twenty-first century, or when offers came to invest in hotels, cafes or restaurants, these traders – as Hassan discussed above – said that they were not interested. One trader told me he had declined the opportunity to invest and become a partner in a new hotel: 'I cannot invest in a business where alcohol will be served, just as I do not want to use Syrian banks. All tourist and most leisure ventures involve alcohol because it makes them profitable.'

The lack of interest on the part of many of my informants in taking an active part in such ventures should not, I think, be interpreted as mainly against alcohol per se, but as a way to avoid too close contact with representatives of the public sector. Traders who engage in tourist and leisure projects must, almost daily, rub shoulders with, and depend on, public employees, by working out leases of land, building codes or health regulations. Many of my informants in the bazaar do not like this. Furthermore, most of my trade informants are not advocates of urban life where, among other things, men and women mix for fun and not out of necessity. They, or their out-of-town partners, might enjoy some of the services provided by many modern hotels, cafes and restaurants, but they have no wish to promote them, or the gender-mixed lifestyle associated with them.

The presence of female traders from the former Soviet Union illustrates how a specific local gender ideal is juxtaposed against ideas of foreign women. Between the late 1980s and the mid 1990s Aleppo benefited from a great trade boom with Russia and the former Soviet republics. In many parts of the medina there were signs in Russian to attract the mainly female traders – *rosiaat* – who came to buy large quantities of textiles and cheap clothes, much of which was produced directly for these markets (cf. Rabo 2005: 143). This trade had an important impact on tourist businesses such as (inexpensive) hotels and restaurants. But the presence of these female traders also became locally contested. Along with 'real' traders, so called 'artists' arrived, working in the local nightclubs in the city centre and attracting local and regional 'tourists' to these establishments. Locally, *rosiaat* connoted not only female traders from the former Soviet republics, but also cabaret artists or even prostitutes. Some of my informants told me that the common Aleppo perception, that *rosiaat* traded in sex rather than textiles, made serious female traders turn away from Aleppo. Other informants claimed that trade dwindled because the Syrian state employees made life miserable for these traders. Today, foreign women who are perceived as *rosiaat* still suffer from the taint of being 'artists' rather than 'real traders'.

The presence of *ajaanib* is hence simultaneously attractive and threatening in Aleppo. Such foreigners may give economic benefits to the city, but their presence also reproduces ideas of an amoral West (or Russia) and a virtuous Muslim Orient. These stereotypes are expressed through the bodies of women. Furthermore, by reproducing this dichotomy, differences between local Aleppo Muslims and Christians are also underlined, and even created. Syrian Christians today do not separate women and men in public, and they are often regarded, and regard themselves, as culturally, religiously and socially closer to 'the West', thus reaffirming the division between Christians and Muslims in Aleppo. When traders take a stand *for* gender separation in public space and *against* the serving of alcohol in restaurants, they demonstrate that they are good Muslims. They also underline their difference to local Christians thought to promote 'modern' kinds of tourism.

Competing Opinions on Heritage and Tourism

In 2006 Aleppo was (with Isfahan in Iran) elected *Capital of Islamic Culture* by the Organization of Islamic Countries. People in tourist circles hoped that this would give an enormous boost to the influx of foreigners, especially from Islamic countries, and also increase local awareness about, and interest in, the city's history. But when I visited Aleppo in April 2006, informants and friends with economic interests in tourism or in history and heritage were upset and disgusted.

The year had not taken off as planned at all, and when delegations came, hotels and cultural services were lacking. The city also began major rehabilitation work around the citadel making access to sites of interest quite difficult.[16] Because the start had been so slow, the 2006 Capital of Islamic Culture was prolonged until the end of March 2007. By then Aleppo's city centre was literally stamped with the logo of that event. All shops had to pay a fee and had the official cliché painted on their roll-down iron doors, and all over the city there were huge signs and posters announcing the year.

The work around the citadel is sponsored by the Aga Khan Trust for Culture, and it has caused acid comments among historically interested people outside the medina, just like the rehabilitation of the old Christian quarters.[17] Critics claim that the restoration around the citadel is not based on how the area ever looked. In the view of a well-known Aleppo historian, the dazzling display of black basalt and white marble rather reflects a vision of what it *ought to* have looked in the twelfth century, according to some people in the Aga Khan Trust for Culture, and the Syrian Directorate General of Antiquities and Museum.[18] Another site for local debate is the huge Sheraton Hotel (built with capital mainly from a Kuwaiti investor) which opened in 2007 on part of the 9 ha lot where, as described earlier, houses were demolished in 1979. The presence of this huge hotel in an architectural style decidedly alien to its environment has radically changed the face of that particular corner of the city.

It is not surprising that there are conflicting and competing views on heritage and tourism in Aleppo. The opinions voiced by travel agents, guides, employees in the directorate of tourism, and Aleppo intellectuals concerned with heritage issues, in many ways differ from those of most bazaar traders. The medina as an enchanted heritage site is mainly promoted by the local intelligentsia and people working directly with the project of rehabilitation in the old city. They typically have a professional rather than shop-keeping interest in tourism. For some of them, the coming of foreign – and discerning – tourists is talked about as a means to safeguard the old city against the exploitative interests of the market people. In their view, traders and others in the medina, as well as many public officials, are the worst enemies of the long-term viability of heritage tourism in Aleppo. Since the end of the 1990s, I have frequently been told that traders only think about their short-term gains, and that public officials are corrupt and ready to accept any tourism venture if they can make quick money on it. The different hopes and fears voiced and acted upon, inside and outside the medina, are thus linked to the kinds of tourism and leisure activities, as well as visions for urban development, that the city people have in mind.

Tourists, like the inhabitants of Aleppo, also have diverse interests and tastes, and come for diverse reasons.[19] The regional and the local Syrian tourists – the most economically important – are not 'heritage oriented' in the same way as many *ajaanib* seem to be. When analysing tourism and imaginations of Egypt, Wynn (2007) underlines that Arabs from the Gulf do not travel to Egypt mainly to see the pyramids or any of the other ancient sites. Rather, they come in order to be entertained by way of contemporary popular culture. In a similar vein – according to informants working in hotel and restaurant businesses – local and regional tourists in Aleppo want good service, good food and to have fun. But they typically also visit the citadel and often one or two mosques.

Many of my informants in the medina have themselves been tourists in the region, or in Europe or Asia. When they return they never talk about 'enchanted, unspoilt and authentic heritage sites' they have visited. Not one of the traders in the medina had objections to the changing façade around the citadel. Many also liked the Sheraton Hotel, which people interested in history and heritage issues found so offensively 'un-Aleppian'. One trader said: 'Look. This lot has been derelict and deserted for so long and it is much better to have a grand hotel on it than nothing at all. This will change these quarters which are quite seedy right now.' And from what I hear, a great number of my informants in the bazaar are of the opinion that the gentrification and cleaning-up of many parts of the city is a good sign.

Many Turkish tourists visit Aleppo on their way to Mecca. They do not seem disturbed by the increasingly bricolage character of tourist ventures in the medina. Nor are they 'concerned about seeing behind the scenes in the places they visit' (MacCannell 1989: 96) since they already are – in some way – at home in the medina. For many Turks, a visit to Aleppo is a trip of recognition and helps to reproduce a common Ottoman and Islamic past.

While local and regional tourists have no need to be enchanted and do not look for the exotic or seek the 'authentic Aleppo', they still want a general Old Aleppo ambiance in the medina. In the mid 1990s a Syrian television series called *Khan al hariir* (the silk khan) was broadcast, depicting the economic and political changes of early twentieth century Syria through a story set in the Aleppo medina. This series became very popular in the Middle East and planted specific visual images which made local and regional tourists and visitors know what to expect from Old Aleppo. Thus in a regional and national context Aleppo is, in some ways, packaged and perceived in a different way than other comparable cities.

Ajaanib are not at all as economically important as the regional and local tourists, as discussed earlier. But they have been, and are, important in other ways. Since the inception of European tourism in the region, Aleppo has had its devoted aficionados. Already in the 1960s, certain of the items sold for the internal market in the covered bazaar, such as silk scarves and traditional cotton cloths and clothes, the silver-thread work done by skilled Armenian silversmiths and the famous Aleppo soap, discussed above, were bought by tourists. Many European visitors have developed a long-term interest in the city as artists, writers, researchers or as promoters of Aleppo heritage.[20]

Most *ajaanib* do not want the old city to be too clean, too neat and too obviously staged for tourists. We – *ajaanib* visitors and aficionados – like the Aleppo medina because it is not museum-like and dead, but instead alive. The enchantment of old Aleppo as a site for many Western visitors and tourists hinges on it being a place for continued prosaic interests for those making a living in the bazaar, and those actually living in the medina. In this search for 'enchantment and authenticity',[21] the influence of the urban rehabilitation project -supported also from abroad – and the UNESCO World Heritage List – promoted also by foreigners (see David 1984) – become quite ambiguous. When discussing urban conservation and heritage management in historic towns, Orbasli notes that the label World Heritage 'introduces a new international ownership for heritage, also highlighting a growing inside-outside tension of use and decision-making' (2000: 2).

When I visited Aleppo in April 2008 I was told by an informant interested in heritage issues that Old Damascus might be removed from UNESCO's World Heritage List. She said that in Old Damascus greedy businessmen had opened too many hotels, bars, cafes and restaurants in the old Arabic houses, and that this had changed the character of the heritage site. Old Damascus had been converted into a kitschy new Old Damascus and UNESCO had protested, she said. This informant supported this stand, and stressed that Old Aleppo too would have to be careful in the future.

The Old City of Damascus is still on the UNESCO list. But it is interesting to note that in this instance the conservationist view of this woman, and the views of the self-styled conservative traders in Aleppo, coincide, but from very different positions. While 'conservationists' argue that too many restaurants will threaten the authenticity of the heritage site, 'conservatives' claim that too many restaurants (of the wrong kind) will threatened the moral integrity of Old Aleppo.

Connecting the Local and the Global

This UNESCO rumour also underlines the influence of outside agencies over how 'authentic heritage' should be interpreted and promoted. A number of my medina informants would object to the power of outsiders in their city. Such a rumour about the World Heritage List could quite possibly galvanize some of them into supporting the expansion of what they see as immoral entertainment in the medina. Their ideas about their right to decide about their own quarters, their own bazaar, their own property and their own businesses could, quite possibly, make them act against their ideals of virtue in public space.

It is not surprising, of course, that opinions differ on the future of tourism and leisure activities in the Old City of Aleppo, or that opinions may change over time. Apart from optimistic traders like Khaled and Rami, discussed above, most of my informants in the market still talk about tourism as if they had very little active part in what is going on. Furthermore, my medina informants are weary and suspicious of any project that is likely to make demands on them, and that might block their perceived economic prosperity. The great distrust vis-à-vis the state reinforces ideas that traders should be independent of the state and others. This, in turn, fosters a lack of interest in co-operating with generalized others if they do not see any immediate economic or social gains in that co-operation.

At times traders do criticize their own attitudes and behaviour. Since the late 1990s shops in the medina have opened later and later, for example. Even those parts of the market that cater to the morning trade of visiting villagers remain closed until most of the morning has passed. Many of my informants blame the slack bazaar on the frozen economy, but also admit that a certain type of laziness has emerged in the Aleppo market. According to many traders this laziness is due to the habit of watching satellite television until dawn. In the spring of 2007 there was a small local scandal when a group of important Turkish guests arrived around ten in the morning only to find that everything was closed in the medina. The governor of Aleppo called for a crisis meeting with the Chamber of Commerce, and told traders that things had to change. He demanded that the whole market should be open by nine in the morning. The representatives of the traders agreed to this decree, but after a few weeks shops opened just as late as before this incident.

But many non-traders in Aleppo also underline that while local traders and city and national public officials act as obstacles for the sound development of tourism, the influence of outside factors must not be neglected. Traders in the market often bring this out. They reiterate that Syria is under great pressure and that many *ajaanib* fear travelling to the Middle East. The war in Iraq, the instability in Lebanon and the tensions in Palestinian occupied territories, all combine to keep foreign tourists away, they say. Tourism, and talking through and about tourism, hence simultaneously brings out a complex set of interrelations between economics, politics and morals, where debates about local, national and global issues become interconnected. The ambivalent, evolving and unstable alliances formed between various actors in – and for – the old city of Aleppo illustrate the continued importance of that site.

In the spring of 2007 I saw a group of European tourists walking in the bazaar with earphones. They were, I found out, following a recorded guided tour through the medina. They were cut off from the real noise and bustle of the market, listening to their individual gadgets, and could thus walk in an enchanted, make-believe, world of the bazaar of long ago. Pre-recorded guided tours could be the ideal solution to the question of authenticity and enchantment. They will allow contemporary traders in the market to continue to talk on their mobile telephones about the price of foreign currencies. Traders can plan their next business trips to Italy, China or Indonesia, or they can simply enjoy their part of the market as if it was still their own, blocking out tourists who do not spend money and only use them and their shops as stage-props. At the same time, European tourists can imagine that Aleppo is still part of the Silk Road where, as stated by the Ministry of Tourism 'the traditions of the Arab middle ages do not seem all that remote' (1989: 147).

Notes

1. The site is actually called the 'ancient city of Aleppo' by UNESCO.
2. This article is based on intermittent fieldwork in Aleppo between 1997 and 2007, focusing on how traders view themselves, each other and the Syrian state in a period of economic liberalization. For more details on traders in Aleppo, see Rabo (2005).
3. An analysis of those who work under the tourist gaze is also, as noted by John Urry in chapter 4 of the influential *The Tourist Gaze* (1990), an important task in the study of tourism, leisure and travel.
4. The city is, for example, mentioned in *Macbeth* (Act I, Scene III); '... her husband's to Aleppo gone, master o'th Tiger'.
5. 'Historical tourism' in the Levant/Asia Minor/Near East – linked to trade and leisure – has a long tradition, as underlined by Scarce (2000).
6. The citadel is used as an icon to draw foreign tourists to the city. An advertisement for the Orient Express from 1925 features a painting of the entrance to the Aleppo citadel.
7. For detailed information about this project, see http://gtz-oldaleppo.org
8. According to the GTZ-project, 'The redevelopment measures have already improved conditions for business in the Old City. Tourism in particular has profited, as shown by the many new restaurants and hotels in renovated houses in the Old City.' (http://gtz-oldaleppo.org/rehab/business.php)
9. In the Syrian census, religious or ethnic affiliation is not registered, so percentages are based on educated guesses.
10. *Jdeide* (new) connotes that this is the new area outside the old walled city, where many Christians established themselves in the fifteenth century. *Saliba* connotes the Christian character of the area; *salib* means cross.

11. There is a small but significant move into the medina by well-off Aleppians and foreigners who have bought and restored old Arabic houses for their personal use.

12. Many foreign citizens coming to Syria are probably emigrants coming to visit family and friends. Although they do spend money while on holiday like other tourists, they have not been attracted to Syria because of its ruins, food or tourist ambiance. For many others foreigners Syria is perhaps a transit country.

13. All numbers of foreign entries into Syria come from *Statistical Abstract*, Syria's Central Bureau of Statistics (2007: 262–3).

14. For a brief history and Syrian position on the border conflict with Turkey, see Jörum (2005). For discussion on how Aleppo traders view Turkey, see Rabo (2006).

15. The names of informants are all fictitious.

16. Important and large government, governorate and city bureaucracies are being moved to other parts of the city in order to make way for tourist and leisure investments (and to lessen the congested traffic in the old city).

17. According to the press release after the inauguration of the project in late August 2008, the Aga Khan said: 'We don't do enough to illustrate to the peoples of our world the greatness of Islamic civilisations of cultures of the past' (http://www.akdn.org/press_release.asp?ID=688).

18. In April 2009 I noticed, however, that the work around the citadel is highly appreciated by local and regional visitors. I was also told that the Aga Khan Trust for Culture is promoting Muslim budget tourism by making the former passport and general security building – facing the back of the citadel mound – into a hostel.

19. Typologies and taxonomies of tourists abound, as noted by Crick (1989), but they may fuddle rather than throw light on tourism.

20. The German commitment to the rehabilitation of old Aleppo started with Heinz Gaube and Eugen Wirth (1984), who published a meticulous geographic study of the old city in Aleppo.

21. Enchantment and authenticity are central in many analyses of tourism. In this article I have not discussed how these concepts are constructed among various tourists and non-tourists in Aleppo but I have rather used them as heuristic devises. For illuminating analysis of these concepts see e.g. Selwyn (1996, 2007).

References

Burns, Ross (1994), *Monuments of Syria: An Historical Guide*, London: I.B. Tauris.

Crick, Malcolm (1989), 'Representations of International Tourism in the Social Sciences: Sun, Sex, Sights, Saving, and Servility', *Annual Review of Anthropology*, 18: 3007–44.

David, Jean-Claude (1984), 'Projets d'urbanisme et changements dans les quartier anciens d'Alep', in *Politiques Urbaines dans le Monde Arabe*, Lyon: Maison de l'Orient, pp. 351–65.

Diab, Maysa H. (n.d.), *Guide to Aleppo*.

Gaube, Heinz and Wirth, Eugen (1984), *Aleppo: Historische und geografische Beiträge zur baulichen Gestaltung, zur sozialen Organization und zur wirthschaftlichen Dynamik einer vorderasiatischen Fernhandelsmetropole*, Wiesbaden: Reichert.

Hreitani, Mahmoud and David, Jean-Claude (1986), 'Souks traditionnels et centre moderne. Espaces et pratiques à Alep (1930–1980)', *Bulletin D'Études Orientales*, Institut Francais de Damas, Tome XXXVI, pp. 1–70.

Jörum, Emma (2005), 'The Role of the Origin of the State: Understanding Current Syrian Policy Towards Hatay', in Annika Rabo and Bo Utas (eds), *The Role of the State in West Asia*, Stockholm: Swedish Research Institute in Istanbul, Transactions Vol. 14, pp. 91–103.

MacCannell, Dean (1989), *The Tourist: A New Theory of the Leisure Class*, 2nd edition, New York: Schocken Books.

Maitland, Robert (2006), 'Culture, City Users and the Creation of New Tourism Areas in Cities', in Melanie K. Smith (ed.), *Tourism, Culture, and Regeneration*, Cambridge, MA: CABI Publishing, pp. 25–34.

Ministry of Tourism (1989), *Syria*, Damascus.

Moubayed, Sami (2008), 'Turkish-Syrian relations. The Erdogan legacy', *SETA Policy Brief*, no.25, pp.1–8.

Orbasli, Aylin (2000), *Tourists in Historic Towns: Urban Conservation and Heritage Management*. London: E. & F.N. Spon.

Rabo, Annika (2002), 'Aleppo', in *Encyclopedia of Urban Cultures*, Vol. 1, Danbury, CT: Grolier, pp. 173–80.

Rabo, Annika (2005), *A Shop of One's Own: Independence and Reputation among Traders in Aleppo*, London: I.B. Tauris.

Rabo, Annika (2006), 'Trade across Borders: Views from Aleppo', in Inga Brandell (ed.), *State frontiers: Borders and Boundaries in the Middle East*, London: I.B. Tauris, pp. 53–73.

Scarce, Jennifer (2000), 'Tourism and Material Culture in Turkey', in Michael Hitchcock and Ken Teaugue (eds), *Souvenirs: The Material Culture of Tourism*, Ashgate: Aldershot, pp. 25–35.

Selwyn, Tom (1996), 'Introduction', in Tom Selwyn (ed.), *The Tourist Image: Myths and Myth Making in Tourism*, Chichester: John Wiley & Sons, pp. 1–32.

Selwyn, Tom (2007), 'The Political Economy of Enchantment: Formations in the Anthropology of Tourism', *Suomen Antropologi: Journal of the Finnish Anthropological Society* 32(2): 48–79.

Selwyn, Tom and Boissevain, Jeremy (2004), 'Introduction', in Jeremy Boissevain (ed.), *Contesting the Foreshore. Tourism, Society, and Politics on the Coast*, Amsterdam: Amsterdam University Press, pp. 11–34.

Smith, Melanie. K (2006), 'Introduction', in Melanie K. Smith (ed.), *Tourism, Culture, and Regeneration*, Cambridge, MA: CABI Publishing, pp. xiii–xix.

Syrian Arab Republic, Office of Prime Minister, Central Bureau of Statistics (2007), *Statistical Abstracts*.

Urry, John (1990), *The Tourist Gaze: Leisure and Travel in Contemporary Societies*, London: Sage.

Wynn, L.L (2007), *Pyramids and Nightclubs: A Travel Ethnography of Arab and Western Imaginations of Egypt from King Tut and a Colony of Atlantis to Rumours of sex Orgies, Urban Legends about a Marauding Prince, and Blonde Belly Dancers*, Austin, TX: University of Texas Press.

Internet Sources

http://www.akdn.org/press_release.asp?ID=688)
http://gtz-oldaleppo.org
http://gtz-oldaleppo.org/rehab/business.php.

–7–

Tropical Island Gardens and Formations of Modernity

David Picard

Introduction

This chapter builds upon previous publications on the Indian Ocean island of La Réunion (Picard 2003, 2005, 2008a, 2008b, 2008c, 2009a, 2009b, forthcoming) and has three aims. The first is to describe aspects of the socio-economic transformation of the island from a French colony producing sugar cane, coffee and other agricultural products to a contemporary tourism destination seeking to offer visitors (predominantly from the West) immersion in the tropical gardens and landscapes that constitute central features of the island's tourist offer. The second is discursively to pick out features of recent theoretical discussions about landscape and garden symbolism (Milani 2005, for example) especially those that have discussed the dual role and function of gardens: utilitarian, on the one hand, 'contemplative', on the other. Gardens are indeed good both to grow vegetables in and good to produce the symbolic wherewithal to think the world. Using and developing ideas about the conceptual uses of gardens, therefore, the third aim is to extend the view beyond the boundaries of La Réunion and to consider the place of contemplative gardens in the global scheme of things, and in particular their role in the formation of modernist thought and the development of modern world systems. At this global scale, I will argue that tropical islands are being cultivated as large contemplative gardens to represent – and to touristically evoke and renew – the moral underpinning of modernist conceptions of time and being.

Preparing the Ground

Until the island became a French overseas department in 1946, La Réunion had, as noted above, been dominated by geopolitical and agrarian functions defined by the French colonial centre. As a harbour on the East India trade route, it was a cash crop colony. The postcolonial movement to a tourism economy introduced new value systems based on the aesthetic and symbolic values tourists and tourist developers attached to certain spaces, peoples and their stories. In the terms sketched out above, La Réunion became a large contemplative garden for tourists. In this chapter I follow the metaphor of the island as a garden in the sea and analyse recent tourism-related developments there in terms of ideas of gardens and cultural technologies of gardening that had marked the ambivalent political and representational dialectics between European colonial centres and peripheries since at least the sixteenth century. The symbolic constitution of tropical islands as metaphorical images of paradise, or as material places that have preserved metonymic traces of the original paradise, appear highly influential for the formation of modernist world-views and modern social practices such as tropical island tourism. Spatial policies on the island (as in others in the Indian Ocean) have come to be determined by ideas about gardens such as these.

The anthropology of gardening provides a good conceptual framework to study both the symbolic content and the form of the models underlying these policies, and thus to articulate the significations of tropical islands as gardens-in-the-sea within a wider societal framework of global modernity within what Emmanuel Wallerstein (2004) termed the 'modern world system'. Following the work of Lechner and Boli, who have written about what they term as the 'global polity format' that provides policy-makers with 'a set of cultural rules or scripts specifying how institutions around the world should deal with common problems' (2000: 51), I would suggest that islands such as La Réunion have been, and are being, governed by a polity format in which we may discern a post-nationalist form of governance, containing both symbolic and material aspects, in which larger and more powerful states and global centres 'garden' smaller and less powerful territories. In this particular sense what the story of La Réunion reveals is what I term a 'global gardening state'.

Anthropology of Gardening

Anthropological texts about gardening – Bronislaw Malinowski's (1935) study of gardening among the Trobriand islanders is possibly the most famous one – usually emphasize the symbolic aspects of what Arjun Appadurai (1996) pointedly summarized as 'working the ground'. To all appearances, gardening is in most cases about the organized cultivation of plants, but also other commodities such as salt, fish or domesticated animals within an enclosed space. The word 'garden' originally derives from the Persian *apiri-daeza* ('verger enclosed by a wall') and was adopted by ancient Hebrew as *pardès*, which became *paradeisos* in the early biblical texts (Delumeau 1992: 13) to designate a garden of delightful felicity inside a happy countryside, Eden. As already implied above, most garden theorists distinguish between utilitarian and contemplative gardens (Assunto 1988; Mosser and Teyssot 1991; Milani 2005). The aim of most utilitarian gardens was and still is to produce agricultural outputs, in other words to put seeds into the earth, nurture plants by giving them water, nutrients, sunlight and by keeping flower beds clear of 'bad herbs', hungry birds and other plant-eating creatures. The success of gardening highly depends on the interplay of various 'natural' conditions, for example, propitious weather, abundance of water, absence of parasites. Under any circumstance, the outcome of gardening remains uncertain until the very time the harvest has been brought in. Malinowski and other commentators who have studied garden cultures elsewhere note that, in most cases, the different phases of gardening are accompanied by invocations; spells and rites thought of as to increase or tame chance, to avoid accidents, produce favourable weather conditions and generate rich harvests (Gell 1988). Besides their strictly utilitarian function, gardens are thus always also places to engage with, and thus to bring into being, the supernatural world, the 'forces of nature', the gods and the spirits whose invocation is believed efficient to generate favourable conditions.

In the case of contemplative gardens, the productive agricultural functions disappear to a large degree while the symbolic functions of engaging with, and thus making visible ideas of, the supernatural or otherwise uncertain worlds are elevated as the principal motif. Contemplative gardens in ancient Egypt and China, for example, constituted interstitial spaces to engage the immediate here and now with the uncertain spaces of the past and future, and the geographical spaces that lay beyond the horizon. Through their material displays and ceremonial aspects, they thus made visible highly allegorical images of the world and the nature of its order. They ostentatiously displayed miniature models of the world (Baridon 1998) as a means to socialize the uncertainties of time and space and to symbolically subject them, in most cases, to the will of the powerful. In many cases, these metaphorical qualities were considered a means to invoke the 'power' or 'aura' of the presumed original. Such gardens were used by different ruling classes to convince people about the nature of social order, time and hierarchy. While producing images to think worlds into existence, gardens also create a material space to engage with the world thought of in terms of the very images mediated through the garden. Their metaphorical quality was frequently reinforced by the use of metonymic matter taken, or made believe to be taken, from a presumed authentic original – for example, fauna, flora, artworks, buildings and even humans imported from quasi-mythical places; relics, artforms, texts, leisure practices, etc. associated with meaningful pasts or figures from the past. In other words, contemplative gardens not only formulated mythical worlds able to articulate the uncertainty of time and space into somehow meaningful frameworks, but also provided the garden visitor a privileged access to, a made-belief 'authentic link' (Steward 1993) with, these mythical worlds. In this sense, they were used as what Alfred Gell (1992) suggests should be called a 'technology of enchantment' somehow capable of luring humans into submitting to the rules of often highly unequal social and economic systems.

The format of contemplative gardens was frequently also used by newly emerging ruling classes to contest dominant world visions and forms of governance. A famous European example is related to the emergence of landscape gardens in England, marking the epistemological break in the consideration of nature taking place, which coincidentally accompanied the political emancipation of the English land noblesse during the eighteenth and nineteenth centuries. During the eighteenth century, England had expanded its militaristic and colonial enterprise at the global scale, and it had become a fashion to see it as a 'new Rome'. To articulate their political and economic emancipation, the newly enriched classes of traders and land nobility broke with the formal aesthetic of previous European garden cultures, which had emphasised the principals of symmetry and thus the submission of nature to human order. In a context in which nature was reconsidered as a thing that could be studied and empirically understood, there was no more need for a central fountain as allegory for a life-giving god or god-like king; central features of earlier Arabian and European garden formats that were reconsidered, in the late 18th century, as signs of political despotism (Baridon 1998). English landscape gardens staged asymmetry in nature as a symbol of the human triumph over the supposedly inherent laws of geometry in nature, the ability of history to tame nature and transform it into human formats.

In the same period, forms of gardening also seemed to have entered other political realms not explicitly referred to as gardens. In this sense, similar to contemplative gardens, many planned urban environments, churches, museums, city centres and exhibition sites were made to mediate dominant ideas about political order and the human relation to nature, time and being (Panofsky 1971; Bouquet and Porto 2005). Also, the emergence – or invention – of specific rural (Marie and Viard 1988), mountain (Joutard 1986), seaside (Corbin 1988) and underwater (Picard 2008b) landscapes since the eighteenth century has been considered as a form of *in visu* gardening; of imposing forms and frames of ideal landscape – captured in paintings that circulated among the urban aristocracies and emerging bourgeoisies – upon the land and thus transforming it into picturesque, alpine or bucolic landscapes (Roger 1997). The emergence of environmentalist movements fuelled by the early environmental crisis in the European colonies (Grove 1997: 117) and the creation of nature conservation areas that had become prominent during the nineteenth century seem to translate the concept of contemplative gardening on an even larger scale. Subsequently, throughout the nineteenth and twentieth centuries, vast extensions of land dominated by the Western colonial empires were transformed into nature and game reserves. The ecology of these places was often remodelled according to an idealized vision of endemic wilderness – purified and protected from 'exotic' plants, animals and 'anthropogenic impacts'. Roderick Neumann (2002) demonstrates how humans, especially indigenous peoples, became ontologically and aesthetically assimilated with such imagined gardens of wilderness and were made to contribute to their tourism-related exploitation. Certain groups living inside the newly developed natural parks in the postcolonial contexts of Tanzania were required to remain in a condition considered by the makers of these parks, as 'natural' (among others, the building of concrete houses, the use of cars and modern weaponry was prohibited). More recently, the discourses of sustainable and ecotourism development – emphasizing the use of low-tech infrastructures and local supplies in building material, techniques and produce – seem to have a similar effect of 'cultivating' certain – usually politically marginalized – populations as parts of culturally codified ideal landscapes (Picard 2008a).

Tourism Development and Gardens in La Réunion

Since the 1980s, La Réunion has seen the development of tourism activities that have involved the popularization of the seaside. This has created new social centres along the coasts and sandy beaches, hitherto symbolically and socially marginal spaces occupied by the poorest populations (Picard 2005). At the same time, other formerly marginalized spaces – abrupt landscapes, valleys, volcanoes and mountainous regions – were discovered as new economic resources catering for the touristic quest for the bucolic and picturesque. The consequent competition over these newly priced lands led to, sometimes, violent conflicts between tourism promoters, environmental conservation agencies and local populations. With tourism and the natural conservation lobbies becoming politically more influential during the 1980s and 1990s, local populations, especially fishing people, were progressively excluded from their resource bases and, tagged as poachers, their activities were eventually criminalized. More industrial, capital-intensive offshore fishing and tourism related game-fishing activities replaced much of the traditional fishing. For parts of the population, the new tourism sectors provided opportunities for alternative livelihoods, the building of new professional capacity and new supply markets for local produce. For instance, all local entrepreneurs who had started tourist businesses in La Réunion's valley of Salazie during the late 1990s had effectively learnt their job through previous employments in tourism .and hospitality infrastructures run by French mainlanders.

Tourism subsequently introduced a new value system in which the generation of wealth was no longer related to the fertility of grounds, the productivity of labour or the abundance of natural resources, but to the aesthetic and symbolic values tourists attach to specific landscapes, heritages, folklore and traditional cultural activities. In this new context, land – transformed into landscape – remained the principal economic resource. While good tourism transport and accommodation infrastructures were a necessary condition for tourism development, they did not, or only in marginal cases, represent the main motive of the tourist journey. The touristic appreciation of landscapes – beaches, mountains, villages, etc. – was at the core of the tourism economy. As in most other tropical islands, public tourism development policies in La Réunion included specific urbanistic regulations, which were widely in accordance to the touristic imagery of tropicality. They also included public behaviour change campaigns to ease social interactions between tourists and local populations, the regulation or suppression of informal economic sectors, stricter waste and environmental management protocols, the cleaning of public beaches, natural and urban spaces, and the relocation, or screening off, of poor populations. Through these policies, selected bits of everyday life were reframed and resignified, becoming the means to participate in the social realms of the tourism contact zone. The act of 'working the ground' was no longer a means to generate produce for a global cash crop economy, but a symbolic performance produced in the eye of international tourism audiences. It appeared to formalize a new technology of gardening less interested in the agronomic value of the fruits of the land than in some kind of delight-value associated with the act and outputs of their cultivation. What is this value?

Hotel Gardens

To respond to this question, it would make sense to start the study by focusing on perhaps the 'purest' form of touristic space, the highly controlled space of hotels most closely designed in line with the ideal forms of tourism related tropical insularity. The typical architecture of tropical island hotels relied, since the 1970s, on a model based on a concrete complex in the form of a half circle open to the sea and beach. In La Réunion, several of these types of hotels were built along the sandy west coast during the 1970s. The space inside these complexes invariably included a swimming pool inside a garden with restaurants, bars, shops and diverse entertainment spaces. The gardens of these hotels also staged a lush nature with different types of palm trees, tropical flowers, grassland and access to the beach. Freed from the burdens of actually organizing their time or daily logistics, the tourists were being catered for; they were free to play, read, talk, swim, eat, drink, sleep or just gaze at the reflection of the sun in the water. In a way, this type of hotel space combined in one place the service environment provided by an early European mansion, the Fordist philosophy of a tin can factory and the aesthetic of the Garden of Eden. The hospitality management systems of these tourist hotels seemed to be based on the workings of European aristocratic households, with a housekeeper responsible for rooms, bed linen and reception, a chef de salle responsible for the restaurant, a chief cook responsible for the food, a supply manager controlling stocks and ordering supplies, an atelier and garden service, a human resource director, etc. The production processes in hotels were very much based on a Fordist logic of mass production; hotel rooms were highly standardized to generate economies of scale as a result of more efficient maintenance procedures and standard quality supplied to tour operators. Their features were usually reduced to a large clean bed, a small bathroom, a small table, a small fridge, a small cupboard and a small television. They thus concentrated most of the minimal essential functions of a standard European household in a space of usually less than 20 sq. m. Hotel gardens complemented this approach of condensing social life to essential functions. Through their planted vegetation, different types of pools, cocktail bars, and a minimalist dress code, they lent themselves as allegorical fantasy world of an imagined original condition of being naked in a happy garden of delight. This environment was further refined by the hotels' 'front-office' staff, especially hotel staff employed to take on the role of both 'friends' and facilitators – bringing tourists together, creating a 'friendly' atmosphere and coaching them through the daily programmes. Most hotel directors I interviewed during fieldwork in La Réunion, Indian Ocean, were quite explicit about the role of these staff to make tourists ('clients') happy and keep them inside the hotel, so that they drank at the bar and ate in the restaurant. In some cases, hotel staff did not have to pay for their own bar consumption as long as they made their tourist 'friends' drink.[1]

More recent constructions of upmarket hotel complexes and the renovation of hotels built during the 1970s and 1980s are indicative of a certain ideological shift underlying the design and functions of the hotel space. This shift can be observed in La Réunion, but equally in other tropical islands in the Western Indian Ocean – Zanzibar, Seychelles, Mauritius – and along the East African shore. The classically very compact spatial configurations appear opened up, usually adapting a more fragmented pattern of bungalows, bar huts and fantasy swimming pools. New materials were introduced, especially wood and 'natural' stone, replacing, or screening off, the concrete fashionable during the 1970s and 1980s. Moreover, many upmarket island hotels started to integrate spatial configurations and decorations that were to evoke a new age 'feng shui' style – based on 'oriental' references such as flat water pools, open spaces, organic building material and soft colours. Most hotels also started to offer body and spa treatments and emphasized, through different forms of internal marketing, their efforts to preserve the environment, to reduce water consumption and to treat waste generated by tourism activities. Some top-end 'boutique hotels' were built around the concept of sophisticated 'eco-friendly', low-tech water and energy treatment technologies. Many new hotels also included elements of direct or indirect 'community participation' – through the marketing of 'typical' local food, references to local architecture and folklore, the offer of local language courses and the participation of tourists in mainly hotel controlled 'community develop-ment programmes'. From this point in time, it appears that new age spiritual values, forms of 'community involvement' and environmental protection have become part of the fantasy world brought alive through the hotel space. They have become products for tourist consumption (Picard 2008a).

Designing La Réunion as a Tourism Territory

These recent shifts in the design of hotels seem akin to those that underlie the environmental design of publicly accessible tourist sites and wider regional or national territories, in La Réunion and other tropical places. New tourist fashions – 'integrated tourism', 'ecotourism', 'ethno-tourism', 'cultural tourism' – seem here to explain a reconsideration of destinations, no longer thought of merely in terms of the highly controlled sites of tourism mass production – hotels, beaches, museums and historical urban centres – but as wider inhabited territories that can be experienced and consumed. Reacting to these shifting desires underlying tourism demand, the regional and national development plans of most touristically developed island states started to suggest an 'integrated' spatial redevelopment of the island territories. The production of these plans usually resulted from a consultation process between different government ministries and agencies, economic and political stakeholders and development experts. This process a priori aimed at the integration of different constraints and policy priorities into a coherent development plan. It also reflected the frictions and asymmetrical power relations between different lobby groups, but also between different government services and their respective policy agendas and clienteles. Paradoxically, despite these context-related differences, the model underlying most of the finally approved and implemented tourism development plans seems relatively consistent. It seems to result from a commonly applied technique of structuring the touristic space of tropical islands by formulating spatial axes which connect different types of 'development clusters': white-sand beach and beach hotel clusters; historical, cultural and urban site clusters; natural site and wilderness clusters; endemic human settlement clusters; and logistic clusters allowing tourists to enter and leave the holiday realm.

Following this technique of 'axing' and 'clustering', many inhabited places of touristically developed islands were reformulated and reconfigured in terms of the functional needs of the tourism economy. In La Réunion, the inner spaces of the island became ascribed as 'inner sanctums', as 'places of origin' where 'pure' water streams out of the earth and where 'endemic populations' have preserved a form of 'original authenticity'. These 'inner' places were made accessible through roads and viewpoints that directed the gaze in a certain way. Similar to what happened in many other tropical islands, they were made amenable to tourist experience as a result of specific development actions including subsidies to rural guesthouses, the preservation of rural activities and lifestyles, local incentives for the 'rediscovery' of ancient techniques and recipes, etc. These 'inner sanctums' were in most cases contrasted with the 'outer limits' of the island spaces, the horizon over the sea and the starlit sky. These 'outer limits' too were made amenable to tourist experience through the creation and cleaning up of beaches, the plantation of palm trees, the building of beach huts, the eviction of fishing populations from beaches and the policing of the informal tourism sector. In between these two poles, tourism planners usually situated a mediating zone typically constituted by 'multicultural' settings – colonial harbour towns, multicoloured markets and memory and cultural heritage sites.

Gardening as Local Modernity

During the early 1990s, almost simultaneously with the emergence of mass tourism in La Réunion and the public recognition of tourism as a new livelihood for the islanders, new types of festivals emerged within the island space. Primarily organized by, and destined for, local audiences, these were constituted around various forms of 'local heritage', formulated as a 'primordial value' of the island's identity and being. Analogous to the festivals of former agrarian or fishing societies whose folklore was often built on their respective main produce or activities, these festivals seem to have elevated and celebrated tourism related sign-resources as existential values for the collective being in the world (Picard and Robinson 2006). As in other islands (Picard 1992; Bruner 2005), the initially exoticizing signs associated with the island were 'transculturated' (Pratt 1992; Ortiz 1995) into auto-ethnographic images and stories. Through these transcult-uration processes, the island nation fashioned itself, in the words of Paul Vergès, historical figure of the island's autonomy struggle, who was elected president of the island's regional council during the late 1990s, as a 'model for the world' (MCUR 2008). While being a model for the world became a new symbolic and economic resource, the act of gardening this new 'resource' was elevated as a new means of social participation – both medium of, and symbol for, the exchange with, and the participation in, a wider world outside (Doumenge 1984; Picard 2003, forthcoming).

In 1999, Paul Vergès announced the creation of a new museum, the *Maison des Civilisations et de l'Unité Réunionnaise* (House of the Civilizations and Réunion Unity). In the preamble to the project outline (MCUR 2008), he defined what he called the historical 'miracle' of La Réunion. 'If we can demonstrate,' he explained, 'that our cultural diversity strengthens our society instead of pulling it apart, that it is a binding force for dialogue and cohesion, that we respect others as equals and acknowledge the originality of each respective contribution, then we can talk of a Réunion miracle: we will have managed to creolise all the incoming values without being assimilated by any one of them, whereas the general tendency is to try to assimilate groups different from one's own and make them fit into one's own cultural values.' 'I think that this is Réunion Island's contribution to the world', he concluded. 'Faced with the impending conflicts that the Indian Ocean region will witness tomorrow, unity is our most precious asset.' From this point of view, the island's capacity to demonstrate 'unity' appeared elevated as a specific value that would determine the future terms of the island's participation in the wider world; La Réunion was to become a sign-world within a new form of global cultural economy. The relationships within this new economy seem to invert the colonial logic of centres and peripheries. Everyday life in the island was resignified in terms of being a 'model for the world', playing out ideas of diversity and transcultural living together. This project, which appears able to have a major impact on the formation of the islanders' self-understanding in the next decades, seems to pick up and further earlier, European Renaissance social utopias of ideal island societies. In the current context, the model underlying these utopias hence seems not only formative for modern tourism practice and heritage conservation polity, but also as a means for the economic and symbolic self-fashioning of tropical island nations.

At the same time, this dynamic implies major ambivalences, in particular with regard to the island as a place *in* history, a place where people actually live and possibly contest the idealized vision of 'unity in diversity' – or unity in creolization – projected upon them. Like many other places of utopian projection, La Réunion is not, or not for everyone, a place of earthly delights (Picard 2008c). At the end of the 1990s, almost 40 per cent of the active population were jobless while at the same time seeking to participate in the emerging realm of a local 'modernity' especially through mass consumption. In this context, it appears uneasy to convince the Réunions to source personal pride and identity in a socially performed role of being a model of unity for the world. Life and love do indeed not care much about ideologies, and evolve, in Jorge Luis Borges's words (2004: 20), in an eternal present. They permanently disrupt our carefully nurtured ideals of transhumance and continuity.

Tropical Gardens and Tourism

The analysis of Western tour operators' travel catalogues indicates the presence of a largely generic tropical island imagery and imaginary in the Western world. Whether the island destinations are situated in the Caribbean, the Indian Ocean or the South Pacific, the sign system employed to advertise them remains significantly stable. Representations of tropical islands appear to be built upon three complementary often interconnected sign-worlds, which are structurally similar, once again, to the spatial models implemented as part of the development programmes discussed earlier. They are constituted by (1) a light flooded white-sand, blue-water, blue-sky beach, hotel and sailing boat world; (2) a flowery green-mountain, lush-nature, dramatic-waterfall island inside world; and (3) a pretty-Métis-girl-and-boy, costumed-local-musician, colourful-fruit-market world. Islands appear to become highly symbolic microscopic images of a wider world and being in the world. Through their arrangements, they appear to evoke a specific philosophy of time and being. The modernist nostalgia of a homogeneous, pure and innocent *ur*-condition appears projected into the specific 'inner' space of the island, embodied through the classical image of springs and fountains in the island's centre. It is dissolved through the optimistic model of the Creole, invoked through people and stories situated in the coastal areas. The tropical island thus can be perceived as an allegory of a morally charged idea of time, with a 'pure' and 'authentic' condition of the past situated in the islands' inside, leading (following the metaphorical flow of the rivers) to a heterogeneous, contradictory historical condition of the present (found in the melanges and clashes of life in the coastal sites), ultimately losing itself in a somehow celestial, undetermined anticipation of the future (following the gaze toward the sunset over the horizon, the indefinite sea, the sky). If we consider the contrast between touristic day and night activities and the semiotics of the spaces in which these take place, we are not far from discovering an erotic anti-image of this celestial condition of the future, in the form of lustrous feasts, alcoholic excess, sexual licence and metaphorical devils dancing around the blaze of the beach bonfire arranged by the hotel staff.

The idea of tropical islands being places to symbolize the separations and order of the social world is not a recent phenomenon, but has been observed in earlier times and places, for example, the very common idea of Happy Islands entailing the world in miniature (Delumeau 1992), the figurations of tropical islands as allegories of the world in eighteenth-century fantastic travel writing (Grove 1997: 9; Racault 2003). The transformation of tropical islands into a global art form appears to stem less from the actual grounds in which this transformation took place, in the tropical islands, but from certain centres in which this art form has developed. In his critical analysis of modernist ideologies of the salvage paradigm, James Clifford (1989) describes how different Western 'poetics of culture' – a term introduced by Stephen Greenblatt (2005: 5) – have fashioned 'cultural others' in a largely allegorical way, to make their imagined cultural selves plausible. As a result of the repetition of these poetics and their institution to govern social relations during the colonial period, he suggests, the world has become a global social theatre playing out a story of modernity, which was scripted in the European centres since the Renaissance. Stephen Greenblatt (2005: 9) demonstrates how, during that epoch, the most influential European poets and philosophical writers mobilized tropes of the alien, strange or hostile (as examples, he mentions, the heretic, savage, witch, adulteress, traitor, Antichrist) to fashion themselves as morally superior and legitimate their enterprise to submit the 'threatening other'. In the context of such a global social theatre, tropical islands seem to play a specific role. As the travel catalogue images indicate, they do not appear as threatening others, but rather embody some essential dreams, desires and enchantments embedded in the Western imaginaries which can be invoked through tourism.

In this sense, authors including Nelson Graburn (1977, 1983, 1989) and Victor and Edith Turner (1973, 1978) have analysed tourism in terms of an alternate movement marking social life in the modern world, a festive break between societal life cycles that invites the travelling tourists to recreate the symbolic foundations of social life. Eric Cohen (1992, 2004) explains tourism as a cyclical form of recreation whose motivations he situates between two poles, the quest for spiritual or allegorical centres on the one hand, and the search for social and physical recreation on the other. For Dean MacCannell, tourism is part of the ideological fabric of modernity and fundamentally motivated by a symbolic quest for authenticity (1976), which he sees deeply rooted in the modernist ideology of time and, concurrently, in the nostalgia of a lost primordial condition, a lost Eden. According to MacCannell, this quest is achieved through 'systems of attraction' in the tourist destinations, more or less stage-managed sign-worlds produced within the material and social contact zones of tourism production and consumption. The sign-worlds of tropical islands, mediated through tour operator travel brochures and the production of touristic spaces, appear to allude to specific ideas of a pre-modern condition of innocence, abundance and natural purity. They appear to evoke, or promise tourists the possibility of evoking, a symbolic centre in time; a primordial authentic condition accessed via the journey. MacCannell's theory of systems of attraction cannot only be applied to describe the materially or socially located realms of tourism, but equally the very time frame of the journey. At the end of their ten-day holiday, tropical island tourists have to return home. The very movement of the journey to, through and from tropical islands thus generates a semiotic of time that can be understood in a wider allegorical sense; an evocation of the departures and ultimate returns that mark life, the imagined places of origin and future that embed these departures and returns in forms of symbolic continuity (Eliade 1957; Bataille 2006). Following the earlier arguments by Victor and Edith Turner, Nelson Graburn, and Dean MacCannell, tropical island tourism can be understood as a particular type of modern 'ritual process' marked by a spatially enacted festive rhythm of departure, liminality and return (Robinson and Picard 2009).

From this point of view, tropical islands appear indeed as 'large gardens' allowing the modern tourist-subject to recognize and remediate different facets of their Selves. In particular, they seem to work as allegorical places to connect to a specific cultural logic of existential time moving from a primordial condition of innocence toward a historic condition of social melange. This particular conception of time may well find an *ur*-model in the Garden of Eden and its consequent loss described in the book of Genesis. Adam and Eve, the characters of an allegorical golden age, initiate time by committing the first crime. Harmony is broken, languages and diversity emerge, and all beings live with the burdens of earthly existence. On a structural level, their story seems to remain fundamental to the common modernist thinking of time and being, and the allegories through which this is renewed as part of the tourist journey. Yet, they only mark a departure, a historical beginning, while the image of the Creole which forms an important part of tropical island tourism experience suggests an optimistic model for thinking separations and fragmentations of contemporary social life, and of the future.

Tropical Island Tourism as Part of the Modern World System

In the early days of travel, pleasure tourism was largely the domain of the leisure classes. Thomas Cook and the various technologies associated with his company (from railway transport to travellers cheques) laid the ground for the mass tourism we have become familiar with a century or so after him. With mass travel we are arguably in an age of what Urry (1995) has termed aesthetic cosmopolitanism. During the 1980s and especially the 1990s, the global liberalization of air travel and the huge advances in logistic technologies, achieved among others through the use of electronic information technologies and the Internet, have led to further significant decreases in the costs of long haul travel. Simultaneously, since the early 1980s, international hotel chains started massively to increase their bed capacities in tropical island countries and tropical island tourism became a mass phenomenon.

These economic developments did not happen spontaneously, but were embedded in international polity frameworks, which had considered tourism as an economic development tool for tropical countries as early as in the 1930s (Lanfant 1995). Since the 1960s, international institutions (the World Bank, the World Tourism Organization, UNESCO) actively supported the development of tourism master plans in many developing countries, for example, Tunisia, Bali, Senegal, Mauritius, the Dominican Republic. While tourism was considered a means to economic development in countries seen as having few alternative options (de Kadt 1979), the ambivalence of its 'products' immediately generated controversies among the development community, the cultural elites of these countries and the tourist audiences themselves. Marie-Francoise Lanfant and Nelson Graburn (1992) explain this ambivalence by the tension between two concurrent but respectively – seemingly – exclusive modernist dynamics, one of advocating progress through economic development and one of protecting the idealized landscapes and 'authentic cultures' of tropical islands through conservation polity. In other words, tourism development was caught up in one of the most striking contradictions of modernist thinking – on the one hand, it was considered a pragmatic economic alternative, on the other hand, a spiritually loaded 'economy of the alternative' (Lanfant and Graburn 1992; Wheeller 1993).

This ambivalence was partly solved through the development of international heritage polities, reconsidering 'culture' and 'nature' as 'resources' of a both transnational and transgenerational symbolic economy; as resources to unite humanity through a common world-historical narrative of humanistic development, cultural refinement and diversity, and the embodiment of this narrative in the material culture of initially mainly historical sites, to be 'preserved for future generations'. When international organizations advocating the conservation of heritage were created (such as UNESCO in 1945), the concept of heritage was then not new. It had been mobilized and legally formalized in France, England and the United States two centuries earlier, in particular as a means to display, historically ground and materially embody (among others in public gardens and landscapes) the public stories of kingdoms and emerging nation-states (Héritier 2003). Concurrently, during the post-war period, the concept of heritage was well in place as a tool to imagine and define specific communities through historical continuity (Anderson 1991). UNESCO in particular mobilized this initially nationalist concept to formulate and promote a universal humanity, a world-nation with a world history embodied in a selection of world heritages, which were to belong to, and make visible the story of, this 'universal' humanity.[2] At the same time, 'heritage' also became an economic and symbolic resource mobilized in the – often controversial – processes of nation-building and modernization which marked the postcolonial or post-war contexts in places as varied as Bali (Picard 1992), Kenya (Bruner 2001), Sri Lanka (Crick 1994), Spain (Greenwood 1989), Turkey (Tucker 2002), Indonesia (Adams 2006), Japan (Hiwasaki 2000), the Philippines (Ness 2003) or Mexico (Van der Berghe 1994). From this point of observation, tourism and heritage need to be considered as different facets of a same highly political phenomenon; a more or less disciplined economy of gazes between what is given to be seen and who it is given to be seen (Lanfant 2009). In other words, tourism development becomes a technology not only providing economic growth, as many would like to make us believe, but also of dramatizing a perceived essence of social life and the boundaries of communal life – be they 'national', 'ethnic', 'class', 'gender', 'age', 'raeggaeton', etc. – in the absorbing eyes of tourist audiences. This technology is played out at a global level, co-constituting centres and peripheries within a common social and symbolic framework.

Most authors interested in tropical islands have focused their attention on the political economy of material commodities produced within the realms of global capitalism (Mintz 1986; Ortiz 1995). The historical enchantments of tropical islands as paradises were often approached in terms of a 'symbolic superstructure', a moral aesthetic legitimizing their exploitation and making hierarchies between centres and peripheries appear normal and natural (Ortiz 1995; Hall 1997; Said 2003). Yet, it is not clear whether there is any connection at all between the political economy of material commodities in tropical islands that developed since the sixteenth century and the far older, pre-Christian imaginaries of tropical island paradises. Both phenomena seem parallel in register rather than conspiratorially intertwined, with only occasional (as opposed to systemic) connections. In this sense, the formation of tropical islands as large gardens of delight seems indicative for a yet so far little discussed facet of global modernity, a form of contemplative gardening at the global scale that, I believe, requires the formulation of new ways of thinking. It seems to imply a different form of world order and world society in which tropical islands and other tourism-related spaces are cultivated and touristically accessed in terms of contemplative gardens. These new ways of thinking require a return to the basic conceptual premises surrounding the cultural practice of gardening.

Towards a Global Gardening State?

Since the late nineteenth century, the technology of gardening had also been translated into the language and thinking of public policy-making. Zygmunt Bauman (1998) powerfully demonstrates how the idea of a 'gardening state' had been applied to govern human society and had contributed to the emergence of deeply racist polity formats during the early twentieth century. He shows how a new concept of gardening based on elements of nature romanticism and Darwinist evolution theory had been mobilized to 'cultivate' the human like a gardener would cultivate flowers, by 'purifying' human 'races' through the control of genetic reproduction, by creating human species according to the racist aesthetics of an ideal nature. During the second half of the twentieth century, considering the horrors of the holocaust, of repeated 'ethnic cleansings' and racial segregation and apartheid, strong opposition developed against the concept of a 'gardening state' and its objective to cultivate humans according to racial ideals. While the continued struggles against racial discrimination provoked the progressive abolition of segregation and apartheid regimes, the fundamental principles of the gardening state appear, however, to have remained, shifting into new contexts and embracing new social scales. Accordingly, during the 1980s, some landscape architects and ecologists claimed – quasi paraphrasing the book of Genesis – that the planet earth constituted the ultimate garden that humanity had an obligation to cultivate (Berque 1995, 1996; Mosser 1999). In this context, the idea of cultivating the planet, both in terms of a utilitarian and a contemplative garden, seems to have led to a new form of global governance. The specific cultivation of places that in their structure resemble those of a 'contemplative garden' – museums, heritage sites, historic city centres, landscapes, tropical islands – seems to have become subjected here to post-national forms of political authority or 'governance states' (Duffy 2002; Tsing 2005). In many cases, the cultivation of 'nature conservation', 'cultural heritage' or 'development' started to constitute in itself a new form of governance (Mosse 2005; West 2006). Similarly, people in many tropical islands have started to cultivate Western representations of tropicality to make sense of their own social reality and participation within global society. Paradoxically, the adoption of the different sign-worlds constituting this tropical insularity becomes here a means and sign of local modernity.

The model underlying these transformations appears largely independent from the social realities that mark social life in the very different island states. But there is a clearly discernible generic pattern that emphasizes 'pristine nature', 'eternal sunshine', 'pure water', 'clear blue skies' and 'beautiful islands indigenes'. It seems that this model finds a nucleus in the age-old trope of an eternal garden invoking and thus bringing alive images of a primordial time and nature. This phenomenon is not new but, as the environmental historian Robert Grove (1997) has shown, has been formative for modernity and modernist thinking themselves. In various historical contexts, tropical islands have provided a visual and symbolic theme to represent and to nurture ideas of those mythical places that have helped humanity to think time beyond death, myriad variations of imagined gardens of delight, heavens, islands of the dead, and other places of origin and eternal return that have been studied by anthropologists around the world. The modernist ambiguity with regard to 'nature' both as a nostalgic past and as a condition to be overcome thanks to rational science and humanistic morals can be seen here as a variation playing out this same theme. The contradictory, yet complementary narratives of a utopian return to nature and of the unavoidable forces of history that so much mark modernist thinking seem to source their symbolic underpinning from pre-modern representations. The innovation brought about by modernist thinking seems to lie in the idea and quasi-religious doctrine that the rational study of nature would ultimately lead to Enlightenment and God (Habermas 1985; McGuigan 1999).

This point is important for a more general understanding of tropical island tourism and the transformations many tropical islands underwent as a result of mass tourism development. The actions by various transnational institutions seem to generate them in terms of a theatrical framework that allows tourists to invoke the mythical realm of an unconditional and a-historical nature and, from there, symbolically to reassert the historical logic of their individual and collective lives. In this sense, tourism development in tropical islands appears governed by post-nationalist forms of stateliness – I propose to call this a global gardening state – that impose certain forms of participation and social identity upon island societies. I suggest that this form of post-nationalist governance has today been relocated in different multilateral networks, especially the bodies of international organizations whose programmes and normative actions are largely dominated by the cultural, political and economic agendas of the countries of the North.

Conclusion

Ideas about imaginary gardens have been a familiar feature of human consciousness since the earliest days. Innovations in transport, logistic technologies and economic growth in the West, however, have transformed tropical island gardens from being part of the repertoire of Western dream worlds to being accessible holiday destinations. As I indicated above, the spatial and symbolic reformation of islands such as La Réunion in accordance with international development guidelines designed to ensure their conformity with widely held ideas of what a tropical island should look like (Lanfant and Graburn 1992) has had profound local consequences. The islands have, in effect, become self-referential gardens staging idealized visions of their own tropicalism, rooted as this is in pre-modern and early-modern visions of island paradises. As we have seen above, historians such as Grove (1997) and Delumeau (1992) have argued that these visions have come to define and delimit the boundaries and essence of the modernist being. Tropicalism and modernism thus appear as antipodal entities within a common symbolic system (see also Fabian 1983; Said 2003). Part of the argument of this paper has been that the tourist- and modernist-led spatial reformation of islands such as La Réunion has made the Spinning Jenny, the steam engine, the idea of empire and imperial domination, the World Wide Web, and the tropical garden appear all of a piece.

Notes

1. These observations were made during fieldwork in La Réunion, which involved among others the drawing of detailed architectural plans of all coastal hotels and participant observation as a member of the hotel animation teams of two beach resorts.
2. The organization engaged in several projects aiming at the preservation of 'cultural heritage of outstanding value', according to its own criteria. The first major project consisted of the relocation of the Abu Simbel temple in Egypt, threatened by the construction of the Aswan dam. With the financial support of all major Western nations, including those of Eastern Europe, the

Abu Simbel temple was cut into pieces and relocated to a higher location. Abu Simbel became a symbol for the will of this international community of experts to 'preserve' the remnants of 'past civilizations', with or without the agreement of national governments. In the following years, architectural remnants of various other 'civilizations' or 'high cultures' were preserved. The organization's global involvement in the specific field of heritage preservation (UNESCO works also in many other fields) was legally formalized through the 1972 *Convention Concerning the Protection of the World Cultural and Natural Heritage*. The principles of this convention, especially the understanding of the concept of heritage, were heavily influenced by French and Anglo-Saxon heritage polities that had developed since the early nineteenth century.

References

Adams, K.M. (2006), *Art as Politics: Recrafting Identities, Tourism, and Power in Tana Toraja, Indonesia*, Honolulu: University of Hawai'i Press.

Anderson, B. (1991 [1983]), *Imagined Communities: Reflections on the Origin and Spread of Nationalism*, London and New York: Verso.

Appadurai A. (1996), 'The Production of Locality', in his *Modernity at Large*, Minneapolis: University of Minnesota Press, pp. 178–200.

Assunto R. (1988), *Ontologia e teleologia del giardino*, Milan: Guerini.

Baridon M. (1998), *Les jardins. Paysagistes, jardiniers, poètes*, Paris: Laffont.

Bataille, G. (2006), *Eroticism*, tr. Mary Dalwood, London: Marion Boyars.

Bauman, Z. (1998), 'The Scandal of Ambivalence', in his *Modernity and Ambivalence*, Cambridge: Polity, pp. 18–52.

Berque A. (1996), *Etre humains sur la Terre. Principes d'éthique de l'écoumène*, Paris: Gallimard

Berque, A. (1995), *Les Raisons du paysage. De la Chine antique aux environnements de synthèse*, Paris: Hazan.

Borges, J.L. (2004 [1949]), 'Tlön Uqbar Orbis Tertius', in his *Fictions*, tr. R. Caillois, Paris: Gallimard, pp. 11–31.

Bouquet, M. and Porto, N. (2005), 'Introduction', in their (eds), *Science, Magic and Religion: The Ritual Process of Museum Magic*, Oxford: Berghahn, pp. 1–28.

Bruner, E.M. (2001), 'The Maasai and the Lion King: Authenticity, Nationalism, and Globalization in African Tourism', *American Ethnologist*, 28(4): 881–908.

Bruner, E.M. (2005), 'The Balinese Borderzone', in his *Culture on tour: Ethnographies of travel*, Chicago: University of Chicago Press, pp. 191–210.

Clifford, J. (1989), 'The Others: Beyond the 'salvage' paradigm', *Third Text: Third World Perspectives on Contemporary Art and Culture* 6: 73–77.

Cohen, E. (1992), 'Pilgrimage and Tourism: Convergence and Divergence', in A. Morinis (ed.), *Sacred Journeys: Anthropology of Pilgrimage*, Westport, CT: Greenwood Press, pp. 47–61.

Cohen, E. (2004), 'Tourism and Religion: A Comparative Perspective', in his *Contemporary Tourism: Diversity and Change*, London: Elsevier, pp. 147–58.

Corbin A. (1988), *Le Territoire du vide. L'Occident et le désir du rivage. 1750– 1840*, Paris: Aubier.

Crick, M. (1994), *Resplendent Sites, Discordant Voices: Sri Lankans and International Tourism,* Camberwell, Victoria, Australia: Harwood.

de Kadt, E. (1979), *Tourism: Passport to Development*, New York: Oxford University Press (for UNESCO/World Bank).

Delumeau, J. (1992), *Une histoire du paradis*, Paris: Fayard.

Doumenge, J.-P. (1984), 'Enjeu géopolitique et intérêt scientifique des espaces insulaires', in *Nature et Hommes dans les îles tropicales*, Talence: CEGET-CRET, pp. 1–6.

Duffy, R. (2002), *A trip too far: Ecotourism, politics, and exploitation*, London: Earthscan.

Eliade, M. (1957), *Mythes, rêves et mystères*, Paris: Gallimard.

Fabian, J. (1983), *Time and the Other: How Anthropology Makes Its Object*, New York: Columbia University Press.

Gell, A. (1988), 'Technology and Magic', *Anthropology Today*, 4(2): 6–9.

Gell, A. (1992), 'Technology of Enchantment, Enchantment of Technology', in J. Coote and A. Shelton (eds), *Anthropology, Art, Aesthetics*, Oxford: Oxford University Press, pp. 40–63.

Graburn, N.H. (1977), 'Tourism: The Sacred Journey', in V. Smith (ed.), *Hosts and Guests: The Anthropology of Tourism*, Philadelphia: University of Pennsylvania Press, pp. 17–31.

Graburn, N.H. (1983), *To Pray, Pay and Play: The Cultural Structure of Japanese Domestic Tourism*, Aix-en-Provence: Centre des Hautes Etudes Touristiques.

Graburn N.H. (1989), 'Tourism: The Sacred Journey', in V. Smith (ed.), *Hosts and Guests*, 2nd edition, Philadelphia: University of Pennsylvania Press, pp. 22–36.

Greenblatt, S. (2005 [1980]), *Renaissance Self-Fashioning: From More to Shakespeare*, Chicago: University of Chicago Press.

Greenwood, D.J. (1989), 'Culture by the Pound. An Anthropological Perspective on Tourism as Cultural Commoditization', in V.L. Smith (ed.), *Hosts and Guests*, 2nd edition, Philadelphia: University of Pennsylvania Press, pp. 171–86.

Grove, R. (1995), *Green Imperialism: Colonial Expansion, Tropical Island Edens, and the Origins of Environmentalism, 1600–1860*, Studies in environment and history, Cambridge: Cambridge University Press.

Habermas, J. (1985), 'Modernity: An Incomplete Project', in H. Foster (ed.), *Postmodern Culture*, London: Pluto, pp. 3–15.

Hall, S. (1997), *Representation: Cultural Representations and Signifying Practices*, London: Sage and Open University.

Héritier, A. (2003), *Genèse de la notion de patrimoine culturel: 1750–1816*, Paris: L' Harmattan.

Hiwasaki, L. (2000), 'Ethnic Tourism in Hokkaido and the Shaping of Ainu Identity', *Pacific Affairs* 73(3): 393–412.

Joutard P. (1986), *L'Invention du Mont Blanc*, Paris: Gallimard/Julliard.

Lanfant, M.F. (1995), 'International Tourism, Internationalization and the Challenge to Identity', in M.F Lanfant, J.B. Allcock and E.M. Bruner (eds), *International tourism: Identity and change*. London: Sage Publications, pp. 24–43.

Lanfant, M.-F. (2009) 'The Purloined Eye: Revisiting the Tourist Gaze from a Phenomenological Perspective', transl. by D. Picard, in M. Robinson and D. Picard (eds), *The Framed World: Tourism, Tourists and Photography*. London: Ashgate pp. 239–256.

Lanfant, M.F. and Graburn, N. (1992) 'International Tourism Reconsidered: The Principle of the Alternative', in V. L. Smith and W. R. Eadington (eds), *Tourism Alternatives: Potentials and Problems in the Development of Tourism*, Chichester: John Wiley, pp. 88–112.

Lechner, F.J. and Boli, J. (2000), 'Introduction', in their (eds), *The Globalisation Reader*, Oxford: Blackwell, pp. 49–51.

MacCannell, D. (1976), *The Tourist: A New Theory of the Leisure Class*, New York: Schocken.

Malinowski, B. (1935), *Coral Gardens and Their Magic*, London: George Allen & Unwin.

Marie, M. and Viard, J. (1988), *La campagne inventée*, Arles: Actes Sud.

McGuigan, J. (1999), *Modernity and Postmodern Culture*, Buckingham, Philadelphia: Open University Press.

MCUR (2008), *Maison des Civilisations et de l'Unité Réunionnaise*, http://www. regionreunion.com (accessed 4 November 2008).

Milani, R. (2005), *Esthétiques du paysage*, tr. G.A. Tiberghien, Arles: Actes Sud.

Mintz, S.W. (1986), *Sweetness and Power: The Place of Sugar in Modern History*, Penguin, New York.

Mosse, D. (2005), *Cultivating Development: An Ethnography of Aid Policy and Practice*, London: Pluto.

Mosser, M. (1999), 'Le XXIe siècle sera jardinier', in H. Brunon (ed.), *Le jardin, notre double. Sagesse et déraison*, Paris: Autrement, pp. 231–40.

Mosser, M. and Teyssot, G. (eds) (1991), *Histoire des jardins de la Renaissance à nos jours*, Paris: Flammarion.

Ness, S.A. (2003), *Where Asia Smiles: An Ethnography of Philippine Tourism*, Philadelphia: University of Pennsylvania Press.

Neumann, R.P. (2002), *Imposing Wilderness: Struggles over Livelihood and Nature Preservation in Africa*, Berkeley, CA: University of California Press.

Ortiz, F. (1995), *Cuban Counterpoint: Tobacco and Sugar*, London and Durham, NC: Duke.

Panofsky, E. (1971), *Renaissance and Renascences in Western Art*, New York: Westview Press.

Picard, D. (2003), 'Traditionell sein, um an der Modernität teilzunehmen: Tourismus und Post-Modernität auf La Reunion', *Voyage – Jahrbuch für Tourismusforschung*, 6: 109–26.

Picard, D. (2005), 'La fable des coraux ou la mythification de l'économique: tourisme international et protection des récifs coralliens à La Réunion', in B. Cherubini (ed.), *Le territoire littoral – Tourisme, pêche et environnement dans l'océan Indien*, Paris: L'Harmattan, pp. 147–66.

Picard, D. (2008a), *Regional Strategic Action Plan for Coastal Ecotourism Development in the South Western Indian Ocean*, Mauritius, Quatre Borne: Indian Ocean Commission – RECOMAP.

Picard, D. (2008b), 'Coral Garden Economics: International Tourism and the Magic of Tropical Nature', *Études Caribéennes* 3(9–10): 99–121.

Picard, D. (2008c), 'La relation à l'étranger à La Réunion', in C. Ghasarian (ed.), *Anthropologies de La Réunion*, Paris: Editions des Archives Contemporaines, pp. 77–94.

Picard, D. (2009a), 'Cultivating Human Gardens: Tropical Island Tourism in the South Western Indian Ocean', in P. Gupta, I. Hofmeyr and M. Pearson (eds), *Eyes Across the Ocean. Navigating the Indian Ocean*, Pretoria: UNISA.

Picard, D. (2009b), 'Through Magical Flowers: Tourism and Creole Self-fashioning in La Reunion', in S. Moorthy and A. Jamal (eds), *Indian Ocean Studies: Cultural, Social, and Political Perspectives*, London and New York: Routledge, pp. 374–96.

Picard, D. (forthcoming), *Tourism, Magic and Modernity: Cultivating the Human Garden*, New Directions in Anthropology series, Oxford: Berghahn.

Picard, D. and Robinson, M. (eds) (2006), *Remaking Worlds: Festivals, Tourism and Social Change*, Clevedon: Channel View Publications.

Picard, M. (1992), *Bali. Tourisme culturel et culture touristique*, Paris: L'Harmattan.

Pratt, M.L. (1992), 'Criticism in the contact zone', in her *Imperial Eyes. Travel writing and Transculturation*, New York: Routledge, pp. 1–14.

Racault, J.-M. (2003), *Nulle part et ses environs: Voyage aux confins de l'utopie littéraire classique (1657–1802)*, Paris: Presse de l'Université de Paris-Sorbonne.

Robinson, M. and Picard, D. (2006), *Tourism, Culture, and Sustainable Development*, Paris: UNESCO.

Robinson, M. and Picard, D. (2009), 'Tourism and Photography: Magic, Memory and World Making', in their (eds), *The Framed World: Tourism, Tourists and Photography*, London: Ashgate, pp. 1–38.

Roger, A. (1997), *Court traité du paysage*, Paris: Gallimard.

Said, E.W. (2003), *Orientalism*, London: Penguin.

Steward, S. (1993), *On Longing: Narratives of the Miniature, the Gigantic, the Souvenir, the Collection*, Durham, NC and London: Duke University Press.

Tsing, A. (2005), *Friction: An Ethnography of Global Connection*, Princeton and Oxford: Princeton University Press

Tambiah, S.J. (1969), 'Animals are Good to Eat and Good to Prohibit', *Ethnology* 8(4): 191–229.

Tucker, H. (2002), 'Welcome to Flintstones-Land: Contesting Place and Identity in Goreme, Central Turkey', in S. Coleman and M. Crang (eds), *Tourism: Between place and performance*, New York: Berghahn Books, pp. 143–59.

Turner, V. (1973), 'The Centre out There: Pilgrim's Goal', *History of Religions* 12(3): 191–230.

Turner, V. and Turner, E. (1978), *Image and Pilgrimage in Christian Culture*, New York: Columbia University Press.

UNESCO (1972), *Convention Concerning The Protection Of The World Cultural And Natural Heritage*, Paris: UNESCO Publishing.

Urry, J. (1995), 'Tourism, Travel and the Modern Subject', in his *Consuming Places*, London: Routledge, pp. 141–51.

Van den Berghe, P. (1994), *The Quest for the Other: Ethnic Tourism in San Cristobal, Mexico*, Seattle and London: University of Washington Press.

Wallerstein, I. (2004), 'The Rise and Future Demise of the World Capitalist System', in F.J. Lechner and J. Boli (eds), *The Globalization Reader*, Oxford: Blackwell, pp. 63–9.

West, P. (2006), *Conservation Is Our Government Now: the Politics of Ecology in Papua New Guinea*, Durham, NC: Duke University Press.

Wheeller, B. (1993), 'Sustaining the Ego', *Journal of Sustainable Tourism* 1(2): 121–9.

−8−

Of Jews, Christians and Travellers in Crete
Recovered 'Roots', Unwanted 'Heritage'
Vassiliki Yiakoumaki

Introduction

In this chapter I am concerned with historical, political and economic conjunctures in contemporary European locales which render possible the emergence of 'roots'-and-'heritage' destinations. Particularly I am concerned with the ways supra-local realities at work and established local-level realities become uneasily entangled in this process, and in the ways this relationship of awkward coexistence is sustained (and doomed to continue) without publicized conflict. It is, in other words, a relationship of tension not released, for specific social and political reasons which will be discussed. I engage in this discussion with the case study of a newly emerging travel destination of ethno-religious character in southern Greece, namely the reopened Etz Hayyim synagogue in the city of Chania, Crete.

At first sight, such an event may appear 'banal' in the broader European context today, if one thinks of the emergence of multiple such loci throughout Europe (and largely 'Eastern Europe') during the last couple of decades, that is, restored sites and landscapes of Jewish identity becoming tourist destinations of a certain kind, particularly in places of Jewish absence. Like many other European locales, the city of Chania (as well as the whole of Crete) lost its Jewish population in the war, while the recovered synagogue is reported to be the only remaining site of 'native' Jewish culture on the island. Such a destination comes to signify a recovered homeland for many of the visitors attracted to it today, and a place of return which becomes significant for the collective memory of Jews as an ethnic/religious group formerly inhabiting the place. This is an anticipated course of a kind of tourist development which addresses and attracts specific audiences today. In this text I argue that what makes the Etz Hayyim case less 'banal', in the above sense, is the particular tension produced because of its presence, which is a tension restrained and confined to the 'domestic' realm of the local society, and unavailable for this society's official image. I attribute this tension to the nature of the encounter of long-established mentalities at local (and national) level, and inevitable sociopolitical realities at a more global level.

Thus the objective of the present discussion is to shed light on these worlds, by unfolding the quiet yet uneasy emergence of this destination at the level of local life, and the realities of a more global, or otherwise non-local, character which, on the contrary, made this emergence possible. The synagogue has become a cause for agitation of different states of affairs in local society, being a politically and ideologically laden emergence, which is largely due to the figure of the 'Jew' in the Greek-Christian imaginary. As such, the case of the synagogue exposes a certain incompatibility and lack of congruence between local and supra-local agendas. Specifically the synagogue's visibility has not been a locally originated project, ambition or imperative. Rather, it is owed to a conjuncture of events *superseding* immediately domestic and local agendas, in other words, within a nexus of circumstances *beyond* the Greek national borders. By this I mean developments at the level of EU institutions and broader geopolitical and historical changes, as I shall discuss. In this process, the synagogue emerges as an enterprise necessitated largely from 'outside' or, in addition, from 'above'. Furthermore, in this process, 'Jewishness' is constructed as local heritage, thus causing a conflict with dominant perceptions of history at local level. These events have repercussions in the manner in which the synagogue acquires a place in local society, and becomes the cause for a silent, or publicly non-explicit, tension at local level. This tension inevitably becomes non-explicit and non-publicizeable, in the face of the necessity to adopt 'correct' political and ideological stances in the Greek public sphere as a result of the supra-local agendas in question.

The Etz Hayyim case can draw on and contribute to the already extensive dialogue on 'heritage' tourism, taking for granted the political and social constructedness of heritage, that is, not treating it as a universal value. From the point of view of the traveller-consumer, one way to view Etz Hayyim is as a case of 'niche tourism' (Robinson and Novelli 2005), whereby the speciality commodity made available for consumption is diverse experiences of 'Jewishness' (e.g. as pilgrimage, or as genealogy search).[1] However, what is at stake in the case of Etz Hayyim is not the consumer, who remains an outsider, but the inhabitant of this urban society who 'must' relate to their 'past'. The concept of 'dissonant heritage' (Tunbridge and Ashworth 1996) perhaps offers a more productive way of reflecting on the issue because of the element of conflict and contestation, that is, in the different uses of the past as heritage, or among the social actors/groups laying claims to heritage. In this light, Etz Hayyim is a case of heritage largely undesired at local level. It is, however, a case of heritage which brings about unspoken conflict and hostile sentiment, which is not eligible to be performed in official public arenas.

The nature of this awkward emergence of heritage can be explained by a number of factors: anti-Semitism; the vicissitudes of the nation-state; long-standing mentalities versus official institutions; and encompassing political and historical realities at the level of integrated Europe. In what follows I present them in a manner which renders their entanglement meaningful. The text is divided into two main thematic parts. The first part unfolds the case of the synagogue as emerging destination: historical facts, itineraries under formation globally leading to the synagogue, and public-versus-private domains of life in Chania depicting the uneasy integration of this heritage in local life. The second part is a mapping of historical and political conditions, namely, the forces from 'outside', or 'above',[2] which account for the feasibility of this heritage emergence.

On Site, or A 'Before-and-After' Story

The Jews of Crete were mainly Romaniot and Sephardic, that is, both ancient/ Byzantine Jews and Ladino-speaking Mediterranean Jews who arrived from the Iberian Peninsula in the fifteenth century. The history of the ancient Cretan Jews can be traced back approximately two millennia, to the Hellenistic period, as with many Jewish communities in the area of the eastern Mediterranean. The gradual end of the Ottoman Empire and the emergence of the Greek nation-state in the nineteenth century (which signalled the unification of Crete with Greece in 1913) turned Crete into an unfriendly homeland, and became the cause of Jewish emigration to other countries. The Jewish presence in Crete remained alive – although quite diminished – until the Second World War, a period when most remaining Jews of Crete were living in the city of Chania. In June 1944, just before the end of the German Occupation, the Jews of Crete perished in a very different yet equally tragic manner as compared to other Greek-Jewish communities, thus marking another episode in the history of the Jewish genocide in Europe. Arrested and deported by the Nazis, they died on board a ship which was sunk on its way from Crete to Athens for reasons not entirely known yet (see, e.g., Humphrey 1991). The course of this ship would be the first phase of their journey to Auschwitz, had they reached their destination. This event meant the ultimate end of the living Jewish presence in Chania, as well as the whole of Crete.[3]

At this point it is useful to use two vignettes, both of them at the site of the synagogue, in order to visualize a certain contrast. The first vignette provides a view of the silent past initiated with the above loss. It tells a post-war story. The building of Etz Hayyim, the only synagogue (of the two) in the city which has survived the war, is turning into a dilapidated space. As such, it becomes available for various uses irrelevant to its original identity, such as a home for squatters, a dump or a shed for feeding animals. All Jewish residents were captured unexpectedly, thus they left their homes intact, not knowing that there would be no return. The Jewish quarter, in the heart of the city's Venetian-Ottoman harbour, is now a repopulated Christian neighbourhood, as well as a landscape wounded by the war and a place of an absence never mourned. Many of the local newcomers are destitute, and others have resorted to the city from the countryside during the post-war years of urbanization.

The other vignette offers a view of the same location beginning in 1999 and, in a way, resuming from 'where we left off'. It tells the story of Etz Hayyim as an exquisitely restored small synagogue in the Romaniot style, in the place of the abandoned site. For the first time one sees visitors in the harbour asking for directions to the narrow side-street of the former Jewish quarter, or, in the summertime, flocks of people waiting in line outside the building, on the occasion when a tourist company organizes trips to Chania for Israeli tourists – another novelty for the city.

This is not a crude 'before-and-after' view of things. Undoubtedly the two images represent two different extremes between past and present, and it is important politically to flesh out what we would call conventionally the 'progress'. At the same time, as will be evident later, the continuities between these images are an equally significant matter. The post-war picture tells the story of a sudden ending, yet one unspoken of, which marks the beginning of a new epoch, with the end of the war; an epoch which shapes different types of memory and ways of thinking of the past. During this time the Jewishness of the place becomes invisible, as an inevitable consequence of historical conjunctures at local and national level. The newcomers in the neighbourhood have no historical or emotional connection to the Jewish aspect of its identity,[4] while the post-war climate in Greece does not include the Jewish question as part of the political agenda and as an issue in the public sphere. Thus the neglect of the synagogue and the absence of memory in the entire Jewish quarter are consistent with the general state of silence on the Shoah at the level of official and public discourse in Greece during the post-war period – and until recently. The 'new' beginning, after approximately half a century, entails visibility and is realized by means of an intervention in the urban space's architecture, that is, through the restoration of the synagogue. This time, however, history is made from 'outside'. The project begins in 1996 thanks to the World Monuments Fund's (WMF) Jewish Heritage Program.[5] By acquiring a place in the World Monuments Watch List for that year, the synagogue attracts international financial support for its restoration.[6] By this time, the synagogue is about to reach a stage of collapse. The restoration work aims at maintaining the Romaniot Jewish style[7] in the interior, in what was otherwise a fourteenth-century Venetian building, which appears to have been acquired by the Jewish community of Chania for conversion during the seventeenth century, that is, during the Ottoman occupation.

The two images serve to render a process of resignification, that is, of a landscape which registers into a new value system: from a post-war urban site devoid of 'history', relegated to a state of non-issue for a society's public sphere, to a contemporary post 1990s' 'world monument' with the pertinent value markers attached, such as 'cultural', 'multicultural', 'Jewish', and 'heritage'. In this process the synagogue plays its part in the reframing of the city's historical landscape, by turning a so-far isolated side street leading to a dead end in the heart of the historical Ottoman-Venetian harbour, to one more space made available to the influx of tourists visiting the old town. Thus the synagogue expands the size of urban space available for tourist use, and increases the commercial value of the neighbourhood, at the same time catering for a niche market addressing specific social categories of tourists/travellers and 'conscientious' consumers.

The synagogue is a symbolically loaded tourist destination in the making. There is not merely one layer of reading. Invested with the symbolism of a Jewish homeland (a place to visit or to return to), as well as with the trauma of absence (the 'Final Solution'), it acquires meaning for Jews of local descent, for Romaniot Jews, for Sephardic Jews, and for Jews or non-Jews who view such a route as a reason for a journey or 'pilgrimage'. The site is also invested with an aura of 'uniqueness', as it is probably the only remnant of Jewish culture in Crete today. Other powerful investments are made when 'multiculturalism' and 'tolerance' are attached as values to the project, the synagogue being a reminder of a pre-modern and pre-national past (i.e., the Ottoman past), and the coexistence of Christians, Muslims and Jews in the Empire[8] – a past which is relatively recent for Crete, as it became part of the Greek nation-state as late as 1913.

On Presence and Absence

This discussion aims at bringing up a particular complexity about the synagogue as roots-and-heritage destination, which rests on an incompatibility between 'local' and 'non local' agendas, and 'public' and 'domestic' worlds. The event of the synagogue enjoying a degree of visibility as 'world monument' does not have an effect on local life analogous to the dimension of this event. Affirmative or disapproving, one would expect a more publicly perceptible impact on the life of local inhabitants, that is, one different from silence. The case of Chania, I argue, pertains to a seeming paradox inherent in this city's present: although the synagogue is highly visible and recognizable to a large and pertinent public, from within but also particularly beyond the borders of this locality, it is not so to the inhabitants of the place it 'belongs' to. Despite the 'new' beginning in the 1990s, the synagogue has never become equally important in the city's 'domestic' life. This 'paradox' is amplified if one thinks that the synagogue is located in the city's historic and most touristic part, or that sometimes one queues in order to get in during high season, or also that its importance has been recognized internationally.[9]

In the following two sections, I depict this seeming paradox by offering a glimpse of the two worlds in the city's everyday life, namely, that of the traveller acknowledging and 'consuming' this heritage and that of the local inhabitant unable and unwilling to claim it. In this process the synagogue becomes a very absent presence for its locals and a very present absence for its visitors.

En Route to 'Roots'[10]

Since 1999, the synagogue has functioned as a cultural centre and as a synagogue 'proper', as well as a multifaith meeting place, according to the discourse and projected desire of the local project protagonists.[11] There are no 'native' Jews in Chania or the rest of Crete, since the entire community perished in the war. Thus Etz Hayyim is a synagogue 'without a community', in the sense of a formal congregation.[12] There is, however, a collectivity being formed around it, largely non-Jewish, made up of the few employees, the volunteers and the small number of local inhabitants supporting the cause. This collectivity also has another large part, which is more transitory, as many of its members are seasonal or maintain a steady relationship of returning.

One way to see its emergence as destination is to follow it from the day of the formal opening, or 'rededication', of the synagogue in October 1999, which is the formal launching of the place as 'Jewish' destination. Such an event is 'authorized' by the appropriate persons and rituals to invest it with the necessary 'legitimacy', for example, the ceremony of installation of the Sepher Torah, and the presence of political and religious figures (Jewish and non Jewish) from Greece and abroad, as well as representatives of the Jewish communities, the WMF, local citizens, etc. Another way to see its emergence as destination is to follow it from the moment of its identification as 'monument'. This process involves the preparation of the 'scene', from around the mid 1990s, such as the candidacy, the nomination, the emergence of rubble, the conception of restoration, the uneasiness caused in town, the comments made in the neighbourhood, the new visitors to a so far 'uninteresting' part of the old town, or the shop owners' mixed feelings between the prospect for profit and the awkwardness about the 'suspect' Greekness of the place. It is already from those moments that it emerges as more than a religious destination and more than a destination for 'Jews'. Therefore the place is destined both for a specific public or interest group (Jews), which endows the place with certain *sine qua non* attributes, namely, Jewish origin and the memory of the Shoah, *and* for other interest groups (of Jews and non-Jews), which assign new meanings to the place, to ethnicity, to religion, to travelling, as well as to Jewishness.

Besides the casual tourist who visits Chania, accidentally passes by the synagogue and drops in, many tourists come to the synagogue, who, as (Greek or non-Greek) Jews from different parts of the world, satisfy different types of personal 'quests': to see a 'Jewish' site, or a 'heritage' site, or otherwise a Romaniot and Sephardic site; to participate in the memory making of the Shoah; to 'return' to a place of origin; to pray; to perform a ritual or religious service; or to offer services as volunteers in the synagogue. Thus the journey acquires various nuances pertaining to the 'imagined community', such as pilgrimage, duty, obligation, responsibility, tribute, homage, nostalgia and return (see Lerman 2009).

The synagogue also becomes a destination for a specific category of Jews who originate in Chania or Crete, and/or are descendants of local Jews. These may come from within Greece or may reside in other countries and travel to Chania, for example, for the purpose of tracing genealogies (for instance, through origin of surname), or for verifying information transmitted through family narratives. Ben, one of my informants, finds himself in Chania for both leisure and a small family mission. A teenager, he comes from Tel Aviv and has Cretan roots through his great-grandmother, who used to live across the street from the synagogue. During his stay, he manages to spot the family house, now almost in ruins, and takes a photo of the old building to show his grandmother who – unable to travel – longed for this moment; he also helps perform the Kabbalat Shabbat prayers in the synagogue, goes to Greek pop concerts and makes sure to memorize the songs – which, he says, will also help him work on his Greek. Iossif, a cosmopolitan Athenian and writer among other things, is another informant who was born in Chania but left with his family to Athens before the arrest. He visits the synagogue as an opportunity to 'connect' to his place of origin, and he has traced his old home in the city centre, as well as the building of the pre-war family shop downtown – they imported textiles. He keeps 'returning' home once or twice a year, and declares himself 'Cretan' in his writings and in his social life.

The new route to Chania attracts Jews of all denominations, as well as self-assigned 'cultural' Jews and 'non-religious' Jews.[13] These visitors may originate in the place or may have no connection whatsoever, yet are attracted to it for varying reasons. Jewish couples and families from elsewhere within Greece or even of different nationalities choose Etz Hayyim for their weddings or for bar and bat mitzvahs. Family reunions and Jewish get-togethers also take place (e.g. for Pesach). Such events may mean the attendance of large numbers of people (kin or friends) flying in from different parts of the world. The figure of the 'Israeli tourist' is a new presence in the city in the last few years: large organized tours visit the city particularly for the synagogue, thus forming another new itinerary towards Chania, of a more commercialized character in this case.[14]

There are also the more 'standard' events of the annual calendar which have by now established specific itineraries towards Chania. One is the annual memorial service organized by Etz Hayyim in honour of the Jews of Chania who perished in the shipwreck of 1944, which takes place at the synagogue every June. Other events are the main Jewish holidays, such as Passover; the latter includes an open invitation to an event of commensality (with the opportunity of the Seder). Such events, besides symbolizing unity for Greece's Jewish communities (represented in the events), also become the reason for a systematic mobilization and mixing of individuals of different nationalities and with different relationships to religion, who have become interested via word of mouth, the newsletter, or the synagogue web page. The occasional presence of 'VIP' personalities (e.g. foreign politicians and diplomats) at such events, or on random occasions throughout the year, also marks the place as an 'important' destination. Another largely mobile group is the different volunteers, some of whom are local, while others travel to Chania in order to stay for a certain period of time and offer their services, at the same time pursuing different objectives: study hours in the synagogue library (if students), reflection, recreation, vacation with a 'purpose', pilgrimage, religious initiation.

Thus the synagogue becomes a cause for different 'routes' to be shaped towards its direction, depending on what each individual or group assigns to them. In turn, the synagogue justifies its emergence as such a destination by making itself available to different audiences. In this process, it produces conditions for imagining the 'community', while also producing its own versions of history, Judaism, religious dogma, ecumenism, secularism and other nodal points.[15]

Whose Roots?

Within the last decade, the synagogue has shifted from a state of being a non-place, to being a place with an 'important' identity par excellence. As such, it cannot be smoothly accommodated at the level of everyday life in the immediate locality, to which it purportedly belongs, because – inevitably – it needs to come to terms with its past. The history of this past, which involves the process of nation-state making, a long-established anti-Jewish sentiment and the total absence of local Jews, does not allow for the construction of this sense of belonging.

Chania (and the whole of Crete) was a multi-ethnic society, as a former part of the Ottoman Empire, in which Jews were a constitutive element. Its unification with the Greek nation-state in the early twentieth century meant for Cretan society its simultaneous integration in Greek national history. In other words, Cretan society submitted itself to the larger process of the construction of the nation-state's collective imaginary, which was the pre-condition for integration in the nation-state – as the new historical necessity of the time (see Herzfeld 1982, 1991). The new collective consciousness, as a rule, had to be identified with a mono-cultural national identity, which, in the Greek case, was Christian and Greek-speaking. Hence, in the longue durée, the process of emergence of the nation-state, did not/could not allow for Cretan society to make a place for the Jew in its collective memory – or for any non-'Greek' Other.

In the courte durée, silence was the case on either side. After the war, and for some decades to come, the (surviving) Jews remained silent, whether for reasons of necessity for continuity, or for reasons of the 'absurd',[16] namely, the Shoah being unfeasible and unbearable to speak of. This was the case not only for Greece's Jews but for surviving Jews in general. Particularly in Chania, however, the abrupt and definitive physical absence of the Cretan Jews in 1944 established a condition of absence of memory in the local society as an equally definitive event. Also, albeit secondarily, the post-war climate all the way from the Greek Civil War (1946–9) to the Greek dictatorship (1967–74) contributed to the silence in its way. Imbued with anticommunism, the dominant ideology of that period produced a particular figure of the Other, namely, the persecuted Leftist, which overshadowed other categories of 'different' Greeks, hence would not make room for political and ideological sensibilities such as the memory of the Greek Jew. Nonetheless, the above do not suffice to account for the forgetting in official collective memory. The silence and oblivion for the Jew ought also to be seen in the context of a pre-modern history of (Christian) Greek anti-Jewish sentiment, and of the more 'modern' one of anti-Semitism.

After the Shoah, therefore, there was no ground in Crete, or the rest of Greece, for fostering the memory of the pre-war and pre-national past as a past which would encompass the Other.[17] Furthermore, there was no question of forging a Greek national identity which would be, what in more contemporary terms is called 'multi-ethnic' or 'multicultural'; it would have been incompatible with the then dominant ideological priorities and political realities. The quest for (and rhetoric of) multiculturalism is a historically more recent event, hence it has been placed on the European political agenda only during the last two or three decades.

What contributes to the sense of uneasiness about the synagogue's emergence is a more recent development: the identification of the Jew with Israel and Israeli politics. This is common in particular political circles of the Greek Centre and Left, and it is associated with a pro-Arab sentiment in Greek politics in the last few decades, particularly rekindled since the 1980s, thus also offering refuge to Greek anti-Semitic sentiment. As a consequence, any act of advocacy of Greek-Jewish culture or history finds itself bearing the symbolic burden of the Israeli–Palestinian conflict.

Therefore an interplay of oblivion and ideology (nationalism, anti-Semitism) has rendered the local society both incapable and unwilling to incorporate the synagogue in its life. In the context of the above past, no reshuffling of local history can be made from 'inside', as it would disturb the equilibrium of long-lived mentalities and ideologies. The emergence of the synagogue constituted such a reshuffling of old chapters in the history of local society. Such an act could only be initiated 'outside' of this society. The fact that this act was not rooted in local life, but was inspired and motivated 'outside', or otherwise put, from 'above', rendered the locals an audience which decided to place itself as extraneous to the matter. This audience, domestic on the one hand, yet foreign to the change, has remained passive and unaware, or has chosen to remain distanced, or has been performing various acts of denial. This becomes evident, for example, in a common knee-jerk reaction of 'resistance' when local neighbours are prompted to remember their former Jewish neighbours. Very often they declare not knowing or not remembering anything. Also, there are different ways of denying the existence of the synagogue. Besides silence, there are acts of boycotting, such as not giving the tourists the right directions when asked where the synagogue is. It is common for a tourist to receive an 'I do not know' response, or even to be directed to the next-door bar, also called 'The Synagogue'. Ironically, thanks to the synagogue's restoration, the area has become more marketable for the locals, thus enabling the opening of cafes and restaurants in the surrounding zone.

Until the mid 1990s, the Jewish identity of the neighbourhood, or the building, was not known, or was ignored, or unspoken of by its inhabitants. Because the post-war generations of local inhabitants have had no memory of the Jews from lived experience, or knowledge about the Jews from official education, any references to the Jewishness of this neighbourhood in everyday parlance, even to the present, have been limited to linguistic use of toponyms (i.e. place names) in statements such as 'I live in Ovriakí'. Ovriakí is the local name of this quarter, and it is an idiomatic version of *Evraïkí*, which means 'Jewish'. For this reason, the meaning of the word is not made immediately evident to the user/speaker. Hence, such a statement today, as uttered by a local, may be devoid of the knowledge of the term's history.

Within this condition of silencing, or otherwise of not speaking, the synagogue's nomination (to the World Monuments Watch list) remains an unknown dimension of this site in the eyes of the local society. The local inhabitants are not aware of this event, and it does not become an issue in more public arenas, such as the local media. Furthermore, in spite of its importance this event has not been appropriated by any (national or local) Greek official actor or stakeholder. At the same time, the most common interpretations of the synagogue's emergence, by various residents of Chania, draw on the notorious anti-Semitic theme of Jewish 'conspiracy', and on more 'traditional' sentiments of Jew-phobia from the Christian imaginary of anti-Judaism.

Because silencing does not refer literally to the absence of speech, but also connotes a certain way of treating a subject in speech, even the most public acts of opposition in regard to the synagogue by local citizens writing in the local press, aim at restricting the visibility of the subject matter in public arenas. One version of these arguments is that the synagogue should not function as a 'religious place' but only as a 'museum', since 'there are no Jews in Chania'.

The uneasy placing of the synagogue in local life rests on a condition of incompatibility, or incongruity, between 'inside' and 'outside', official and non-official, domestic and public worlds in Chania. Deeply rooted ideas, attitudes and convictions about the Jew are now coming to terms with official politics and practices of affirmative visibility of the Other in Greek society. In this light, the various acts of denial when it comes to speaking of the Jew are also a consequence of the inability to be publicly vocal against the Jew in an era of official endorsement of multiculturalism; or, otherwise, denial is another word for the inability to be violent against the Jew in ways which were more common in a pre-modern past.

By contrasting the 'public' and the 'private', I do not wish to convey a sense of a physical separation of two different bodies of persons, in other words, a divide between 'natives' and 'visitors', Greeks and non-Greeks, immobile locals and mobile travellers/spectators. The individuals and the itineraries under formation, which render the synagogue a destination, may have varying starting points, within the locality or outside. Rather, by public and private, I mean the production of two different images of local life, depending on where the observer is standing. One is the image more available for public consumption and also, in a way, the official one: an image of tolerance and consensus. The other is the image more available for domestic consumption: one of 'forced' acquiescence.

In a sense, the visibility of the synagogue as a roots-and-heritage destination is only true for an outsider, while the locals remain wilfully blind or unable to communicate with the emerging reality – for reasons which history can explain. Hence, there is continuity between the two vignettes used earlier. Although they depict two different landscapes and two different eras divided by more than half a century, the two images share the consensus on silence.

'Making Up' for the Absence – Or, History Made from 'Above'

The synagogue, therefore, emerges as a roots-and-heritage destination of a certain importance 'outside' of the locality, but remains almost a non-issue within the confines of the locality it belongs to. As such, the emergence of the synagogue rests on an inconsistency between the public and the private, the official and the non-official, the local and the supra-local. Although a politically significant event at the level of Greek official institutions, this event is a complex and awkward emergence as experienced at local level: not only is an alleged heritage 'recovered', but also it is recovered from 'above'.

Resorting to terms such as 'outside' or 'above' is not an oversimplification of the matter but serves heuristic purposes. Although the state and other supra-local or supra-national entities are indeed implied, the terms are not used to connote a cynical idea of a top-down ideological imposition, or any sense of enforce-ment of a state of affairs on to the local society. Rather, they connote processes in the making at supra-local level which *counteract* and/or *surpass* local (and national) realities, or do not originate in the locality, yet shape its present. These are historical events and conjunctures of a larger scale, or new sociopolitical agendas emerging in the framework of Europe at the level of official institutions, as I elaborate below. It is as a result of such processes that the project of the synagogue, as well as the various other instances of the visibility of Jewishness in the Greek public sphere, is realized. In other words, the synagogue has become a feasible reality as a result of supra-local actors, forces and realities at work, not of local or national sociopolitical agendas or priorities. The synagogue has not been a 'bottom-up' initiated and inspired project, historically necessitated by local (or national) realities, aspirations and world-views of one or more social groups or classes. This condition has rendered the local society both unable to cope with the change and resistant to it. In this section I sum up some of the main parameters of this condition, which enables officially endorsed visibility; as such, at the same time it produces undesired heritage.

There are certain parameters of this condition which pertain more strictly to Jewish identity and history. A main one is the identification of Jewishness with the Shoah and the Jewish 'memory boom' worldwide. Particularly from the 1980s onwards, there has been a massive 'liberation' of discourse on the Jewish genocide,[18] which has taken various forms: the publication of testimonies and memoirs, the emergence of 'Holocaust' historiography, the establishment of 'Holocaust studies' in the academic world, the founding of Jewish museums and 'Holocaust memorials', and the construction of Jewish monuments, primarily in the USA and Europe.[19] The roots of this memory boom can be traced in the 1960s and 1970s, an era of gradual integration of the Shoah in Jewish memory, hence resignification of the Shoah as *topos* of empowering identification of Jews far and wide.[20] The 'triggering' of memory as part of the management of the Shoah towards a new construction of Jewishness is particularly activated by events and situations in different fields, such as the focus on 'identity' and 'memory' as academic objects of study culminating in the 1980s and 1990s; a rise of anti-Semitism and the revisionist trends in Europe relativizing or disputing the Shoah in the 1980s; the visibility of 'eastern' European Jewry after 1989; the role Israel has played in the tense geopolitical situation in the Middle East (particularly since the Six-Day War in 1967). The synagogue becomes part of this larger process of constructing Jewishness, drawing on the Shoah as a major point of reference. The practice of commemoration has been one of its constitutive and self-defining elements from the day of the synagogue's rededication.[21] Since then, one part of the travellers/visitors attracted to the synagogue form their itinerary by virtue of the fact that they will experience a place marked by the genocide, or that in this process they will be paying homage to an 'ancestral' land. In this process, besides being a site of Romaniot and Sephardic 'heritage', Etz Hayyim also functions as another Jewish site of pilgrimage/heritage tourism participating in the construction of Jewish memory as Shoah memory.

One parameter closely related to the above, is the changed geopolitical map of Europe post-1989, and the integration in the EU of what was formerly known as 'Eastern bloc'. The collapse of regimes that did not make the Jewish issue available to the public sphere throughout the cold war period triggered a Jewish memory boom and publicization of Jewish culture and history, in European locations with a strong Jewish presence historically, such as Poland, Hungary, the Baltic countries, the Czech Republic, but also Austria, Germany (the 'eastern' part), Italy, etc.; or, otherwise, in locations where a strong Jewish presence in the past is today counteracted by Jewish absence. More specifically, a major aspect of this new condition is what appears as a Jewish 'revival', and pertains to practices such as the preservation or restoration of Jewish cemeteries, synagogues and former Jewish quarters (e.g. Krakow), the opening of Jewish museums and the creation of 'Holocaust' monuments (e.g. Berlin), the publishing of life histories, the launching of Jewish studies programmes in European universities, the teaching of the Hebrew language, 'roots' tourism and recreational packages for travellers interested in 'Jewish' destinations (e.g. 'tours' of Auschwitz).[22] This production of Jewish culture involves both a devoted intention to 'restore' Jewish memory and a commercialization of Jewishness – as perceived. There is an emerging market of cultural commodities, such as travel routes in search, or in memory, of Jewish 'roots'[23] and a host of products with 'Jewish' identity (e.g. 'traditional' Jewish cuisine and music) available in these European locations. The emergence of these Jewish destinations, with a smaller or larger consumerist agenda underlying this process, is based on the element of (Jewish) absence. The deployment of absence is conducive to the production of versions of imaginary Jewishness for the visitor, thus investing the journey with affect, a sense of belonging, and a necessary and pertinent aura of history.[24] The Etz Hayyim project is acquiring a place on the larger European map of 'Jewish' memory destinations.[25] Currently without a commercialized profile for tourist consumption,[26] the synagogue, nevertheless, finds itself participating in a European network of Jewish memory spaces, whereby the traveller/consumer is already endowed with a certain culture: to view their journey both as experience of 'identity' and as recreation. Regardless of its own set agendas, therefore, the synagogue has been implicated from the start in a process of cultural production whereby memory and commodity are interchangeable features. In this process, objects or spaces with symbolic value, such as an abandoned synagogue, can function both ways: *both* as products of 'politically correct' practices making history visible, *and* as sites of construction and commercialization of 'heritage', Jewish heritage in this case.

There are other parameters which pertain to broader issues or political develop-ments in Europe. One is the 'normalization' of Otherness as cultural and political imperative in Europe today. By this I mean Greece's alignment with European politics on ethnic Others, such as the prioritization of 'rights' in the European political agendas and the emergence of legal frameworks regarding 'minorities'.[27] Specifically, during the last couple of decades, that is, approximately since the beginning of the 1990s, Greece has entered a new moment in regard to the management of ethnic difference. For historical reasons pertaining to the formation of Greek national identity within a tradition of ethnic nationalism, Greece viewed 'difference' as a national handicap and practically treated it as non-existent, hence appearing excessively 'sensitive' in international fora when it came to speaking about its 'minorities'.[28] The new historical moment was initiated as a result of its gradual integration in the European unification process, and as a result of the fact that, since 1989, Greece has found itself coming to grips with the pressing issue of the presence of new Others in massive numbers within its borders – as has the rest of Europe. In this context, beginning in the 1990s, Greek (political and intellectual) elites have promoted the agendas of 'multiculturalism' and 'tolerance' at the level of official rhetoric and practice, hence giving them the necessary 'legitimacy' in the Greek public sphere. Although such rhetorics are not easily adopted at the level of non-official actors and raise contentious ideological issues among different interest groups and social categories in the Greek population, and although engagement in such politics is subject to political conjunctures, the official state has been obliged to harmonize itself with these agendas; hence it has become possible during this time to articulate different (or alternative) definitions of Greekness in the public sphere, which are not compatible with the dominant – and hegemonic – definition of (Christian-Greek) national identity.[29] The adoption of terms such as 'multiculturalism' is almost a prerequisite in the official discourse of politicians, NGO activists, various actors in local government and other stakeholders.

This is, in other words, a historical moment whereby Greece engages in the politics of 'political correctness' as a necessary political step for its public image in the European and international political community, and for coping with geopolitical and demographic changes of the last couple of decades as an EU member. The politics against anti-Semitism in the context of various legal frameworks and NGO actions within Europe in recent years is also a product of this new historical moment shaping the official Greek stance.[30] It is within this new state of official 'consent' (i.e. against 'intolerance') that the synagogue is made visible in Crete, something which could not have taken place at an earlier moment in time, that is, without an anticipated social tension made more public. The emergence of the synagogue as destination is part of the larger process of engagement in the rhetorics and politics of 'cultural diversity' in Europe;

otherwise put, it is part of a process of normalization of 'visibility' in Europe. As in the rest of Europe, discussed above, Jewish visibility in Greece entails the official endorsement of incorporation of Jewish memory in Greek public life, by the state and various state actors, particularly utilizing the Shoah as point of reference. Specifically, this means an anticipated 'monumentalization' process (construction of 'Holocaust' monuments, naming of squares and streets drawing on Greek-Jewish history, restoration of synagogues and Jewish quarters),[31] the inclusion of 'Holocaust Remembrance Day' (since 2004, by decree of Parliament) in the calendar of national commemorations and the incorporation of the Shoah in education curricula (in teaching material by the Ministry of Education) among others. The process also includes the publicizing of 'testimonies' and a development of historiography on the Jewish issue.[32] Therefore the case of Etz Hayyim as emerging destination ought to be seen, on the one hand, in the context of European politics during integration and shifting geopolitical realities, and, on the other hand, in the context of a society (Chania, or Crete) where the Jews (or other non-'Greek' Others) were not a subject of public dialogue or a subject for inclusion in collective memory.

Another parameter is the action on the part of supranational entities, be it from the world of institutionalized politics or the world of civil society. In the case of the synagogue, one example is entities such as the World Monuments Fund, whose function is to assign the marker of 'heritage' to the site and to mobilize the necessary networks of donors or sponsors. Another example is the EU as supranational political entity funding 'European research' in academic institutions such as universities, a fact which applies particularly in the case of the synagogue and the fieldwork I was able to conduct there as anthropologist. As in the larger EU political agenda mentioned above, the prioritization of agendas, such as that of 'minorities' and 'multiculturalism', is manifest in the philosophy of the funded research programmes. The research in question was realized in the context of Euromed Heritage,[33] a European Commission-funded cluster of programmes on Mediterranean cultures.[34] Within a consortium of a number of city-partners across Europe and the Mediterranean littoral, the research focused on urban spaces, and particularly 'Mediterranean' neighbourhood spaces. The local research in Crete had the city of Chania as study-object, while the Jewish aspect of the city's history became one main theme in the process of anthropological mapping of the city's multi-ethnic character.

Concluding Remarks

One of the main points of this discussion is that in a process of a roots-and-heritage destination under construction, the heritage in question may be unwanted by the local society or community it 'belongs' to, yet never publicly disowned. More specifically, with the Etz Hayyim case, which is aimed at contributing to a study of the political economy of heritage destinations in tourism, I discuss a sociopolitical conjuncture which renders heritage an undesirable yet inevitable reality for the society possessing it. I attribute this seeming anomaly to the incompatibility of priorities between local and supra-local realities: on the one hand, there are global and encompassing historical, political and economic processes which are conducive to the emergence of Etz Hayyim synagogue as Jewish heritage for the immediate location (identity politics, the European unification process and growing markets for commodities); on the other hand, there is a local society in Crete 'possessing' this Jewish history yet unable and unwilling to claim it.

The emergence of the synagogue as (tourist) destination is, for the society of Chania, essentially an experience of Otherness as knowledge coming from 'above' within a broader political climate of endorsing cultural 'diversity' and of 'restoring' Jewish memory. In other words, this society is 'discovering' about itself today that it is 'multicultural' and 'tolerant', while having been conditioned historically to perceive itself as 'Greek', by narratives of Hellenism and Christianity inherent in the process of the Greek nation-state making. For this reason, this process of new knowledge of the collective self, with the opportunity of the synagogue, is politically correct yet by all means inconvenient. In other words, while the local society is not conditioned to 'see' the Other, the political climate projects a very different necessity, namely, to make the Other visible and part of the collective self – to make the absent Jew a present Jew. In this process, diversity and tolerance emerge as both politically necessary values and marketable objects. For the above reasons, although this society embraces the cause rhetorically (i.e. by means of its official actors), it does not appear willing to embrace it in practice.

The official and public image of this society tells the story of a successful and celebrated restoration project which helps construct tourist itineraries attracting audiences from all parts of the world, while also drawing on the new legitimate ethos concerning the management of 'difference'. The 'private' life of this society, on the other hand, keeps such an event in its universe of unspoken facts, in a collective process of exclusion nurtured by traditions of nationalist and anti-Jewish sentiment. The sense of Jewish roots and imagined homeland in Chania is emerging 'outside' of the immediate concerns of this society, and without its actual participation. As a roots destination, this heritage is glorified by the many and disowned by the few.

I have used the case study in question as an example of the complex and conflictual nature of the emergence/construction of heritage, in this case of tourist destinations which make claims on roots and emerge by means of investing on the collective memory of a social group. With the above mapping of local and supra-local processes, I illustrate that such an emergence cannot be the smooth outcome of social consensus, or of unitary action by the social actors/social partners involved. On the verge between mentalities and institutions, public and private, official and non-official, reality and political necessity, this 'destination' is a highly politicized event.

Acknowledgements

I would like to thank Nikos Stavroulakis, Director Emeritus of the Jewish Museum of Greece and Director of the Etz Hayyim project, for his illuminating presence and support in the course of the research, and for the inspiration.

Notes

1. 'Dark tourism' (Lennon and Foley 2000), as a particular 'niche', might also apply, since the synagogue emerges also as a landscape affected by death and disaster (see below on the tragic death of the entire Jewish community).
2. In the second part, I account for the use of these spatial designations, which, because of the implied binarisms, may give the impression of a certain oversimplification (of an otherwise complex situation).
3. The number of the victims is reported to be approximately 265. The Synagogue web page is a well-informed site on local Jewish history (http://www.etz-hayyim-hania.org). On the history of Crete's Jewry, see also, e.g., Starr (1942), Humphrey (1989), Stavroulakis (1990), Schoenfeld (2007).
4. The Synagogue website has the following to say about the fate of local Jewish properties after the war: 'By 1957 the problem of the unclaimed Jewish property of Hania was in the process of being resolved ... Squatters were given permission to purchase property at nominal prices and thus Kondylakis street formally ceased to be a Jewish Quarter. Only the synagogue of Etz Hayyim remained and by this time, as in the case of all "abandoned" communal Jewish property in the form of synagogues, midrashim and schools, it had become the property of the Central Board of Jewish Communities of Greece. The squatters moved out and the synagogue was left to the mercy of the neighborhood. From this date encroachments were made into the two courtyards of the synagogue...' (http://www.etz-hayyim-hania.org/_synag/reconstr.html)
5. See http://www.wmf.org. The organization is known for raising awareness on 'conservation' of 'architectural heritage'. To a large degree this includes religious buildings. Specifically (I am quoting), 'launched in 1996 and issued

every two years, the World Monuments Watch calls international attention to cultural heritage around the world that is threatened by neglect, vandalism, conflict, or disaster.' (http://wmf.org/watch.html)

6. Etz Hayyim functions as a non-profit organization relying on donations. The Etz Hayyim project has a director (and an executive board since 2008), who acts on behalf of the Central Board of Jewish Communities in Greece. Some of the main donors for the restoration were the Ronald S. Lauder, Rothschild, Rosenberg, Rose and other foundations, as well as a number of individuals.

7. To quote the Synagogue website on its history and architecture: 'This layout is quite different than that of the Sephardi synagogues in Greece and can be found in Venice, elsewhere in Italy, and occasionally in Turkey and North Africa. In keeping with all synagogues the Ehal is located on the East wall but as is typical of Romaniot synagogues, the Bema is located axially opposite to it against the West wall.' (http://www.etz-hayyim-hania.org/_synag/arch.html). On the reconstruction and renovation, see also: http://www.etz-hayyim-hania.org/_synag/reconstr2.html.

8. It is certainly an anachronism to apply such terms as 'multiculturalism' to a pre-modern historical era (namely, the empire), let alone to imply an idealized coexistence of ethnically different populations. To my knowledge, however, it is used strategically by the actors in the Synagogue project, for reasons of fostering the idea of coexistence in 'modern' times, which have been marked by ethnic conflict – that is, within the nation-state.

9. By being placed on the World Monuments Watch list, the Synagogue is placed in the same company as other 'important' monuments worldwide. See http://www.wmf.org/watch_all.html. Having said this, I am not implying a 'high' and 'low' culture divide as a criterion for judging the value of monuments. Furthermore, one cannot stress enough that the selection of a site as 'monument' is an act governed by historical and political circumstances.

10. Although an exhaustively utilized play on words, I confess I found 'routes' and 'roots' to be quite convenient here. I cannot acknowledge the one who coined it, but I am borrowing it from my own anthropological readings, such as Gilroy (1993) and Clifford (1997), at a time when the authenticity of roots was a favourite subject of reflection.

11. See, e.g., http://www.jewish-heritage-europe.eu/confer/prague04/papers/Stavroulakis.pdf

12. On the other hand there is a small number of Jews, Greek or non-Greek, living in Crete today who established themselves there more recently for family, business or other reasons.

13. These terms were used in the interviews by the informants themselves.

14. In Feldman (2007), there is a useful ethnographic example of a transformation of the tourist/traveller to pilgrim, and of the visited land, to land with religious

significance. See also Ebron (2000) on the construction of a tourist destination and its 'pilgrim'.

15. See http://blog.etz-hayyim-hania.org.

16. That is, the Shoah as an 'absurd' crime.

17. Needless to say, this is not only true for the Jews. The historically inevitable, and necessary, 'amnesia' in Cretan society as part and parcel of the nation-state making, also includes other Others, such as the Cretan Muslims. These non-'Greek' Cretans began to depart from Crete as the end of the Ottoman Empire was nearing, and finally had to leave with the exchange of populations between Greece and Turkey in 1923.

18. See, e.g., Wieviorka (2005), ch.12, which, through the emblematic case of Auschwitz, provides a detailed mapping of the emergence and inter-nationalization of Jewish memory, beginning from the early post-war years.

19. See Young's renowned work on the emergence of 'Holocaust' memorials (1993). See also Stier (2003) on the different ways and settings through which the emerging 'memorial' culture of the 'Holocaust' is materialized.

20. From being a silenced issue, the Shoah became a key element of Jewish identity. In the post-war period Israel, as a new state, did not deploy the Shoah as constitutive element of its national identity, neither did it identify itself with the European Jewry. The Jewish genocide was not 'appropriate' as nationalist narrative for the new nation. At the same time, the diasporic Jews of the USA opted for successful assimilation in American society rather than identification with a 'victimized' identity such as that of the Shoah. Well into the 1960s, the construction of a new sense of nationhood took place in Israel by means of affirmative integration of the Shoah in Jewish 'collective' memory – as is known at present. This was largely owing to the political circumstances which resulted in a rise of Jewish nationalism, specifically a well-established sense of national sovereignty for Israel (particularly its sense of being a powerful actor in the tense relations with the Arab world), along with an increasing self-confidence and powerful presence of Jews in American society. See Tom Segev (2000), for a discussion of the redefined national identity and of the multiple uses of the Shoah in Israeli society and politics.

21. The performance of mourning and remembrance rituals are central in this process of imprinting the Shoah in local Jewish history, e.g., the annual memorial service, the placing of the names of the victims on a synagogue wall, and the reading of the names out loud during this service every June.

A self-assigned mission for the synagogue is, among others, to act 'cor-rectively' vis-à-vis the rupture in local memory: '... Chania is the only town in all of Greece that had a Jewish community that was lost, or decimated, or fractured, that does not have a monument to the dead Jews. The only town in the whole of Greece ...' (interview with the Etz Hayyim project director, in Yiakoumaki 2005)

22. There is no intention in this text to idealize this 'revival'. As is known, the collapse of the 'Eastern bloc' also brought about revisionist trends in historiography regarding the Jewish genocide, and a resurgence of anti-Semitism.

23. See, e.g., Feldman (2008) on organized trips of young Israelis to Poland as a means of constructing Holocaust memory and Israeli national identity today; and Kugelmass (1992) on American Jews travelling to Poland and rites of 'returning'.

24. Gruber (2002) is a useful ethnographic research on a number of these European locations 'reviving' Jewishness, on the commodities available, and the play on 'absence'. A very useful case study is Kugelmass and Orla-Bukowska (1998) on the 'rediscovery' of Kazimierz, the large Jewish quarter in Krakow.

25. See also institutionalized events, such as the European Day of Jewish Culture, held every September. This year (2009) Etz Hayyim was the Greek participant (http://www.jewisheritage.org/jh/edjc.php).

26. See note 6.

27. For example, the *Framework-Convention for the Protection of Ethnic Minorities* (1995) of the European Council, or the *Document of the Copenhagen Meeting* (1990) by OSCE (Organization for Security and Co-operation in Europe).

28. With the exception of the 'Muslim minority' in Thrace. Although this community, too, has been 'invisible' in the past in many ways, it is the only population with the official status of minority in Greece (Treaty of Lausanne, 1923).

29. A useful source on such developments, albeit from the point of view of an NGO providing an anticipated critical approach on Greece's course, is the Greek branch of Helsinki Monitor, http://www.greekhelsinki.gr.

30. See, e.g., the *Berlin Declaration* (2004) by OSCE; *Perceptions of Antisemitism in the European Union* (2004), by FRA (European Union Agency for Fundamental Rights, http://fra.europa.eu, formerly EUMC, European Monitoring Centre on Racism and Xenophobia); *Manifestations of Antisemitism in the EU, 2002–2003* (2004) with a country-report on Greece. Within Greece, see, e.g., http://www.greekhelsinki.gr/bhr/greek/special_issues/antisemitism.html.

31. Particularly in this area private initiatives are more common, while the official state is not the main actor, or even may be absent – albeit always 'endorsing'.

32. Needless to say, this is merely a brief and indicative mention of what is otherwise a highly politicized process and product of specific politics within Greece and outside – hence deserving a discussion of its own.

33. http://www.euromedheritage.net.
34. The specific name of our project was 'Mediterranean Voices: Oral History and Cultural Practice in Mediterranean Cities', Contract no. ME8/ AIDCO/2000/2095-05, with a time span from 2002 to 2006 (see http://www. med-voices.org).

References

Clifford, J. (1997), *Routes: Travel and Translation in the Late Twentieth Century*, Cambridge, MA: Harvard University Press.

Ebron, P. (2000), 'Tourists as Pilgrims: Commercial Fashioning of Transatlantic Politics', *American Ethnologist* 26(4): 910–32.

Feldman, J. (2007), 'Constructing a shared Bible Land: Jewish Israeli guiding performances for Protestant pilgrims', *American Ethnologist* 34(2): 351–74.

Feldman, J. (2008), *Above the Death Pits, Beneath the Flag: Youth Voyages to Poland and the Construction of Israeli National Identity*, Oxford: Berghahn Books.

Gilroy, P. (1993), *The Black Atlantic: Modernity and Double Consciousness*, Cambridge, MA: Harvard University Press.

Gruber, R.E. (2002), *Virtually Jewish: Reinventing Jewish Culture in Europe*, Berkeley, CA: University of California Press.

Herzfeld, M. (1982), *Ours Once More: Folklore, Ideology, and the Making of Modern Greece*, Austin, TX: University of Texas Press.

Herzfeld, M. (1991), *A Place in History: Monumental and Social Time in a Cretan Town*, Princeton: Princeton University Press.

Humphrey, J. (1989), 'The Jews of Crete under German Occupation 1941–44: I', *Bulletin of Judaeo-Greek Studies* 5: 18–26.

Humphrey, J. (1991), 'The Sinking of the *Danae* off Crete in June 1944', *Bulletin of Judaeo-Greek Studies*, 9: 19–34.

Kugelmass, J. (1992), 'The Rites of the Tribe: American Jewish Tourism in Poland', in I. Karp, C.M. Kreamer and S.D. Lavine (eds), *Museums and Communities: The Politics of Public Culture*, Washington, DC: Smithsonian Institution Press, pp. 382–427.

Kugelmass, J. and Orla-Bukowska, A. (1998), '"If You Build it They Will Come": Recreating an Historic Jewish District in Post-Communist Krakow', *City & Society* 10(1): 315–53.

Lennon, J. and Foley, M. (2000), *Dark Tourism: The attraction of death and disaster*, London: Continuum.

Lerman, A. (2009), 'Crete's extraordinary synagogue', *The Guardian*, 30 July. Available online at http://www.guardian.co.uk/commentisfree/belief/2009/ jul/30/crete-synagogue-etz-hayyim

Robinson, M. and Novelli, M. (2005), 'Niche Tourism: An Introduction', in M. Novelli (ed.), *Niche Tourism: Contemporary issues, trends and cases*, Oxford: Butterworth-Heinemann Ltd, pp. 1–14.

Schoenfeld, A.J. (2007), 'Immigration and Assimilation in the Jewish Community of Late Venetian Crete (15th–17th Centuries)', *Journal of Modern Greek Studies* 25(1): 1–15.

Segev, T. (2000), *The Seventh Million: The Israelis and the Holocaust*, New York: Holt Paperbacks, Henry Holt and Co.

Starr, J. (1942), 'Jewish Life in Crete under the Rule of Venice', *Proceedings of the American Academy for Jewish Research*, 12: 59–114.

Stavroulakis, N. (1990), *The Jews of Greece*, Athens: Talos Press.

Stier, O.B. (2003), *Committed to Memory: Cultural Mediations of the Holocaust*, Amherst, MA: University of Massachusetts Press.

Tunbridge, J.E. and Ashworth, G.J. (1996), *Dissonant Heritage: The Management of the Past as a Resource in Conflict*, Chichester: John Wiley & Sons.

Wieviorka, A. (2005), *Auschwitz, 60 ans après*, Paris: Robert Laffont.

Yiakoumaki, V. (2005), *Etz Hayyim-Tree of Life: Voices Surrounding a Synagogue*, 'Mediterranean Voices' & London Metropolitan University. Documentary film (DVD).

Young, J.E., (1993), *The Texture of Memory: Holocaust Memorials and Meaning*, New Haven, CT: Yale University Press.

Internet Sources

Berlin Declaration (2004), http://www.osce.org/item/8250.html (accessed 14 September 2009).

Document of the Copenhagen Meeting (1990), http://www.osce.org/documents/odihr/1990/06/13992_en.pdf (accessed 14 September 2009).

Framework-Convention for the Protection of Ethnic Minorities (1995), http://conventions.coe.int/Treaty/EN/Treaties/Html/157.htm (accessed 14 September 2009).

Perceptions of Antisemitism in the European Union (2004), http://www.europarl.europa.eu/studies/eumc_report/eumc_interviews_en.pdf (accessed 14 September 2009).

Manifestations of Antisemitism in the EU, 2002–2003 (2004), http://eumc.europa.eu/eumc/as/PDF04/AS-Main-report-PDF04.pdf (accessed 14 September 2009).

Tourist Attractions, Cultural Icons, Sites of Sacred Encounter

Engagements with Malta's Neolithic Temples

Kathryn Rountree

Introduction

Drawing on a decade of fieldwork among local people and visitors to Malta, this chapter focuses on sacred places, the uses of ancient monuments in contemporary tourism, and the diverse ideas and embodied experiences generated through a variety of engagements with sites: in short, about multiple discourses of legitimacy, ownership and appropriation. I claim that the familiar bipartite categories of hosts and guests, indigenes and visitors, tourists and pilgrims are not especially relevant when trying to understand the many interpretations, values and functions of these monuments. Interest groups contesting the meanings and management of sites cross-cut these binary categories and individuals within them find both unexpected allies and dissenters. Moreover, the constitution of different stakeholder groups and the pattern of relationships among them are constantly changing and realigning. Amidst this variety of local and foreign attitudes and approaches to Malta's Neolithic monuments, a national heritage project within the country is increasingly employing the sites as iconic symbols of Maltese cultural identity in a postcolonial context, while the tourism industry uses them to represent Malta to overseas visitors. Beneath the radar of such official, organized and publicly visible projects, Malta's Neolithic sites are also attracting a thin but steady stream of visitors who come for religious or spiritual reasons. Most of my fieldwork has focused on these pilgrim-tourists.

The phenomenon of religious tourism dates to antiquity, and is arguably as old as tourism itself, especially given the difficulty of disentangling the sacred and secular within the motives, destinations, experiences and narratives of tourists' journeys. Myra Shackley (2001: 17) has suggested that religious tourism may date back to the Palaeolithic, based, for example, on evidence of early humans visiting Lascaux in south-western France around 16,000 years ago to paint the cave walls or view the magnificent murals. Over three decades ago Victor and Edith Turner acknowledged the complex intertwining of sacred journeys and tourism in their claim that 'a tourist is half a pilgrim, if a pilgrim is half a tourist' (1978: 20).

One particular instance of modern religious tourism involves the journeys made by contemporary Pagans, Wiccans and Goddess-followers – participants in a fast-growing, global new religious movement – to sites once connected with ancient religions.[1] Indeed, the phenomenon of Pagan pilgrimage seems to have come full circle. In classical times, pilgrims made arduous journeys to consult the oracle at Delphi, to pay homage to Artemis at Ephesus, Zeus at Olympia and Aphrodite at Paphos. Popular destinations for today's Pagans include Stonehenge, Avebury, Glastonbury, Brú Na Bóinne (Newgrange), Crete, Malta, Ephesus, Çatalhöyük, Luxor, Machu Picchu, Chichén Itzá, Uluru (Ayers Rock, Australia) and a host of others. Karen Tate's book *Sacred Places of Goddess: 108 Destinations* (2006) is billed in the promotional material as 'an encyclopaedia of Goddess allowing one to visit her sacred sites and discover Goddess culture around the world'.[2]

Some modern Pagans journey from one side of the globe to the other to visit sacred sites, while others drive or walk to sites near their homes. Some join guided tours designed especially for them – in particular, Goddess tours – some design their own itineraries and some join tours for regular tourists.[3] These pilgrim-tourists sometimes perform individual or group rituals at sites, light candles, leave offerings, chant, sing, dance, write poetry or prose, paint, pray and meditate (Rountree 2002b; Blain and Wallis 2004, 2007). Like other pilgrims visiting the holy places of their religions, Pagan pilgrims are often searching for an experience of the numinous; connection with the past; and physical, emotional or psychological healing. But often they are outwardly indistinguishable from other tourists – quietly admiring the remains, studying the guidebook, listening to the tour guide, taking photographs and chatting with companions. On tour they participate in many of the activities enjoyed by other tourists: relishing local cuisines and learning about local cultures; visiting sites of local interest, museums, galleries and markets; and pursuing various leisure pursuits such as shopping, swimming and hiking (Rountree 2002b).

Before discussing Pagans' visits to sacred sites further, I should briefly introduce contemporary Western Paganism for readers unfamiliar with it. Harvey (1997: vii) summarizes it well as 'a religion at home on Earth, an ecological spirituality, a somatic philosophy of life'. It is an umbrella term for a large number of modern Western Nature religions, the most common being Wicca (or modern Witchcraft), Druidry, contemporary Western Shamanism, Goddess Spirituality and Heathenism (which draws on Germanic and Scandinavian traditions). A great many modern Pagans do not, in fact, embrace a single spiritual path, preferring to call themselves 'eclectics' and choosing whatever appeals to them from various traditions to create a personally customized path. There are now Pagans in all

Western countries, thousands of websites, and hundreds of thousands of Pagans worldwide who use them. The following principles are shared by many:

- *Love for and kinship with nature, reverence for the life force and its cycles of life, death and regeneration.* These cycles are widely celebrated in eight annual seasonal festivals (two solstices, two equinoxes and four other days: Imbolc, Lammas, Beltane and Samhain).
- *The concept of Goddess and God as dual, complementary expressions of the Divine reality.* Modern Pagans are variously polytheists, animists, pantheists and panentheists. Those involved in Goddess spirituality tend to refer only to Goddess, rather than to God and Goddess.
- *Personal freedom and autonomy,* along with responsibility to others, including other-than-humans, expressed as: 'Do what you will, but harm none.'
- *The inter-relatedness and interdependence of everything* – all matter and energy – often expressed in urgent concerns about ecology and ideas about karma.

In the last twenty or so years, the Mediterranean island nation of Malta has become a relatively popular destination for modern Pagans because of its remarkable and extensive Neolithic heritage, which incorporates at least twenty-three megalithic temples dating to around 3,600 BCE, thought to be associated with the ancient veneration of a fertility or Mother Goddess. Pagan pilgrim-tourists to Malta claim a spiritual affinity with (what they believe were) the earth-and-woman honouring beliefs of the temple-builders, want to learn more about the Neolithic past and see for themselves its remains, and often seek a personal spiritual experience at sites. The most frequent Pagan visitors to the temples are women connected with the Goddess movement, and since the early 1990s Goddess tours have been organized – usually several per year – mostly by North American and British women who are themselves part of the movement.[4] Tours are patronized mostly by Americans, but also by Canadians, British, continental Europeans and Australasians. Participants are of all ages; however the majority are middle-aged (perhaps because they are better able to afford the cost), university-educated feminists. Occasionally women bring their mothers or daughters for a special bonding, educational, healing or initiatory experience (girlhood to womanhood, or middle-aged woman to wise elder), and some make return visits. I know of Dutch and English Pagans, for instance (men as well as women), who travel to Malta's temples frequently, and claim to experience in doing so a kind of 'home-coming'.

While the Pagan contingent of visitors to Malta's Neolithic temples is relatively new, the sites – the oldest free-standing stone monuments in the world (Renfrew 1973: 161) – have long attracted foreign tourists and are an important component of heritage or cultural tourism within the country. In 1980 the twin temples of Ġgantija, along with the magnificent Hal Saflieni Hypogeum, a beautifully preserved underground temple-tomb descending three levels below the street, were designated UNESCO World Heritage sites because of their exceptional cultural value. In 1992 five more temple sites – Mnajdra, Haġar Qim, Tarxien, Ta' Haġrat and Skorba – were added to the World Heritage list (Figure 9.1).[5] Modern Pagans constitute only a tiny portion of visitors to these sites (it is impossible to know what proportion), but their prehistoric counterparts were perhaps more numerous. A tourism video entitled 'Sacred Island', which screens regularly at the Emigrants Commission in the nation's capital Valletta, suggests that the islands and its temples may have first become a destination for pilgrims several millennia

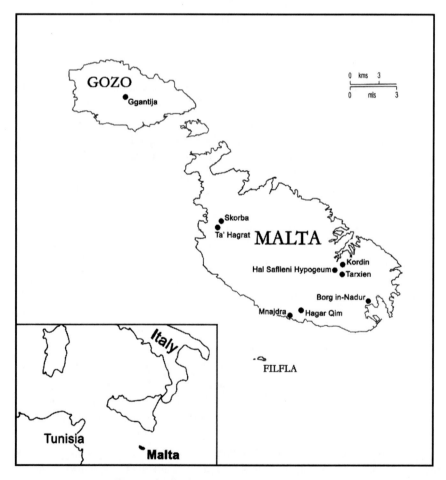

Figure 9.1 The key Neolithic temple sites in Malta.

before Christ, based on the large number of temples within a relatively small land area (Malta is 27 by 14 km, about the size of the Isle of Wight).

Malta has a long history of colonization, and from the Bronze Age onwards, the temples were appropriated and contested, reinterpreted and reused by a host of foreign and local groups for a variety of economic, cultural, historical, scientific and religious purposes (Trump 1990; Cassar 2000).[6] It has to be said that for most Maltese and most tourists today, the temples are not regarded as part of a contemporary sacred landscape, at least not in the religious sense of 'sacred'. While the sites and their associated artefacts are increasingly employed as cultural icons in the creation of a postcolonial Maltese national identity and as unique attractions in tourism advertising, for most local people they have no contemporary spiritual importance. Their values have to do with history, science (particularly archaeology) and the economy. While they are important symbols of heritage and cultural identity, interestingly this is not linked with a strong sense of cultural ownership. Maltese people insist that as UNESCO World Heritage sites, the temples are 'to be shared by everyone'; they are not *owned* by Maltese, simply on Maltese soil.

My interest in undertaking fieldwork in Malta was sparked initially by a desire to understand the meanings and values of the Neolithic heritage for Maltese people in the light of their valorization by the slow but steady stream of foreign Pagan pilgrim-tourists who visited them. My early research (1998–2000) turned up a variety of local discourses in relation to the temples, with contesting meanings and interpretations determined by the agendas of those who generated them (Rountree 2001, 2002a). At the beginning of this research, I knew nothing about an indigenous Maltese Neo-Pagan community or any agendas it might have with respect to the temples. The movement was then, and still is, fairly well concealed, and in the late 1990s was in its infancy. It was not until 2004 that I learnt, via an email from someone in Malta I had never met, that contemporary Western Paganism had made it to Malta, and that a small but passionate network of Maltese Witches and Pagans was coalescing below the surface of the overwhelmingly Catholic mainstream society. Between 2005 and 2009 I carried out ethnographic fieldwork in this community and came to understand, among other things, how the country's Neolithic monuments functioned within these people's beliefs and practices (Rountree 2010).

Maltese Relationships with the Temples

It is difficult to generalize about Maltese people's relationships to the Neolithic past and the temples. Local villagers and communities, farmers and hunters who live or carry out their activities near temples are likely to have different attitudes and concerns from urban-dwellers. People working for heritage organizations, archaeologists, tourism operators, historians, politicians, policy-makers, planners, artists, temple guides and custodians all have different standpoints, and the variety of views within any of these stakeholder groups – which together comprise only a small minority of the Maltese population – is considerable.

It needs to be acknowledged that while many Maltese feel a strong affinity with, and passion for, the temples, and particularly the landscape in which they are embedded, many more do not. This is partly due to the fact that most Maltese perceive no connection between themselves and the people of the temple period. Archaeological opinion has long held that the temple culture was entirely wiped out by, or became extinct before the arrival of, waves of later peoples: Bronze Age people, Phoenicians, Romans and so on (Bonanno 1997; Trump 1990: 31). Therefore, in the eyes of most, the temple builders were not their remote ancestors, but a quite separate, little-understood people that once occupied these islands thousands of years before Christ. Indeed, until the twentieth century and the scientific excavation of sites, the Neolithic remains were something of a mystery. One of the earliest accounts, published in 1647, suggested that the temples were built by cyclopean giants. It later turned out that the skulls of these 'giants' belonged to an extinct species of dwarf elephant found in the islands (Mifsud and Ventura 1999: 3). It was not until the turn of the twentieth century that archaeologists began attributing the temples to a prehistoric culture (Grima 1998: 34).

When I talked with Maltese people in an effort to understand the temples' meanings and importance, it became clear that most, while proud that Malta was home to such remarkable monuments, saw them as primarily things that tourists were interested in. Apart from middle-class and educated people and those with a special interest in the sites, it seemed that most Maltese grew up with a sense of the temples as a taken-for-granted part of the Maltese landscape and their cultural heritage, but this sense was vague and seldom thought about. Their relative lack of interest in the temples contrasted sharply with their pride, interest and knowledge in relation to other historic buildings, especially churches and structures built during the period when the Knights of St John ruled Malta (1530–1798). As a Maltese university student told me: 'We see the link with the Maltese of the time of the Knights because they were Christians like us, but somehow the link is lost throughout the millennia it took between us and the people of the temple period.'

The absence of a felt connection – ancestral or cultural and certainly not religious – with the temple culture is perhaps hardly surprising given its antiquity and the paucity of knowledge about it. The temples constitute the remains of a past so distant that it can scarcely be imagined, let alone identified with. Writing in the late twentieth century about nineteenth-century painting, Maltese anthropologist Paul Sant Cassia (1993: 359) concluded that the Neolithic ruins were 'mute testimonies of an unknown silent past with very little connection to contemporary realities'. He showed how the relationship between the Maltese, Christianity and their pre-Christian 'pagan' past was constructed as a very different kind of cultural narrative from, for example, that constructed by Greeks about their relationship with their 'pagan' (Classical) past. Since the birth of the independent Greek state in 1834, Acropolis Hill and its monuments in particular were chosen as the national symbol of the new state, forging a link between past and present (Fouseki 2006: 534). Sant Cassia (1993: 358) says that Malta's Neolithic temples did not become a symbol of nationhood in the way that Greek temples did, at least for a long time. In Malta nationhood began with Christianity and literacy. For Maltese, he writes (1993: 359), the arrival of St Paul on the island in 60 CE following his shipwreck en route to martyrdom in Rome marked not only the beginning of their history, but also their designation as a 'chosen people, having been selected by divine Providence to become Christians before the rest of Europe'.

It is not only that many Maltese have chosen not to construct a strong link with the Neolithic past. Reuben Grima argues that the otherness of the past has been 'reinforced by a long history of exclusion. During the early nineteenth century, when Malta was a British colony, the people actively interested in these sites were almost exclusively foreign and primarily British' (Grima 1998: 39). For Maltese, Grima claims, the conclusion has been that 'it is the foreigner who can relate to these stones and make them speak'. The 'prehistoric sites have not yet been appropriated by Maltese culture at its grass-roots'. In particular, Grima says, the communities which live closest to the temples located in rural settings have seen them as places of foreign interest and activity. This interest is not always welcomed, especially by those who have traditionally used the countryside around the temples for bird-trapping and hunting, activities which do not complement tourism. The government's creation of a heritage park on a section of the beautiful southern coast encompassing Ħaġar Qim (Figure 9.2) and Mnajdra temples particularly enraged some of these hunters and trappers who felt that their traditional, God-given rights were being curtailed.

In 1996 the southern Mnajdra temple was spray-painted with graffiti which included the name of Malta's Green party (with which the hunters are para-doxically associated) and 'RTO' (an abbreviation of *Reservato*, used in the countryside to mark where a hunting or trapping concession has been rented out). Grima interpreted the vandalism to the temple as 'a perverse but eloquent cry of dispossession' from those who see an intrusive state as 'the direct successor of a foreign colonial power' (1998: 42): the temples had become symbols of the established order rather than a proud national heritage. On Friday, 13 April 2001 there was an even more devastating attack by vandals, who cut through the flimsy wire fence around Ħaġar Qim and Mnajdra and, armed with crowbars and other tools, managed to dislodge, topple and smash sixty megalithic stones. In

Figure 9.2 Façade of Ħaġar Qim. (Photograph courtesy of author.)

the wake of this tragedy, there was a huge public outcry and strong call for much better security, conservation and protection (from the weather as well as vandals) for the temples. But the hunters' anger about what they see as the curtailment of their hunting rights persists. In March 2007 'Mnajdra RIP' was daubed in paint on the roadside leading to the temples following numerous threats of violence and vandalism posted on the web forum of the hunters and trappers' federation (FKNK).[7]

Despite these isolated events and the more generalized distancing described by Sant Cassia and Grima, the temples have been and are widely regarded as important symbols of Maltese identity, particularly since the end of the colonial era, and this importance is growing noticeably in the twenty-first century. Sparked by Maltese independence from Britain in 1964 and by the broader global questing of the period, the 1960s saw an intellectual and artistic renaissance in Malta, along with a questing for self-understanding, roots and identity. Academics, artists, philosophers, musicians, writers, historians, scientists and linguists were all exploring what it meant to be Maltese, and the temples came to be employed as symbols of an essentially Maltese identity.[8] A class of students I spoke with at the University of Malta, children of parents who grew up during the 1960s, emphasized that the temples were part of their heritage and cultural identity. They grew up learning poems which romanticized the sites, engendered patriotic pride and formed a part of their national consciousness.[9] But they also acknowledged that while the temples had been co-opted as symbols to support the artistic revival and nationalistic agenda of the post-independence era, 'the populace' was probably much less aware of this essentially middle-class project. This was echoed in my own early fieldwork in Malta.

In the contemporary context as the colonial period recedes further, the heritage industry grows, more people are coming to value the uniqueness of the Neolithic remains and EU funding is available for temple preservation, the temples have undoubtedly become symbols of nationhood for Maltese. (Malta was admitted to the European Union on 1 May 2004.) While they are important cultural icons and unique tourist attractions with historic, economic and scientific values, they are not, however, or not yet, termed 'sacred sites' – even in a nationalistic sense – in official Maltese heritage discourse.

Comparisons with Greek and British Sites

The Maltese situation is quite different from that in Greece, as described by Fouseki (2006: 541), where, following independence in the nineteenth century, Acropolis Hill was imbued with 'sacredness' in an effort to transform 'the remains of the glorious, classical past of the Acropolis and its landscape into a monumental place in time and space'. Sacredness in this context refers to feelings of respect, national pride and admiration for the aesthetics of the monuments, Fouseki says, and the notion has powerfully helped shape Greek people's identities and perceptions. Of course the iconic importance of the Acropolis is equally enormous for foreign tourists in signifying Greekness.

Malta's temples can also be compared with powerful British cultural icons like Stonehenge. Stonehenge, which is 1,500 years younger than the Maltese sites, is, like them, a UNESCO World Heritage site, sacred to modern Pagans, and vital to tourism. Its meanings, preservation and management have also been contested by a range of interest groups and stakeholders, although the debate over Stonehenge has gone on a great deal longer and been more heated with a higher political profile than the one over Malta's temples (Bender 1993, 1998). One of the groups with an interest in Stonehenge is the diverse and fast-growing British Pagan community, which has, after a chequered history of engagement with the site and with heritage managers, achieved managed open access Solstice celebrations at Stonehenge. As Blain and Wallis (2004: 238) have illustrated, a number of other ancient sites across Britain have also become the focus of Pagans' attention, whether they are visiting sites, conducting ceremonies at them, campaigning for their preservation, protesting about damage or potential damage to them, contributing to community education about heritage, trying to get Pagan interpretations of sites recognized, or to have input into heritage management plans. As a result of political activity and negotiations by British Pagans over a number of years, the work of scholars like Bender and endeavours like Blain and Wallis's 'Sacred Sites, Contested Rights/ Rites' project (Blain and Wallis 2007), Stonehenge and some other high-profile sites are now defined in British heritage discourse as 'sacred site', 'spiritual place' or 'special place' to acknowledge that for some people, including Pagans, the sites hold these values. It should be acknowledged, however, that not all involved in British heritage who use the term 'sacred' are using it in the religious sense. Some are referring to the sense of respect, admiration and national pride that a wide range of people have for these sites.[10]

This is where heritage discourses in Britain and Malta differ. To be fair, Maltese Pagans have not, as a group, entered the political contest over the interpretation, use and management of prehistoric sites in the way that British and other much larger, longer-established cohorts of Pagans have. Modern Greek Pagans, for example, gained international media coverage in January 2007 when, to the great consternation of the Greek Orthodox Church, they performed a dramatic costumed ritual at an ancient sanctuary to Zeus in the heart of Athens, ignoring a ban by the Greek culture ministry. A high priestess within the group, Doreta Peppa, was quoted as saying, 'We are Greeks and we demand from the government the right to use our temples.'[11]

While a few Maltese heritage managers know about the local Pagans, it is likely the majority have never heard of them or know little about them. In any case, they are easy to overlook because of their small numbers (perhaps fewer than 200 people), relatively youthful demographic, necessarily low profile and lack of a defined or coherent political stance in relation to the temples. By and large, the importance of the temples to Maltese Pagans goes unregistered in the wider public consciousness around heritage because it is simply not known about. When special access to Mnajdra and Ħaġar Qim is organized by Heritage Malta at dawn on the equinoxes and solstices – times when remarkable astronomical alignments can be witnessed within the temples – it is so that people (tourists and local people who can afford to join the tour) can be informed by Heritage Malta employees about the scientific aspects of the events (figure 9.3), rather than for Pagans to celebrate their holy days in ways they might deem appropriate.[12]

Maltese Artists and Writers

Four and a half millennia of foreign appropriation and two millennia of Christianity have resulted in a great many Maltese feeling disconnected from these monuments and the past they represent. Even so, some Catholics, including

Figure 9.3 Summer Solstice 2006, Mnajdra. Archaeologist addressing tour group. (Photograph courtesy of author.)

priests, see the temples as 'primitive people's attempts to worship God', and there are Maltese with various backgrounds and interests for whom the temples are deeply important, not only for their historical and heritage values. I met some employed as temple guides and guards who felt personally – as well as professionally – deeply engaged with these places; people from various spiritual paths, including Catholics, who go to the temples to meditate or find peace at times of stress; and individuals whose passion for Maltese history and landscape is more than academic or nationalistic.

Before I met Maltese Pagans, however, the group of Maltese I encountered who were most passionate about the temples comprised artists – painters, writers, architects, sculptors and ceramicists – among whom there has been a fresh renaissance of interest in the legacy of the Neolithic. Some had been working with these themes and images since the 1960s, while others had grown up in the post-independence era and saw the temples as sources of indigenous symbols and global connections. I visited studios and galleries, talked with art critics, and interviewed ten Maltese artists who had worked with temple imagery. Those interviewed had diverse motivations for using Neolithic symbols and themes, but all were concerned with questions of individual and/or national identity and had a strong ecological awareness. They spoke with feeling about their sense of intimate connection with the temples, expressed in terms of nationalistic pride, spiritual rootedness, and a deep reverence and love for the landscape in which the temples are embedded. These configurations of earth, stone, sea and sky were places in which they felt energized and inspired, where spirit and artistic muse were awakened. They talked about their respect for the Neolithic artists, the metaphor of the earth as Mother, of the birth–death–rebirth cycle, and of the Neolithic society as peace-loving and earth-honouring. One woman, writing about an installation she had created inspired by the temples, wrote: 'I am left with the strange feeling of stretching through time ... a sense of being ancient and yet unborn'.[13] Another, who had received permission to paint at some sites, told me that when she entered the Hypogeum to work: 'I would feel like I'm going home ... comfortable and protected.' The ardour with which these indigenous artists – none of whom identified as Pagan – spoke about the temples was at least equal to that of the foreign Pagan pilgrim-tourists I encountered.

Whether they are foreigners or Maltese, Pagan or Catholic, people for whom the Neolithic sites constitute sacred space often indicate that in the context of the temples a series of common binaries dissolve and become continuities: human body and earth body, past and present, inner and outer worlds, self and other, human and deity. A profound connection to the earth and Malta's 'metaphysical heritage', for example, is poignantly evoked in Maltese poet Marlene Saliba's volume of poems *Time-faring* (1994). In 'To the Earth, my Mother' (1994: 15) the protagonist's relationship to the earth and all beings is expressed in terms of vital, loving kinship, concluding:

Lying within the beat of your maternal heart
I listen to your whispers as you tell me
that united in cosmic harmony and understanding
infinite space is infinite love
So here I am my dearest earth
Today and all the days my soul breathes within you.

A sense of kinship with, reverence for, and timelessness within a sacred landscape is similarly explored in many of Maltese writer and architect Richard England's poems (1980, 1994). In 'This Holy Earth' the protagonist kneels on the earth and prays that the 'spirits of this place / may once again attain / their long-lost custody of this land'. The temple's winding paths mirror his life's journey; the stones 'carve alchemies in my changing bones / and guide me through the walls of time' (England 1994: 36–7). Kinship with 'Mother Earth' is also potently expressed in some of the works of Antoine Camilleri, one of Malta's best known artists of the twentieth century, where he embeds self-portraits in his paintings of Neolithic statues found in the temples.[14]

Clearly, perceiving the temples as sacred places and feeling a spiritual bond with them is not the sole prerogative of the foreign Pagan pilgrim-tourists or local Maltese Pagans. Other Maltese too, albeit a minority, view them this way and often did so long before the emergence of contemporary Paganism in Malta in the mid-to-late 1990s. For these people the temples are not mute testimonies to an unknown past; the stones do speak (cf. Sant Cassia and Grima above).

Maltese Pagans

It would be difficult to argue that Maltese Pagans, as a whole group, have a substantially different relationship with the temples from the minority of other Maltese for whom they are special, sacred places. For Pagans, too, the temples are a source of mystery and national pride, something of an enigma in terms of deciphering their meanings with certainty or understanding the society that built them. One of my research participants eloquently expressed what I also heard from non-Pagans:

> I think that something important in the Maltese setting is what I may call the illusion of 'absence of myth'. While modern Greeks, Romans, Scandinavians, British and Irish have a large corpus of myths from their own ancestors to draw from, in Malta little is known about the mythology of our prehistoric cultures. I am not saying that Maltese people do not have access to other mythological cycles and pantheons, but I do think that this lack of knowledge about the people who lived in our islands in times gone by is something significant, for better or worse.

Unlike Pagans in other countries which harbour prehistoric sites once connected with ancient pre-Christian religions, Maltese Pagans have not overtly claimed the temples as part of a specifically Maltese Pagan identity. Like other Maltese, local Pagans emphasize that the temples are World Heritage sites for all to share, and they do not seem to feel that their indigenous status gives them any kind of special claim or connection to them over foreign Pagan visitors, or other non-Pagan people. Unlike British prehistoric sites or temple sites in Greece, Malta's temples have not become places where local Pagans have openly asserted and performed their religious identity by conducting organized, publicly visible ceremonies (although surreptitious rituals and ceremonies are held in them from time to time, as discussed below). They have not explicitly used the temples to legitimize the indigenous roots of their contemporary Paganism, and some Maltese Pagans seem to feel just as strongly drawn to ancient sacred sites overseas – Glastonbury in particular is a much-loved destination of several. The temples have not been incorporated into a programme of regular holy day celebrations, become sites of protest, or the focus of other political claims and activity. Individual and group rituals are more likely to be carried out in Pagans' homes or, occasionally, in public places where they can find a private place away from prying eyes. Far from making dramatic displays or contentious claims to sites in terms of interpretation, management, access, or the legitimization of their contemporary religious path, Maltese Pagans have been deliberately unobtrusive.

Maltese Pagans *do* pray, meditate and conduct rituals at temples, but these activities are mostly carried out quietly by individuals, or by small ad hoc groups (Figure 9.4). As far as I am aware, the largest indigenous Pagan ritual held in a Maltese Neolithic temple so far was the Wiccaning (baby blessing, equivalent of a Christening) of a Pagan couple's infant son, held at Summer Solstice 2008, attended by some thirty people. Some Pagans claim special connections with particular temples: one woman has a strong connection with Mnajdra and frequently goes there to pray, leave offerings and connect with the Goddess (Figure 9.5). When she returns from a trip overseas, she goes straight from the airport to this temple before going home. Indeed for her it is 'home', her literal touchstone for reconnecting with Malta.

Another woman who has had a key role in the local Pagan community for around ten years, on the other hand, has seldom visited the temples, and none of the rituals she has organized have been conducted at temples. The Lammas ritual a small group of us did on a scorching hot afternoon at Mnajdra in August 2005 was not only the first time she had participated in a ritual held in a Maltese temple, it was also the first time she had ever visited Mnajdra. (She had, however, frequently visited Tarxien, a temple complex near her home.) This occasion was one that pointed up the contested nature of Pagan and tourist engagements with these Neolithic monuments. While a steady stream of tourists meandered through the officially accessible areas of the temple, chatting and posing for photographs, the Pagans chose a quiet moment to slip under the cordon intended to keep visitors out of the apses and quietly set up their altar in a concealed apse, conducting the ritual in hushed tones, watchful for tourists who might glimpse (and possibly complain about) them. In official terms, the tourists were there for legitimate purposes, the Pagans were not. Yet the Pagans occupied an inner, private space within the temple, while the tourists were confined – confined themselves – to the restricted space designated for visitors on the other side of the cordon. While the site is explicitly constructed as a place for tourists (including local tourists, perhaps accompanying their visiting overseas relatives), Pagans slipped beneath the radar of this official construction, feeling that their spiritual identification with the ancient temple builders gave them valid access.

To say that the temples have not been employed as symbols of an essentially Maltese Paganism does not mean that they are unimportant to Maltese Pagan identity or imagination. To some extent, the temples function for Maltese Pagans in ways similar to their functioning for other Maltese, like the artists discussed above, who are passionate about them. As one young man told me:

Figure 9.4 Maltese Pagan priestess at Ħaġar Qim temple. (Photograph courtesy of author.)

The temples have always been very sacred to me. Standing near Mnajdra and Ħaġar Qim, I get such a feeling of deep calm – maybe that is also connected to the landscape out there; the land slopes off to a magnificent view of the sea and [the island of] Filfla poking out of the waves. To sum up, I'd say it's a feeling of connection, with the world and with the past which still touches us today.

Figure 9.5 Maltese Pagan at southern Mnajdra temple. (Photograph courtesy of author.)

These are places of energy, prayer, communication with ancestors and spontaneous insights about the ancient culture. Like other Maltese for whom the temples are special places, Pagans visit them when they have a particular problem to solve or feel stressed, or simply to experience the special energy they feel there.

But for Pagans the temples are also more than this: they are places of worship which feel more potently charged with sacred meaning and energy than Christian churches. 'They are more representative of our inclination to the spiritual in my eyes than the largest, most frilly, Gothic cathedral,' one person said. Like the foreign Pagans who visit the temples, Maltese Pagans make a connection between their own contemporary spiritual path and what they understand to be the religion of the temple period, particularly with respect to reverence for the earth Goddess and nature's cycles. They make this connection not as a political claim for Pagan legitimization; it is something felt in the deepest part of a person, in the soul and in the bones. One Pagan man who has worked at the temples for thirty years wrote to me:

> the more I came in contact with the temples, the more I felt connected with them ...
> spiritually, as if the sound of the wind that blew through the fissures of the rock turned
> into words I could understand, as if the spirit of those that built them were trying to

communicate something important to me. I came to understand some of the techniques used to build these magnificent temples just by looking beyond the physical structures and listening. Anyway, I find it always hard to express my experiences in words. I saw people being healed of physical and psychological stress.

Hearing about this experience of the stones coming alive reminded me of one an American Goddess pilgrim described to me, where she heard the stones breathing beneath her while she sat meditating in a temple.

Maltese Pagans talk a lot about the energy of the temples. A Pagan of Maltese descent living in Canada described feeling 'a lot of built up and very old energy' which connected her with particular ancestors. For some Pagans the megalithic stones themselves are reservoirs of enormous energy, while for others the stones are channels of the earth's energy. One Wiccan woman described the stones as working the way a lightning rod does when it earths lightning – except that the stone is channelling energy from the earth below. A friend of hers felt that the temples' energies were generated not so much by the individual stones, but by the interaction of the built structures with the sacred landscapes in which they are embedded. When stones are removed from sites and placed in the National Museum of Archaeology to preserve their decorations better, he cannot feel their energy so strongly. One young woman told me of her frustration when the temples are seen as mere commodities for tourism, when for her and others they are 'sacred space, an area for worship that for some can be more spiritual than a church':

> I do tend to get quite annoyed when temples are marketed as a dead relic of the past, as a stone structure devoid of spirit, as one of the many secular attractions Malta has to offer to tourists. This is not to say that temples should not be promoted, yet I am very much against their commercial exploitation, very much against the sullying of the surrounding landscape, which is part and parcel of the sacred space itself. The temples, whose essential significance has remained unchanged throughout the ages, are testimony to the living soul of the past.

Apart from Pagans' apprehension around current conservation plans in relation to the temples (see below), there seem to be no tensions so far between Maltese archaeologists, heritage managers and local Pagans. As noted above, this is because Pagans have kept a low profile, have not acted as a lobby group, and most heritage managers do not know they exist as a recognizable community distinguishable from other Maltese individuals who love the sites. Maltese Pagans who visit them regularly are more likely to be well known to people who work at the sites – temple guards, guides and site officers – with whom they have developed friendships. It is the foreign pilgrim-tourists, and particularly their tour leaders, who are better known to those who have power over the sites in terms of interpretation and management decisions.

The mostly American Goddess tour leaders have been in regular dialogue with local archaeologists, museum staff and heritage personnel for around two decades, longer than modern Maltese Paganism has been around. An American woman who set up a non-profit foundation to help foster international and local appreciation for Malta's prehistoric heritage has been involved in several temple conservation projects, written a novel about the temples, prepared material for Maltese classrooms, and organized an international conference in Malta for 'Exploring the Maltese Prehistoric Temple Culture'.[15] Her foundation has donated an archaeology laboratory to the University of Malta and chairs for the Museum of Archaeology's seminar hall. Maltese archaeologists give talks on Malta's prehistory to Goddess tour groups and experts on the temples have been flown to the United States to talk to Goddess enthusiasts. Over the years, Goddess tour groups have arranged special access to temple sites – some of which are not normally accessible to other visitors – for educational tours and rituals. This kind of official access arranged by foreign Goddess tour leaders through formal channels contrasts with the informal, friendly and somewhat surreptitious arrangements made by Maltese Pagans with guards on site with whom they communicate in Maltese. The latter negotiations follow the pattern of traditional Maltese patronage relationships where favours are sought through unofficial approaches using local social networks. Being local gives a convenient invisibility to Maltese Pagans' activities, but also means any claims they might have go unregistered.

Some Maltese Pagans have intermittent contact with foreign Pagan visitors to the temples, often as a result of a first meeting through Internet-based groups. Local women are occasionally invited to participate in the activities of American Goddess tour groups, and on two of my field-trips I was introduced to Priestesses of Avalon who were on pilgrimages from England. Such occasions provide opportunities for mutual learning, rituals, temple tours and the making or deepening of valued friendships. Occasionally Maltese Pagan women have been co-opted by foreign Goddess tour leaders as indigenous priestesses to authenticate and embellish the tour experience and to advise and help with local arrangements. While local Pagans are quick to embrace such opportunities for sharing, their time and expertise have not always been recompensed, which has, on occasion, led to a feeling of being taken for granted. Given that Goddess tours can reap considerable financial rewards for their overseas organizers, this could seem to be a form of exploiting local goodwill and generosity.

Temple Conservation

Having survived five and a half thousand years, Malta's Neolithic temples are a remarkable testimony to endurance, but they are under continuing, accelerating threat. The vandals' attacks of 1996 and 2001 wreaked instant, devastating damage, but ongoing weather damage from storms, salt-laden winds, harsh sun, fluctuating temperatures and humidity cause daily erosion and occasionally major destruction. Other threats such as quarrying and a threatened landfill in the vicinity have caused concern and occasioned protest over the years. Interestingly, I was told, it was only when the Catholic Church joined voices with those opposing the landfill scheme and the archbishop claimed that the temples were sacred space, that the scheme was dropped.

In 2003 an international competition was launched to design protective shelters for Mnajdra and Ḥaġar Qim. The winning entry, submitted by a Swiss architect, involved erecting 'tents' constructed of an opaque, Teflon-like textile stretched over steel frameworks and tethered by wire ropes attached to the ground using an anchoring system grouted in boreholes (Figure 9.6). Two-thirds of the funding for the tents was to be funded by an EU Regional Development Fund, with the remainder provided by the Maltese government.[16] The project was finally completed in 2009.

The prospect of placing tents over the temples caused vigorous debate among people passionate about them irrespective of their religious affiliation or local or foreign status. Some thought the 'space-age' appearance of the proposed tents was uncomplementary to the environment of the temples and an aesthetic crime. Some struggled with the idea of any kind of covering for the temples because it would alter the relationship between stones, sea and sky integral to the natural beauty and sacred atmosphere of the area. This group included some of those who visited the temples for solace, artistic inspiration and quiet reflection, including artists and Pagans, both foreign and local. A few people told me that they almost preferred that the temples erode away naturally altogether, rather than be severed artificially from the environment in which they are embedded. To this, others replied that the temples were originally roofed, not open to the sky (although a twenty-first-century Teflon tent is a far cry from a corbelled roof of limestone slabs). A number of local and foreign Pagans worried about how the energy of the temples would be affected by the steel and Teflon structures. Others pointed out that the tents might provide protection from the elements, but not from vandals. Their detractors replied that additional security personnel, an illumination system, a more robust boundary fence and closed-circuit cameras would hopefully deal with the problem of vandals. Some foreign Goddess tour leaders vowed not to bring any future groups to Malta. A local Pagan was so upset at the thought of the temples being shrouded by a synthetic tent that she declared she 'might as well pack up and leave Malta if I can't even save my temples!'

Figure 9.6 Conservation 'tent' covering Ħaġar Qim. (Photograph courtesy of author.)

Conclusion

Clearly Pagan ideas about what it means to 'save the temples' differ from policy-makers', architects' and archaeologists' ideas. For Pagans, indigenous and foreign, the temples are more than cultural icons, tourist attractions and unique feats of Neolithic engineering comprising megalithic monuments susceptible to erosion. They have a timeless numinous energy which is also vulnerable to erosion from the very sources intended to stall the erosion caused by weather damage. As the tents at Mnajdra and Ħaġar Qim have become a physical reality during 2009, there has been a reluctant but pragmatic acceptance among some Maltese Pagans that conservation of the temples is urgent and essential, and some form of roof over them is unavoidable if they are to be preserved. They are somewhat comforted by the fact that the shelters are 'temporary' (designed to last thirty years) and can be removed in the future should some better conservation solution be found. There are still many, though, non-Pagan and Pagan, who are distressed and horrified by the impact that the coverings have had on the sites. One Catholic woman, an artist, told me she was sick for three days and had to take to her bed after first seeing the steel and Teflon structures now covering Ħaġar Qim. On her second visit, however, she felt a lot better about them; the stones' power seemed as strong as ever. Another woman, Pagan, told me she believes the energy of the sites has changed and that the stones will not tolerate what has happened and will somehow get rid of the coverings (by some natural event – she suggested that the storm that ripped one of the tents soon after it was erected constituted a warning about such an event). When I visited the sites myself in July 2009, I noted an unexpected result of the tents: almost all visitors spoke in hushed voices within the temples, as they might visiting a cathedral, perhaps because the presence of a 'roof' separated them from the surrounding landscape and made them feel more like sacred places. This seemed a marked contrast from the days when children ran noisily through the sites and tourists spoke loudly to each other as they snapped photographs.

This chapter disrupts the often taken-for-granted categories of hosts and guests in relation to Malta's Neolithic monuments by demonstrating that attitudes to the temples do not divide along foreign/local lines. Nor do attitudes divide along Pagan/non-Pagan lines. For those Maltese who are passionate about them – whether Pagan, Catholic or something else – the temples hold a similar place in people's imagination and experience: they are sites of sacred heritage, numinous encounter, connection with landscape, peace and beauty. Catholicism and Paganism might seem very different religions, but the strong feelings and attachment the temples generate within such individuals are expressed in similar terms. This affinity with the sites has more to do with class, level of education, and attitudes to heritage, landscape, ecology, history and archaeology than to do with an individual's particular religious or spiritual path. There are still many Maltese for whom the sites do not evoke a sense of heritage, even less the sacred.

Nor is there a categorical difference between Maltese people and foreigners, hosts and guests, in terms of feelings about and engagements with these sites. Foreign Pagan pilgrims and some tourists express feelings of awe, affinity and gratitude that are similar to those expressed by some local people. Foreign Pagan visitors, Maltese Pagans and indeed some Maltese Catholics make the claim that the ancient religion connected with these sites was the distant ancestor of their own contemporary religious path. Overseas Pagans as well as local ones frequently comment that visiting the temples feels like 'coming home'.

While the temples have not (yet) been co-opted in terms of a specifically Maltese Pagan identity – unlike British and Greek sites, for example – they are increasingly being co-opted in the development and public presentation of a postcolonial Maltese identity. Visitors arriving at Malta's recently refurbished national airport at Luqa are now greeted by a replica of the Mother Goddess and temple imagery, along with paraphernalia associated with the Knights of St John and the country's Christian heritage. The pre-Christian past is now being incorporated more obviously and comprehensively in official discourse about Maltese origins, including tourism discourse. A great deal more money is being spent on caring for and promoting the Neolithic sites. After being closed to the public for many years, the Hypogeum reopened to the public in 2004 following major conservation work and the building of a small visitors' centre above the subterranean temple-tomb complex. It is now a premium tourist attraction, with visitors needing to make reservations weeks in advance of their visit. The contentious conservation project associated with Mnajdra and Ħaġar Qim has sparked sporadic but animated public debate in the media over at least the last four years. As I complete revisions of this chapter in July 2009, Heritage Malta is in the final phase of a public consultation campaign regarding a 'Draft Management Plan for the Megalithic Temples', concluding a process begun in July 2006. Such a plan is a requirement for all sites on the UNESCO World Heritage list. The aim of the management plan, according to information panels in the foyer of the Museum of Archaeology, is to 'balance different aspects which affect these sites such as archaeological research, visitor facilities, nature conservation, farming, land use and other local concerns'. No mention is made of sacred values in relation to the sites. The finalized plan is due to be adopted in November 2009.[17]

Art exhibitions in Malta continue to regularly feature work inspired by the temples. Some of the artists are local and some live abroad. Spiral and 'tree-of-life' designs used in Neolithic architecture and decoration commonly appear in tourism material and souvenirs. The variety and availability of temple-inspired souvenirs for sale has increased considerably. When I began this research a decade or so ago, souvenir shops sold an assortment of miniature replicas of Goddess figurines. The figurines are still available, but Goddesses and temple imagery now also appear on a wide range of souvenir commodities, including T-shirts, clocks, aprons, money-boxes, tote-bags, candle-holders and finely crafted silver jewellery. While the importance of the temples should not be overstated – there are still plenty of Maltese who see nothing remarkable about them and deride tourists who make a big deal over 'a pile of old stones' – it is nonetheless evident that a sense of national pride and collective concern about these unique monuments is slowly growing in Maltese society.

Acknowledgements

I am indebted to many people in Malta, above all the Maltese Pagan community who welcomed me into their lives, and the artists and writers I interviewed. I am deeply grateful to Massey University, and in particular the School of Social and Cultural Studies, for supporting my fieldtrips to Malta over the years.

Notes

1. Paganism is now the eighth largest religious grouping in the United Kingdom, with 42,336 people selecting it as their faith in the 2001 British Census (Lewis 2007: 15). The Pagan Federation of Great Britain, which represents many of the faith groups from Wiccans to Druids, estimates the number of Pagans at between 50,000 and 200,000. See Cahal Milmo, 'Paganism and Prejudice', *The Independent* (London), 29 May 2006. http://findarticles.com/p/articles/mi_qn4158/is_20060529/ai_n16433217 (accessed 21 April 2009).
2. See Karen Tate's website: http://www.karentate.com/Tate/sacred_places.html (accessed 27 April 2009).
3. Goddess tours are the most common organized tours. For example, feminist theologian Carol Christ has been running Goddess Tours in Greece since 1993 (http://www.goddessariadne.org/ariadne.htm); Cheryl Straffon and Lana Jarvis run Goddess Tours to Crete, Cornwall and Ireland (http://www.goddess-tours-international.com); and Kathy Jones runs Goddess Tours of Glastonbury (http://www.kathyjones.co.uk/goddesstours.html). There are many others. (Websites accessed 21 April 2009.)
4. The majority of those who run tours do not live in Malta. The notable exception is Clotilde Mifsud, a half-American, half-Maltese woman who set up Goddess Tours to Malta in 1992, and continues to run customized tours to Malta and Gozo (http://www.goddesstourstomalta.com/).
5. 'International Council on Monuments and Sites', ICOMOS, World Heritage Lists no. 130 and no. 132 http://whc.unesco.org/archive/advisory_body_evaluation/132.pdf and http://whc.unesco.org/archive/advisory_body_evaluation/130.pdf (accessed 26 April 2009).
6. Malta was first settled around 5,000 BCE from Sicily and the Temple Culture emerged about 3,600 BCE. Attracted by the islands' strategic position and excellent natural harbours, a stream of settlers, colonizers and rulers followed over successive millennia: Bronze Age people (2,500 BCE), Phoenicians

(800 BCE), Carthaginians (550 BCE), Romans (218 BCE), the Byzantine empire (by at least 535 CE), Arabs (870), the Normans under Count Roger (1090), Swabians (1194), Angevins (1266), Aragonese (1283), Castilians (1410), the Knights of St John (1530–1798), the French under Napoleon (1798–1800) and the British (1800–1964). Malta became a republic on 13 December 1974. See Trump (1990: 20) and Cassar (2000).

7. Editorial, *Malta Today*, Sunday 1 April 2007, p. 19.

8. Some of those who became well known in Malta during this period were Richard England (architect, artist and poet), Father Peter Serracino Inglott (philosopher, academic), Charles Camilleri (music), Francis Ebejer (dramatist/novelist), Antoine Camilleri (artist), Gabriel Caruana (sculpture/ceramics) and Envin Cremona (artist).

9. Examples of such poems are '*Il-Ggantija T'Ghawdex*' and '*F'Hajar Qim*' by Gorg Pisani. Both poems invoke ancient scenarios where maidens are being sacrificed in the temples for their beloved country, either to save it from famine or from foreign invasion. There is, however, no archaeological evidence that human sacrifice ever occurred in the temples (Trump 1990: 30).

10. Email communication, Jenny Blain, 1 February 2007. Blain says that for some in heritage management, defining a site as 'sacred' may be intended to mean a place that was once sacred and needs quiet contemplation.

11. Helena Smith, 'By Zeus!', *The Guardian*, 1 February 2007, http://www.guardian.co.uk/g2/story/0,,2003096,00.html (accessed 28 April 2009); *New Zealand Herald*, 23 January 2007, B3.

12. I was fortunate to be able to join one of these tours at Summer Solstice 2006, and it was a well organized, informative and very enjoyable event, but not one intended to offer a numinous experience.

13. Ruth Bianco, writing on her 'Veils of Absence' exhibition, 1999, text provided to me by artist.

14. In the exhibition 'Antoine Camilleri: A Retrospective Exhibition', 5 June–2 July 1999, such works included 'Mother Earth with Self-portrait', 'Embracing Mother Earth', 'Back in Time: The Patrimony of our People'. Camilleri died on 23 November 2005. I was very fortunate to have the opportunity to interview him in January 2000, shortly before his seventy-eighth birthday.

15. The foundation is called the OTSF (Old Temples Study Foundation). See http://www.otsf.org/index.html and http://www.otsf.org/LindaEneix.htm (accessed 28 April 2009). Linda Eneix's novel is titled *People of the Temples*.

16. http://www.timesofmalta.com/core/article.php?id=256648. Article by Fiona Galea Debono, *The Times*, Thursday 29 March 2007.

17. http://www.heritagemalta.org/resources/mtdraft.html (accessed 3 July 2009).

References

Bender, Barbara (1993), 'Stonehenge: Contested Landscapes (Medieval to Present-day)' in Barbara Bender (ed.), *Landscape: Politics and Perspectives*, Providence/Oxford: Berg, pp. 245–79.

Bender, Barbara (1998), *Stonehenge: Making Space*, Oxford: Berg.

Blain, Jenny and Wallis, Robert (2004), 'Sacred Sites, Contested Rites/Rights: Contemporary Pagan Engagements with the Past', *Journal of Material Culture* 9(3): 237–61.

Blain, Jenny and Wallis, Robert (2007), *Sacred Sites, Contested Rites/Rights*, Brighton, Portland: Sussex Academic Press.

Bonanno, Anthony (1997), *Malta: An Archaeological Paradise*, Malta: M.J. Publications.

Cassar, Carmel (2000), *A Concise History of Malta*, Malta: Mireva.

Eneix, Linda (1997), *People of the Temples*, Sarasota, Florida: OTS Foundation and Malta: Progress Press.

England, Richard (1980), *Island: A Poem for Seeing*, Malta: M.R.S.M.

England, Richard (1994), *Selected Poems: Eye to I*, Malta: Dormax Press.

Fouseki, Kalliopi (2006), 'Conflicting Discourses on the Construction of the New Acropolis Museum: Past and Present', *European Review of History*, 13(4): 533–48.

Grima, Reuben (1998), 'Ritual Spaces, Contested Places: The Case of the Maltese Prehistoric Temple Sites', *Journal of Mediterranean Studies* 8(1): 33–45.

Harvey, Graham (1997), *Listening People, Speaking Earth: Contemporary Paganism*, London: Hurst & Company.

Lewis, James (2007), 'The Pagan Explosion: An Overview of Select Census and Survey Data', in Hannah Johnston and Peg Aloi (eds), *The New Generation Witches: Teenage Witchcraft in Contemporary Culture*, Aldershot, Hampshire and Burlington, VT: Ashgate, pp. 13–23.

Mifsud, Anton and Charles Ventura (1999), 'Introduction', in Anton Mifsud and Charles Ventura (eds), *Facets of Maltese Prehistory*, Malta: Prehistoric Society of Malta, pp. 1–23.

Renfrew, Colin (1973), *Before Civilization*, Harmondsworth: Penguin.

Rountree, Kathryn (2001), 'The Past is a Foreigners' Country: Goddess Feminists, Archaeologists, and the Appropriation of Prehistory', *Journal of Contemporary Religion* 16(1): 5–27.

Rountree, Kathryn (2002a), 'Re-inventing Malta's Neolithic Temples: Contemporary Interpretations and Agendas', *History and Anthropology* 13(1): 31–51.

Rountree, Kathryn (2002b), 'Goddess Pilgrims as Tourists: Inscribing the Body through Sacred Travel', *Sociology of Religion* 63(4): 475–96.

Rountree, Kathryn (2010), *Crafting Contemporary Pagan Identities in a Catholic Society*, London: Ashgate.

Saliba, Marlene (1994), *Time-faring*, Malta: Formatek Ltd.

Sant Cassia, Paul (1993), 'The Discovery of Malta: Nature, Culture and Ethnicity in 19th Century Painting', *Journal of Mediterranean Studies* 3(2): 354–77.

Shackley, Myra (2001), *Managing Sacred Sites: Service Provision and Visitor Experience*, London and New York: Continuum.

Tate, Karen (2006), *Sacred Places of Goddess: 108 Destinations*, San Francisco: CCC Publishing.

Trump, David (1981), 'Megalithic Architecture in Malta', in Colin Renfrew (ed.), *The Megalithic Monuments of Western Europe*, London: Thames and Hudson, pp. 64–76.

Trump, David (1990), *Malta: An Archaeological Guide*, Malta: Progress Press.

Turner, Victor and Turner, Edith (1978), *Image and Pilgrimage in Christian Culture: Anthropological Perspectives*, Oxford: Basil Blackwell.

−10−

'Hotel Royal' and other Spaces of Hospitality
Tourists and Migrants in the Mediterranean
Ramona Lenz

Hospitality and the host–guest relationship are central issues not only of anthropological and socio-scientific tourism studies, but also of the respective practitioner literature. In this chapter, I will pick up some studies from both genres and critically discuss the provided notions of hospitality and the host–guest relationship against the backdrop of ethnographic data from Crete and Cyprus. I suggest that a broader concept of hospitality has to be applied in tourism studies, which offers more than a culturally conservative or an economic rationale approach, and goes beyond the dichotomy of sedentary local hosts and mobile tourist guests. In view of the fact that many tourist regions in the Mediterranean have become hotspots for migration, I will especially stress the need for an understanding of hospitality that considers the various actors involved in or affected by host–guest relationships in Europe and not only the usual suspects of tourism studies.

The Host–Guest Relation

In 1974, the American Association of Anthropologists organized a symposium on tourism and cultural change where several case studies on the host–guest relationship in tourism were presented. These case studies were published three years later in a volume with the title *Hosts and Guests: The Anthropology of Tourism* (see Smith 1992: 187). Since then the host–guest paradigm has become central in tourism studies far beyond the USA.

The dichotomy of hosts on the one hand and guests on the other is related to other oppositions like locals and foreigners or home and away, which imply information about belonging and non-belonging. In the second edition of *Hosts and Guests* (Smith 1989), it is admitted that tourism does not inevitably destroy the cultures visited, but may even have contrary effects. However, the opposition of mobile tourists versus a sedentary local community, whose members act as hosts and are bearers of a certain territorially limited culture, persists. This opposition is enforced by the seemingly obvious differentiation between metropolitan centres

(= countries of origin of tourists) and touristic peripheries (= destination countries of tourists), which especially Dennison Nash (1989: 47) proclaims. Moreover, when tourists are conceptualized as 'temporarily leisured persons' (Smith 1989: 1) the opposition between work and leisure is stressed as a basic and insurmountable difference between 'hosts' and 'guests': 'In sum, tourists are separated from their hosts by the facts of strangerhood, the work-leisure distinction, and whatever cultural differences they obtain in a particular situation' (Nash 1989: 46). Hence, it is assumed that the gap between 'hosts' and 'guests' and the negative effects of tourism grow with an increasing number of tourists (Smith 1989: 11 et seq.).

Critical reflection on these prominent theses on the touristic relation between 'hosts' and 'guests' may start from a number of different aspects. Julio Aramberri (2001), for example, criticizes the fact that most of the contributions to the volume conceptualize the populations of tourist destinations as static and homogeneous communities. According to him, the host–guest paradigm is completely unsuitable for an analysis of modern mass tourism, since it was based on the idea of interaction between members of pre-industrial communities and modern societies which, however, was an exception. In the case of tourism, based mainly on the production and consumption of commodities, services and signs, it was the logic of the market, rather than features like reciprocity, which were central for the relationship of tourists and those who are toured. For this reason, Aramberri considers it to be more appropriate to speak about 'service providers and customers' rather than 'hosts and guests'.

However, there are case studies which show that the relationship between tourists and those who are visited is characterized by more than a merely commercialized interaction (see e.g. Schrutka-Rechtenstamm 1997). Moreover, the tourism sector is often called the 'hospitality industry', and there are many colleges that teach hospitality skills. In tourism management studies, hospitality is considered to be central with regard to the quality of the provided service (see e.g. Pechlaner and Raich 2007). Hospitality and the host–guest relation – however commercialized – thus still deserve research, especially in terms of the service providers and those who teach the respective skills. In socio-scientific and anthropological studies on the host–guest relation, the aspect of service, however, is often neglected as, for example, Valene L. Smith (1992: 192) states. Even though this observation still seems to be correct, I do not agree with Smith's idea that socio-scientific and anthropological research on the host–guest relation in the tourism sector should basically concentrate on the evaluation of service quality (1992: 196), which would subordinate it to the rationale of business management. Nor do I agree with Peter M. Burns (1999: 129 et seq.) who stresses a tension between the tendency to standardization in the tourism industry on the one hand and the tourists' demand for locally unique 'emotional products' like hospitality on the other, and suggests that hospitality should be analysed as a dilemma of globalized 'hospitality and tourism firms'. Too many arbitrary assumptions and simplified dichotomies, for example about the global and the local, are implicit in this argument.

Even though I am sceptical about the above mentioned attempts to adapt the host–guest model to the globalized and commercialized reality of tourism and to narrow down the concept of hospitality to certain business-related research questions, I think we should not completely abandon the issue of hospitality from tourism research, as Aramberri suggests. Rather, I suggest that tourism should be studied in the context of other relevant social phenomena, and that tourism studies can profit from approaches to hospitality that have been developed in other academic fields. If we take into account that service jobs in certain destinations are increasingly staffed by immigrants and seasonal workers from abroad, it may be useful to take the tourism-related host–guest model as a starting point, but question the equation of hosts with locals, and guests with tourists. In this way attention may be directed towards the interchanging roles of locals, service providers and tourists, and their complex interconnections that are constitutive for the tourist destination but also beyond it. Against this backdrop, the questions that arise go further than the concerns that are usually addressed through the host–guest model in tourism studies. Challenging the seemingly self-evident classification of hosts and guests and including various relevant participants in the host–guest interaction, we might ask more generally: Who is welcome as a guest and who is not? Who has the necessary resources at his or her disposal to act as a host and who has not? How do we conceptualize people who participate in host–guest relations but cannot be unambiguously defined either as 'hosts' or as 'guests'?

A privileged place to study different aspects of hospitality is the hotel, a building explicitly set up for the accommodation of guests. The hotel has been used as a chronotope for certain modern lifestyles in the urban centres of the Old World (e.g. Clifford 1997), contrasted by the motel as a metaphor for a rather postmodern way of life (e.g. Löfgren 1995). Both metaphors have been criticized because of their biased presentation of travel that does not reflect class, race and gender inequalities, and ethnographic interest has turned to women, servants and hotel staff (e.g. Adler and Adler 2004) in order to compensate for a predominant travel historiography that concentrates on privileged travellers. In the following, the hotel will not only be considered as a working place for locals and migrants, but also as a potentially multifunctional building that allows for different utilizations from tourist accommodation to detention camp. I will first give an example of the discourse that may be triggered when migrants compete with locals for the role of 'hosts' in so far as they take up jobs in the tourism industry. Then I will explore an example of how the tourist infrastructure is redefined for the accommodation of unwelcome migrant 'guests'. Both examples – the first derives from my fieldwork in Cyprus, the second from my fieldwork in Crete[1] – may illustrate that migrants and refugees have become undeniable participants of what happens in the European 'pleasure periphery' and challenge the touristic host–guest arrangement. In the conclusion, I will then take up concepts of hospitality that are not only relevant with regard to tourism but also with regard to mobilities in Europe in a broader sense.

'Unsettling Hosts'

In the 1980s, the Republic of Cyprus had one of the highest rates of growth of all Mediterranean tourist destinations (Sackmann 1998: 408). Since then the island has constituted an important part of the Mediterranean 'pleasure periphery' (Scott 2000) for many tourists from Western and Northern Europe as well as increasingly for Russians. With more than 50 per cent of all tourists, Britons, however, constitute by far the largest group.[2] The growth of the tourism industry has also had positive effects on other branches of the economy, such as the construction sector.[3]

The general economic growth in the Republic of Cyprus between 1970 and 1990 brought about an increasing need for labourers. The majority of jobs created between 1980 and 1995 – more than eight out of ten – were in the tertiary sector, most of them in hotels and restaurants. In other branches of the service industry, however, which were directly or indirectly related to tourism, the number of gainfully employed persons also augmented. Thanks to the growing tertiary sector the number of gainfully employed persons also rose in total, even though it was declining in the primary sector. In the 1980s, part of the need for workers could be satisfied by population growth, employees from the receding primary sector and returnees from abroad. Mainly, however, it was the increasing number of female workers entering the labour market who filled the vacancies in the tertiary sector. But even the enormous rise in the number of women on the labour market was not enough to meet the growing requirements (Ayres 2000: 119–20).

In 1990, the increasing demand for workers, together with the deceleration in economic growth and the rise in the inflation rate, led to a radical change in the migration policy of the Greek-Cypriot government. For the first time, migrants in large numbers were given work permits in order to boost the Cypriot economy. Since then, immigration from the global East and South has steadily increased, with external factors such as the end of the cold war also playing an important role (Trimikliniotis 2001: 57–8). With a total population of 790,000 for the Republic of Cyprus as a whole,[4] the number of foreign workers who entered the country legally has almost tripled, from 20,713 in 1998[5] to 61,483 in 2006. Around three-quarters of them came from so called 'third countries', the rest from countries of the European Union.[6] According to official estimations, by the end of 2006 there were more than 40,000 migrants living illegally in the Republic of Cyprus (*Cyprus Mail*, 14 October 2006). Most migrants work in poorly paid jobs in labour intensive activities. There is a particularly high demand for foreign workers in the tourism industry, the most important sector of the Cypriot economy.[7] It is especially in this sector, however, that the employment of non-Cypriot staff is highly controversial, and this has to do with a current trend to what is called 'quality tourism', in combination with popular essentialist constructions of what constitutes hospitality.

In the face of unintended side effects and stagnant or declining income from the tourism industry, since the 1990s Cyprus and other Mediterranean tourist destinations have increasingly focused on the diversification of their touristic products, which up to now have been based mainly on the mass touristic consumption of sun and sea, and hence are highly seasonal and concentrated on the coastal regions. 'Sustainability' and 'quality' have become keywords and have been dealt with in several tourism studies on Cyprus since the mid 1990s (Godfrey 1996; Beck and Welz 1997; Ayres 2000; Amato 2001; Sharpley 2003; Sharpley and Forster 2003; Paphitou 2007; Welz 2007). In the wake of this debate, it is demanded that not only the economic, but also the ecological and social effects of tourism development are considered and given more priority. In this context, the local population is taking on greater significance in tourism studies (Akis, Peristianis and Warner 1996; Saveriades 2000) and their degree of 'hospitality' seems to have become a benchmark for the well-being of locals as well as tourists in terms of 'sustainability' and 'quality'.

As with 'hospitality' discourses on other Mediterranean tourist regions, to which especially guidebooks contribute, 'Cypriot hospitality' is often represented as a threatened or already destroyed attribute of an autochthonous population that needs to be protected against commercialization for the well-being of the locals.[8] At the same time, it is declared to be an essential quality feature that is typical for a specific region and makes it interesting for tourism, as, for example, the following passage from an op-ed article in the *Cyprus Weekly* of October 2005 may illustrate:

> Friendliness and hospitality are normal characteristics of most Cypriots in the services… One of the problems of Cyprus tourism today is that there is a labour shortage, and not enough locals to go round in the hotel trade. How do you get a local flavour in the hotels when most of the staff is foreign? What type of hospitality can you get from a Romanian employee who arrived a couple of weeks ago, speaks a crude form of pidgin English and does not know what halloumi means? (quoted from the *Cyprus Mail*, 1 June 2008)

This attitude, expressed in many guidebooks and the aforementioned newspaper article correlates with theses that have been developed in research literature on tourism in Cyprus, which maintain, for instance, that 'hospitality' is a characteristic of Cypriot people and that tourists are keen on it, without giving empirical data apart from subjective impressions. Stephen F. Witt, for example, states: 'In Cyprus, hospitality forms an integral part of the culture, and the people have a welcoming attitude towards foreigners' (1991: 43) and Ron Ayres claims: 'In the past traditional warmth and the friendliness of Cypriots have scored high on consumer satisfaction' (2000: 125). Just as Ayres sees little need to prove his thesis on the relation between hospitality and consumer satisfaction empirically, so does he neglect to give any evidence for how he comes to the conclusion that the tourism industry in Cyprus is discredited by the increasing employment of untrained staff. He simply asserts: '[A]s the industry has grown and taken on large numbers of untrained workers the service provided in some instances has become more mechanical and formal' (2000: 125).

Often foreign staff are per se declared to be unqualified. If it is assumed that 'hospitality' can only be provided by locals, foreigners are qua origin considered to be less qualified for service jobs in the tourism sector. After having blamed the trade unions for the declining productivity and poor service quality in the tourism industry, Richard Sharpley weighs up economic pros and cons of hiring foreign staff for individual entrepreneurs and for the national economy: 'However, likely membership of the EU will make it easier to recruit (cheaper) overseas staff although, importantly, a greater proportion of foreign workers is likely to dilute the traditional hospitality for which Cyprus is renowned, further diminishing the island's competitiveness.' (2003: 253)[9]

Apart from the fact that Sharpley's estimation concerning the easier recruitment of cheaper overseas staff after EU accession is to be doubted, his thesis implies further problematic implications concerning foreign workers. According to Sharpley, they are cheaper and that's why it is entrepreneurially reasonable to employ them. However, the fact that they are foreigners would inevitably contribute to the destruction of 'traditional Cypriot hospitality' – in effect, a contradiction in terms – and would eventually diminish the competitiveness of the island and hence harm the national economy. In this logic, foreign workers can neither experience hospitality, nor can they offer it. Even though there are a lot of private colleges in Cyprus which specialize in providing their students with the necessary qualifications for jobs in the 'hospitality industry' and which profit especially from the fees that foreign students pay (Li 2007), where the Cypriot labour market is concerned, 'hospitality' is considered to be an exclusive characteristic of locals that can not be learned by foreigners. In the presumed host–guest model, foreign staff are either totally disregarded or perceived as a disturbing factor.

A lecturer at the Higher Hotel Institute – a public college in Nicosia which operates as a Department of the Ministry of Labour and Social Insurance and offers educational programmes in Hotel and Catering Studies – explained in an interview:

> Hoteliers in the last few years have taken the easy option by hiring foreign staff, especially in the house and in service positions, in the kitchen, in restaurants and so on, primarily because they are cheaper. They are a cheaper labour force as opposed to Cypriots who are unionized and they have lots of benefits etc. But they create problems to the image of the industry.... You as a national of the country, you go to the restaurant and you cannot communicate with the waiter in your own language, let alone the tourists'.... If the CTO's direction is to transform Cyprus into a quality destination, that's not the best way to do it. You have to start from the workforce.

For quite a few years now the CTO (Cyprus Tourism Organization) has been promoting 'quality tourism' in Cyprus in order to counteract the problem of decreasing per capita spending of tourists. 'Human Resource Development' is defined as one of the three main areas in their strategy plan for tourism between 2000 and 2010, which aims at the proliferation of 'quality tourism'. In the wake of their efforts to turn Cyprus into a destination of 'quality tourism', the CTO commissioned a study that, among other things, focused on foreign personnel in touristic enterprises, as one officer of the CTO told me in 2005. They were, however, not satisfied with the results. Since many migrants worked illegally in Cyprus, the researchers had not been able to conduct interviews nor could they deliver any numbers. Hence, the study was broken off. Summarizing the provisional result, the CTO officer said that most of the respondents – largely tour operators and tourists – did not mention foreign workers at all. Those who did mention them had complained about their dishevelled appearance and lack of language skills: 'They don't speak our language, that's why Cypriots are dissatisfied, and they don't speak any other common European language, that's why the tourists are dissatisfied.'[10] Even though most tourists didn't mention foreign workers at all, and the preliminary results of the study are obviously very sketchy, the CTO's strategy plan (n.d.: 71 et seq.) continues to define the most important means of increasing quality as: 'To cover needs in human resources mainly by Cypriots.'

Employers in the tourism sector appreciate foreign workers not only because they often cost less than locals, but also because as 'third country nationals' their residence and work permit depends on their employer, and they cannot easily change their employer. Hence, in contradiction to the official government policy that aims at a reduction of 'third country nationals' in favour of EU citizens, employers stress how hardworking and reliable they are. Many employers would, however, agree that 'hospitality' can only be properly performed by locals and in this way justify the fact that they hire migrant personnel basically for backstage jobs, as cleaners or dishwashers, and hide them from the 'tourist gaze'. A personnel manager of a big five star hotel in one of the main tourist areas in Cyprus, for example, rejected the employment of 'third country nationals' in jobs with direct customer contact, stating that he feared the eventual damage to the image of Cyprus as a country of exceptional hospitality. Although he stressed that he was very content with his foreign employees, he regretted that hiring foreigners had become an imperative for Cypriot hoteliers: 'We don't have enough staff, so we ended up hiring foreigners and changing the general image.' In a similar way, the manager of a small hotel in a rather remote area of Cyprus was afraid that the authenticity of the tourist experience was impaired by foreign staff. She said: 'I mean, it's nice to go to Cyprus to meet Cypriots, not to meet Bulgarians or whatever, because you want to see the culture.' Foreigners were not used to the local cuisine and didn't know how to prepare traditional Greek food properly. She had two employees from Sri Lanka, but they only worked for the family and not for the hotel guests.[11]

The discourse on foreign workers and their (in)ability to offer hospitality not only has to be analysed against the backdrop of the increased prominence of 'quality' and 'sustainable' tourism in Cyprus and in Europe, but also in the context of the changing Cypriot labour market after EU accession. Defining 'hospitality' as an exclusive characteristic of locals gives a decisive advantage to Cypriot employees, who, since EU accession, have to compete for jobs with citizens from all over the European Union. At the same time, this notion of hospitality can be used by the government in order to implement a more restrictive policy with regard to the employment of 'third country nationals', and entrepreneurs can justify their personnel policy of allocating foreign workers to the exhausting and badly paid jobs backstage. Against this backdrop, socio-scientific or anthropological research does fall short of the touristic reality if it continues to conceptualize 'hospitality' as a threatened or exclusive characteristic of an autochthonous population that is only defined by locals and tourists. There are many more actors and interests that have to be taken into account with regard to the host–guest relation, and 'hospitality' can be considered as the contingent product of transnational negotiation processes.

'Unsettling Guests'

As in Cyprus and other Mediterranean countries, the number of tourists in Greece has – with some intermittent vacillations – increased enormously in the last decades (Reimelt 2004: 14). While in 1950, only 30,000 tourists were counted (Reimelt 2004: 12), in 2006, 17.3 million arrivals of foreign tourists were registered (NSSG 2008a: 211).[12] One important trigger for this expansion was the fact that in the

1960s the Greek government started to invest in tourism planning. In this context, it examined the potential of various Greek regions – for example, of Crete – for systematic tourism development.[13] This initiative was enlarged from 1967 onwards by the military junta, which promoted tourism by tax relief, the extension of the infrastructure and cheap credits. In Crete and elsewhere in Greece, this policy was a major cause of the construction of huge tourism facilities. The building boom and the relatively low level of prices in Greece contributed decisively to the massive increase in tourist arrivals (Kousis 1989: 321; Reimelt 2004: 12). As in Cyprus and other Mediterranean countries, this development had consequences for the employment structure. In 2007, 1.1 million people were legally employed in 'trades, restaurants and hotels', which hence constitutes the most important employment sector in Greece, followed by the manufacturing industry and the sector 'agriculture, livestock and fishing' (NSSG 2008b: 7). Not least because of the significance that tourism has gained over the years, there is a clear trend from the primary to the tertiary sector (Reimelt 2004: 11–2). It is estimated that about 40 per cent of employees in bars, restaurants, taverns and hotels are foreigners, mainly from Albania, Russia, Ukraine, Poland and other countries of the former Eastern block (Kathimerini, quoted from *Griechenland Zeitung*, 8 July 2003).

Within Greece, Crete has become the most important tourism destination. The tourism industry is the principal sector of the island's economy and has been growing even more than in other regions of Greece. The overnight stays in Crete constitute more than one-fifth of all stays in the whole country (Reimelt 2004: 33). They have increased from 3,767 in 1954 to 12.58 million in 2001 (Reimelt 2004: 24).[14] It is estimated that approximately 40 per cent of the 600,000 registered Cretans (NSSG 2008a: 39) directly or indirectly work in the tourism industry (Andriotis 2005: 70–1). Since the 1970s, the employment structure has shifted to the tourism sector, while there is a labour shortage in other sectors, especially in agriculture,[15] whereas areas of the secondary sector like the food and the construction industry profit from the tourism development (Velissariou 1999: 51 et seq.). As in Cyprus and elsewhere the need for workers for labour-intensive and poorly paid jobs in different sectors of the economy – in agriculture as well as in tourism – is increasingly met by workers from abroad. There are a lot of workers from Albania, Bulgaria, Serbia and countries of the former Soviet Union, many of them working illegally (Meyer-Bauer 2003: 25; Reimelt 2004: 43 et seq.) Moreover, there are many people from Western and Northern EU countries in Crete who are not necessarily working in more privileged positions but also compete for the same jobs with people from less wealthy countries.

Even though tourism is still prospering, local entrepreneurs notice stagnation or even decline in their revenues. Hence, they not only employ cheaper foreign staff, but have also started to rent out their hotels and guesthouses more permanently to workers, students and refugees. During my fieldwork in Crete in spring and late summer 2004, I stayed in different tourist accommodations. All of them were occupied not only by people spending their holidays in Crete, but also by people who stayed there for other reasons. A hotel that, in summer, was booked by international tour operators for tourists from Germany, Austria, Poland and Hungary, in winter turned into an accommodation for mainland Greek students attending the nearby university. A small guesthouse in the historic city centre of Réthimnon, where my fieldwork was principally located, was partly rented out to Erasmus students from France, and the cockloft of another guesthouse was permanently occupied by a German who had emigrated to Greece. The youth hostel in the same town was inhabited by various groups of people. There were backpackers as well as seasonal workers from Britain or Albania and street traders from Israel and Senegal. Since the time span of my fieldwork in Crete was limited, these are, of course, only snapshots. The composition of the 'guests' changes frequently.

Taking the example of the 'Hotel Royal', which is located a few kilometres away from the Cretan capitol of Iráklion, I will try to illustrate some consequences of the fact that the various 'guests' in Mediterranean tourist destinations have become a constant characteristic of the region and unsettle conventional notions of touristic or migrant host–guest relations. In summer, 'Hotel Royal' serves as a tourist accommodation for less privileged Greek citizens from the north of Greece who are once a year entitled to state-sponsored vacations on one of the Greek islands. When we – a political scientist, a sociologist and myself, a cultural anthropologist, from Germany – visited the 'Hotel Royal' in September 2004, the touristic peak season had already come to an end. However, about 140 persons were said to be staying currently in the hotel, though, when we arrived, no one could be noticed on the balconies and the entrance hall was totally deserted. We were told that the hotel guests were not allowed to leave the first floor of the building or to use the balconies.

When we went upstairs we found three men sitting in the corridor playing cards. Two of them were wearing uniforms of the Greek navy. They kept an eye on the guests and made sure that no one escaped from the hotel. The third card player – like the rest of the hotel guests – was a refugee from Egypt or Palestine. The men had left Alexandria heading for the Italian coast. A week before, their ship had almost sunk in the middle of the Mediterranean Sea. Greek coastguards rescued the passengers and brought them to Crete. Originally, the ship's crew had consisted of six persons. Since two of them had disappeared, the police arrested the remaining four and one of the passengers. The other passengers were temporarily accommodated in the 'Hotel Royal', which in the low season serves as a detention camp. The same personnel that in summer had served the tourists now catered for the refugees, with the kitchen staff adjusting the menu to cook without pork.

We spoke with some passengers. One of them introduced himself as the headmaster of a school in Egypt. He explained that he had paid €2,000 for the crossing to Italy. He was told that they were going to bring him to a big ship where he would be provided with a passport and a visa. Nothing like that happened in the end and he was left with no official documents at all. Others had similar stories to tell. After the Cretan coastguards had brought the ship from Alexandria under their control, one of their first actions was to separate out the tour operators who, due to the difficult mobility conditions at the external borders of the European Union, are usually called 'smugglers of human beings'. Thus, the first gathering of the new arrivals, which took place in the lobby of 'Hotel Royal', was not for the welcome cocktail but to let the passengers identify the members of the ship's crew. In this way the border police were able to separate the 'villains' from the 'victims'. Even though this dichotomy is highly problematic with regard to the actual practices of border crossing, it is central for the legitimization of European migration politics. It allows for a certain management of migration: with the official objective of smashing 'trafficking networks' and 'smuggling gangs', intensified border controls may be legitimized as humanitarian measures, which serve the prosecution of crimes and the protection of 'victims'. Through this process those involved in the 'movement of migration' are split up into 'villains' on the one hand and 'victims' on the other (Bojadžijev and Karakayalı 2007: 206).

Scholars have acknowledged that the mobility of people has caused the erosion of the immobilizing equation of 'territory, identity and nationality' (Beck and Grande 2004: 193).[16] With the undermining of the nexus of 'state, nation (birth) and territory', the nation-state entered a state of crisis, and in this crisis the camp has gained ground, as Giorgio Agamben (2002 [1995]: 185) explains. What happens in the camp, according to Agamben, is the stable spatial installation of the state of exception, which was originally only a temporary abolition of the legal order. Agamben puts it as follows: 'The camp is the space, which opens up when the "state of exception" begins to become the rule.' (2002 [1995]: 177). He explicitly stresses that the camps of today can be found in seemingly harmless places such as hotels. If we follow Agamben's argumentation, places like 'Hotel Royal' actually define a space where the normal order is in fact abolished. In such a place, what happens with its inhabitants no longer depends on the law, but on the civility and ethics of the police, who temporarily act as sovereign here (2002 [1995]: 183–4).

During our visit to the 'Hotel Royal', we learned that most inhabitants were waiting for their deportation. Some of them were planning to apply for the status of asylum seekers. The Egyptians among them would rather not do so, because, in the case of their very probable deportation, they would have to fear imprisonment for treason once back in Egypt, and new attempts to migrate would become more difficult, as a representative of Amnesty International Iráklion explained to us later. The fears of deportation are absolutely justified, because organizations like the UNHCR (United Nations High Commissioner for Refugees) or the IOM (International Organization for Migration) and other powerful actors of the European border regime, which have taken on the responsibility concern for human rights issues from the nation-states, usually proceed in such cases in accordance with the principle that people should live where 'their homeland' is, where their 'folks' are 'at home' (Düvell 2002: 107–8).

However, it is by no means inevitable that an illegal journey into the European Union ends in repatriation, even if one is caught and placed in a detention camp. An application for asylum, made in a camp in Greece, can help one to obtain a temporary residence permit in the country. Only a very small number of applications for asylum are accepted in the end, but the application offers the possibility of getting legal residence status until the case is dealt with, and once you are there, you may try to overstay illegally. From other camps in Greece it is known that camp inhabitants are released after three months with a document that calls on them to leave the country 'voluntarily' within a fortnight 'in a direction of their choice'. That gives them the possibility of continuing their journey to mainland Greece and Europe. It may take one to two years until it finally comes to an interview with the applicant. 'This administrative practice documents an openly admitted political calculation: that the migrants don't show up for the interview and remain illegally in the country or continue their journey', as Efthimia Panagiotidis and Vassilis Tsianos (2007: 72–3) put it.

Hence, we wouldn't understand the camp properly if we considered it to be a place of total immobilization. On the contrary, it can become an entrance ticket to the West. It may be regarded as 'as the spatialized attempt to temporarily control people's movements by administering their routes' (Panagiotidis and Tsianos 2007: 79). Detention camps obviously do not aim at the total prevention of illegal border crossings, but rather at their regulation according to the needs of the labour market. So we were not too surprised when, a few days after our visit, we learned that a small group of the refugees had managed to escape from the hotel-camp and disappear. Rather than representing moments of total immobility, the camps seem to be a means 'to control mobility by deceleration' (Panagiotidis and Tsianos 2007: 81).

Doubtless the situation of the men from Alexandria whom we met in the 'Hotel Royal' differs significantly from that of the tourists who had occupied the hotel a few weeks before. The mere fact that they were accommodated in the same place doesn't make them travellers of the same class. In an often quoted passage about the antagonistic difference between 'tourists' and 'vagabonds', Zygmunt Bauman says:

> The tourists stay or move at their heart's desire. They abandon the site when the new, untried opportunities beckon elsewhere. The vagabonds, however, know that

they won't stay for long, however strongly they wish to, since nowhere that they stop are they welcome. The tourists move because they find the world within their reach irresistibly attractive; the vagabonds move because they find the world within their reach unbearably inhospitable. (1998: 309)

The stress on a fundamental difference between 'tourists' and 'vagabonds' according to whether they are welcome or not, not only misses out the various intersections of tourism and migration, but also the structural proximity of the different mobility forms in terms of their consequences for the polity. The example of 'Hotel Royal' illustrates that migration and tourism in Europe materialize in similar infrastructures. The often provisional solutions for the accommodation of people who stay for a limited period of time have a 'hybrid, multifunctional character' (Holert and Terkessidis 2006: 251) and allow for different utilizations. Often they are equipped with similar technologies, used for different purposes. From the perspective of technological progress, the night sensing equipment that is used by the border police to detect migrants who try to enter the European Union illegally seems to be equivalent to the monitoring cameras that are installed in order to protect the vacation colonies of the tourists, the houses of returned former emigrants and the apartments of the residents from the north.

Apart from that, the refugee camps as well as the vacation colonies seem to have similar consequences for the polity. With the provisional accommodations and camps for migrants and the building projects of the tourism industry, a whole world of strange interim solutions, of seasonal or temporarily occupied places, sometimes overcrowded, sometimes totally deserted, is created, as Tom Holert and Mark Terkessidis (2006) maintain. Increasingly, these accommodations become what we paradoxically might call 'permanent interim solutions' (2006: 48) for 'people who are absent, who commute, who pass by in summer, who wait' (2006: 127). Especially in the Mediterranean, the European pleasure periphery at the external borders of the European Union, more and more 'zones in the permanent state of exception' (2006: 169) come into being. Not only are many migrants often without papers, but so are many of the tourists who occupy these zones. Even though Europeans are allowed to move without restrictions within the European Union, they have to register when they stay for a longer time in a country different from their country of passport. However, only very few actually do so (2006: 181). Even if they do, many of them are not interested in local politics. 'Water, electricity, and a highway seem to be sufficient as connection to the polity' (2006: 139). Hence, at the edges of Europe – but also in its presumed centres – more and more places without a public seem to emerge: places which are inhabited by people who either don't possess political rights or don't care for political participation. Holert and Terkessidis come to the conclusion: 'What is in the making here and all over Europe are whole cities without citizens.'

Conclusion

Hospitality is apparently more than an act of courtesy or the result of a simple cost-benefit calculation, which can be reduced to the interaction of tourists and local service providers, especially when it is no longer obvious who the host is and who the guest. According to Emil Beneviste, the drawing of borders in the process of nation building has fundamentally changed host–guest relations: when an 'ancient society becomes a nation, interpersonal relations as well as those between clans weaken. Only the distinction between what is internal and external to the civitas remains relevant' (Beneviste quoted in Heidrun Friese 2004: 69). Hence, hospitality becomes an issue that affects not only interpersonal relations, but also relations between states, as well as between states and individuals.[17] Jacques Derrida differentiates between ethics of unconditional, absolute hospitality, and laws or politics of limited hospitality. The latter conform to the interests of nations or states, which constitute themselves by defining borders and which confirm their territorial sovereignty by being hospitable to some and denying access to others. In contrast to the *politics* of hospitality, the *ethics* of hospitality implies an unconditional opening of borders and doors for everybody, putting up with the greatest risks (Germann Molz and Gibson 2007: 4–5). Implicit in both notions of hospitality is an ambivalent concept of the guest, who may be a friend or an enemy.[18] Against that backdrop, hospitable gestures may aim at minimizing the risk by creating 'reliability, durability and continuity' (Friese 2004: 70). They can be understood as 'more or less formalized rites of integration' that regulate the transformation of strangers or guests into 'human and social beings' with a determined place in the social geography. The stranger 'must be "transformed into a relative or a citizen" to receive rights and to assume duties and responsibilities' (2004: 71).

Problems arise when the guest stays but his or her status doesn't change. Mireille Rosello (2001: 18) maintains that in postcolonial Europe the host–guest relation is rather consolidated. According to her, the differentiation between hosts and guests goes along with a series of other problematic opposition pairs like power and powerlessness, property and expropriation, stability and nomadism. She states: '[I]f the guest is always the guest, if the host is always the host, something has probably gone very wrong' (2001: 167). In the same vein, Karima Laachir reflects on the 'inclusive exclusion' which is implied in the consolidation of the host–guest relation in Europe that Rosello highlights: 'Descendants of post-war immigrants believe themselves to "belong" to Europe, but they are still widely perceived as outsiders whose cultural, religious and social values will never be reconciled with "European values". This may be perceived as an attempt to turn postcolonial settlers into migrants long after immigration came to a halt.' (2007: 185) As long as colonial and postcolonial migration is not considered to be an integral part of European history, and immigrated people are not perceived as equal members of the society but as 'guests' at the most, 'hospitality' has to be seen as an expression of continuing colonial power relations, she concludes (2007: 186).

With regard to Southern European countries like Greece and Cyprus, the postcolonial situation is somewhat different. The settlement of foreigners there can only in part be directly connected to the colonial past as, for example, in the case of Britons who establish their retirement home in Cyprus. However, the problem that the guests remain guests, although they spend most of their time in the country, is not only relevant with regard to the postcolonial situation in Western Europe, but also with regard to the Mediterranean countries of Southern Europe, which have become hotspots for tourism and migration. Refugees on their way to Europe, who are picked up at the Mediterranean coasts and are temporarily arrested in hotels and other touristic buildings, disturb the host–guest arrangement between locals and tourists, as well as migrants who work in the tourism industry. If refugees or migrants stay in the country and yet work in the 'hospitality industry', they are neither perceived to be 'guests' like the tourists nor are they considered to be in the position of a 'host' who is able to properly provide the hospitality that their job demands. Their status is kept in abeyance. The same is true for former tourists who have settled in the Mediterranean or spend most of the year there but still behave like 'guests' in so far as they don't care for or don't get access to the social and political life of the place where they live. What unites these different groups of people is that they – voluntarily or not – do not participate in the polity but rather stay in the position of welcome or unwelcome 'guests'.

A concept of hospitality that is able to grasp the conditions of a globalized world full of migrants, tourists and other mobile people needs to question the territorial notion of 'home' and has to look into the complex flows and circulations of hosts, guests and objects as they can be found in the Mediterranean (Germann Molz and Gibson 2007: 13). Jennie Germann Molz and Sarah Gibson put it as follows:

> We want to illuminate the paradox of hospitality – that it evokes both home and movement – in order to destabilize the way power relations are congealed within the paradigmatic discourses in tourism and migration studies. We hope to figuratively mobilize the concept of hospitality across disciplines and to de-couple associations of the host with home, territory, stability, and ownership on one side, and of the guest with mobility, estrangement and un-belonging on the other. (2007: 16)

This approach is not only useful regarding Western European countries with a migrant population that derives from a recent imperialist history, but also for an analysis of mobilities at the south-eastern borders of the European Union, where tourism and migration interrelate in various ways. In view of these multilayered interactions, hospitality is not adequately captured as the characteristic of a sedentary local population, but rather as the product of various discourses and practices by which people negotiate and perform their position in changing social geographies.

Acknowledgements

I would like to thank Miriam Wallraven for her invaluable proof-reading and the Frankfurt Graduate School for the Humanities and Social Sciences (FGS) which provided the funding for this.

Notes

1. My fieldwork was conducted in spring and summer of 2004 (Crete) and 2005 (Cyprus) within the framework of my recently completed doctoral thesis. In Crete, I was primarily located in Réthimnon, a town in the north of the island. 'Hotel Royal', which is discussed in this paper, however, is located a few kilometres away. My fieldwork in Cyprus mainly concentrated on a village at the west coast of the Republic. In Cyprus as well as in Crete, I also spent time in the respective capital city, where I conducted a series of expert interviews.
2. Between January and September 2008, 1,965,855 arrivals of tourists were counted in the Republic of Cyprus (exclusive of the Turkish occupied northern part of the island), which was 0.3 per cent less than in the same period of the year before; 81.5 per cent of all tourists came from EU countries. Tourists from the United Kingdom constituted the largest group with 52.4 per cent of all arrivals, followed by Russians with 7.7 per cent, Swedes with 5.4 per cent, Greeks with 5.2 per cent, Germans with 4.8 per cent, Norwegians with 2.8 per cent, Danes with 1.7 per cent and French with 1.5 per cent (Statistical Service of the Republic of Cyprus 2008: 7–8).
3. As in many other Mediterranean countries, many former tourists have acquired real estate in Cyprus and the island has become their first or secondary residence, which has led to an enormous increase in building activities on the island.
4. According to the demographic report of the Statistical Service of the Republic of Cyprus, the total population was 789,300 by end of 2007 (Statistical Service of the Republic of Cyprus 2007).
5. See Statistical Service of the Republic of Cyprus (2003: 59).

6. According to more recent estimations, the total number of foreign workers in the Republic of Cyprus amounts to 150,000, of which about 40,000 come from other European Union countries and more than 80,000 entered legally from so called 'third countries', mainly from Sri Lanka and the Philippines. The rest is supposed to have entered and stayed in the country illegally. Moreover, around 8,000 people wait for the processing of their asylum application (*Cyprus Mail*, 3 October 2007).

7. According to the director of the Cypriot Tourism Organization, tourism is the largest source of income for the Republic of Cyprus: 13–15 per cent of the Cypriot economy was directly, and another 20 per cent indirectly, dependent on tourism (*Cyprus Mail*, 20 September 2006). With 8.9 per cent of the economically active population who in 2004 worked in the hotel, restaurant and catering sector, the numbers in Cyprus were proportionally more than double the EU average, and the highest of all the (at this point) 25 EU member states (Eurostat quoted from *Cyprus Weekly*, 14 October 2005).

8. See, for example, passages in the German guidebooks on Cyprus by Korst and Hoff (2002: 95) or by Braun (2005: 10).

9. See also Sharpley and Forster (2003: 689).

10. This assumption is much too sweeping, if, for example, you consider the fact that there are many Russian-speaking waiting staff in Cyprus and that Russians have become the second largest group of tourists in Cyprus.

11. See also the study of Gisela Welz (2007: 343–4) about an agrotourism entrepreneur who, in accordance with sustainable tourism criteria, prefers to recruit employees from Cypriot villages. In his eyes, Cypriots add zest to the service for customers and offer a special human warmth.

12. Most of the foreigners who arrive in Greece come from the United Kingdom, followed by Germany and Albania (NSSG 2008a: 212). Tourists predominantly arrive in summer, two-thirds of them between June and September (Reimelt 2004: 17).

13. For a critical assessment of the Greek tourism policy today, especially with regard to Crete, see, for example, Andriotis (2001) or Reimelt (2004: 14 et seq.).

14. Three-quarters of all foreign tourist arrivals are concentrated in the months May to September (Reimelt 2004: 29). Regarding the problem of seasonality in tourism and attempts to prolong the season in Crete, see, for example, Donatos and Zairis (1991) or Reimelt (2004: 55–6).

15. At 38 per cent, the number of workers in agriculture in Crete is, however, still very high and far beyond the Greek average (Reimelt 2004: 22; see also Meyer-Bauer 2003: 27–8).

16. All English quotation from German texts (see references) have been translated by Ramona Lenz.

17. In his reflections on cosmopolitanism, Kant maintains that universal hospitality between states is the condition for universal peace, whereby he considers the principle of reciprocity as central to hospitality. Karima Laachir (2007: 179) criticizes Kant for not taking into account the problem of unequal distribution of power and resources between states. She concludes that his cosmopolitanism is basically reserved for wealthy and powerful states that impose their principles on the rest. Seyla Benhabib (2008), however, offers a different interpretation of Kant's hospitality concept. She also stresses that the concept is predominantly related to the interaction of states (2008: 27 et seq., 131–2), but in contrast to Laachir she seems to be convinced that it implies a critique of hierarchical power relations between states when she interprets Kant's theses as a 'jeremiad against Western imperialism' (2008: 133).

18. In her postcolonial critique of concepts of hospitality, Mireille Rosello (2001: 12–13) points out that only the guest is perceived as potentially dangerous, whereas the threat that may emanate from the hosts – for example, in the form of racist assaults – is not considered.

References

Adler, P. A. and Adler, P. (2004), *Paradise Laborers: Hotel Work in the Global Economy*, Ithaca, NY and London: Cornell University Press.

Agamben, G. (2002 [1995]), *Homo sacer: Die souveräne Macht und das nackte Leben*, Frankfurt/M.: Suhrkamp Verlag.

Akis, S., Peristianis, N. and Warner, J. (1996), 'Residents' attitudes to tourism development: the case of Cyprus', *Tourism Management* 17(7): 481–94.

Amato, F. (2001), 'Nachhaltigkeit als Hoffnung für das zypriotische Hinterland: Neue Konzepte in Denkmalpflege, Regionalentwicklung und Tourismus', in G. Welz and P. Ilyes (eds), *Zypern. Gesellschaftliche Öffnung, europäische Integration, Globalisierung*, Frankfurt/M.: Kulturanthropologie Notizen, pp. 173–98.

Andriotis, K. (2001), 'Tourism Planning and Development in Crete: Recent Tourism Policies and their Efficacy', *Journal of Sustainable Tourism* 9(4): 298–316.

Andriotis, K. (2005), 'Community Groups' Perceptions of and Preferences for Tourism Development: Evidence from Crete', *Journal of Hospitality and Tourism Research* 29(1): 67–90.

Aramberri, J. (2001), 'The Host Should Get Lost: Paradigms in the Tourism Theory', *Annals of Tourism Research* 28(3): 738–61.

Ayres, R. (2000), 'Tourism as a Passport to Development in Small States: Reflections of Cyprus', *Journal of Social Economics* 27(2): 114–33.

Bauman, Z. (1998), 'On Glocalization: Or Globalization for Some, Localization for Some Others', in Z. Bauman (ed. by P. Beilharz), *The Bauman Reader*, Malden, MA and Oxford: Blackwell Publishers, pp. 298–311.

Beck, S. and Welz, G. (1997), 'Naturalisierung von Kultur – Kulturalisierung von Natur: Zur Logik ästhetischer Produktion am Beispiel einer agrotouristischen Region Zyperns', *Tourismus Journal: Zeitschrift für tourismuswissenschaftliche Forschung und Praxis* 1(3–4): 431–48.

Beck, U. and Grande, E. (2004), *Kosmopolitisches Europa: Gesellschaft und Politik in der Zweiten Moderne*, Frankfurt/M.: Suhrkamp Verlag.

Benhabib, S. (2008), *Kosmopolitismus und Demokratie: Eine Debatte*, Frankfurt/M. and New York: Campus Verlag.

Bojadžijev, M. and Karakayalı, S. (2007), 'Autonomie der Migration. 10 Thesen zu einer Methode', in Transit Migration Forschungsgruppe (ed.), *Turbulente Ränder. Neue Perspektiven auf Migration an den Grenzen Europas*, Bielefeld: Transcript Verlag, pp. 203–9.

Braun, R.R. (2005), *Zypern*, Erlangen: Michael Müller Verlag.

Burns, P.M. (1999), *An Introduction to Tourism and Anthropology*, London and New York: Routledge.

Clifford, J. (1997), *Routes. Travel and Translation in the Late Twentieth Century*, Cambridge, MA and London: Harvard University Press.

Cyprus Mail (20 September 2006), 'Sun and sea are not enough'.

Cyprus Mail (14 October 2006), 'How will Romania and Bulgaria affect our workforce?'

Cyprus Mail (3 October 2007), 'Migrant numbers pass 150,000 mark'.

Cyprus Mail (1 June 2008), 'Tourism plagued by lack of vision'.

Cyprus Tourism Organization (n.d.), *Strategy Plan for Tourism 2000–2010*, Nicosia.

Cyprus Weekly (14 October 2005), 'Cyprus tops in hotel employees league'.

Donatos, G. and Zairis, P. (1991), 'Seasonality of Foreign Tourism on the Greek Island of Crete', *Annals of Tourism Research* 18(3): 515–19.

Düvell, F. (2002), *Die Modernisierung des Migrationsregimes. Zur neuen Einwanderungspolitik in Europa*, Berlin and Hamburg: Assoziation A.

Friese, H. (2004), 'Spaces of Hospitality', *Angelaki: Journal of the theoretical humanities* 9(2): 67–79.

Germann Molz, J. and Gibson, S. (2007), 'Introduction: Mobilizing and Mooring Hospitality', in J. Germann Molz and S. Gibson (eds), *Mobilizing Hospitality: The Ethics of Social Relations in a Mobile World*, Aldershot: Ashgate, pp. 1–25.

Godfrey, K.B. (1996), 'Towards Sustainability? Tourism in the Republic of Cyprus', in L.C. Harrison and W. Husbands (eds), *Practicing Responsible*

Tourism: International Case Studies in Tourism Planning, Policy and Development, New York: John Wiley & Sons, pp. 58–78.

Griechenland Zeitung (8 July 2003), 'Hoher Ausländeranteil in der Touristenbranche'.

Holert, T. and Terkessidis, M. (2006), *Fliehkraft: Gesellschaft in Bewegung – von Migranten und Touristen*, Köln: Kiepenheuer & Witsch.

Korst, M. and Hoff, E.P. (2002), *Zypern Handbuch*, Rappweiler: Reise Know-How Edgar Hoff Verlag.

Kousis, M. (1989), 'Tourism and the Family in a Rural Cretan Community', *Annals of Tourism Research* 16: 318–32.

Laachir, K. (2007), 'Hospitality and the Limitations of the National', in J. Germann Molz and S. Gibson (eds), *Mobilizing Hospitality: The Ethics of Social Relations in a Mobile World*, Aldershot: Ashgate, pp. 177–90.

Li, H.Y. (2007), 'Studying Abroad in Cyprus – Taking Part in a Globalised World? Chinese Students and the Greek-Cypriot Higher Education System after EU Accession', Final Report of the Field Research Course 2005–6 *New Europeans: Cyprus after EU Accession*, Working Paper No. 1, Frankfurt/M.: Institut für Kulturanthropologie und Europäische Ethnologie.

Löfgren, O. (1995), 'Leben im Transit? Identitäten und Territorialitäten in historischer Perspektive', *Historische Anthropologie* 3: 349–63.

Meyer-Bauer, D. (2003), *Europäische Integration – Kultureller Wandel in Westkreta*, Dietrich Reimer Verlag: Berlin.

Nash, D. (1989), 'Tourism as a Form of Imperialism', in V.L. Smith (ed.), *Hosts and Guests: the Anthropology of Tourism*, 2nd edition, Philadelphia: University of Pennsylvania Press, pp. 37–52.

NSSG (National Statistical Service of Greece) (2008a), *Concise Statistical Yearbook 2007*, Pireas.

NSSG (National Statistical Service of Greece) (2008b), *Greece in Figures*, Pireas.

Panagiotidis, E. and Tsianos, V. (2007), 'Denaturalizing "Camps". Überwachen und Entschleunigen in der Schengener Ägäis-Zone', in Transit Migration Forschungsgruppe (ed.), *Turbulente Ränder. Neue Perspektiven auf Migration an den Grenzen Europas*, Bielefeld: Transcript Verlag, pp. 57–85.

Paphitou, N. (2007), 'Same route, different tourists: methodological issues in tourism research', ASA Conference '*Thinking through tourism*', London Metropolitan University (E-Paper).

Pechlaner, H. and Raich, F. (eds) (2007), *Gastfreundschaft und Gastlichkeit im Tourismus: Kundenzufriedenheit und -bindung mit Hospitality Management*, Berlin: Erich Schmidt Verlag.

Reimelt, M.P. (2004), *Kreta: Fallstudie für ein nachhaltiges Tourismuskonzept*, Sindelfingen: Libertas.

Rosello, M. (2001), *Postcolonial Hospitality: The Immigrant as Guest*, Stanford: Stanford University Press.

Sackmann, B. (1998), 'Tourismus', in K.D. Grothusen, W. Steffani and P. Zervakis (eds), *Südosteuropa-Handbuch, Vol. VIII: Zypern*, Göttingen: Vandenhoeck & Ruprecht, pp. 408–36.

Saveriades, A. (2000), 'Establishing the Social Tourism Carrying Capacity for the Tourist Resorts of the East Coast of the Republic of Cyprus', *Tourism Management* 21: 147–56.

Schrutka-Rechtenstamm, A. (1997), 'Gäste und Gastgeber: touristische Ritualisierungen diesseits und jenseits der Bezahlung', *Tourismus Journal: Zeitschrift für tourismuswissenschaftliche Forschung und Praxis* 1(3–4): 467–81.

Scott, J. (2000), 'Peripheries, Artificial Peripheries and Centres', in: F. Brown and D. Hall (eds), *Tourism in Peripheral Areas: Case Studies*. Clevedon: Channel View Publications, pp. 58–73.

Sharpley, R. (2003), 'Tourism, Modernisation and Development on the Island of Cyprus: Challenges and Policy Responses', *Journal of Sustainable Tourism* 11(2–3): 246–65.

Sharpley, R. and Forster, G. (2003), 'The Implications of Hotel Employee Attitudes for the Development of Quality Tourism: the Case of Cyprus', *Tourism Management* 24: 687–97.

Smith, V.L. (ed.) (1989), *Hosts and Guests: the Anthropology of Tourism*, 2nd edition, Philadelphia: University of Pennsylvania Press.

Smith, V.L. (1992), '"Hosts and Guests" Revisited', *American Behavioral Scientist* 36(2): 187–99.

Statistical Service of the Republic of Cyprus (2003), *Labour Statistics*, Nicosia.

Statistical Service of the Republic of Cyprus (2007), *Population of Cyprus*, Nicosia.

Statistical Service of the Republic of Cyprus (2008), *Tourism Statistics*, January–September 2008, Nicosia.

Trimikliniotis, N. (2001), 'The Location of Cyprus in the Southern European Context: Europeanisation as Modernisation?', *The Cyprus Weekly: A Journal of Social, Economic and Political Issues* 13(2): 47–73.

Velissariou, E. (1999), 'Tourismus und Wirtschaft – Bilanz der ökonomischen Entwicklung', in *Tourismus auf Kreta. Bilanz, Gefahren, Perspektiven. Zu den Grenzen touristischen Wachstums*, Bensberger Protokolle 93: 43–58.

Welz, G. (2007), 'Ein Wohltäter des Landes: Der Agrotourismus-Unternehmer', in B.J. Warneken (ed.), *Volksfreunde: Historische Varianten sozialen Engagements: Ein Symposium*, Tübingen: Tübinger Vereinigung für Volkskunde, pp. 339–48.

Witt, S.F. (1991), 'Tourism in Cyprus: Balancing the benefits and costs', *Tourism Management*, March: 37–45.

–11–

Anthropology, Tourism and Intervention?
Simone Abram

Introduction

The question of anthropological intervention in tourism policy raises a number of conceptual problems. Put simply, it begs some rather fundamental questions about what intervention is, what tourism is and what the particular contribution of anthropologists might be. Both 'intervention' and 'tourism' are pseudo-categories, which present us with significant difficulties for taking debates forward, and many tourism-anthropology debates have stumbled around this central question. Most anthropological debates are based on what we might call 'fuzzy concepts', or what Needham called 'polythetic classifications', and generally the attempt to define a concept is inconclusive. This is not to say it is not helpful, though, and the struggle to define may also help us to clarify what we are not dealing with, as well as what we are. Although we cannot precisely denote what either 'tourism' or 'intervention' is, the interrogation into their referents helps us to clarify our preconceptions and assumptions. This chapter interrogates the concepts at the core of an anthropology of tourism, and raises questions about the moral imperatives often pressed on its practitioners. Rather than accept existing chastisement about the ineffectiveness of anthropologists in the public domain, I would challenge the expectations of what makes anthropology distinctive, and call for anthropologists not merely to 'toe the line' like good consultants, but to think laterally about what their potential roles might be in the world of tourism.

By interrogating assumptions about what tourism is, where it is to be found and how it is run, a new range of activities is made apparent not only for activism but also for research. Similarly, moving beyond assumptions about what anthropologists can 'do', that is, taking account of a history of applied anthropology which has radically broadened in recent years, the notion of 'intervention' takes on a more layered complexion than we might initially assume. The chapter is not and could not offer a history of applied anthropology, of course, but through reference to some of the central concerns in the field, and in a context of changing anthropological objects, it is possible to recast ideas about the role of anthropologists both within and outside academia. It also reminds us of a complementarity that we must maintain between valuing theoretical and abstract conceptualization and analysing empirical detail. Despite recent critiques of postmodern deconstruction, anthropology is one of few disciplines which actively maintains a link between theory and practice through its commitment to ethnographic research, but its special focus on questioning categories and concepts poses problems in relation to daily action. Rather than trying to solve such problems (e.g. by making ethnography look more like 'evidence'), it could be profitable to re-evaluate the utility of this central tension, and acknowledge the intellectual and practical benefits it brings. On a more pragmatic level, we should also acknowledge the role of scholarly articles in supporting activists through political and legal battles in concrete contexts.

Tourism as Ways of Seeing, Ways of Being, an Ontology?

A key criticism of tourism studies, and of early anthropologies of tourism, is that they often begin from a position which conceptualizes tourism as an external research object, and most particularly in economic terms (see also Abram and Waldren 1997). As Franklin and Crang have argued, *'our understanding of tourism has become fetishized as a thing, a product, a behaviour'* (2001: 6). In the more practitioner-oriented disciplines within tourism studies (tourism development, event management, etc.), this concept of tourism as a sector of business is taken for granted, but in anthropological studies, as might be expected, many authors have taken a much more critical approach.

A series of analytical approaches to tourism have reframed it away from the industry-led preoccupation with maximizing economic gain, reconceptualizing tourism as cultural practice, whether the pursuit of authenticity in the face of modernity (e.g. MacCannell 1992) or as an extension of imperialism (Nash 1989), as a way of seeing (Urry 1990), a form of hybrid culture or, as Franklin would have it, as a form of ordering (2004). Franklin's approach contemplates tourism as a historically situated social development that goes beyond a specific set of economic practices, and he is more interested in questions of how the *desire* to indulge in tourist practices was created and is maintained and pursued. Reconceptualized in this perspective, Franklin defines tourism as a significant rhizomic global phenomenon, often enchanted by the machinic (in relation to travel), multilayered and diverse. But this sort of approach also suggests that it may be increasingly difficult to distinguish tourism from global modernity or postmodernity. If tourism is less a definable set of practices and more a way of living and organizing our socio-technical relations (in relation to the understanding of social life as exhibition, e.g. Mitchell 1991), then as an abstract concept, it may in fact be irreconcilable with the notion of 'intervention'. If it is a defining concept of our age, then, to echo Wildavsky (1973), if tourism is everything, maybe it is nothing.

While this may well be the case, we cannot simply drop the recognition that at present a large part of the global economy and many national and local economies are categorized as tourism, and that this categorization includes businesses based on the exploitation of leisure, the encounter with difference (place, people, time), or at a basic level, staying in hotels. Whether or not we agree that tourism is a useful aggregating concept, we still know that building, supplying and servicing hotels causes all sorts of social, economic and environmental effects, often to the detriment of people who are poor, exploited – almost by definition – or otherwise excluded from the benefits of the kind of capitalism that envelops much of the contemporary world. We know that watering the greens of golf courses or filling hotel swimming pools can withhold the water needed for the survival of neighbouring populations, for example, and we know that transforming traditional rituals into tourist performances can change the way they are experienced, for better or worse (Boissevain 1992).

With the relatively simple idea that tourism is a particular kind of development industry, the question of intervention arises almost automatically. Development implies a power relation, and anthropologists have often seen the effects and sympathized with those who suffer in the name of development. The urge to intervene has been channelled through advocacy to participation and what Gardner and Lewis have called 'facilitation' (1996: 48). Discussion has thus changed from a concern with intervention to one of collaboration, as Hart and Woolf argue (2006). Within anthropological studies of development, attention has moved to the developers themselves, to try to understand what and how they gain from development and how development that leads some people to impoverishment continues in the name of improvement (Mosse 2005, 2006). Yet anthropologists do not intervene in development as lone actors in simple encounters between developers and locals. On the contrary, development is embedded in long-standing and often complex regimes of planning and economics. Contemporary planning systems often emphasize some sort of participation of the stakeholders to development, and the performance of participation could be argued to make the intervention of interested (or disinterested) outsiders somewhat more complex and less effective than simple elitist regimes. In any case, it is hard to envisage a development context where an anthropologist might have the authority or the legitimacy to simply wade in and change the balance of power. So what is it that we refer to when we talk of intervention in tourism, and what does the notion of intervention suggest?

Intervention: Active, Passive, Policy and Practice

Intervention is a term used in many fields including medicine, international relations and economics, sometimes adopted as a euphemism for interference, regulation, imperialism or aggression, including war. Intervention implies modification or hindering, but the term is relational: it requires an object, singular or plural. Is it a category that includes its relatives such as intercession, intermediation or interpretation? What kind of social role does intervention imply, and how does it differ from subversion, protest, engagement or management? Intervention implies an action that changes the course of events, a reactive force or a pressure against the flow of events, and we can think of this happening at different levels of engagement. In its broadest sense, the question of intervention in people's activities is the question of government. How should people be governed, and by whom? Who has the right, or duty, to interfere in the government of people, and how are those persons legitimized? However, intervention radically presumes an externalized situation into which intervention may be inserted. That is, it presumes a pre-existing state either static or moving in one direction that the intervention attempts to divert, whereas we may prefer to see the world as a set of relations and tensions already pulling in different directions, rather than as an equilibrial balance of power, for example. Re-grounding questions of development in the theories and principles of political philosophy allows us to reconceptualize the notion of intervention and move it beyond a narrow personal or moral question to an institutional dilemma. By implication, this also means grounding the question of tourism intervention in a broader debate about development anthropology, as I outline below.

To the extent that tourism is governed, it is the economics of tourism development which is most plainly subject to governmental regulation. For anthropologists too, economics becomes a prioritized arena in relation to the transformation of social relations, whether that is in relation to concerns about commodification of rituals, the transformation of hospitality into commercial transactions or the construction of national economies which demand particular property relations, and the incorporation of local markets into a globalized capitalism. Deborah Root (1996) argues that commodification is part of the pattern of colonial expansion, suggesting that the commodification of traditional objects and practices is not merely an effect of the introduction of tourism, but is a symptom of a broader economic expansion enacted by investors with the support and encouragement of governments and of international organizations. In this context, the institutions of global economics are key to the patterns of colonial expansion that Root identifies.

The World Bank is one of these organizations, and it has been through various phases in its policy of using tourism as a means of economic development, seeing tourism as a 'value chain', a means by which growth in gross national product can be generated (Hawkins and Mann 2007: 250). During the 1960s, the Bank invested heavily in tourism development, funding private sector development to maintain import substitution for foreign exchange earnings, while in the 1970s, investment was targeted to public infrastructure as what it called 'capacity building' (2007: 354). By the 1990s, they had apparently decided that tourism had become so profitable that the private sector could manage on their own,[1] and they more or less handed over intervention in tourism development to the UNDP and the World Tourism Organization. The bank continued to support tourism projects, notably *'to examine micro-policy reform, to decentralize institutional structures, and to promote public-private partnerships'* (2007: 358).

Recently, the World Bank's Board of Directors elected to halt funding of tourism development, judging the industry to be 'unstable and volatile, with destinations at the mercy of trends and fashions for their popularity, dependent upon fluctuating political and economic conditions worldwide, and impacted by natural/human-made disasters and political instability' (2007: 359). These 'challenging externalities' are not thought to assist the Bank in its supposedly core business of poverty reduction. Interestingly, the only other area where funding has been halted has been in the field of nuclear energy. Yet the World Bank continues to fund tourism projects under other guises, and its volatile policy in relation to tourism reveals layers of ambivalence and changing fashions in both tourism and development policy.

Yet it is not only international institutions that are involved in the regulation of tourism. Many governments – although far from all – have tourism-specific policies too. Whether or how governments should be involved in tourism development in the first place would seem like a question that anthropologists might wish to contemplate. Certainly the arguments put forward by economic determinists ('fatalists' might be a better term) like Jenkins and Henry (1982) that, 'in many if not all developing countries, government has to undertake an entrepreneurial role to ensure that "pioneer" activities are initiated' strike the reader now as extraordinarily pessimistic, not only about the inevitability and desirability of tourism development and the incapability of developing countries to resist the pressures of international capital, but also about the nature, strength and capabilities of governments themselves. From a less deterministic perspective, Hall (1994) argues very strongly not only that governments should have policies in relation to tourism, but that the politics of tourism should be studied more seriously. Yet this study needs to be embedded in a wider understanding of polit-ical process. He points out that '[d]ecisions affecting tourism policy, the nature of government involvement in tourism, the structure of tourist organizations, and the nature of tourism development emerge from a political process' (1994: 3). Hall has particularly harsh criticism of the kind of political literature that describes idealized political processes – accounts of rational decision-making that bear little relation to the reality of political practice. He reminds us that, '[t]ourism is not the result of a rational decision-making process' (1994: 3), in contrast to what one might imagine from the descriptions written by some political scientists. Yet this is true of any realm of policy analysis, whether that is related to health, welfare, transport or any other field of government. Policy is by definition politically framed, and the role of rationality in political process is well recognized as problematic (see, for example, Abram 2005 on the role of science in policy-making). However, the style of political analysis that Hall criticizes is very different to that found in anthropological research. Boissevain and Theuma's account of the politics of tourism development in Malta (1998), for example, points clearly towards the realpolitik of corruption and influence, as does Waldren's account of Mallorquin road-building (1998), a well-known case of corruption that used tourism development as a ruse to cover the siphoning of EU funds. These two cases have been framed as corruption, which for the sake of simplicity can be described as the illegal compromise of political process, yet political process is always compromised to some extent, and this is often framed as 'successful policy implementation', as 'realpolitik' or as 'implementation'.

Us and Them: Governors, Interveners and Other Activists

Yet despite these examples, a common approach to the role of anthropologists in tourism development is exemplified by Carson Jenkins, who argues a familiar normative line in urging academics to engage in commercial practice in order to be taken seriously by practitioners (1999). For Jenkins, academics and their insular world of peer review lie on one side of a typological distinction between academics and practitioners. For him, academic writing is preaching to the converted, while practitioners with their project-specific, profit-driven aims encounter academics only when the latter move into the world of project consultancy. He argues that it is only through implementation that projects have any impact on development, and that academics can influence this only through a 'real-world participatory function which should benefit the project', where 'the experience gained would also benefit teaching and future research' (1999: 63). In this view, academic knowledge for its own sake is the opposite of practical knowledge, and academic influence is only achieved through tourism-development-project management.

Jenkins can be admired for his energy in trying to make anthropology relevant to business, or in urging anthropologists to have the confidence to engage in business development even when practitioners appear to be uninterested in academic research findings. But the trouble with this kind of intervention is that it takes for granted the premises of the world of commerce, and leaves the academic vainly scratching at the gate, a bit-part player in somebody else's game, whether that is private commerce or public policy. There is no challenge here to the all-powerful image of the World Bank and its economic definition of tourism as a strategy for economic development, nor of the definition of tourism as an economic process with cultural 'effects' and 'impacts', nor any Boal-like attempt to change political or economic structures (Boal 1998). Jenkins's vision of commercial and governmental institutions as immutable fails to recognize the contingency and historicity of both companies and governments, and gives no inkling of the complex social relations behind the façade. What is needed instead is a critical approach, not merely to the performance of academics in commercial contexts, but to the constitution of such commercial and policy contexts themselves. If we do not understand how modern states and business work, how can we expect to be effective in promoting anthropological insights?

In particular, any approach to 'intervention' requires a more sophisticated analysis of how states or commerce work, either respectively, or relatively. That is, we need also to understand the relations between state and commerce. We cannot, for example, continue to imagine governments as singular entities when it is thirty years since Philip Abrams observed that Bentham, in turn, argued that government is a word which gives 'spurious concreteness and reality to that which has a merely abstract and formal existence' (1988 [1977]: 58). There is sufficient ethnography of government available now that we cannot avoid seeing the fractions and struggles that government officers and politicians engage in to produce the effect we know as 'the state'. We know, too, that 'markets' are illusory effects of cumulative transactions and transactional practices, and that the collective actions of competing commercial agents resemble crowd behaviour rather than any rational equation of demand and supply. Given this complexity, the idea of intervening may appear daunting at best, or hopeless at worst. Yet even in the knowledge of the messiness of state and market, we can still approach them as 'black boxes' and argue, for example, that where 'state' processes meet the 'market' of commercial transactions, a 'moment of opportunity' may open up, where the outcome of a process becomes temporarily unstable and the potential for change is greatest. It is clear in urban regeneration, for example, that while developers are lobbying politicians and civil servants for access to development opportunities, spaces are opened up where community groups and third-sector organizations can bid to take over public services themselves (see Abram 2008). It may be the point at which policy or practical intervention is most effective; although at moments of state instability outside intervention is often excluded, if new ideas attract public attention, they can often be seized upon to fill a vacuum left by the instability of existing policy. This very tangible approach appeals to people who are skilled in activism, but for many academic anthropologists, it may seem to be beyond their scope, in terms of time and energy as well as political skills. How, then, can we move forward and find new ways of conceptualizing intervention?

A New Vocabulary of Tourism Management, a New Role for Anthropologists?

One way to move the problem forward is to reconceptualize it by adopting a different vocabulary, to cast a new theoretical perspective on the issue. The language of actor-networks, or actant-rhizomes (Latour 1999), has been particularly useful for this, and frames a tourism encounter as the product of a complex network of relations that enable persons to be transported 'on holiday'. The change is not merely of vocabulary, but allows us to give serious attention to the technologies that are woven into social relations. A tourist does not miraculously appear in a holiday destination, but is aided not only by agents who make arrangements, but also the technologies that transport people, offer information, and provide goods and services through an often international supply chain. As these technologies change, the practical details of tourism also change, from cheap air travel facilitating mass transport, to techniques of reinforcing concrete that made multi-storey hotels cheap enough to build en masse along beaches. Callon uses the example of a man going on a ClubMed holiday, being the result of an alignment of processes and products, including,

> computers, alloys, jet engines, research departments, market studies, advertisements, welcoming hostesses, natives who have suppressed their desire for independence and learned to smile as they carry luggage, bank loans and currency exchanges. (1991: 139)

He also points to the gradations of the permanence of existing arrangements, inviting us to examine the fragile temporary stability of certain techno-economic networks, and their reliance on a range of 'hybrid intermediaries', including texts and other inscriptions (1991: 138). With such a perspective, rather than seeing the anthropologist as a lonely wanderer seeking a way in to the solid edifice of development policy or commercial deals, we can instead become the vehicle for particular kinds of intermediary intervention, a hybrid actor – working with both the texts and technologies of our discipline and the actors of our fieldwork – who might play a crucial role in the reordering of existing tourism assemblages. This approach also opens up the workings of tourism industries to anthropological investigation – it becomes apparent that the role of a travel agent or the activities of a ferry-designer are critical links in a wider web of activities that have hitherto been more or less ignored. Who is publishing ethnography with hotel designers,[2] for example, or currency exchange organizations? Despite the arcane language of ANT, there is something of the political and historical common sense about Callon's observations. The historian's game of 'what if' the outcomes of a revolution had been different alerts us to the possibilities for change when longstanding networks are destabilized, and canny administrators know that they stand the best chance of making radical policy changes during regime changes (or 'moments of opportunity', as noted above). The liminal moments that such changes provide allow for radical action to occur. This is, indeed, the meaning of the liminal in ritual process, which demands the ritual work of re-creating stability after radical upheaval.

What does this mean for the intervention of anthropologists in tourism? While Jenkins focuses on the role of policy consultant, this is by no means exclusive nor necessarily the most effective form of intervention. Consultancy brings its own demands, and may corner an anthropologist into behaving, even thinking, like any other consultant. On the other hand, anthropologists, by definition, are not typically the kind of academic who never ventures out of their study. On the contrary, many anthropologists have been directly involved in political struggles in their chosen fields, and the commitment to the participative element of participation-observation has only deepened through the course of the discipline's history. Turner argues that we have moved from a modernist paradigm of nation-state homogeneity (with the nationalist ideal of society as a uniform multitude of citizens united in relation to a unique centre, the sovereign state), to what he calls 'synchronic pluralism' as the axiom of the current dominant frame of anthropological analysis, or 'chronotope' (form of social space-time) (2006: 17). According to Turner, this represents a decoupling of nation and state through increased authority at an international level, such as that for human rights, which local activists have been quick to exploit to legitimize their claims to self-determination. He further argues that anthropologists ought to have spent more intellectual energy considering what this means for the discipline and its subjects, and the implications for the notion of popular sovereignty. In his view, the eclipse of nation-state holism for a 'synchronic cultural pluralism with multiculturalism and identity politics as its main ideological expressions', meant that 'culture' and cultural difference took on new political meanings for many groups (2006: 18). Whereas a sociological understanding sees inequality resulting from, and resulting in, stigmatization of sectors of the population, in the world of identity-politics, difference becomes a claim to legitimacy, even respect. In his view, the anthropological response has been ambivalent, yet it is clear that the pervasion of uncertainty and the rise of ethical debate have resulted in a similarly strengthened diversity of anthropological approach as well.

One consequence is that we are increasingly sensitive about defining our relations in the field in terms of 'informants', acknowledging thereby that postcolonial anthropology must face head-on the power-relations of fieldwork, whether that work is with people who are oppressed or whether it 'studies up' to the centres of power. This is reflected in debates about who it is we are working with when we perform both fieldwork and academia. Marianne Gullestad proposes replacing 'informant' with terms such as 'consultant', 'participant', 'conversation partner' or 'partner', 'terms that would reflect, more accurately, the high importance of the contribution of the people we work with' (2006: 321). The problem is not merely one of renaming the informant, but of redefining the power relations between ethnographer and those among whom participant-observation is conducted. Angie Hart and David Wolff suggest that as well as changing terms, building community–university partnerships offers academic researchers a way to root their work in a 'sense of place and a commitment to engage with issues of locality' (2006: 121). In promoting university–community partnerships, Hart and Wolff do not denigrate academic research, but attempt instead to find ways to mutualize that knowledge. I cannot endorse their suspicions that theorizing may be a displacement activity from what they call the harder work of improving services (2006: 125), implying as it does a moral hierarchy of intellectual efforts. Yet the work that goes into differentiating academic discourses from practitioner discourses does have the potential both to offer greater insight, and to risk irrelevance. Theoretical developments certainly do emerge into practitioner and popular consciousness, even if we are not always clear over the routes they take. Our problem is that we cannot necessarily predict in which direction our theorizing might travel, nor when theoretical speculation may spark the interest of practitioners, journalists or politicians.

My argument is that theoretical academic research need not necessarily be defined in opposition to practical knowledge, even though it should require me to counteract a central dichotomy in Western society, typified by the differentiation referred to above between an academic intellectual work defined as 'pure',[3] and knowledge handled outside academic described, for example, by Gibbons et al. (1994) as 'applied, problem-centred, transdisciplinary, heterogeneous, hybrid, demand-driven, entrepreneurial, network-embedded'. The efforts to define the first as pure and the second polluted have bedevilled the history of what has been called 'applied anthropology', as Wright and Mills make clear (Mills 2006; Wright 2006), yet certainly since the 1980s and the development of BASAPP, and later Anthropology in Action, many anthropologists have worked strenuously to dissipate the dichotomy. In bringing the notion of active or politically engaged anthropology to the question of tourism, we might recast the notion of intervention.

'Direct' Intervention in Policy-Making, but What is Policy? An Example

How, then, should anthropological knowledge become power in the context of tourism? The temptation is to leap directly at policy as the root of action, or the solution to threatening action. Given the discussion of the state and commerce, above, it is worth being a little wary of approaching policy as some kind of magic tool. Indeed, it is the idea of policy, not as a straightforward independent text to be implemented, but as a process that plays out conflict, tension, drama and compromise, that is implied by the neologism 'policy-act'. Policy gathers around it a host of actors of different kind (including technology, if we are to follow Latour's line (1996)), status, capital, etc. who engage in a process whose result might be concretized as a policy, either written or enacted, sometimes both, although the two never wholly coincide. It is difficult to talk meaningfully about policy in abstract terms, so I will pin my discussion down to a particular field. A field of policy which is often most relevant to tourism is development or land-use policy, which, theoretically, aims to regulate the externalities of building projects. Although there are outstanding works on this theme in anthropology (e.g. Robertson 1984), most anthropological attention has been focused on planning for what we might call 'overseas development', especially with regard to indigenous or subjugated ethnic groups, and the tendency here is to focus on the area of anthropological expertise, being those ethnicities, rather than the question of planning as a field of governmental activity per se (with Robertson as a notable exception). Only recently have anthropologists returned to these questions, and a more substantial field of anthropology of planning (planned development) is only now emerging (Abram and Waldren 1998; Boholm 2000; Müller and Neveu 2002; Abram and Vike 2003; Boholm and Lofstedt 2004). What it requires is both a model of how people imagine government processes ought to work and a knowledge of practice. Just as in anthropological studies of kinship we need to understand the models people think with, as well as how they practise kinship in everyday life (and on special occasions), such an approach is equally valid in studies of government.

An illustration will help us imagine alternative modes of intervention. While tourism development is often approached by anthropologists through the problem of cultural exploitation or ethnic conflict between parties we might conceptualize as developers and developed, I would argue that the dilemmas of planning are intrinsic to planning itself, and merely exacerbated by cultural difference. Many of the dilemmas referred to above are equally evident in local development (as illustrated in Abram and Waldren 1998).

Development policy's domain is explicitly about the governance of external-ities. What effect will the building of your house have on your neighbour? What effect will the building of a housing estate have on the environment (particular or general) or on the market for existing or future houses? Who is liable for the loss of hotel business if a new industrial plant is built on a neighbouring plot? It is the element of planning for future effects, as well as for effects on existing societies, which makes development policy into a complex negotiation between competing interests and conflicting world-views. For many years, planners and political scientists have debated the role of citizens in forming policy about development, not only in so-called 'developing', but also 'developed' countries,[4] where the term 'developed' refers effectively to countries for whom the discourse and practices of development are wholly normalized, even if they are contested in the particular. Such debates go to the heart of philosophical questions about the nature of democracy and the degree of rule by citizens, the form of representation and the potential for participatory democratic government.

In Britain, planning is tied into a model of representative democracy which presumes that different and conflicting individual and collective interests can be represented by individuals as spokespersons for groups. The idea of repres-entation is so embedded that recent experiments with more participatory models of democracy still rely on the idea that collectives can be represented by individuals. Indeed, individuals are only legitimate participants in political debates as representatives for wider groups. At public enquiries into planning legislation, the key legitimizing effect for a person wishing to speak or submit comments to a public enquiry is who they represent, and how their representation is formalized (e.g. elected representatives of a group carry more legitimacy than 'self-appointed' representatives). After many years of campaigns about community self-determination (see Ellis 2000, 2007), recent planning laws for England and Wales oblige local authorities to demonstrate that they have a policy on 'community involvement'. Involvement is not clearly defined, and although the demand for a 'Statement on Community Involvement' could be used to experiment with new democratic practices, cash-strapped local authorities seem mostly inclined to satisfy this demand by making public announcements about policy or by staging one-off public exhibitions about new developments.[5] However, the key principled debates about participative democracy address the risk of policy processes being derailed by strongly motivated minority interests (e.g. what if your local community wants to adopt racist plans?), and the problem of how to make decisions when several competing collectives seem to have equally valid proposals. Planning theorists have gone so far as to propose that planners can perform a sort of community therapy between conflicting ethnic groups (Sandercock 2000), although this approach dissolves the question of rights into a desire for consensus. Still, British planning law requires that a new major plan (the official name has changed regularly in recent years) is subjected to some form of public inquiry, a process of judicial review presided over by a member of Her Majesty's Planning Inspectorate. It is at such inquiries that push comes to shove, and those opposing any clause in a plan prepared by a local authority may be allowed the opportunity to voice their objections (subject to the decision of the Inspector). In such inquiries, the old fashioned intimidation of witnesses by hierarchical status or class can still be seen, with barristers employed by the authorities to demolish the arguments of local residents or other interested parties. Crookes, for example, reports local authority officers sniggering at residents giving evidence, and independent objectors being accused by barristers of being 'meddling busybodies', and, in particular, qualitative evidence being dismissed as unobjective (Lee Crookes, pers. comm.). This serves as a reminder, if we needed it, that objectivity is still an important quality of knowledge that can be enlisted by barristers in these semi-judicial environments, where statistical or economic information is considered more authoritative than anything that can be associated (even by inference) with sentiment or preference. In this context, what activists require is not an anthropological advocate or interpreter, but a body of evidence that can stand up to cross-examination. Here anthropologists are often sadly under-trained, and our published work has rarely been written with the interrogative lawyer in mind. And yet it is here we could provide skilful knowledge that would be extraordinarily valuable to activists, either untrained or trained in other disciplines. Opening debates with practising barristers might not only allow us to produce an ethnography of legal process, but offer us sharper insights into how barristers may use different kinds of knowledge and what kind of statements we perhaps unwittingly use that can undermine the potential exploitation of our work. While anthropologists are perhaps more familiar with requests to be expert witnesses in cases of immigration or extradition, it is rare to see ethnographic texts used in other legal fields.

It is not only in the planning courts that evidence has a role, of course. The British Academy recently published a response to the British government's long-standing call for what it describes as 'evidence-based policy', a nomination thought by many still to be an oxymoron and not, sadly, a tautology (e.g. Wilson 2008: 29). The report points to the gap between what policy-makers require and what academics provide, which mainly revolve around the need for quick-win easily interpreted facts and opinions for policy-makers, versus in-depth understanding of debates in current research that academics are best positioned to offer. Undoubtedly, the latter offers a privileged position from which to critique policy proposals, yet civil servants are often trying not to upset the status quo rather than thinking critically about the effects that policy directions may have in practice. Engelke also urges us to introduce a stronger debate about the notion of evidence in anthropology, albeit with the proviso that evidence is not necessarily a concept of knowledge that sits easily with an ethnographic approach that tries to avoid both positivism and normativity (2008: S3). What Engelke's interrogation into the notion of evidence in ethnographic practice usefully reminds us is that evidence need not only provide certainty or indubitability, but can also be evidence of uncertainty, of lack of proof. Anthropological knowledge need not be limited to advising on questions of what Good identifies as 'cultural evidence' (2008) but his outline of the 'cultural defence debate' raises important questions about what kind of 'expert witness' an anthropologist can be and how their representations to courts of law can be interpreted.

Readers may think that a discussion of the law is not relevant to the question of anthropological intervention in tourism, since not all tourism is policy, and even if it were, not all policy processes go through public inquiries or courts of law, even if most policy processes go through some examination by governmental body (apart perhaps from in dictatorships). What the consideration of legal process does offer us, though, is a sharper focus on the linguistic games involved in the presentation of evidence to policy-makers, and it is the everyday politics and politicking that have most impact on policy. If anthropological knowledge is to emerge in policy processes, either as advice to policy-makers or as evidence in judicial reviews of policy, we must be aware of the networks that policy-processes gather about them, the roles available, and the potential to create new ones. Existing roles in the policy process might be typified by activity (instead of organizationally), such as decision-making, lobbying, representing, protesting, promoting, providing expert opinion or advocating. But there are many background roles, such as that of the public servant constructing the context of a policy debate in the shape of background papers, or further back, the consultants shaping the type of information or knowledge accepted as relevant, particularly through the choice of statistical constructs which are so often taken as 'fact' at the start of any policy development (see Abram 2002). If our role is constantly to try to counteract the dominance of statistical scenarios at the point of policy decision-making, then we will always be fighting a rearguard action. It is the equivalent of throwing oneself in front of bulldozers at the end of a long political process in which significant investment of time, energy and capital has been made – it may be effective, but is more likely to be purely symbolic. Although Actor Network Theory has been criticized for imagining that socio-technical networks emerge around egotistical humans only acting in self-interest (Skodbo 2005), studies like Latour's *Aramis* (1996) make visible the long tendrils of policy development in time, space and sociality, and show how decisions are fragile moments in long arcs of labour-intensive time and space.

Reinventing Anthropological Intervention in Tourism

We have, as a discipline, been here before, of course, not least in the campaigns for 'applied anthropology' (see Pink 2006). ASA monograph 23, *Social Anthropology and Development Policy*, offers many of the key points mentioned above (Grillo and Rew 1985). At the time, Conlin noted that agricultural economists were more effective in influencing technocratic decisions in government departments, and urged anthropologists to 'learn the ethnography' of the organization (1985: 72). While the ethnography of the Overseas Development Administration may have changed, the importance of understanding political and bureaucratic process has not, and Conlin offered a bureaucrat's view of how anthropologists often misunderstand the policy process, and where they might be most effective. Grillo also emphasized the need for an anthropology of development that would offer an analysis of 'the project' and the rhetoric of policy (1985: 29), a challenge taken up by several authors since (notably Ferguson 1990; Mosse 2005, 2006). Angela Cheater, on the other hand, offered an acute analysis of what might be called the politics of policy, illustrating the gap between policy process, document and implementation (1985). She argued that governments may well recognize that anthropologists hold valuable information that they need, but lack. However, as soon as anthropologists become involved in the formulation of public policy, she argues, academic detachment can be illusory: '[i]n reality the anthropologist is entering the political domain of decision making, which should be recognized for what it is' (1985: 69). Worse, she suggests, anthropologists' 'professional ability to survive in the corridors of power is questionable' (1985: 69) She cites the work of Chavunduka (1979) who attempted to sensitize law makers to the practical realities of colonial legislation on witchcraft, which was met with outright hostility from a Zimbabwean government who preferred to claim that witchcraft was either false or evil (Cheater 1985: 61). However, Cheater also notes that where Chavunduka's research had been useful in formulating legal policies, for example, it had not been done with policy goals in mind, nor had the anthropologist acted as a consultant (1985: 61), a significant aside that I return to below.

Norman and Ann Long prefaced their 1992 volume with the argument that the separation of pure and applied research,

> encourages field practitioners and intervention experts to adopt a sanguine view of the possibilities of fundamental research contributing to the solution of concrete problems, and at the same time shields the researcher from having to struggle seriously with issues of practical concern. (1992: 3)

On the contrary, they argue, they are so closely interwoven as to be essential. Their response is to take an 'actor-oriented approach' based in everyday life experiences of all actors, from poor peasants to bureaucrats or researchers (1992: 5). Similarly, Katy Gardner and David Lewis argue that a key role of anthropology of development is to 'deconstruct the assumptions and power relations of development' (1996: 77), but they also refer to the problematic separation of pure and applied anthropological knowledge, and to Johannsen's proposal for 'steering a new path between trying to solve posed problems (applied anthropology) and representing a cultural system by one's own writing (interpretive anthropology)' (1996: 41). Both approaches, they argue, imply that 'the practice of anthropology itself is essentially an *intervention* of some kind' (1996: 41; emphasis in original), and suggest that anthropologists can enable people in communities to identify the nature of, and solutions to, their problems. If anthropology itself is intervention, we are coming closer not only to a rejection of the pure/applied dichotomy, but to the idea that all actors are, in a sense, intervening either in creating new assemblages or resisting them. It also allows us a new perspective in which to consider how classic academic anthropological knowledge has a role in such assemblages, either as the underlying theoretical framework for 'practical knowledge' or as objects of 'evidence' in the negotiations over policy acts.

Lambert has recently criticized a weakness among anthropologists, which she interprets as an immaturity of the discipline of anthropology: a collective failure to specify the nature of the evidence that anthropology deals in. Part of the difficulty is that anthropologists have interrogated the notion of evidence itself, and this is seen as the opposite of taking control of it. Lambert (2009) suggests that this is symptomatic of some kind of excess of postmodern deconstructionist zeal, yet she too, like many before, is unable to see a way through to an idea of evidence that meets the demands of the new audit-based evidence approach, or of legal hearings. Rather than admire the legal professions for the precision of their concepts of evidence, we might better enter into a dialogue with them to consider how their definition of evidence falls short of making justice available to all those who need it. This might be thought presumptuous: the legal profession is much longer established than anthropology, but no discipline or institution is immune to change, and law and its professions are always under revision. Anthropologists have tended in recent years to enter a contest of ideas, rather than one of evidence, and despite calls for a return to empiricism (to which Lambert refers), it would be another kind of dereliction if this return caused us to withdraw from the battle of ideas itself.[6] If our interrogation into the notion of evidence is used to clarify empiricism, rather than to scare us away from it, then the apparent choice between theorization and empiricism will show itself to be a false dichotomy.

Where Do We Go Next?

Perhaps unsurprisingly, this chapter will not end with a formula for effective anthropological intervention in tourism. On the contrary, it has aimed to show that 'anthropological intervention' is a rather odd idea in itself. As politically active persons, and as citizens, we may choose to try to intervene in tourism development policy or practice, and that needs no further comment. However, the question of how we might intervene 'as anthropologists' is more challenging. In the light of the discussion above, we must argue that Jenkins is wrong to imagine that academic debate does not reach into development contexts. Although they may not read academic publications, tourism and development practitioners are undoubtedly influenced by the discourses and debates which circulate within it, and not least by occasionally critical attention in more serious public media about tourism and its consequences.[7] Popular debate does not pass by those involved in tourism business, and sometimes intellectual messages reach wide new audiences. Michael Wesch's five-minute YouTube clip on the mutability of online text and human–machine relations has probably been read by more people than any other anthropological text, with over 2 million viewings at the time of writing (Wesch 2007a,b; Wesch et al. 2007). Critical and incisive reflections on the world about us, which build on our capacity for subversive and creative thought, offer great potential for changing dominant practices and hegemonic concepts.

In other words, intervention in tourism may not only mean diverting economic processes or attempting to change the wording of public policy. Even if those remain the desired outcomes, the means to achieve them may be more closely related to anthropologists' core realm of expertise. If an anthropologist is an expert, then it is an expertise tied to participant observation, distanciation, analysis and representation. The academic training of anthropologists is directed towards analysing and making representations, whether that is in texts, images, filmed, audio, plastic or other media, just as much as it is in making oral representations. A well-timed article in the media can have as much effect as a long campaign of persuasion over policy or local conditions, and with equally unpredictable outcomes. We may also note that 'intervention' is a term adopted by artists to describe a particular form of commentary, an intervention which provokes a rethinking of the familiar, or a reconceptualizing of mainstream assumptions or perceptions. Sometimes, too, architects are described as making interventions in the landscape or the built environment, and these rather different versions of intervention offer us a useful alternative route to imagining the interventions possible for anthropologists.

They also serve as reminders to be wary of the anti-intellectualism and false dichotomies of thought and knowledge implied in the calls for academics always to make the imaginary journey across into policy or commerce. If we are to move beyond normative moralizing pressures to make our own voices heard in alienating economic or legal institutions, we must rethink what intervention is and how it might be imagined. At the same time, calling for anthropological intervention risks assuming a common moral or ethical stance towards engagement, which may or may not reflect a meaningful commonality among anthropologists. Members of the ASA are expected to abide by its ethical code, but not all anthropologists are members of the ASA, and the title 'anthropologist' is an adjective, not a protected professional appellation. Anthropology is a broad discipline, and its literature may appeal – or not – across the political spectrum, implying quite different understandings of legitimacy of intervention in different circumstances. We know of anthropologists who support covert activity by the CIA and who apparently also carry out such activities (see Gonzalez 2008; Keenan 2008; Lutz 2008), and we are aware of people adopting anthropology and ethnography to support racist regimes (see Lang 2005). We also know of debates in which anthropologists apparently decrying racism themselves reinforce race-based thinking (see Gullestad 2006). Why should we imagine that all anthropologists share a political stance in relation to their public role, and why, further, in relation to tourism? Anthropology is not a corporation with an agreed public image, but a discipline and a debate. We are constantly in the process of reproducing anthropology yet always aware that our definitions are not universally shared. Rather than imagine academics intervening in practice, we may need to abandon the metaphor of intervention with its implication of modifying existing trajectories, and adopt a more open question of action in contingent worlds, the creation of new rhizomic nodes, or gathering of otherwise dispersed forces.

Anthropologists have been well positioned to give accounts of what happens 'on the ground', seen often from the perspective of the less powerful. Yet only recently have accounts of the process of government from the perspective of politicians and administrators begun to appear in any number, and we certainly have to look outside the field of tourism for such studies. If we adopt the more recent approach to tourism as a form of ordering, a colonizing mentality, rather than as the description of an industry, we have a rather more complex challenge if we are to think about intervention. The question is at once larger – should or could we intervene in the maintenance of this way of thinking, how could we alter it – and less tangible – what is there to intervene in? If intervention implies a relation, where is the relation within the process of ordering? With detailed studies of the politics and policies of tourism in practice, with knowledge of this most complex of social fields, we may be better equipped to answer the question of what kind of intervention would be anthropological.

Notes

1. Or, in their own words, 'that the markets and the private sector were the most appropriate growth engine and that focused lending would not be necessary' (Hawkins and Mann 2007: 355)
2. *Editors' note:* But see chapter by Picard, this volume
3. 'pure, disciplinary, homogenous, expert-led, supply-driven, hierarchical, peer-reviewed and almost exclusively university-based' (Hart and Wolff: 123).
4. Generally speaking, economic development depends on concrete constructions in time and place, and certain forms of infrastructure which join these together, and it is this arena that is regulated through a web of legislative and practical processes. Trends in development policy do cross over between the overseas development and domestic planning policy, even though they appear to be segregated both politically and academically.
5. Even assuming there is goodwill, cf. Wilson (2005).
6. Nor is it entirely clear that anthropologists have really been so dismissive of empiricism at all, even if holistic ethnographic monographs have been slightly thinner on the ground – in response to a healthy critique of their position of authority and changing trends among publishers.
7. The tourism anthropologists at London Metropolitan University have themselves cultivated good relations with journalists, campaigners and industry to help bring their research findings into broader public domains.

References

Abram, S. (2002). 'Planning and Public-Making in Municipal Government', *Focaal* 40: 21–34.

Abram, S. (2005), 'Science/Technology as Politics by other means', *Focaal, European Journal of Anthropology* 46: 3–20.

Abram, S. (2008), 'Transparency and Participation: Partnership and Hierarchies in British Urban Regeneration', in C. Garsten and M.L.D. Montoya (eds), *Transparency In A New Global Order: Unveiling Organizational Visions* London: Edward Elgar Publishing, pp. 201–22.

Abram, S. and Vike, H. (2003), 'Antropologi, styring og forvaltning', *Norsk Antropologisk Tidsskrift* 14: 53–69.

Abram, S. and Waldren, J. (1997), 'Introduction', in S. Abram, J. Waldren and D. Macleod (eds), *Tourists and Tourism: Identifying with People and Places*, Berg: Oxford, pp. 1–12.

Abram, S. and Waldren, J. (1998), *Anthropological Perspectives on Local Development: Knowledge and Sentiments in Conflict*, London: Routledge.

Abrams, P. (1988 [1977]), 'Notes on the Difficulty of Studying the State', *Journal of Historical Sociology* 1(1): 58–89.

Boal, A. (1998), *Legislative Theatre: Using Performance to Make Theatre*, London: Routledge.

Boholm, Å. (2000), *National Objectives – Local Objections: Railroad Modernization in Sweden*, Göteborg: Center for Public Sector Research (CEFOS) Univ. Göteborg.

Boholm, Å. and Löfstedt, R.E.V. (eds) (2004), *Facility Siting: Risk, Power and Identity in Land Use Planning*, London: Earthscan.

Boissevain, J. (ed.) (1992), *Revitalizing European Rituals*, London: Routledge.

Boissevain, J. and Theuma, N. (1998), 'Contested Space: Planners, Tourists, Developers and Environmentalists in Malta', in S. Abram and J. Waldren (eds), *Anthropological Perspectives on Local Development: Knowledge and Sentiments in Conflict*, London: Routledge, pp. 96–119.

Callon, M. (1991), 'Techno-Economic Networks and Irreversibility', in J. Law (ed.), *A Sociology of Monsters*, London: Routledge, pp. 132–61.

Chavunduka, G.L. (1978), *Traditional Healers and the Shona Patient*, Gwelo: Mambo Press.

Cheater, A.P. (1985), 'Anthropologists and Policy in Zimbabwe: Design at the Centre and Reactions at the Periphery', in R.D. Grillo and A. Rew (eds), *Social Anthropology and Development Policy*, London: Tavistock Publications, pp. 58–72.

Conlin, S. (1985), 'Anthropological advice in a government context', in R.D. Grillo and A. Rew (eds), *Social Anthropology and Development Policy*, London: Tavistock Publications, pp. 73–87.

Ellis, H. (2000), 'Planning and Public Empowerment: Third Party Rights in Development Control', *Planning Theory and Practice* 1: 203–17.

Ellis, H. (2007), *CLG Planning White Paper Committee 11 June 2006, evidence by Friends of the Earth*, London: Friends of the Earth.

Engelke, M. (2008), 'The Objects of Evidence', *Journal of the Royal Anthropological Institute* Special Issue 2008, S1–S21.

Ferguson, J. (1990), *The Anti-Politics Machine: "Development", depoliticization, and bureaucratic Power in Lesoth*. Cambridge: Cambridge University Press.

Franklin, A. (2004), 'Tourism As an Ordering: Towards a New Ontology of Tourism', *Tourist Studies* 4(3): 277–301.

Franklin, A. and Crang, M. A. (2001), 'The Trouble with Tourism and Travel Theory?' *Tourist Studies* 1(1): 5–22.

Gardner, K. and Lewis, D. (1996) *Anthropology, Development and the Post-Modern Challenge*, London: Pluto.

Gibbons, M., Limoges, C., Nowotny, H., Schwarzman, S., Scott, P. and Trow, M. (1994), *The New Production of Knowledge: The Dynamics of Science and Research in Contemporary Societies*, London, Sage.

González, R.J. (2008), '"Human Terrain": Past, Present and Future Applications', *Anthropology Today* 42: 21–6.

Good, A. (2008), 'Cultural Evidence in Courts of Law', *Journal of the Royal Anthropological Institute* Special Issue 2008, S47–S60.

Grillo, R.D. (1985), 'Applied Anthropology in the 1980s: Retrospect and Prospect', in R.D. Grillo and A. Rew (eds), *Social Anthropology and Development Policy*, London: Tavistock Publications, pp. 1–36.

Grillo, R.D. and Rew, A. (1985), *Social Anthropology and Development Policy* (ASA Monographs 23) London: Tavistock.

Gullestad, Marianne (2006), *Plausible Prejudice*, Oslo: Universitetsforlaget.

Hall, C.Mi. (1994), *Tourism and Politics: Policy, Power and Place*, Chichester: John Wiley and Sons

Hart, A. and Wolff, D. (2006), 'Developing Local "Communities of Practice" through Local Community–University Partnerships', *Planning, Practice and Research* 21(1): 121–38.

Hawkins, D.E. and Mann, S. (2007), 'The World Bank's Role in Tourism Development', *Annals of Tourism Research* 34(2): 348–63.

Jenkins, C.L. (1999), 'Tourism Academics and Tourism Practitioners: Bridging the Great Divide', in D.G. Pearce and R. Butler (eds), *Contemporary Issues in Tourism Development*, London: Routledge, pp. 52–64.

Jenkins, C.L. and Henry, B.M. (1982) 'Government Involvement in Tourism in Developing Countries', *Annals of Tourism Research* 9: 499–521.

Johannsen, A.M. (1992), 'Applied Anthropology and Post-Modernist Ethnography', *Human Organisation* 51: 71–81.

Keenan, J. (2008), 'US Militarization in Africa: What Anthropologists Should Know About AFRICOM', *Anthropology Today* 24(5): 16–19.

Lambert, H. (2009), 'Evidentiary Truths? The Evidence of Anthropology through the Anthropology of Medical Evidence', *Anthropology Today* 25: 16–20.

Lang, Andrea (2005), 'Picking up the Relay Baton: Translating Traditions in Apartheid and Democratic South Africa', *Focaal* 25: 36–53.

Latour, Bruno (1996), *Aramis, or the Love of Technology*, Cambridge, MA: Harvard University Press

Latour, Bruno (1999), 'On Recalling ANT', in J. Law and J. Hassard (eds), *Actor Network Theory and After*, Oxford: Blackwell Publishers, pp. 15–25.

Long, N. and Long, A. (1992), *Battlefields of Knowledge: the Interlocking of Theory and Practice in Social Research and Development*, London: Routledge.

Lutz, C. (2008), 'Selling Ourselves? The Perils of Pentagon Funding for Anthropology', *Anthropology Today* 24: 1–3.

MacCannell, Dean (1992), *Empty Meeting Grounds: The Tourist Papers*, London: Routledge

Mosse, David (2006), 'Anti-social Anthropology? Objectivity, Objection, and the Ethnography of Public Policy and Professional Communities', *JRAI (N.S.)* 12: 935–56.

Mosse, David (2005), *Cultivating Development: an Ethnography of Aid Policy and Practice*, London: Pluto Press

Mills, D. (2006), 'Dinner at Claridges? Anthropology and the "Captains of Industry", 1947–1955', in S. Pink (ed.), *Applications of Anthropology: Professional Anthropology in the Twenty-First Century*, New York/Oxford: Berghahn, pp. 55–70.

Mitchell, T. (1991), *Colonising Egypt*, Berkeley, CA: University of California Press.

Müller, B. and Neveu, C. (2002), 'Mobilising Institutions – Institutionalising Movements: An Introduction', *Focaal* 40: 7–19.

Nash, D. (1989), 'Tourism as a Form of Imperialism', in V.L. Smith (ed.), *Hosts and Guests: The Anthropology of Tourism*, Philadelphia: University of Pennsylvania Press, pp. 33–47.

Pink, S. (ed.) (2006), *Applications of Anthropology: Professional Anthropology in the Twenty-First Century*, Studies in Applied Anthropology vol. 2, New York and Oxford: Berghahn.

Robertson, A.F. (1984), *People and the State: An Anthropology of Planned Development*, Cambridge: Cambridge University Press.

Root, D. (1996), *Cannibal Culture: Art, Appropriation, and the Commodification of Difference*, Oxford: Westview Press.

Sandercock, L. (2000), 'When Strangers Become Neighbours: Managing Cities of Difference', *Planning Theory and Practice* 1(1): 13–30.

Skodbo, S. (2005), Enrolling Genetic Technology in Regulation: Struggles for Recognition by Biotechnologists in Norway', *Focaal* 46: 91–106.

Turner, T. (2006), 'Anthropology as Reality Show and as Co-production: Internal Relations between Theory and Activism', *Critique of Anthropology* 26: 15–25.

Urry, J. (1990), *The Tourist Gaze*, London: Sage.

Waldren, J. (1998), 'The Road to Ruin', in S.A. Abram and J. Waldren (eds), *Anthropological Perspectives on Local Development: Knowledge and Sentiments in Conflict*, London: Routledge, pp. 120–40.

Wesch, M. (2007a), 'The Machine is Us(ing) Us', http://www.youtube.com/watch?v=6gmP4nk0EOE (accessed 5 April 2007).

Wesch, M. (2007b), 'The YouTube Project', http://mediatedcultures.net/ksudigg/?page_id=85 (accessed 5 April 2007).

Wesch, M. et al. (2007), 'Introducing our YouTube Project', http://www.youtube. com/watch?v=tYcS_VpoWJkandmode=relatedandsearch= (accessed 5 April 2007).

Wildavsky, A. (1973), 'If Planning is Everything, Maybe it is Nothing', *Policy Sciences* 4(2): 27–153.

Wilson, A. (2008), *Punching Our Weight: the Humanities and Social Sciences in Public Policy Making*, A British Academy Report, London: British Academy.

Wilson, N. (2005), 'The Dark Side of Community Development', *Planning Theory and Practice* 6(4): 519–26.

Wright, S. (2006), 'Machetes into a Jungle? A History of Anthropology in Policy and Practice, 1981–2000', in S. Pink (ed.), *Applications of Anthropology: Professional Anthropology in the Twenty-First Century*, New York and Oxford: Berghahn, pp. 27–54.

Postlude

Nelson Graburn

In drawing this volume to a close, I will make four reflections on certain aspects of it that contain implications for the anthropology of tourism and social anthropology more generally.

The first concerns hospitality. Shuzo Ishimori (1995) has described how he obtained a government grant for the Japanese National Museum of Ethnology to establish a three-year seminar on the anthropology of tourism. The grant enabled scholars from other universities and research institutions in Japan and elsewhere to visit the museum every month. The first year was spent discussing hospitality. Apart from giving us an example of how to do things properly, the fact lends credibility to the suggestion in this volume that hospitality is indeed one of the founding issues of the field. Part of the reason that Ishimori himself placed hospitality in such a position was that it was a term well placed to make the link between the anthropology of tourism on the one hand, and Japanese cultural ideas and practices on the other. Such 'bridging ideas' are invaluable.

The second has to with tourism and home. The fact that so *familiar* a concept in Japan as hospitality was taken to be the starting point of Ishimori's seminar series raises the intriguing possibility that the anthropology of tourism is as much about *us* at home as it is about the *other* out there. Many, if not all, the chapters in this volume are concerned in various ways with home and who *we* are (or would like to be) rather than with how *they* are. The idea is not new despite the fact that most would associate the anthropology of tourism with relations between 'us' and 'them' – 'hosts and guests' to coin a phrase. But over twenty years ago (Graburn 1983) I encouraged the idea that the study of domestic tourism was an important part of the subject and that familiarity was just as significant a tourist attraction as alterity.

Thinking about the link between tourism and home raises a significant issue, namely that visiting friends and relatives, VFR as it is termed in the trade, is not only the commonest form of tourism but also not discussed at all in this volume. However, VFR tourism has begun to surface on the research radar and we do have the beginnings of promising work on the subject (e.g. Basu 2004; Bruner 2005; Leite 2005; Leite and Graburn 2009).

The third reflection I have relates to the question of anthropology and intervention. The fact is that, throughout its existence, anthropology as an academic discipline has coexisted with various forms of anthropological intervention. For example, social scientists who we might have recognized as anthropologists were active in the international human rights organization, the Aboriginal Protection Society (1837–1909) which fought against the ill treatment of indigenous peoples all over the colonized world and which perhaps spurred one of the earlier indigenous resistance movements, the Aboriginal Rights Protection Society, founded in 1897 in West Africa. In the early and middle parts of the twentieth century, Malinowski headed the Rockefeller-funded International African Institute, while Radcliffe-Brown became *amicus curiae* on the side of groups of southern African peoples legally defending their customary marriage payments in the face of accusations of bride purchase. Later, scholars such as Evans-Pritchard in the Sudan and George Foster in Rhodesia intervened with the colonial government on behalf of those with whom they were working as ethnographers. Postcolonial intervention often took the form of working with those threatened with dispossession (Tom Sazaki on behalf of the Navajo, Fred Eggan on behalf of the Hopi, for example). Later, in the 1950s and 1960s (cf. Graburn 2006) the Canadian government employed anthropologists (including Jean Briggs, June Helm, John Honigmann, Asen Balikci, and Diamond Jenness) to work as intermediaries in questions of housing, schooling, medical and welfare provisions among the Inuit and Athapaskans in the context of government settlement policies. My own research (Graburn 1963) served to save and revive a very healthy Inuit community threatened with government policies. But scholars have not been universal in their praise of such work. My own involvement in Inuit art, for example, was strongly criticized by the art historian George Swinton for 'introducing the concept of originality' to Inuit artists in Povirnituk when I organized an art competition there (de Courval 1968). More recently still, anthropologists, some involved in tourism research, have been active in fields such as environmental protection (Mbaiwa and Stronza 2009), pro-poor tourism (Zhang 2006), human rights, human trafficking, labour conditions and the international trade in human organs (cf. Scheper-Hughes 2000). *Tourism Concern*, the well-known non-governmental organization active in tourism related affairs (in all the above fields as well as others) was partly born out of the first Masters course in the UK in the Anthropology of Tourism set up at the University of Surrey (Roehampton) in 1992.[1]

This brings me to my fourth and final reflection. This is that, in the UK, the anthropology of tourism has unquestionably come in from the cold (as it has done for slightly longer in the USA and (arguably) France). Few anthropologists work in regions in which tourism does not play a significant role. As far as professional identities and distinctions are concerned, my own graduate seminar at Berkeley, 'Tourism, Art, and Modernity', pays less attention to the formal disciplinary background of the researchers with whom we work than we do to their commitment to obtaining data and testing theories through intensive long-term field research. If they do that, then we count them as anthropologists even if the titles they wear on their lapels have sociologist, geographer, historian or anything else written on them. But this is a point at which we may draw a distinction between anthropologists and those working in the field of cultural studies whose approaches to data gathering and analysis sometimes appear to us opportunistic (MacCannell 1976).

Whither, we may thus ask, the anthropology of tourism? To start with, to emphasize the point, it has unquestionably achieved its place among such academic siblings as medical anthropology, ethnomusicology and the anthropologies of food, migration, art, landscape and so on. However, as this volume has so clearly demonstrated, the breadth of its ethnographic and theoretical reach suggests that the anthropology of tourism no longer needs the protective and/or defensive boundaries characteristic of a sub-group. Large parts of the wider social anthropological canon and curriculum are increasingly affected in some way or another by tourism and the issues with which it is associated.

Notes

1. See Nash (2007) for an account of the Surrey (Roehampton) MA. For information about *Tourism Concern*, see http://www.tourismconcern.org.uk.

References

Basu, P. (2004), 'Route Metaphors of "Routes Tourism"', in S. Coleman and J. Eade (eds), *Reframing Pilgrimage*, London: Routledge, pp. 150–74.

Bruner, E. (2005), 'Tourism in Ghana: Representations of Slavery and the Return of the Black Diaspora', *American Anthropologist* 98(2): 290–304.

de Courval, M. (1968) 'Les Nouvelles Sculptures de Povungnituk', *North* 15(6): 14–17.

Graburn, N. (1963), *Lake Harbour, Baffin Island: The Decline of an Eskimo Community*, Ottawa: Government of Canada, NCRC-63–2.

Graburn, N. (1983), 'The Anthropology of Tourism', *Annals of Tourism Research* (special issue on the anthropology of tourism) 10(1): 9–34.

Graburn, N. (2006), 'Canadian Anthropology and the Cold War', in J. Harrison and R. Darnell (eds), *Historicizing Canadian Anthropology*, Vancouver: University of British Columbia Press, pp. 242–52.

Ishimori, S. (ed.) (1995), *Japanese Civilization in the Modern World, IX: Tourism*, Osaka, National Museum of Ethnology, Senri Ethnological Studies, 38.

Leite, N. (2005), 'Travels to an Ancestral Past: On Diasporic Tourism, Embodied Memory, and Identity', *Antropologicas* (Porto) 9: 273–302.

Leite, N. and Graburn, N. (2009) 'Anthropological Interventions in Tourism Studies', in T. Jamal and M. Robinson (eds), *The Sage Handbook of Tourism Studies*, London, Sage, pp. 35–64.

MacCannell, D. (1976), *The Tourist: A New Theory of the Leisure Class*, New York: Shocken.

Mbaiwa, J. and Stronza, A. (2009) 'The Challenges and Prospects for Sustainable Tourism and Ecotourism in Developing Countries', in T. Jamal and M. Robinson (eds), *The Sage Handbook of Tourism Studies*, London, Sage, pp. 333–53.

Nash, D. (ed.) (2007), *The Study of Tourism: Anthropological and Sociological Beginnings*, Amsterdam: Elsevier.

Scheper-Hughes, N. (2000), 'The Global Traffic in Organs', *Current Anthropology* 41(2): 191–224.

Zhang, X. (2006), *Symbols and Rituals: An Illustrated Introduction to the Civilization of the Guizou Mountains*, Guiyang: Guizhou ren min chu ban she.

Index

Anthropology, xiii–xiv, xvii, 1–9, 11–12,
16–19, 37, 52–5, 67, 71–2,85–6, 140,
209, 231–2, 234, 236, 239–41, 243,
245–6, 248, 255–7
applied, 231, 240, 245–6
consultancy, 2, 16, 236, 239
funding, 2, 21, 175, 235
institutional affiliations, 129, 201
Anti-Semitism, 162,169, 172, 174
Archaeology, 187–8, 193, 199–200,
202–4
Art/Artists, 15, 149, 192–4, 196, 201,
203–7, 256–7
Authenticity, xiii, xvii–xx, 5–7, 18, 133,
135, 147, 150, 216, 232

Bodies
and death, 53, 562, 65, 68, 154, 194
sexualized, 11, 19, 35, 41–4
Borders
and mobility, 85–6, 119, 220–1, 223
and refugees, 85, 125, 212, 217–8, 219,
220, 223

Children, xvi, 42–3, 52, 79, 100, 105, 119,
123, 190, 203
Citizenship, 43, 72, 81–2, 100, 110, 125,
129, 166, 171, 215–6, 218, 221, 239,
242, 247
Civil society, 13, 19, 93, 99–101, 175
non-governmental organisations, 98,
102, 106, 108, 110
Class, 7, 17, 19, 27, 31, 51, 56, 72–3,
77–9, 84–6, 100, 119, 127, 129, 141–2,
151–2, 172, 188, 191, 203, 211, 220,
243
Colonialism, 3, 99
Comfort, 35, 42
Commodification, 5, 51, 93, 97, 110, 234

Consumption, xviii, 7, 9, 18–9, 27–8, 31,
40, 42, 56, 145–6, 148, 150, 162, 171,
173, 210, 213
Corruption, 53, 67, 121, 236
Culture
Aga Khan Trust, 131
cultural studies, 17–8, 257
performance of, xvii–xx, 3, 7, 11, 36,
44, 144, 233, 237

Development
cottage, xv, 12, 71–86
post-conflict, 2
property, 12, 19, 101,106,109–11
pioneer, 12, 77–83, 86, 235
policy, 98–9,101
settler, 76, 78, 82, 84, 95–6, 109, 222
Dress, 52, 59–63, 65, 122, 129, 145
Drink, xviii, 27, 29, 30, 35, 37, 40–1, 44,
78, 127, 129, 144–5
Durkheim, 19, 33

Embodiment, 52, 152
Enchantment, 13, 29, 33, 42, 117,128,
131–3, 134, 135, 142, 150, 153, 232
Ethics, 219, 222
Ethnicity, 3, 7, 27, 34, 37, 41, 43, 63, 72,
79, 83–6, 122, 129, 152–3, 161, 168–9,
174–5, 241–2
Europe, 185, 189, 212, 215–6, 220–3
European Union (EU), xv, 8–9, 14–15,
27, 37, 98, 101, 109, 162, 173–6, 191,
201, 212, 214–7, 219–21, 223–5, 236
Exhibitions, 142, 204, 232, 242

Femininity, 28, 42, 51, 55, 57, 64–7
Food 10, 19, 27, 29–31, 36–38, 40, 42, 44,
103, 117, 125, 132, 145–6, 216–7, 257
Free market, 43, 97, 99, 101

Gender, xix, 7, 27–8,42–4, 51–2, 55, 57–9, 61–2, 64–8, 72, 128–30, 152, 211
Golf courses, 98, 233
Globalization, 5, 27, 51, 55, 85
Government/s, xxii, 2, 9, 17, 56, 61–2, 67, 93, 95–101, 105, 110, 136, 146, 156, 174, 189, 192, 201, 212, 215–7, 234–7, 241–5, 255

Habitus, 28, 37, 40
Heritage, 1, 3, 7–8, 13–15, 19, 28, 37, 54, 83, 85,93, 95, 99, 102–3, 105, 109–10, 117–8, 121, 124, 130–3, 143, 147–50, 152, 154, 161–7, 171–7, 183, 185–95, 199–200, 203–4
Holocaust, 153, 172–3, 175, 179–80
Hospitality, xix, 1, 6, 8–9, 15–6, 33, 53, 143–4, 209–16, 222–4, 234, 255
Hotels, 5, 9–10, 14, 29–30, 95, 98, 106, 108, 119, 122, 125, 128–31, 133, 144–6, 212–3, 217, 219, 223, 233, 238
Human rights, 220, 239, 256

Images, xviii, 5, 9–11, 14, 16, 20, 33, 42, 57, 60, 63–4, 66, 73, 77, 105, 132, 140–1, 147, 149–50, 154, 164–5, 171, 193, 247
Immigrants, 76, 81, 83, 85, 211, 222
foreign workers, 211–7
Import substitution, 235
Informants, 6, 7, 121–30, 132–4, 167, 239
Intervention, 2, 15–6, 18, 20, 164, 231, 233–41, 244–8, 255–6

Labour, 15, 53, 74, 77–9, 81–3, 85, 143, 212–7, 220, 244, 256
Leisure, 6–7, 9, 13–4, 16, 31, 40–1, 52, 55, 74, 77, 79–80, 82, 84, 98, 108, 122, 124, 127, 129, 131, 134, 141, 151, 184, 210, 233

Marx, 19, 93
Masculinity, 28, 42, 54, 56, 64, 66
Mauss, 6
Media, 11–12, 20, 53, 55, 57–61, 64–5, 67–8, 74–5, 101, 170, 192, 204, 247
Medina, 13, 117, 120–4, 126–8, 130–4

Memory, 8, 14, 36–7, 62, 71, 81, 85, 95, 147, 161, 164, 166–7, 169–70, 172–3, 175–7
see also Heritage
Military, 34–5, 42, 94–8, 217
Minorities, 14, 174–5
Modernity/Modernism, 79, 81, 85, 120, 139–40, 147–8, 150, 153–4, 232, 256
Monuments, 10, 15–6, 72, 95, 98, 120, 126, 129, 131, 135, 164, 170, 172–3, 175, 183, 185, 187–9, 191–2, 196, 202–4
Morality, xviii, 51–3, 55, 59, 62–5
Multicultural/ism, 14, 54, 147, 165, 169, 171, 174–6, 239
Murder, 10–11, 53, 55, 57–61, 64–5, 67–8

Names, 7, 11, 29, 31–6, 38, 42, 59, 167, 170, 175, 240, 243
Nation/Nationalism, 7, 8, 10–11, 12, 14, 16–7, 19, 20, 27, 30–1, 34, 36–7, 42–4, 54, 61, 63–4, 66, 71–3, 76–7, 80–3, 85–6, 93, 95, 99–101, 105, 111, 118, 120, 123–4, 132, 134, 146–8, 152, 154, 156, 161–5, 168–70, 172, 174–6, 179, 183, 185–7, 189, 191–3, 195, 199, 204, 214–6, 219–20, 222, 233–4, 239, 255
Neighbourhood, xv, 164–6, 170, 175
Neolithic, 8, 15, 20, 183, 185–9, 191, 191, 193–4, 196, 200, 202–4

Objects, 9, 13, 16, 20, 172–3, 176, 223, 231, 234
souvenirs, 2, 10, 31–2, 204

Paradigm, 4–5, 8, 15, 110, 149, 209–10, 223, 239
Paradise, 51, 63, 140, 153, 155
Partnerships, 235, 240
Performance, xviii, xix–xx, 3, 7, 11, 36, 44, 233
Population density, 3, 9, 11, 13, 15, 31, 67,73,75–6, 83, 85, 93, 97, 108, 118, 122, 143–4, 146–8, 161, 174, 188, 210, 212–3, 216, 223–4, 233, 239
Postfeminism, 51, 67
Postmodernism, 4–5, 10, 211, 232, 246
Power relations, 146, 223, 239–40, 246

Pro-poor tourism, 256
Public domain, 5, 162, 164–5, 172–4, 231

Religion, 14, 15, 56, 120, 122, 161, 163, 165–72, 175, 184, 186–7, 192–5, 198, 201, 203
    and sacred sites, 10, 14, 15, 20, 94–5, 122, 142, 161–76, 183–5, 187–204, 245

Security, 42, 84, 194, 201
Sex
    education, 56
    sexual assault, 59–61, 63, 67
    sexuality, 11, 20, 42, 44, 51–2, 54–5, 56, 57, 62–4, 66–8
    sex tourism, 11, 51–5, 64–7
Sustainability, 30, 213
Swimming pools, 40, 98, 107, 128, 145, 233
Symbols, 5, 7, 10–11, 13–14, 16, 19–20, 29, 33, 37, 40–1, 43–4, 62, 71, 86, 139–41, 143–4, 147–50, 152–5, 165, 173, 244

Tourism
    and imperialism, 3, 54, 232
    industry, xii, 7–8,11, 15, 20, 28–30, 33, 41, 45, 56, 65, 67, 97–8, 128, 183, 210–5, 217, 221, 223, 232, 235, 248–9
    policy/planning, 2, 16, 231, 235

    practitioners, 5, 15, 18, 231, 236, 240, 247
    sustainable, xi, 143, 216, 225
    Tourism Concern 256
Tourists
    cultural, 4, 98
    domestic, xiv, xvii, xx, 71, 86
    regional, 10, 117, 132
    and migrants, xiv–xviii, xx–xxi, 8, 15, 76, 81, 83, 85, 123, 136, 186, 209, 211–3, 215, 220–3
    VFR, 255
    see also Visitors

Trade/traders, 8–10, 13, 20, 117–8, 120–3, 126–35, 142, 218

UNESCO, 15, 117–8, 120–1, 124, 133, 151–2, 186–7, 191, 204
Urban rehabilitation, 117–8, 121, 133

Value chain, 234
Veblen, 7
Visitors, xiii, xiv, xix–xx, 9, 12, 29, 51, 56, 72, 95, 106, 110, 119, 124–5, 127–8, 132–3, 139, 161, 164, 166–7, 171, 173, 183, 185–6, 195–6, 200, 203–4
    see also Tourists

Water, xiv, 40, 76, 78, 83, 104, 107, 110, 140–141, 146, 154, 221, 233
World Bank, 151, 234–5, 237
World Monuments Fund, 164, 175

LaVergne, TN USA
04 February 2011
215260LV00003B/29/P

9 781847 885319